anges for Engineers

Engineer VI	Engineer VII	Engineer VIII	Engineer IX
ull technical responsibility for interpreting, or-ing, executing, and coordinating assignments and develops engineering projects concerned unique or controversial problems which have portant effect on major organization programs involves exploration of subject area, definition ope and selection of problems for investigation, evelopment of novel concepts and approaches ains liaison with individuals and units within or de his organization with responsibility for act-dependently on technical matters pertaining to eld. Work at this level usually requires exten-rogressive experience	Makes decisions and recommendations that are recognized as authoritative and have an important impact on extensive engineering activities. Initiates and maintains extensive contacts with key en-gineers and officials of other organizations and companies, requiring skill in persuasion and negotiation of critical issues. At this level individu-als will have demonstrated creativity, foresight, and mature engineering judgment in anticipating and solving unprecedented engineering problems, de-termining program objectives and requirements, organizing programs and projects, and developing standards and guides for diverse engineering ac-tivities.	Makes decisions and recommendations that are recognized as authoritative and have a far-reaching impact on extensive engineering and related ac-tivities of the company. Negotiates critical and controversial issues with top level engineers and officers of other organizations and companies. In-dividuals at this level demonstrate a high degree of creativity, foresight, and mature judgment in plan-ning, organizing, and guiding extensive engineering programs and activities of outstanding novelty and importance.	An engineer in this level is either (1) in charge of programs so extensive and complex as to require staff and resources of sizeable magnitude (e.g. research and develop-ment, a department of government responsible for extensive engineering programs, or the major component of an organi-zation responsible for the engineering required to meet the objectives of the organization); or (2) is an individual researcher or consultant who is recog-nized as a national and/or international authority and leader in an area of en-gineering or scientific in-terest and investigation.
rvision received is essentially administrative, assignments given in terms of broad general tives and limits	Supervision received is essentially administrative, with assignments given in terms of broad general objectives and limits	Receives general administrative direction	
or more of the following. (1) In a supervisory city (a) plans, develops, coordinates, and di-a number of large and important projects or a ct of major scope and importance, or (b) is onsible for the entire engineering program of an nization when the program is of limited com-ty and scope. The extent of his responsibilities rally require a few (3 to 5) subordinate super-s or team leaders with at least one in a position barable to level V. (2) As individual researcher orker conceives, plans, and conducts research oblem areas of considerable scope and com-ty. The problems must be approached through ies of complete and conceptually related es, are difficult to define, require unconven-l or novel approaches, and require sophisti-l research techniques. Available guides and edents contain critical gaps, are only partially ed to the problem, or may be largely lacking due e novel character of the project. At this level, dividual researcher generally will have contrib-inventions, new designs, or techniques which f material significance in the solution of impor-oblems. (3) As a staff specialist serves as the ical specialist for the organization (division or any) in the application of advanced theories, epts, principles, and processes for an assigned of responsibility (i.e., subject matter, function, of facility or equipment, or product). Keeps ist of new scientific methods and developments ting his organization for the purpose of recom-ding changes in emphasis of programs or new ams warranted by such developments	One or both of the following. (1) In a supervisory capacity is responsible for (a) an important segment of the engineering program of an organization with extensive and diversified engineering requirements, or (b) the entire engineering program of an organiza-tion when it is more limited in scope. The overall engineering program contains critical problems the solution of which requires major technological ad-vances and opens the way for extensive related de-velopment. The extent of his responsibilities gener-ally requires several subordinate organizational segments or teams. Recommends facilities, per-sonnel, and funds required to carry out programs which are directly related with and directed toward fulfillment of overall organization objectives. (2) As individual researcher and consultant is a recognized leader and authority in his organization in a broad area of specialization or in a narrow but intensely specialized field. Selects research problems to further the organization's objectives. Conceives and plans investigations of broad areas of considerable novelty and importance for which engineering precedents are lacking in areas critical to the overall engineering program. Is consulted extensively by associates and others with a high degree of reliance placed on his scientific interpretations and advice Typically, will have contributed inventions, new de-signs, or techniques which are regarded as major advances in the field.	One or both of the following. (1) In a supervisory capacity is responsible for (a) an important segment of a very extensive and highly diversified engineering program, or, (b) the entire engineering program when the program is of moderate scope. The pro-grams are of such complexity that they are of critical importance to overall objectives, include problems of extraordinary difficulty that often have resisted solution, and consist of several segments requiring subordinate supervisors. Is responsible for deciding the kind and extent of engineering and related pro-grams needed for accomplishing the objectives of the organization, for choosing the scientific ap-proaches, for planning and organizing facilities and programs, and for interpreting results. (2) As indi-vidual researcher and consultant, formulates and guides the attack on problems of exceptional diffi-culty and marked importance to the organization or industry. Problems are characterized by their lack of scientific precedents and source material, or lack of success of prior research and analysis so that their solution would represent an advance of great signifi-cance and importance. Performs advisory and con-sulting work for the organization as a recognized authority for broad program areas or in an intensely specialized area of considerable novelty and impor-tance	
s, organizes, and supervises the work of a staff gineers and technicians. Evaluates progress of taff and results obtained, and recommends r changes to achieve overall objectives. Or, as dual research or staff specialist may be as-d on individual projects by other engineers or nicians	Directs several subordinate supervisors or team leaders, some of whom are in positions compara-ble to Engineer VI, or, as individual researcher and consultant, may be assisted on individual projects by other engineers and technicians	Supervises several subordinate supervisors or team leaders, some of whose positions are comparable to Engineer VII, or individual researchers some of whose positions are comparable to Engineer VII and sometimes Engineer VIII. As an individual re-searcher and consultant may be assisted on indi-vidual projects by other engineers or technicians	
or or Principal Engineer, Division or District eer, Production Engineer, Assistant Division, ict or Chief Engineer, Consultant, Professor, or County Engineer	Principal Engineer, Division or District Engineer, Department Manager, Director or Assistant Director of Research, Consultant, Professor, Distinguished Professor or Department Head, Assistant Chief or Chief Engineer, City or County Engineer	Chief Engineer, Bureau Engineer, Director of Re-search, Department Head or Dean, County Engineer, City Engineer, Director of Public Works, Senior Fel-low, Senior Staff, Senior Advisor, Senior Consul-tant, Engineering Manager	Director of Engineering, General Manager, Vice President, President, Partner, Dean, Director of Public Works
presentations, gives lectures, provides training, etc			
220% — 300%	260% — 360%	300% — 450%	Open Negotiated

COST ESTIMATING

NEW DIMENSIONS IN ENGINEERING

Series Editor

RODNEY D. STEWART

SYSTEMS ENGINEERING: CONCEPTS AND APPLICATIONS
BENJAMIN BLANCHARD

NEW DIMENSIONS IN LOGISTICS
LINDA L. GREEN

DESIGN TO COST
JACK V. MICHAELS
WILLIAM P. WOOD

COST ESTIMATING, SECOND EDITION
RODNEY D. STEWART

COST ESTIMATING

Second Edition

RODNEY D. STEWART

A WILEY-INTERSCIENCE PUBLICATION
JOHN WILEY & SONS, INC.
NEW YORK / CHICHESTER / BRISBANE / TORONTO / SINGAPORE

Copyright © 1991 by John Wiley & Sons, Inc.

Library of Congress Cataloging-in-Publication Data:

Stewart, Rodney D.
  Cost estimating / Rodney D. Stewart. — 2nd ed.
    p. cm. — (New dimensions in engineering)
  Includes bibliographical references and index.
  ISBN 0–471–85707–6 (cloth)
  1. Costs, Industrial—Estimates. I. Title. II. Series.
HD47.S76 1991
658.15′52—dc20   90–35943
                                        CIP

Printed in the United States of America

20 19 18 17 16 15 14 13 12 11

STEWART'S LAW

There are losses and inefficiencies in every endeavor accomplished by mankind. The secret to true competitiveness is to minimize these losses.

Rodney D. Stewart, 1990

CONTENTS

FOREWORD

This second edition of *Cost Estimating* by Rodney D. Stewart is being included in a series of books entitled: "New Dimensions in Engineering." This series will be published during the coming years by John Wiley & Sons, Inc.

Mr. Stewart has devoted a considerable amount of time gathering together data on the cost estimating and cost analysis processes. As there are no texts or highly technical treatises on the mathematical and statistical aspects of cost estimating and cost analysis, this book provides coverage of a primary nature.

Mr. Stewart has arranged the topics within this book to provide the readers with a logical, straight-forward approach to cost estimating. Within this second edition some of the examples, data, and techniques have been updated to help the reader better understand the processes involved. The two new chapters on computer-aided cost estimating and cost analysis and software cost estimating are the first that I have reviewed on these two timely subjects.

One of the hardest tasks for writers who are describing elemental theorems on a technical subject is to not over-portray themselves as experts on the subject. Mr. Stewart clearly explains that the basic theorems and processes he describes must be subject to intensive review and verification by further individual research of the reader.

As both a Certified Professional Estimator and a Certified Cost Analyst, I look forward to additional books produced within this series and especially a scientific study into the intricacies of cost estimating and cost analysis.

I applaud the efforts of Mr. Stewart and recommend that this and other books within this series should be considered for addition to our personal libraries.

Maximilian F. Steinbuchel, C.P.E., C.C.A.

Past President, National Estimating Society

Publisher's Note: Mr. Maximilian F. Steinbuchel has been active in the Cost Accounting, Cost Estimating and Cost Analysis professions for more than 20 years with companies in food processing, sports equipment manufacturing and the aerospace industry.

Mr. Steinbuchel is both a Certified Professional Estimator and a Certified Cost Analyst. He is a member of both the Society of Cost Estimating and Cost Analysis and the International Society of Parametric Analysts. He has served his profession as the president of the National Estimating Society from 1985 through 1987.

PREFACE TO THE SECOND EDITION

In this second edition of *Cost Estimating,* I have retained those features that attracted readers, reference users, and teachers of cost estimating to the first edition, and I have added some new features that should make the book even more useful as a reference and instructional guide. Questions at the end of chapters, added with the help of Dr. Larry D. Gahagan, a Certified Professional Estimator and Certified Cost Analyst, will help readers in self-testing to determine comprehension, assist seminar and short course leaders in student evaluation, and provide a basis for expanded testing for undergraduate or graduate students of cost estimating.

All chapters have been updated to provide currently applicable examples, data, and techniques, and two new chapters (Chapters 12 and 13) have been added. Chapter 12 provides information on computer tools and models for cost estimating. Chapter 13 covers the important area of software cost estimating with special emphasis on the effect of computer-aided software engineering (CASE) tools on software productivities and resulting software costs. A complete set of inflation tables is included to permit conversion from any year dollars to any other year dollars from 1959 through 1997—based on the most recently available government projections of inflation and escalation.

The book retains its comprehensive coverage of the elements needed to embark on a cost estimating task. Manufacturing standards for hardware and electronics are retained, as are handy tables for determining the costs of engineering, design, documentation, drafting, and testing. The most valuable parts of the book, those designed to inform the estimator how to produce a competitive and credible cost estimate, have been strengthened. These features are among those that prompted the National Estimating Society to include *Cost Estimating* in its recommended list of study guides for use in preparing for the Certified Cost Estimator examination and that have convinced universities, colleges, trade schools, and continuing education departments to adopt this book as a textbook on cost estimating.

I am confident that you will find the information, techniques, and suggestions gained during many years in the cost estimating field useful and profitable in preparing competitive cost estimates.

As a final note, I would like to thank Mr. Ed Yates for reviewing the completed manuscript and for spotting several corrections that needed to be made.

RODNEY D. STEWART

Huntsville, Alabama
September 1990

PREFACE TO THE FIRST EDITION

In many years of working in the fields of project management, procurement, and cost estimating, I have found that a common thread of methodology and practice exists in virtually all cost estimating situations. There are certain principles, practices, and procedures that hold true whether it is an industrial process, a manufactured product, a multimillion dollar construction project, or a business service that is being estimated. This book describes these principles, practices, and procedures; provides a simple cost-effective, step-by-step methodology for cost estimating; and points out pitfalls, problems, mistakes, and inaccuracies that can occur in cost estimates that can determine the difference between success and failure. The book is organized so that you can view the overall picture or delve more deeply into each step of the cost estimating process. It is not a highly technical, sophisticated treatise on the mathematical and statistical aspects of cost estimating. Rather, this book is a simple, straightforward exposition of the basic concepts and steps required to develop industrial engineering type, labor-hour and material-based, and parametric cost estimates. It is designed for the shelf of any professional who is a cost estimator, price estimator, cost analyst, price analyst, or systems cost analyst, and it will be equally useful to those working in a university, a small firm, a large corporation, or a government agency. It is a necessary constituent of the library of any business or organization that is interested in making a profit consistently and achieving maximum results for dollars spent.

As you read and apply the principles, practices, and procedures presented in this book, you will find that you will more fully appreciate the connection between the content of a work activity and the resources required to accomplish that activity. You will realize the sizable benefits of good estimating. Further, after having applied an organized approach to estimating the cost of your work activity or work output, you will have a better appreciation for the value of the work to you as a producer and to the consumer.

Good luck—good reading—and good estimating.

RODNEY STEWART

Huntsville, Alabama
May 1981

LIST OF SOFTWARE TRADEMARKS

Aaron Model

Ability Plus

ACEIT

ADAM

Advanced Project Workbench

Advanced Revelation

Aerospace Model

ALECM

ARC

ARTEMIS (2000,6000, 7000, 9000)

Ask Sam

BBEST

Boeing Model

BPM

CAAMS

   CAAMS-H

   CAAMS-RISNET

   CAAMS-MICRO COST

   CAAMS-WBS TREE

   CAAMS-L

CACES

CARP

Clarion Professional

Clipper

COBRA

COCOMO

COLOG

Cost Drivers

COSTIMATOR

Cost of Money Factors

CP^3

Cricket

CSS

Curvefit

Dataease Developer

Dataease

DataPerfect

dBASE

dBASE MAC

dbXL

DENEB

Doty Model

EASYBASE

EASYTRAK

ECM

Estiplan

ET/CETERA

ET/GATEWAY

EXEL

EXPERT
Farr Model
FAST
FATES
Formula
foxBASE+
Framework
G.B. Stat
GAUSS Mathematics and
  Statistical System
GRC Model
Harvard Project Manager
Javelin Plus
Jensen Model
Kustanowitz Model
LASER
LCURVE
LOGAM
Lotus 1-2-3
Lucid 3-D
McMax
MacProject II
Mainstay
MICAS
MICRO Cost Model
Micro-Planner
Microsoft Project
Microsoft Works
MicrostatII
Milestone
MULTI/CAM
NASA/SEL
Nelson Model
NICE
NWA StatPak
Paradox
PC/Focus
PFS First Choice
PFS: Professional File

PFS: Professional Plan
PICES
PlanPerfect
Plantrac
Prestige-PC
PRICE-H
PRICE-HL
PRICE-M
PRICE-S
PRICECOM
Primavera Project Planner
Pro-Path Plus
PROJECT/2
Project Scheduler
Project Workbench
Promis
PSM
Q&A
QRCM
Quattro
Quicksilver
Quiknet Professional
RAMLOG
R&R
RBASE
REVIC
RISNET
RISNET/A
Ruby Model
SCANS
SCATS
Schneider Model
SCM
SDIOLCCM
SHAZAM
Silk
Smart Spreadsheet
Smart System
SNAP

Softcost-R

SPACETRAN

SPANS

SPSS/PCplus

StatGraphics

StatPac Gold

Supercalc

SuperProject

Symphony

SYSTAT

TEAM

Tecolote 2

Tecolote Expert Selection System

Thinktank

TIGER

Time Line

Trapeze

20/20

VES

Viewpoint

Vis1on

WBS/Tree

WingZ

Wolverton Model

COST ESTIMATING

1
WHY COST ESTIMATING?

For which one of you, when he wants to build a tower, does not first sit
down and calculate the cost to see if he has enough to complete it?
Otherwise, when he has laid a foundation, and is not able to finish, all who
observe it ridicule him, saying, "this man began to build and was not able
to finish."

Luke 14:28–30

ESTIMATING IN A WORLD OF LIMITED RESOURCES

Almost a generation ago, Frank Borman, the first human to orbit the moon, was interviewed on the "Today" show. Colonel Borman's commentary went something like this:

When our Apollo Spacecraft came out from behind the moon for the first time, I saw a wondrous sight—the beautiful green earth—about the size of a basketball, against the bleak horizon of the moon's landscape. It was then that I realized how much our earth is like a self-contained spacecraft.

There it was, a tiny ball with a very thin atmosphere—an atmosphere that must sustain all of known human life. I realized then that the earth, like our Apollo Spacecraft, has a finite amount of air, water, food, and natural resources. I also realized that, unlike my spacecraft (which would be jettisoned and discarded after we had used up all of the supplies and left our wastes there) the earth must continue to sustain life for years and years to come if the human race is to survive. Further, with the population increasing at an ever expanding rate, natural resources will continue to be used more rapidly and could be depleted sooner than we think.

Borman's viewpoint emphasized that the earth's material resources are limited and that the use of these resources must be planned and controlled carefully in order to ensure our continued survival on this planet. We are like someone stranded on a desert island with a limited amount of food or an airplane pilot lost over the ocean with a limited amount of fuel. Each must estimate and plan consumption of the most valuable resource based on the time or distance to be covered and the quantity of the

1

resource available. The solutions to either of these problems of scarce or limited resources require the best possible estimate of future occurrences.

Natural resources are only one type of limited resources that are used by a society. There are other limited productive resources, including labor, capital, and equipment. The main problem facing any society is how best to allocate and distribute these scarce resources. These resources can be combined by using various technologies to produce combinations of goods and services. The objective of cost estimating is to describe adequately the cost of using the appropriate combination of the limited resources to achieve the required level of goods or services for the society. Good cost estimating will enhance the potential for the efficient utilization of resources.

The law of supply and demand says that the more limited the supply is at a given demand rate, the greater is the cost or price of a raw material, commodity, or service. This is one of the reasons that the cost of nonrenewable resources such as fossil fuels and precious metals tends to increase steadily. In an environment of continuing cost increases, it is necessary to have techniques and tools readily available that can rapidly and accurately estimate the costs of processes, products, projects, and services. The increasing costs of materials, equipment, and labor are compounded by the facts that money is more costly to borrow and that the materials required and skills needed to produce higher-technology products are becoming sophisticated and costly over time. Good cost estimating will keep the price to be charged for work activities or work outputs abreast of changing market conditions.

The inflationary cycle that brings about a need for continuing application of good cost estimating techniques is shown on **Figure 1.1**. As shown, (1) depletion and use of our natural resources results in a reduction of available resources. (2) The increase in demand for higher-technology, more sophisticated processes, products, projects, and services, coupled with the reduction of resources available to produce these outputs, causes prices to increase. (3) Increasing costs, coupled with a limited

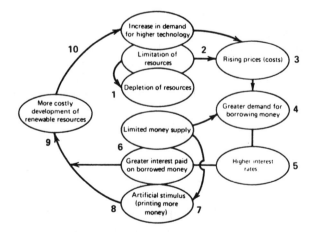

Figure 1.1 Inflationary cycle.

money supply, cause a greater demand for borrowed money. (4) This greater demand, and the limited money supply, result in sustained or increased interest rates. (5) Because of the need for money to lend, financial institutions give greater interest rates and help pay for this by the higher interests they charge their customers. (6) Greater interest that must be paid on borrowed money tends to restrict the flow of dollars and continues to limit the money supply. (7) In the meantime, the federal government continues to bolster the money supply by approving budgets that require a greater output of dollars than is taken in through taxes and other income. To do this, more money is printed than can be backed by income or gold reserves. This practice reduces the buying power of the dollar and results in higher costs of renewable resources and higher costs of the high-technology products needed to satisfy increasing demand (steps 8–10). Thus, the inflationary cycle is completed and starts again. Because of the dynamic nature of this cycle, estimating the costs of a work output must be done frequently and periodically to keep estimates accurate and credible.

Specific factors that should be tracked to keep estimates abreast of the latest inflationary trends are (1) changes in employee fringe benefits, (2) changes in the consumer price index, (3) changes in wages based on merit, contract negotiation, productivity, or the minimum wage, (4) changes in material prices, (5) changes in energy costs, (6) changes in the cost of taxes, insurance, depreciation, or meeting government regulations, (7) changes in the company's productivity level, and (8) changes in required *combinations* of resource requirements (natural, labor, or capital resources). Good cost estimating will permit prices to accurately reflect changing inflationary trends.

INCREASED PRODUCTIVITY AS A SOLUTION

One way to stretch the availability of limited, natural, labor, and capital resources judiciously is to increase productivity. Increased productivity does not necessarily mean increased production; rather, it means obtaining a greater output of goods or services for a given amount of natural, manufactured, financial, or human resources. Increased productivity can be achieved by improving the efficiency, economy, and effectiveness of any form of work output. The ability to plan, schedule, estimate, and carry out an activity therefore has a significant impact on the effective use of resources. The development of realistic estimates of the projected cost of an activity will result in adequate resource allocation and, as a result, more likely project completion. If more projects are completed within their original cost estimates, greater productivity will result. Fewer projects or work activities will be cancelled for lack of funds when they are partially completed (see the Scripture at this chapter's beginning). Better cost estimates for all work activities may result in fewer being started because it will become apparent that all desired projects cannot be started within the limit of resources available. But those that are started will have a greater likelihood of being completed if realistic estimates are made. Good cost estimating will pinpoint areas for needed productivity improvements and will assist in the avoidance of potentially unprofitable ventures.

PRODUCTIVITY AND THE PROFIT MOTIVE

Making a profit and providing the best possible work output, whether a process, a product, a project, or a service, are two motivators in increasing productivity. These two forces or motivations are not always given equal emphasis in a particular work activity, but one or both are present in all successful ventures. Both are significant factors in the continuing improvement in the quality of life—and they affect our overall productivity as a nation.

To ensure maximum productivity, it is necessary to have an accurate estimate of the costs required to accomplish a job before it is started and to manage the job efficiently and effectively within the cost constraints established. Too often we fail in one or both of these respects, and underestimates or cost overruns result. The accuracy and credibility of a cost estimate or series of cost estimates, in fact, can be the source of success or failure of a business, commercial activity, or government project. A commercial or industrial activity that consistently produces cost estimates that are too high and bases its prices on these estimates may fail because its work output is not cost competitive in the marketplace. A company whose bids or estimates are consistently too low will not make a profit and eventually may face bankruptcy. Any business or corporation that wants to continue operating profitably must continually improve its estimating and pricing methods. (Some companies and businesses have become successful without employing good cost estimating and pricing techniques, but very few of these companies *stay* successful without them). Many companies employ "loss leaders" (products priced below their cost) to capture a market or to draw customers to other products of the same company, but to stay in business, these companies must have a mix of profit and loss that results in an overall profit in the long run. Good cost estimating will provide greater assurance that a profit can be made in a venture.

Excess profits are often criticized by consumers or small businesspeople who believe that they are being victimized by larger corporations or monopolies. The potential ability to make not only a profit but a large profit is what makes business risks both feasible and attractive for an industry or investor. Without these risks, the advancements in technology and improvements in the standard of living we have experienced would not have been possible.

The subject of productivity is far more complex when it comes to the activities of state, local, and federal government departments and agencies. Since the profit motive does not exist in government, it is even more important to be able to predict and control costs. Cost estimating by independent organizations within government departments and agencies is on the increase because taxpayers are becoming more concerned about the need for efficiency, economy, and effectiveness in government. Since tax-based income levels are relatively fixed in proportion to gross earnings, government tends to look for the most work output per dollar rather than the lowest cost per work output. Both approaches require a form of cost estimating. The latter requires an "estimating-to-cost" or "design-to-cost" technique that provides a work output based on the resources available. This technique is more difficult than the simple process of defining a work output and estimating its cost because it requires an iterative process of defining-estimating-redefining-reestimating, and so on until a work output is defined that can be accomplished within the funds allotted. More about this procedure will be discussed in Chapter 10.

AT STAKE, THE ORGANIZATION'S REPUTATION

The cost estimating and pricing policy of a company or a government organization will have a profound effect on its business reputation. Accurately estimating a job and performing it within the estimated cost will go a long way toward building a reputation that will enhance an organization's future business potential and will help to retain a good long-term business base.

If you want to stay in business for a long time, you must avoid "buying in" to jobs or tasks that you cannot complete within the allotted resources. There is a danger that larger companies may fall into this mode of operation when long-term, high-cost projects are undertaken because even a company that is going out of business pays its executives, and those in the marketing and management roles may be tempted to underbid unrealistically just to get the job in the hope that they will obtain "bail-out" changes or follow-on contracts later.

Most successful companies do not resort to this tactic if they desire to stay in operation. They fully realize that they will lose a certain percentage of their bids, and they take pride in offering a better service, better facilities, more qualified personnel, or an innovative design. A credible and realistically low bid can be achieved through good planning, organization, and design rather than through the use of an arbitrarily low or misleading cost estimate.

A company's reputation in performing work within the cost target established is becoming an increasingly important factor in selection to do important work in both the private and public sectors. The use of advanced technology in design, manufacturing, and administration is a key factor in producing a competitive cost estimate. If a company is innovative and up-to-date in its management and technical approach, it will perform cost analyses of new techniques as they become available and will adopt those techniques that result in reasonably high life cycle cost savings (see Chapter 10 for a description of how to compute life cycle cost savings). The only way to know if advancements will pay off is to develop a detailed cost estimate that uses the best available inputs and assumptions and to perform an economic analysis to determine the costs versus benefits of an innovation.

A company can also protect its reputation in cost estimating and bidding by maintaining a competitive salary mix and skill mix. There is a danger of salary creep if the turnover of a company is so low that the percentage of senior employees grows each year. The solutions to this problem are (1) maintaining steady growth, (2) adding most of the new employees at the bottom of the salary structure, or (3) retiring or laying off employees once their skills and related salaries exceed the level that can support a competitive bid. Clearly the former solution is much more satisfactory than the latter. A good detailed cost estimate, along with an analysis of cost estimates prepared over a two- or three-year period will provide management with the knowledge of potential grade and salary creep above that which could be attributed to inflation. Good cost estimating, accompanied by astute hiring and promotion practices, will help to ensure a continuing competitive skill mix.

IN-DEPTH COST ESTIMATING

There are two general categories of cost estimating: the "top-down," or parametric approach, and the "bottoms-up," or industrial engineering approach. The parametric approach uses historical data from previous work and projects the costs of new work based on cost determining variables such as increased or decreased quantity, size, weight, power level, or other factors for the new work. Adjustments can then be made for quantity, volume and/or rate, and schedule. The industrial engineering approach requires estimation of the labor-hours and materials of each element and subelement of work and pricing and accumulating all the costs of the elements and subelements into a total cost estimate. Both methods of estimating are satisfactory, but for different phases of the acquisition cycle; the parametric method is used early in the acquisition cycle when there is less product definition, while the industrial engineering approach is used later in the acquisition cycle when there is greater design detail. The two approaches become more closely related, and even become one and the same, as definition proceeds toward lower levels of the work. For instance, the number of minutes or seconds needed to accomplish a single assembly line operation, an input to an industrial engineering type of estimate, is really a parametrically derived value based on past experience. The two methods are essentially the same, except that the parametric estimate has been traditionally used at a much higher level in a work operation. The use of a dollar-per-square-foot value to estimate the cost of a house (versus the minutes or seconds required to install an electrical socket) would be an example of the traditional use of a parametric estimate. Most large organizations use both types of estimates for their projects and combine the knowledge derived from these two estimates to develop their final cost estimate.

The top-level parametric estimate has limitations from the standpoints of visibility of estimate components, identification of major cost drivers, isolation of inflation effects on each cost element, and adjustment of costs to reflect subtle changes in the work output; but has the advantage of rapid preparation.

When a detailed definition of the work is available, the most credible, supportable, usable, and accurate cost estimate is one where an in-depth analysis of the work and estimation of work elements is accomplished. This in-depth cost estimating procedure usually consists of one or more of the following types of activity:

1. Preparation of a complete list of all drawings, documents, publications, materials, and parts required to perform the job and analysis of these items to

establish a make-or-buy decision on each. In software cost estimating, it requires a listing of each task to be accomplished and a listing of all of the tools and equipment (computers and software) required to accomplish these tasks.

2. Detailed manufacturing or process planning, including a preliminary design of each major tool and piece of special equipment, and a complete analysis and description of the manufacturing or process flow. In software cost estimating, the planning, analysis, and design must be done to schedule and describe when each task must be accomplished and its relation with other tasks.

3. Application of work standards and adjustment to account for expected performance against these standards. In software cost estimating, this includes adjustments required to accommodate computer-aided software engineering (CASE) tools.

4. Definition of each administrative, engineering, manufacturing, assembly, testing, shipping, and support task by discipline and the use of standard industrial engineering methods, staffing techniques, judgment of skilled personnel, and historical experience to arrive at a detailed estimate. In software estimating, this includes estimates of efforts required to prepare flow diagrams, specifications, coding, testing, and documentation of software.

5. Application of standard catalog prices; recent purchase order data; vendor quotations for materials, parts, equipment, and software; the solicitation of quotations; and the competitive solicitation of quotations for subcontracts.

6. Use of the latest available information on labor rates, travel costs, fringe benefits, overhead costs, general and administrative expenses, inflation, and profit objective.

Through the use of these techniques, sufficient detailed data can be accumulated to estimate accurately the most probable costs to accomplish any given work output and to adjust the cost estimate to allow for subtle changes in product definition, schedule timing, and inflationary effects.

FIGHTING INFLATION AND ESCALATION

Through the use of an in-depth cost estimate, sufficient knowledge of the effects of two of the largest cost drivers—inflation and escalation—can be gained to permit the development of a competitive yet credible cost estimate. Chapter 11 provides a detailed discussion of the history, causes, and approaches to dealing with inflation and cost escalation. Subdivision of costs into the various components of labor, materials, overhead, general and administrative expenses, fringe benefits, and travel costs permits the analysis and identification of the effects of inflation and escalation on each one of these factors. The importance of this work is underscored by the rapid fluctuation in inflation rates that has been experienced in recent years, as well as the trend for certain costs to be computed based on current inflation rates. From 1974 to 1976, for example, the U.S. inflation rate dropped from about 13 percent per year to less than 6 percent per year. Over the next three years, the inflation rate went back up to 13.3 percent. More recently, inflation rates have receded to the earlier values.

Economists are able to segment or subdivide inflation into its various components, permitting a more finely tuned analysis of the effects of inflation on each of the work elements of a process, product, project, or service. For example, 2.2 percent of the 13.3 percent inflation in 1979 was attributable to energy price increases. Economists expect similar energy price increases in the 1990s. If your work output is energy dependent, you will have to base your estimates on a potentially higher inflation rate than if it is not. An in-depth cost estimate will allow you to isolate and identify the energy-dependent cost elements and work elements. Other factors that you must keep track of to allow you to keep your estimates abreast of the latest inflationary trends are fringe benefits; cost-of-living salary increases; merit increases; raw material costs; increases in the minimum wage level; increases in travel, transportation, and lodging costs; and increases in interest rates. Inflation cannot be avoided, but knowledge of your work activity gained through an in-depth estimate and projection of inflationary trends for specific product and service areas will allow you to evaluate its effects more accurately.

Escalation, the tendency for work output per dollar to decrease, causing increased prices, can be controlled or counteracted by productivity increases.

THE COST ESTIMATE AS A PLANNING TOOL

Experienced estimators know that the cost estimating *process* is just as valuable as if not more so than, the cost estimate itself. The answer to the question "What is the cost?" is often a barrage of other questions: "What is the schedule?" "Who is going to do the work?" "Where will the work be done?" "Exactly what does the work consist of?" Those requesting cost estimates frequently give very little advanced thought to these and other important questions. Often a cost is quoted without qualifications as to the conditions on which the estimate is based—one reason for frequent misunderstanding and confusion concerning the costs of an activity. Whenever a cost of a process, product, project, or service is quoted, it should be accompanied by the following information: (1) a full description of the product or work output at completion, (2) the starting date and key milestones for the activity, (3) the geographical location of the work, (4) the skills and organizations assumed available to perform the work, and (5) the expected quality and service life of the work output.

By providing this information along with the cost estimate, the estimator avoids the common problem of having the recipient think the estimate is for an entirely different work output than that estimated. This precept may seem elementary, but a clear definition of what is included in an estimate and the estimate ground rules and assumptions will help to avoid later problems.

There is considerable value in having the individuals who are going to perform the work assist in preparing the cost estimate. This practice will familiarize the performer with the work and will have the added advantage of allowing him or her to set goals. In this respect, preparation of a cost estimate is one of the best training tools available for those who are about to perform the job they are estimating. Estimators will have to go through the procedures and actions mentally that will be required to get the job done and will have to ask themselves questions like, "Do I have the proper equipment to do this job?" "Are the right materials available?"

Since good planning and good estimating go hand in hand, the cost estimate itself is an excellent planning tool. With a meticulously prepared cost estimate in hand, a firm is in a position to identify the planned use of labor, materials, tooling, and other resources; plan for adequate profit for the firm; and predict and control costs—the most important reasons any company would want to invest adequate resources in the process of cost estimating itself because they affect hiring objectives, facility expansion requirements, equipment purchases, financial needs from stockholders, and assurance of a return to the investors.

POSSIBLE: A STANDARDIZED BASIC ESTIMATING PROCEDURE

Another answer to the question "Why cost estimating?" is that, despite the fact that many different estimating methods, techniques, policies, and procedures exist, the steps required in cost estimate preparation can be standardized into a uniform procedure. Little standardization in estimating procedures occurred until lately because of the competitive nature of the process. The competitive content and resulting sensitivity to competitive exposure of a cost estimate, however, are usually in the levels or magnitudes of resource predictions rather than in the methods or techniques used in making the estimate. Removal of the competitive content (the estimated resource values themselves) has made standardization of estimating *procedures* possible. Cost estimating has become a profession in which standard procedures and techniques can be applied by experienced professionals to provide realistic and comparable cost estimates. This standardized approach to cost estimating is explored in the remaining chapters.

QUESTIONS

1.1. What are three reasons for requiring good cost estimating?

1.2. What are two contributing factors to inflation?

1.3. What are three factors that should be tracked to keep estimates abreast of the latest inflationary trends?

1.4. List three of the seven requirements that make a credible, supportable, accurate, and detailed cost estimate.

1.5. Industrial engineering type, labor-hour, and material quantity based estimates are used in the early phases of programs.   (True)   (False)

2
THE BASICS OF ESTIMATING

Having had perfect understanding of all things from the very first . . .

Luke 1:3

FOUR KINDS OF WORK OUTPUT

There are four basic outputs or areas of work under which virtually every type of productive activity can be categorized: (1) processes, (2) products, (3) projects, and (4) services. Each specific productive activity within these output categories represents an industrial or commercial activity that uses specialized skills, equipment, materials, techniques, and knowledge unique to that field of endeavor. Examples of productive activities that fall into each of these output categories are shown in Tables 2.1 through 2.4.

Processes

Processes are industrial or commercial activities that alter or convert one or more raw materials or substances into other useful products or substances through physical or chemical change. The processing industries are characterized by their need for large investment in capital equipment, the use of a large amount of energy, and the importance of environmental protection and pollution control techniques. Rapidly increasing costs in each of these three areas emphasize the need for using up-to-date cost estimating techniques. The production of minerals, inorganic chemicals, and organic chemicals represents a large segment of the U.S. economy—an estimated $100 million to $150 million per year—and the processing industries represent one of the fastest growing of all industrial or commercial activities. The processes shown in **Table 2.1** are typical of those major industries.

Products

Products are commercial items or goods sold in quantity to private or industrial consumers. **Table 2.2** shows only a few of the myriad of products manufactured and

TABLE 2.1   Examples of Processes

Aluminum, magnesium, and titanium production
Cement, glass, gypsum, and lime production
Ceramics
Coal, coke, and carbon compounds
Elastomers
Fiber production (cotton, wool, silk, rayon, acetate, nylon)
Film developing
Gas liquefaction (cryogenics)
Gaseous state processing
Liquid state processing
Land excavation and earth moving
Nitrogen compounds
Oil refining
Paper and wood pulp
Petroleum and natural gas production/refining
Phosphorus compounds
Plastics and rubber
Powder metallurgy
Radioactive materials processing
Raw material extraction
Raw material processing
Raw materials refining
Salt compounds
Solid state processing
Steel and iron production
Sulfur compounds
Waste treatment
Water treatment
Welding, soldering, and brazing

sold by U.S. business and industry. Important elements in the cost of products are advertising, marketing, distribution, servicing, and operational costs. Often these costs far exceed that of initial production or acquisition. Competition is the significant factor that sets the price, production and sales quantity, design, and utility of a product. The difference between making a profit or losing money on a product is often a matter of how accurately the cost is estimated and the price established. Product design and the mix of products constantly change to meet the evolving needs of a growing society.

Projects

Projects are multidisciplinary activities that frequently advance the state of the art of technological knowledge. They require great skill and care in estimating because of the presence of unknown factors that are difficult to foresee at the time of project

TABLE 2.2   Examples of Products

Agricultural products
Automotive products
Beverages
Cameras and photographic and projection equipment
Clothing, textiles, fabrics, and fibers
Communications equipment
Construction and building materials and supplies
Electrical and plumbing supplies and equipment
Electronic products
Farm, construction, handling, and earth-moving equipment
Food products
Health and Hygiene supplies
Heating, cooling, and ventilation equipment
Jewelry, watches, and clocks
Manufacturing and production equipment and tools
Marine products
Military products (e.g., ammunition)
Office and business machines, computers
Optical equipment
Paints, varnishes, lacquers, and coatings
Petroleum, coal, and natural gas
Recreation and entertainment equipment, sporting goods, and toys

planning. The size of a project activity, the need for multiple skills, and the span of time usually required result in the need for precise planning, scheduling, estimating, and management. **Table 2.3** shows several categories of projects. Because of the size and funding requirements for projects, they are frequently supported or funded by state, federal, or local governments.

TABLE 2.3   Examples of Projects

Aerospace projects
Airport construction
Building construction: homes, commercial buildings, civic centers
    and entertainment facilities, factories, and laboratories
Dams and hydroelectric plants
Highway and bridge construction
Military weapons systems
Nuclear plants
Research and development projects
Transportation systems (mass transit)
Urban renewal
Utility distribution and collection systems
Water and waste treatment facilities

Services

Services are labor-intensive activities that provide assistance to private, commercial, or industrial consumers by furnishing useful work for consumers. This work can be in the form of advice or information, or it can be in the form of useful work performed on or with a product. Services usually have a continuing or repetitive nature that contributes to the growth and profit of a company or business. **Table 2.4** shows some typical services. Price, cost, and competition are significant factors in providing services. Because of their repetitive or continuing nature and the high degree of personal contact they require with consumers, company reputation and customer satisfaction are of great significance in planning and estimating services.

COST ESTIMATING DEFINED

An estimate is a judgment, opinion, forecast, or prediction. A cost estimate, therefore, is a judgment or opinion of the cost of a process, product, project, or service. It is a prediction or forecast of what a work output or work activity will cost. The

TABLE 2.4   Examples of Services

Appliance, electrical, and plumbing repair
Architectural and engineering services
Automotive repair
Cleaning and laundry
Computer programming and software services
Consulting
Dental, medical, health care, and physical fitness services
Educational services
Entertainment
Employment services
Financial, accounting, and banking services
Geological, mapping, and geographical exploration
Graphics and art
Insurance
Laboratory research
Landscaping
Law enforcement
Legal and patent services
Marketing and advertising
Personal and beauty care
Photography
Printing, reproduction, and publications
Secretarial services
Shipping, moving, and transport
Utilities
Veterinary medicine and animal care

verb "estimate" means to appraise, evaluate, value, rate, or assess.[1] According to the Society of Cost Estimating and Analysis (SCEA), estimating is "the art of approximating the probable worth or cost of an activity based on information available at the time." The society further states that the estimating profession includes "those concerned with the accumulation and reporting of costs, those involved in the establishment of standards for labor hours and material costs, and those persons whose occupations are concerned with estimating and its derivative functions as listed: cost estimating, price estimating, pricing, price analysis, cost analysis, systems cost analysis, life cycle cost analysis, and economic analysis."[2]

"COST" AND "PRICE" EXPLAINED

Notice that in these definitions, the terms "price estimating" and "cost estimating" are used side by side. Those who have been in business or industry quickly learn the difference between cost and price. The *cost* of a product is the summation of the resources required to produce the product. The *price* is the value that will be used in marketing the work. It may be equal to the cost or may be adjusted to conform to the most likely market demand for the item. The price is the value placed on the item for sale by the producer, and it is usually more than the production and marketing cost by the amount of profit anticipated and required by the seller.

Prices paid for goods and services are significant drivers in the overall economic system. Prices control the amount of money to be paid for goods and services. For individual consumers, prices set the standard of living. For every business transaction, there is a buyer and a seller. The seller wants the price to be high in order to make a substantial profit. The buyer wants the price to be as low as possible to save money or to buy more goods and services for the same amount of money. Prices are directly related to profit, the basis of the nation's economy. The technical definition of price is seen in the following formula:

$$Price = Cost + Profit.$$

The price of an item is based on the economic principle of supply and demand. When the item is in increasing demand, the price tends to increase. When the supply of the item is greater than the demand, the price tends to fall. How does this relationship affect industry? When prices are high, the resources needed to produce (natural, human, and capital) are allocated to the industry, and production is increased. When the prices decline, usually demand for the item has fallen, and buying has fallen. The resources that were attracted by the industry during higher prices are drawn into other, more active industries. This scenario describes the competitive economy where prices set the pace for allocation of limited resources.

THE ESTIMATING PROCESS: INGREDIENTS AND TOOLS REQUIRED

The process of cost estimating is itself a valuable activity that accomplishes useful goals. Later we will examine how to determine the costs of producing a cost estimate and the benefits of the estimate and the estimating process. But first it is necessary to know something about the ingredients and the tools required to produce a credible, accurate, and competitive cost estimate.

Basic Ingredients

The basic ingredients of a cost estimate are labor-hours, materials and subcontracts, travel costs, other direct costs (such as computer services), labor rates, indirect costs, administrative costs, and fee or profit. Throughout the cost estimating process, these ingredients combine and interact to result in a cost estimate.

Labor-Hours. Labor costs are the origin of all costs. A quantity of raw material in the ground or ocean costs little. A very small portion of its costs is determined by the mineral rights of the owner. Its *primary* costs are incurred when labor (human effort and time) is used to extract the material from its natural state. Even the machinery used to extract and refine the item of raw material is a product of human labor. Thus the principal element of cost of a work activity or output is traceable back to reimbursement for the human labor invested. This labor, usually stated in labor-hours, -months, or -years, is performed by individuals with various labor rates or wages based on various degrees of proficiency, skill, training, and experience. Labor-hours are usually estimated for each broad labor category or skill. The proficiency, skill, training, and experience of the worker usually set the value placed on the work, which establishes a labor rate or wage. Since multiple skills are used to accomplish most activities at various labor rates, it is necessary to separate labor-hours into labor skills. The mixture of skills used to accomplish a given job is called a "skill mix."

Materials and Subcontracts. Materials are the tangible items that must be bought or otherwise procured to perform the task or set of tasks being estimated. These can be categorized as parts, raw materials, supplies, equipment, and tools. In cost estimates, these elements are referred to as "materials." "Subcontracts" are activities to be performed or products to be supplied by organizations other than the principal performer. Materials and subcontracts are usually categorized together because they represent outside purchases.

Travel Costs. Travel costs include the per diem reimbursement for personal living expenses incurred by an individual while traveling, as well as the costs of transportation and other travel expenses. Travel costs usually do not include the employee's hourly labor costs or salary.

Other Direct Costs. Labor-hours, materials and subcontracts, and travel costs are considered direct costs; that is, they are costs directly incurred in design, manufacturing, testing, or production of the product itself. Added to these direct costs is the category "other direct costs," which includes such elements as computer services, reproduction services, and training.

Labor Rates. To convert direct labor-hours to direct labor costs, it is necessary to determine and then apply the appropriate hourly, weekly, monthly, or yearly direct labor rate. This rate will vary depending on the skill, experience, and proficiency of the individual. A composite labor rate, usually an average of direct labor rates of various labor categories within a broader labor category, is normally used to develop the labor costs for a given estimate.

Indirect Costs. Indirect costs—those not directly attributable to a project but that must be borne by all of the units of an organization—usually consist of labor burden, material burden, and overhead. Organizations vary widely as to the types of costs included in each of these categories. The overall list of costs included in all three will serve as a convenient checklist to ensure that all indirect cost elements are included in the cost estimate. Labor burden usually includes items such as bonuses, health insurance (company's contribution), paid holidays and vacations, sick leave, social security (company's contribution), supervisor's salary, and pension contributions (by the company). Material burden includes costs such as material handling, inventory control, purchasing costs, and material packaging, storage, and preservation. Overhead costs include amortization of facilities and equipment, bid and proposal costs, claims, communications costs, custodial services, depreciation costs, industrial relations, insurance costs, lighting, maintenance, operating supplies, power, rental of buildings, waste disposal, and water.

Administrative Costs. Most large companies have a cost category called general and administrative (G&A) expense. It includes corporate or home office expenses. G&A expenses usually cover administration, advanced design, advertising, corporate expenses, executive salaries, finance, marketing, personnel, research, training, and corporate taxes. Warranty costs, hazardous pay, and license fees can be included in G&A or in other categories, depending on the organization and accounting practices of the company.

Fee or Profit. Fee, profit, or earnings are funds that are returned to the company stockholders, used for reinvestment, or expended for capital equipment, facilities, or tooling. In economic terms it represents the payment made to the owners for risking their capital in performing the work.

Basic Tools

There are five basic tools used to combine the basic ingredients into a good cost estimate: (1) a team of estimators or an estimator, (2) a methodical approach, (3) knowledge or data concerning the project, process, product, or service, (4) a computation capability, (5) and a publication capability.

Estimators. The principal resource and most important tool required to develop a good cost estimate is a qualified estimator (or a team of estimators) who can devote undivided attention to the preparation of the estimate. If a team approach is used, a cost estimate manager or coordinator is needed who is competent in estimating techniques and should have a general knowledge of the work being estimated. This person does not necessarily require a detailed knowledge of the work activity or output at the outset because the best estimating methodology uses the skills and knowledge of the work performers to provide the data required. To develop a good estimate, a single individual must be primarily responsible for planning, organizing, and carrying out the activity. The number and type of estimators chosen will depend on the size, complexity, and diversity of the task being estimated.

Methodical Approach. The second important tool required is a methodical approach. A standard methodology or approach is applicable to a wide variety of estimating situations. The estimator must have a definite plan of action in mind. Many estimates have failed because a helter-skelter approach was used. Estimates not made in a methodical manner can end up being inaccurate, nonsupportable, unclear as to exactly what was estimated, or ambiguous as to work content, ground rules, and assumptions. A good estimator or estimating team using a methodical approach will be able to develop a credible, supportable, accurate, and useful cost estimate.[3]

Knowledge and Data Concerning the Work Activity or Work Output. The third tool required for a good cost estimate is the best knowledge and data available concerning the process, product, project, or service being estimated. Knowledge of the resources required to do a job can be gained from handbooks or from the judgment and experience of individuals who perform or have performed the same type of functions being estimated. The best estimator is one who has had to do the work being estimated. This person is the one most likely to be able to envision the time, materials, equipment, tools, facilities, and skills required. He or she need not be a skilled estimator but must have the ability to visualize the activity or portion of an activity being estimated and to convert this concept into a staffing, labor-hour, or shop-hour estimate. With the aid of a skilled estimator, this worker can then quantify the various resources required to perform a job. If a task or project is complex, a number of skilled performers may be consulted by the estimator. The cardinal rule when estimating is to ask the expert. Involvement of the performer or performing organization is essential because this person or organization will be responsible for doing the work within the estimated resources once the job is accepted.

Computation Capability. Although any estimate can be computed by hand, organizations that produce estimates for their own or other organizations regularly find that a computer system for carrying out the computations required is vital. Software is available ranging from simple basic programs to highly sophisticated "vertical market" costing and pricing systems. (Vertical market systems are those that apply to only one of the processes, products, projects, or services listed in Tables 2.1 through 2.4.) In general, an estimator who spends more than 10 percent of work time performing the computations is not properly applying other estimating skills. A computer system has the advantages of rapidly computing and producing a printout in a readable, organized, accurate, and consistent format. This type of output has virtually replaced handwritten or typed cost estimates because of greater consistency and accuracy.

Publication Capability. An organization or individual desiring to produce a cost estimate must have the capability of publishing one or more organized, concise, readable, and easily used cost estimate documents. Ideally the document should have a hard cover for durability; be plainly marked with the title, date, sensitivity, and organization; and should be index tabbed for quick referencing. The document should be legible and organized for ease of reference, and all pertinent primary and backup data should be included. Clerical support, reproduction services, and appropriate supplies are needed to produce the document. An ideal combination is a desktop publishing system that can import both tabular and graphic results of cost estimating computations from applications software programs or vertical market cost estimating software programs.

THE COST ESTIMATOR: THE HUMAN ELEMENT

The cost estimator has emerged as a key professional employee in many business, industrial, and governmental organizations. Cost estimating has grown into a profession that is beginning to equal the professions of accounting, marketing, and industrial engineering in importance. In the past, cost estimators came from a large variety of backgrounds and usually obtained their knowledge from on-the-job training. Very few had had formal training in cost estimating. The principal deterrent to the elevation of the cost estimator to a stature equal to a financial manager, accountant, or industrial engineer was the slow development of standardized procedures, professional qualifications, certifications, and formal training programs. Recent efforts by organizations such as the Society of Cost Estimating and Analysis, the American Society of Professional Estimators, the American Association of Cost Engineers, and many universities have paved the way for removal of these deficiencies and have provided focal points for improving the cohesiveness of the profession.

Skills required for cost estimating vary as widely as the types of work activities and work outputs being estimated. The disciplines involved include engineering, accounting, statistics, mathematics, economics, and industrial management. Although no formal degrees are offered in the field of cost estimating, most universities and colleges teach all of the disciplines required. Generally a cost estimator will have formal training in one or more of the fields just named. The motivation of the individual cost estimator is just as important a factor in assuming top performance in this field as it is in ensuring top performance in other fields. In the 1990s cost estimators will become increasingly important because of continuing scarcity of resources, increasingly larger high-technology content of work outputs and work activities, and greater competition from abroad.

Other factors that affect the cost estimators' performance include their interaction with others within and outside of the cost estimating organization, the use to which the estimate is applied, the feedback received in response to the estimating activities, possession of the right tools and data, and access to information on actual costs incurred in the performance of the work. A typical cost estimating situation will include the interaction of technical specialties, business or financial specialties, and accounting, mathematical, or statistical skills. The makeup of skills in the cost estimating group or activity depends to a large degree on the work being estimated. Generally an individual or group is assigned the task of estimating the cost of a work activity or work output; this individual or group can call on other individuals or groups within the organization for advice, information, and assistance. Indeed, the development of cost estimates typically requires this interaction. Therefore a cost estimating group is usually formed consisting of individuals with the appropriate technical, business, financial, marketing, and mathematical skills. Like any other formal or informal organization, this group needs a leader, variously called an estimate manager, proposal manager, estimate coordinator, or cost estimate leader or cost estimator, to bring together the appropriate skills, information, and knowledge required to produce the cost estimate.

Like any other professional, the cost estimator must have a code of professional standards and responsibilities. The three key responsibilities of a cost estimator are (1) independence, (2) integrity and objectivity, and (3) technical competence. Because of the constant and sometimes fierce competition that exists in a world of limited financial and physical resources, the cost estimator is often subject to pressures to compromise one or more of these responsibilities. Many businesses, industries, and government organizations purposely place their cost estimating activities outside the organization's line authority to protect the estimators and their estimates from inordinate or excessive pressures. Since the value of a cost estimate to management is a function of credibility and accuracy, it is important to retain this independence.

The most important motivating factor for a cost estimator is effective use of the cost estimate. Organizations have been known to spend considerable sums of money, labor-hours, and materials in developing a cost estimate and then fail to consider that estimate in their overall business, financial, and marketing plans. Assuming that an accurate and credible cost estimate has been prepared, it is a mistake for management to fail to use this tool. A principal problem of management in this regard is a failure to recognize that the "bottom line," or total cost number, is not the principal output of the estimate but that the details of the estimate itself should be used to adjust the available funds to the work content (or vice versa, as discussed in Chapter 10).

Once an organization is convinced of the value of cost estimating and is effectively using its estimates, the estimator or estimating group will be motivated to continue to provide a high level of integrity, objectivity, and technical competence.

THE ANATOMY OF AN ESTIMATE

The cost estimating process, like the manufacture of a product, is comprised of parallel and sequential steps that flow together and interact to culminate in a completed estimate. **Figure 2.1** shows the anatomy of an estimate. It depicts graphically

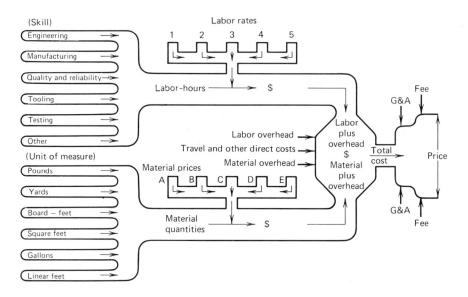

Figure 2.1   Anatomy of an estimate.

how the various cost estimate ingredients are synthesized from the basic labor-hour estimates and material quantity estimates. Labor-hour estimates of each basic skill required to accomplish the job are combined with the labor rates for these basic skills to derive labor dollar estimates. In the meantime, material quantities are estimated in terms of the units by which they are measured or purchased, and these material quantities are combined with their costs per unit to develop direct material dollar estimates. Labor overhead or burden is applied to direct material costs. Then travel costs and other direct costs are added to produce total costs; G&A expenses and fee or profit are added to derive the "price" of the final estimate.

The labor rates applied to the basic labor-hour estimates are usually "composite" labor rates; that is, they represent an average of the rates within a given skill category. For example, the engineering skill may include draftsmen, designers, engineering assistants, junior engineers, engineers, and senior engineers. The number and titles of engineering skills vary widely from company to company, but the use of a composite labor rate for the engineering skill category is common practice. The composite labor rate is derived by multiplying the labor rate for each skill by the percentage of labor-hours of that skill required to do a given task and adding the results. For example, if each of the six skills has the following labor rates and percentages, the composite labor rate is computed as follows:

Skill	Labor Rate ($/Hour)	Percentage in the Task
Draftsman	$ 9.00	7
Designer	$12.00	3

(Continued)

Engineering assistant	$15.00	10
Junior engineer	$19.50	20
Engineer	$22.00	50
Senior engineer	$27.00	10
Total		100

Composite labor rate $= (0.07 \times \$9.00) + (0.03 \times \$12.00) + (0.10 \times \$15.00) + (0.20 \times \$19.50) + (0.50 \times \$22.00) + (0.10 \times \$20.00) = \$19.39.$

Similar computations can be made to obtain the composite labor rate for skills within any of the other skill categories.

Another common practice is to establish separate overhead or burden pools for each skill category. These burden pools carry the peripheral costs related to and a function of the labor-hours expended in that particular skill category. Assuming that the burden pool is established for each of the labor skills shown in Figure 2.1, we can write an equation to depict the entire process. This equation is shown in **Figure 2.2**.

So far we have considered only a one-element cost estimate. The addition of multielement work activities or work outputs will greatly increase the number of mathematical computations, and it becomes readily evident that the anatomy of an estimate is so complex that computer techniques for computation are essential.

Time, Skills, and Labor-Hours Required to Prepare an Estimate

The resources (skills, calendar time, and labor-hours) required to prepare a cost estimate depend on a number of factors, one of them the estimating method used. Chapter 4 describes various estimating methods and their effect on the time required for estimating, as well as their influence on estimate accuracy and credibility. Another factor is the level of technology or state of the art involved in the job or task being estimated. A rule of thumb can be used to develop a rough idea of the estimating time required. The calendar time required to develop an accurate and credible estimate is usually about 8 percent of the calendar time required to accomplish a task involving existing technology and 18 percent for a task involving a high technology (e.g., nuclear plant construction, aerospace projects). These percentages are divided approximately as shown in **Table 2.5**.

Note that the largest percentage of the estimating time required is for defining the output, a subject covered in considerable detail in Chapter 3. This area is most important because it establishes a good basis for estimate credibility and accuracy, as well as making it easier for the estimator to develop supportable labor-hour and material estimates. These percentages also assume that the individuals who will perform the task or have intimate working knowledge of the task will assist in estimate preparation. Hence the skill mix for estimating is similar to that required for performing the task.

$$C_T = \Big\{ \ [(E_H \times E_R) \times (1 + E_0)] + [(M_H \times M_R) \times (1 + M_0)] + [(TO_H \times TO_R) \\ \times (1 + TO_0)] + [\ (Q_H \times Q_R) \times (1 + Q_0)] + [(TE_H + TE_R) \times (1 + TE_0)] \\ + [(O_H \times O_R) \times (1 + O_0)] + S_D + S_0 + [M_D \times (1 + M_{OH})] \\ + T_D + C_D + OD_D \Big\} \times \Big\{ GA + 1.00 \Big\} \times \Big\{ F + 1.00 \Big\}$$

(a)

$$C_T = \Big\{ \ [(L1_H \times L1_R) \times (1 + L1_0)] + [(L2_H \times L2_R) \times (1 + L2_0) \ldots + \\ [(LN_H \times LN_R \times (1 + LN_0)] + S_D + S_0 + [M_D \times (1 + M_{OH})] \\ + T_D + CD + OD_D \Big\} \times \Big\{ 1 + GA \Big\} \times \Big\{ 1 + F \Big\}$$

Where: $L1, L2, \ldots LN$ are various labor rate categories

(b)

Symbols:

$C_T =$ total cost

$E_H =$ engineering labor hours

$E_R =$ engineering composite labor rate in dollars per hour

$E_0 =$ engineering overhead rate in decimal form (i.e.: 1.15 = 115%)

$M_H =$ manufacturing labor hours

$M_R =$ manufacturing composite labor rate in dollars per hour

$M_0 =$ manufacturing overhead rate in decimal form

$TO_H =$ tooling labor hours

$TO_R =$ tooling composite labor rate in dollars per hour

$TO_0 =$ tooling overhead in decimal form

$Q_H =$ quality, reliability, and safety labor hours

$Q_R =$ quality, reliability, and safety composite labor rate in dollars per hour

$Q_0 =$ quality, reliability, and safety overhead rate in decimal form

$TE_H =$ testing labor hours

$TE_R =$ testing composite labor rate in dollars per hour

$TE_0 =$ testing overhead rate in decimal form

$O_H =$ other labor hours

Figure 2.2 Generalized equation for cost estimating.

O_R = labor rate for other hours category in dollars per hour

O_0 = overhead rate for other hours category in decimal form

S_D = major subcontract dollar

S_O = other subcontract dollars

M_D = material dollars

M_{OH} = material overhead in decimal form (10% = 0.10)

T_D = travel dollars

C_D = computer dollars

OD_D = other direct dollars

GA = general and administrative expense in decimal form (25% = 0.25)

F = fee in decimal form (8% = 0.08)

Figure 2.2   (*Continued*)

Labor-hours required for preparation of a cost estimate can be derived from these percentages by multiplying the task's calendar period in years by 2000 labor-hours per labor-year, multiplying the result by the percentage in Table 2.5, and then multiplying the result by 0.1 and by the number of personnel on the estimating team. Estimating team size is a matter of judgment and depends on the complexity of the task, but it is generally proportional to the skills required to perform the task.

Examples of the application of these rules of thumb for determining the resources required to prepare a cost estimate follow:

1. A three-year high-technology project involving 10 basic skills or disciplines requires the following number of labor-hours to estimate:

$$3 \times 2000 \times 0.18 \times 0.1 \times 10 = 1080.$$

TABLE 2.5   Estimating Time as a Percentage of Total Job Time

	Existing Technology (%)	High Technology (%)
Defining the output	4.6	14.6
Formulating the schedule and ground rules	1.2	1.2
Estimating materials and labor-hours	1.2	1.2
Estimating overhead, burden, and G&A	0.3	0.3
Estimating fee, profit, and earnings	0.3	0.3
Publishing the estimate	0.4	0.4
Total	8.0	18.0

2. A six-month "existing-technology" project requiring five skills or disciplines requires the following number of labor-hours to estimate:

$$0.5 \times 2000 \times 0.08 \times 0.1 \times 5 = 40.$$

These relationships are drawn from my experience in preparing and participating in a large number of cost estimates and can be relied on as a guideline in preparing for the estimating process. But remember that these are rules of thumb, and exercise caution and discretion in their application.

DISCUSSION OF TYPES OF COSTS

Table 2.6 provides examples of costs for various work outputs. Each of the types of costs are described in the following section.

Initial Acquisition Cost

Businesspeople, consumers, and government officials are becoming increasingly aware of the need to estimate accurately and to justify the initial acquisition cost of an item to be purchased, manufactured, or built. The trade-off between the initial acquisition costs and the benefits to be derived from an expenditure are covered in considerable detail in Chapter 11. When we speak of initial acquisition costs, we are usually referring to the total costs to develop, procure, install, and put into operation a piece of equipment, a product, or a structure. Initial acquisition costs do not consider costs associated with the use and possession of the item. Individuals or businesses that purchase products are beginning to give more serious consideration to maintenance, operation, depreciation, energy, insurance, storage, and disposal costs before purchasing an item, whether an automobile, home appliance, clothing, or industrial equipment. Because of inflation, it is as important to estimate accurately the most probable initial acquisition cost as it is to consider the cost savings brought about by use of the item being acquired. Initial acquisition costs include planning, estimating, designing, and or purchasing the components of the item; manufacturing, assembly, and inspection of the item; and installing and testing the item. Initial acquisition costs also include marketing, advertising, and markup of the price of the item as it flows through the distribution chain.

Fixed and Variable Costs

All four categories of productive outputs (processes, products, projects, and services) have both fixed and variable costs. The relationship between fixed and variable costs depends on a number of factors, but it is principally related to the kind of output being estimated and the rate of output. "Fixed cost" is that group of costs involved in an ongoing activity whose total will remain relatively constant regardless of the quantity of output or the phase of the output cycle being estimated. An

TABLE 2.6 Examples of Costs for Various Outputs

	Process	Product	Project	Service
Initial acquisition costs	Plant construction costs	Manufacturing costs, marketing costs, and profit	Planning costs, design costs, manufacturing costs, test and checkout costs, and delivery costs	Building rental
Fixed costs	Plant maintenance costs	Plant maintenance costs	Planning costs and design costs	
Variable costs	Raw material costs	Labor costs	Manufacturing costs, test and checkout costs, and delivery costs	Labor costs
Recurring costs	Raw materials costs	Labor and material costs	Manufacturing costs, test and checkout costs, and delivery costs	Labor costs
Nonrecurring costs	Plant construction costs	Plant construction costs	Planning costs and design costs	Initial capital equipment investment
Direct costs	Raw materials	Manufacturing costs	Planning, design manufacturing, test and checkout and delivery costs	Labor and materials costs
Indirect costs	Energy costs	Marketing costs and profit	Energy costs	Energy costs

example would be leasing costs for the manufacturing facility. "Variable cost" is the group of costs that vary in relationship to the rate of output. An example would be the raw material costs. Therefore, where it is desirable to know the effect of output rate on costs, it is important to know the relationship between the two forms of cost as well as the magnitude of these costs. Fixed costs are meaningful only if they are considered at a given point in time, since inflation and escalation will provide a variable element to so-called fixed costs. Fixed costs may be truly fixed only over a given range of outputs. Rental of floor space for a production machine is an example of a fixed cost; its use of electrical power will be a variable cost.

Recurring and Nonrecurring Costs

Recurring costs are those that are repetitive in nature and depend on continued output of a similar kind. They are similar to variable costs because they depend on the quantity or magnitude of output. Nonrecurring costs are those that are incurred to generate the first item of output. It is important to separate recurring and non-recurring costs if it is anticipated that the costs of continued or repeat production will be required at some future date.

Direct and Indirect Costs

Direct costs are those that are attributable directly to the specific work activity or work output being estimated. Indirect costs are those that are spread across several projects and allocable on a percentage basis to each project.

COLLECTING THE INGREDIENTS OF THE ESTIMATE

It is important to define the ingredients of an estimate and to give a preview of the techniques and methods that will be used to collect these estimate ingredients. (Chapter 6 discusses in detail how to collect the ingredients of the cost estimate.)

Labor-Hours

Since the expenditure of labor-hours is the basic reason for the occurrence of costs, the estimating of labor-hours is the most important aspect of cost estimating. Labor-hours and staffing requirements are estimated by five basic techniques: (1) use of the methods, time, and motion (MTM) techniques; (2) the staffing technique; (3) direct judgment of labor-hours required; (4) the use of labor-hour and staffing estimating handbooks; and (5) the use of parametric or statistical models for determining labor-hours.

MTM methods are the most widespread methods of deriving labor-hour and skill estimates for industrial processes. They are available from and taught by the MTM Association for Standards and Research, located in Fair Lawn, New Jersey. The association is international in scope and has developed five generations of MTM systems for estimating all aspects of industrial, manufacturing, and machining operations. The MTM method subdivides operator motions into small increments that can be measured and provides a means for combining the proper manual operations in a sequence to develop labor-hour requirements for accomplishing a job. Typical terms used in MTM are shown on **Table 2.7**. [An example of an MTM analysis was shown in **Figure 2.3**.] Standard times are computed using MTM and other similar methods.

The staffing technique is perhaps the simplest and most widely used method for estimating the labor-hours required to accomplish a given job. In this method, the estimator envisions the job, the work location, and the equipment or machines required and estimates the number of people and skills needed to staff a particular operation. The estimate is usually in terms of a number of people for a given number of days, weeks, or months. From this staffing level, the estimated on-the-job labor-hours required to accomplish the task can be computed.

Another method, closely related to the staffing technique, is the use of direct judgment of the number of labor-hours required. This judgment is usually made by an individual who has had experience in performing or supervising a similar task.

Finally, the use of handbooks is a widely used and accepted method of developing labor-hour estimates. Handbooks usually provide larger time increments than the MTM method and require a specific knowledge of the work content and operation being performed.

Materials and Subcontracts

Materials and subcontract dollars are estimated in three ways: (1) drawing "takeoffs"—a direct measurement of length, area, volume, or quantity from a drawing—and handbooks, (2) dollar-per-pound relationships, and (3) direct quotations or bids. The most accurate way to estimate *material costs* is to calculate material quantities directly from a drawing or specification of the completed product. Using the quantities required for the number of items to be produced, the appropriate materials manufacturer's handbook, and an allowance for scrap or waste, one can accurately compute the material quantities and prices. Where detailed drawings of the item to be produced are not available, a dollar-per-pound or dollar-per-square-foot relationship can be used to determine a rough order of magnitude cost. Firm quotations or bids for the materials or for the item to be subcontracted are excellent ways of developing a materials estimate because the supplier can be held to the bid.

Labor Rates and Factors

The labor rate, or number of dollars required per labor-hour, is the quantity that turns a labor-hour estimate into a cost estimate; therefore the labor rate and any direct cost factors added to it are key elements of the cost estimate. Labor rates vary by skill, geographical location, calendar date, and the time of day or week they are applied. Labor rates vary from over $4 per hour for hourly paid personnel to over

TABLE 2.7 Terms Used in MTM

Motion Element Term	Abbreviation	Description of Subelements
Apply Pressure	AP	
Crank	C	
Disengage	D	
Eye Focus	EF	
Eye Travel	ET	
Grasp	G	
Move	M	
	MA	Move object to other hand or against stop
	MB	Move object to approximate or indefinite location
	MC	Move object to exact location.
Position	P	
	P1	Loose fit
	P2	Close fit
	P3	Exact fit
Reach	R	
	RA	Reach to object in fixed location or to object in other hand
	RB	Reach to single object in varying location
	RC	Reach after a "search and select" operation
	RD	Reach to a very small object (accurate grasp required)
	RE	Reach to indefinite location, body balance, or positioning
Release	RL	
Turn	T	

Operation: Printed Circuit Assembly: Assemble Revision   Page 1 of 1

Date: 6/25/91   1/4 W to 1/2 N, Axial   S.D. > Ref# 2.1.3

Left Hand	Analysis	Time Management Unit[a]	Analysis[b]	Right Hand
		14.2	R12C	Reach to get resistor
		12.9	G4C	Get resistor
		2.5	MIA	Move from bin
		2.8	(50%) G2	Orient part
			MA	Move close to board
Look to sample or print	ET (16 × 16)	15.2		
Identify location	2 EF	14.6		
Look to board	ET (16 × 16)	15.2		
Identify point of assembly	2 EF	14.6		
		10.1	M6C	Move to position to board
		26.6	P2N5D	Position to board
		6.6	P2152	Align and insert 2nd end
		2.0	RL1	Release Resistor
			R A	Clear hand
Inspect assembly	EF	7.3		
Verify color code	EF & IN	12.35		
	Total	156.95		

Standard Minutes 0.094

Seconds: 5.65

Analyst: _____

Approval: _____

[a]Values are derived from Rodney D. Stewart and Richard M. Wyskida, *Cost Estimator's Reference Manual* (New York: Wiley, 1987), Chapter 11.

[b]Indicates the number of time measurement units (0.036 seconds) required for each operation. R = Reach; G = Grasp; M = Move; P = Position. (See Table 2-7).

Figure 2.3   An example of MTM analysis.

$30 per hour for salaried personnel. Labor rates vary geographically by a factor of 2.61 to 1 in the continental United States and 3.61 to 1 if Alaska is included. The calendar date affects the labor rate because inflation must be added each year to adjust wages to the cost-of-living increases encountered during that year. Shift premiums, overtime pay, and hazardous duty pay are also added to hourly wages to develop the actual labor rate used in developing a cost estimate. Wage rate structures vary considerably depending on union contract agreements. Once the labor rate is applied to the labor-hour estimate to develop a labor cost figure, other factors are commonly used to develop other direct cost allowances, such as travel costs and direct material costs.

Indirect Costs, Burden, and Overhead

Burden or overhead costs for engineering activities often are as high as 100 percent of direct engineering labor costs, and manufacturing overheads go to 150 percent and beyond. A company that can keep its overhead from growing excessively or even trim the overhead can place itself in an advantageously competitive position. Since overhead more than doubles the cost of a work activity or work output, trimming the overhead has a significant effect on reducing overall costs.

Administrative Costs

Administrative costs range up to 20 percent of total direct and indirect costs for large companies. G&A costs are added to direct and overhead costs and are recognized as a legitimate business expense.

Fee, Profit, or Earnings

The fee, profit, or earnings will depend on the amount of risk the company is taking in marketing the product, the market demand for the item, and the required return on the company's investment. This subject, treated in more detail in Chapter 8, deserves considerable attention by the cost estimator. Basically the amount of profit depends on the astute business sense of the company's management. Few companies will settle for less than 6 or 7 percent profit, and many will not make an investment or enter into a venture unless they can calculate a 20 to 30 percent return.

Assembly of the Ingredients

Once resource estimates have been accumulated, the process of reviewing, compiling, organizing, and computing the estimate begins. This process is divided into two general subdivisions of work: (1) reviewing, compiling, and organizing the input resource data and (2) computing the costs based on desired or approved labor rates and factors. A common mistake made in developing cost estimates is the failure to perform the first of these work subdivisions properly. In the process of reviewing, compiling, and organizing the data, duplications in resource estimates are discovered and eliminated, omissions are located and remedied, overlapping or redundant effort is recognized and adjusted, and missing or improper rationale, backup data, or supporting data are identified, corrected, or supplied. A thorough review of the cost estimate input data by the estimator or estimating team, along with an adjustment and reconciliation process, will accomplish these objectives. With the basic ingredients and basic tools available, we are now ready to follow the steps required to develop a good cost estimate. The following chapters describe these steps in detail. All steps are needed for any good cost estimate. The manner of accomplishing each step, and the depth of information needed and time expended on each step, will vary considerably depending on the work activity or work output that is being estimated. These steps are as follows:

1. Define the product, process, project, or service.
2. Develop a methodology and estimate schedule.
3. Formulate a project schedule.
4. Prepare estimate ground rules.
5. Estimate labor-hours and materials and other direct costs.
6. Review, compile, organize, reconcile, and compute the estimate.
7. Analyze the resulting estimate for credibility, competitiveness, completeness, comprehension, and compatibility with budget constraints.
8. Revise, if required, and publish the estimate.
9. Use the estimate.

NOTES

1. *Webster's New Collegiate Dictionary* (Springfield, Mass.: G. C. Merriam Co., 1981), p. 388.
2. National Estimating Society, *By-Laws* (March 1978).
3. A 12-step methodological estimating approach is presented in Rodney D. Stewart and Richard M. Wyskida, eds., *Cost Estimator's Reference Manual* (New York: Wiley, 1987), chap. 1.

QUESTIONS

2.1. What are the four kinds of work output?

2.2. Define cost estimating.

2.3. Explain the difference between cost and price.

2.4. What are the basic ingredients of an estimate?

2.5. What are the five basic tools of the estimating process?

2.6. Travel can be considered as a separate element of cost.   T   F

2.7. For a typical cost estimating exercise, number in chronological order the following events:

    a. Develop a methodology for estimating and a schedule for doing it.

    b. Prepare the estimating ground rules.

    c. Review inputs; then compile, organize, and compute the estimate.

    d. Formulate a schedule for the work to be estimated.

    e. Use the estimate.

    f. Publish the estimate.

    g. Estimate all labor, materials, and other direct costs.

    h. Define the work to be done.

3

DEFINING THE WORK

As a wise master builder I laid a foundation, and another is building upon it. But let each man be careful how he builds upon it.

1 Corinthians 3:10

THE FIRST QUESTIONS TO ASK (AND WHY)

When you are estimating the cost of a process, product, project, or service, there are some basic questions to ask in order to get started. These questions relate principally to the requirements, descriptions, location, and timing of the work.

In government projects, and in many commercial projects, the Statement of Work is the source document that defines what is to be accomplished and, for our purposes, what is to be estimated. The Statement of Work is the most important document in defining the effort. Any work not found listed in it should not be included as part of a responsive estimate. This document is the primary source for answering the following questions about the work.

What Is It?

A surprising number of cost estimates fail to be accurate or credible because of a lack of specificity in describing the work being estimated. The objectives, ground rules, constraints, and requirements of the work must be spelled out in detail to form the basis for a good cost estimate. First, it is necessary to determine which of the four generic work outputs (process, product, project, or service) or combination of work outputs best describes the work being estimated. Then it is necessary to describe the work in as much detail as possible.

What Does It Look Like?

Work descriptions usually take the form of detailed specifications, sketches, drawings, materials lists, and parts lists. Weight, size, shape, material type, power, accuracy, resistance to environmental hazards, and quality are typical parameters described in detail in a specification. Processes and services are usually defined by the required quality, accuracy, speed, consistency, or responsiveness of the work. Products and projects usually require a preliminary or detailed design of the item or group of items being estimated. In general, more detailed designs will produce more accurate cost estimates. The principal reason for this is that as a design proceeds, better definitions and descriptions of all facets of this design unfold. The design process is an interactive one in which component or subsystem designs proceed in parallel; component or subsystem characteristics reflect upon and affect one another to alter the configuration and perhaps even the performance of the end item. Another reason that a more detailed design results in a more accurate and credible cost estimate is that the amount of detail itself produces a greater awareness and visibility of potential inconsistencies, omissions, duplications, and overlaps. Next to the statement of work, the technical specifications are most important.

When Is It To Be Available?

Production rate, production quantity, and timing of production initiation and completion are important to establish before starting a cost estimate. Factors such as raw material availability, labor skills required, and equipment utilization often force a work activity to conform to a specific time period. It is important to establish the optimum time schedule early in the estimating process, to establish key milestone dates, and to subdivide the overall work schedule into identifiable increments that can be placed on a calendar time scale. A work output schedule placed on a calendar time scale will provide the basic information needed to compute start-up costs, fiscal year funding, and inflationary effects. The delivery schedule is next in importance in defining a total program.

How Is The Work Structured?

In defining a total program, the next most important question to be answered is "How is the work structured?". The work structure should be as detailed as program definition will allow. The work breakdown structure is a hierarchy of work elements and subordinate tasks; and these tasks can be assigned to performing organizations for estimation and subsequent performance.

Who Will Do It?

The organization or organizations that will perform an activity, as well as the skill and salary levels within these organizations, must be known or assumed to formulate a credible cost estimate. Given a competent organization with competent employees, another important aspect of developing a competitive cost estimate is the determination of the make-or-buy structure and the skill mix needs throughout the work activity. Judicious selection of the performers, and wise time phasing of skill categories and skill levels, can rapidly produce prosperity for any organization with a knowledge of its employees, product, and customer.

Where Will It Be Done?

Geographical factors have a strong influence on the credibility and competitive stature of a cost estimate. In addition to the wide variation in labor costs for various locations, material costs vary substantially from location to location, and transportation costs enter heavily into the cost picture. The cost estimator must develop detailed ground rules and assumptions concerning location of the work and then estimate costs accurately in keeping with all location-oriented factors.

The most important input to a cost estimate is the Statement of Work, followed by the technical specifications, the delivery schedule, and the work breakdown structure.

THE ESTIMATE SKELETON: THE WORK BREAKDOWN STRUCTURE

The first step in developing a cost estimate of any type of work output is the development of a work breakdown structure (sometimes called a work element structure). The structure serves as a framework for collecting, accumulating, organizing, and computing the direct and directly related costs of a work activity or work output. It should be used for managing and reporting resources and related costs throughout the lifetime of the work. There is considerable advantage in using the work breakdown structure and its accompanying task descriptions as the basis for scheduling, reporting, tracking, and organizing, as well as for initial costing. Hence, it is important to devote considerable attention to this phase of the estimating process. A work breakdown structure is developed by subdividing a process, product, project, or service into its major work elements, breaking the major work elements into subelements, subelements into subsubelements, and so on. There are usually five to 10 subelements under each major work element.

The purpose of developing the work breakdown structure is sixfold:

1. To provide a lower-level breakout of small tasks that are easy to identify, staff, schedule, and estimate.
2. To provide assurance that all required tasks are included in the work output.
3. To reduce the possibility of overlap, duplication, or redundancy of tasks.
4. To furnish a convenient hierarchical structure for the accumulation of resource estimates.
5. To give greater overall visibility as well as depth of penetration, to the makeup of any work activity.
6. To provide a basis of comparison for the actual work completed versus the estimate.

THE HIERARCHICAL RELATIONSHIP OF A
WORK BREAKDOWN STRUCTURE

A typical work breakdown structure is shown in **Figure 3.1**. The relationship resembles a hierarchy where each activity has a higher activity, parallel activities, and lower activities. A basic principle of work breakdown structures is that the resources or content of each work element are made up of the sum of the resources or content of elements below it. No work element that has lower elements exceeds the sum of those lower elements in resource requirements. The bottom-most elements are estimated at their own level and sum to higher levels. Many numbering systems are feasible and workable. The numbering system shown is one that has proved workable in a wide variety of situations. Many complex structures use alpha characters to expand the available levels and elements.

One common mistake in using work breakdown structures is to try to allocate effort to every block, even those at a higher level. Keep in mind that this should not be done because each block or work element contains only that effort included in those elements *below* it. If there are no blocks below it, then it can contain resources. If there is a need to add work activities or resources not included in a higher-level block, add an additional block below it to include the desired effort. Level 1 of a work breakdown structure is usually the top level, with lower levels numbered sequentially, as shown. The "level" is usually equal to the number of digits in the work element block. For example, the block numbered 1.1.3.2 is in level 4 because it contains four digits.

FUNCTIONAL ELEMENTS

The major subdivisions of a work activity or work output can be either functional or physical elements. In fact, the second level in a work breakdown structure usually consists of both functional and physical elements if a product or project is being estimated. For a process or service, all second-level activities could be functional. Functional elements of a production or project activity can include activities such as planning, project management, systems engineering and integration, testing, logistics, and operations. A process or service can include any of hundreds of functional elements. Typical examples of the widely dispersed functional elements that can be found in a work breakdown structure for a service are advising, assembling, binding, cleaning, fabricating, inspecting, packaging, painting, programming, projecting, receiving, testing, and welding.

PHYSICAL ELEMENTS

The physical elements of a work output are the physical structures, hardware, products, or end items that are supplied to the consumer. These physical elements

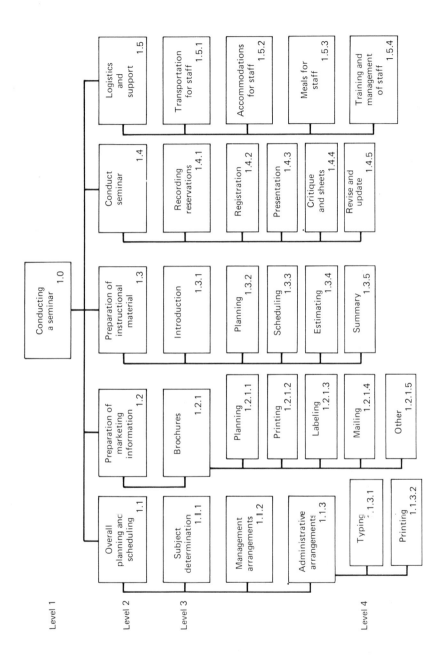

Figure 3.1 Typical work breakdown structure.

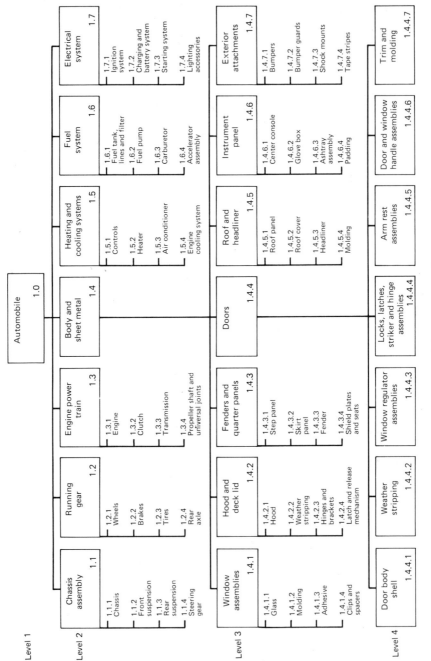

Figure 3.2 Work breakdown structure for an automobile.

represent resources because they take labor and materials to produce. Hence, they can and should be a basis for the work breakdown structure.

Figure 3.2 shows a typical work breakdown structure of the physical elements of an automobile. The figure shows how one automobile company chose to subdivide the components of its product. For any given product or project, the number of ways that a work breakdown structure can be constructed are virtually unlimited. For example, the company could have included the carburetor and engine cooling system as part of the engine assembly (this might have been a more logical and workable arrangement since it is used in costing a mass production operation). Note that the structure shows a level 3 breakout of the body and sheet metal element, and the door (a level 3 element) is subdivided into its level 4 components.

This physical element breakout demonstrates several important characteristics of a work breakdown structure. First, notice that level 5 would be the individual component parts of each assembly or subassembly. It took only three subdivisions of the physical hardware to penetrate to a point where the next-level breakout would be the individual parts. One can see rapidly that breaking down every level 2 element three more levels (down to level 5) would result in a very large work breakdown structure. Second, to convert this physical hardware breakout into a true work breakdown structure would require the addition of some functional activities. To provide the labor as well as the materials required to procure, manufacture, assemble, test, and install the components of each block, it is necessary to add an assembly, fabrication, or installation activity block.

TREATMENT OF RECURRING AND NONRECURRING ACTIVITIES

Most work consists of both nonrecurring activities, or "one-of-a-kind" activities needed to produce an item or to provide a service, and recurring or repetitive activities, which must be performed to provide more than one output unit. The resources requirements (labor-hours and materials) necessary to perform these nonrecurring and recurring activities reflect themselves in nonrecurring and recurring costs.

Although not all estimates require separating nonrecurring and recurring costs, it is often both convenient and necessary to separate them because one may need to know the costs for an increased work output rate. Since work output rate principally affects the recurring costs, it is desirable to have these costs readily accessible and identifiable.

Nonrecurring and recurring costs can be separated in two ways through the use of the work breakdown structure concept. First, the two costs can be identified, separated, and accounted for within each work element. Resources for each task block would, then, include three sets of resource estimates: (1) nonrecurring costs, (2) recurring costs, and (3) total costs for that block. The second convenient method of cost separation is to start with identical work breakdown structures for both costs and develop two separate cost estimates. A third estimate, which sums the two cost estimates into a total, can also use the same basic work breakdown structure.

Elements unique to each cost category can be added to the appropriate work breakdown structure.

WORK BREAKDOWN STRUCTURE INTERRELATIONSHIPS

As the automobile example shows, the work breakdown structure provides considerable flexibility concerning the placement of physical elements. (The same is true with functional elements.) Because of this and because it is necessary to define clearly where one element leaves off and the other takes over, it is necessary to provide a detailed definition of what is included in each work activity block. For example, in the automotive example, the rear axle unit could have been located and defined as part of the power train or as part of the chassis assembly rather than as part of the running gear. Where does the rear axle leave off and the power train begin? Is the differential or part of it included in the power train? These kinds of questions must be answered before a detailed cost estimate is generated, in the form of a work breakdown structure dictionary. The dictionary describes exactly what is included in each work element and what is excluded, it defines where the interface is located between two work elements, and it defines where the assembly effort is located to assemble or install two interfacing units. An example of a detailed work breakdown structure dictionary is shown in Appendix III.

A good work breakdown structure dictionary will prevent many problems brought about by overlaps, duplications, and omissions because detailed thought has been given to the interfaces and content of each work activity.

Skill Matrix in a Work Breakdown Structure

When constructing a work breakdown structure, keep in mind that each work element will be performed by a person or group of people using one or more skills. There are two important facets of the labor or work activity for each work element: skill mix and skill level. The skill mix is the proportion of each of several skill categories that will be employed in performing the work. Skill categories vary widely and depend on the type of work being estimated. For a residential construction project, for example, typical skills would be bricklayer, building laborer, carpenter, electrician, painter, plasterer, and plumber. Other typical construction skills are structural steelworker, cement finisher, glazier, roofer, sheet metal worker, pipefitter, excavation equipment operator, and general construction laborer. On the other hand, professional skills such as those of lawyers, doctors, financial officers, administrators, project managers, engineers, printers, and writers, are called on to do a wide variety of direct labor activities. Occasionally skills will be assembled into several broad categories (such as engineering, manufacturing, tooling testing, and quality assurance) that correspond to overhead or burden pools.

Skill levels reflect the experience and salary level of individuals working within a given skill category. For example, engineers are subdivided into various categories such as principal engineers, senior engineers, engineers, associate engineers, junior engineers, and engineering technicians. The skilled trades are subdivided into skill level categories and given names that depict their skill level; for example, carpenters could be categorized as master carpenters, carpenters, journeymen carpenters, apprentice carpenters, and carpenter helpers.

Because skill categories and skill levels are designated for performing work within each work element, it is not necessary to establish separate work elements for performance of each skill. A work breakdown structure for home construction would not have an element designated carpentry because carpentry is a skill needed to perform one or more of the work elements (e.g., roof construction, wall construction).

Organizational Relationships to a Work Breakdown Structure

Frequently all or part of a work breakdown structure will have a direct counterpart in the performing organization. Although it is not necessary for the work breakdown structure to be directly correlated to the organizational structure, it is often convenient to assign the responsibility for estimating and for performing a specific work element to a specific organizational segment. This practice helps to motivate the performer, since it gives the performer responsibility for an identifiable task, and it provides the manager greater assurance that each part of the work will be accomplished. In the planning and estimating process, early assignment of work elements to those who will be responsible for performing the work will motivate them to do a better job of estimating and will provide greater assurance that the work will be completed within performance, schedule, and cost constraints because the functional organizations have set their own goals. Job performance and accounting for work accomplished versus funds spent can also be accomplished more easily if an organizational element is held responsible for a specific work element in the work breakdown structure.

DEFINING THE ESTIMATE INGREDIENTS

Equipment

Personnel, equipment, and facilities are the three resources that provide a business, industry, or governmental organization with the capability of performing useful work. Usually all three are required for any continuing or recurring business activity. Even many organizations that are principally service oriented require equipment and facilities to provide their service. By the time an organization grows to a size of more than just a few employees, it usually acquires some type of equipment for performance of its work. Often it is the use of specialized equipment, coupled with skilled and experienced personnel, that gives one company or organization the competitive edge over another.

Equipment costs are an important part of an organization's expense and enter into an overall cost estimate in several ways. First, equipment costs can be considered as a directly related or direct cost to the job being done. If the equipment is sufficiently specialized and will be used only for the task being estimated, it is added to the direct costs of performing the work. More frequently, however, equipment is purchased as a capital investment item and is used for a number of different activities related to a given type of work output. Occasionally equipment lease costs will be charged directly to a project for the time that the specific project or work activity uses the equipment.

Facilities

Facilities are most often estimated as part of a company's overhead, general and administrative expenses, or capital investments derived from profit or fee. Facilities usually consist of land, buildings, or fixed installations that belong to the performing organization and are operated to support a continuing business activity. The cost of maintaining and operating a facility is one of the largest elements in overhead costs.

Labor

As one of the major cost elements in doing any type of work, labor costs have received the most attention of planners, schedulers, and estimators in the past. Labor costs make up 50 to 95 percent of direct costs; moreover, they are more susceptible than other costs to increases or decreases in productivity. Because labor costs are such a large part of any work activity, motivation of the work force to produce maximum output can have a significant impact on the cost-effectiveness and the competitive stature of a work output.

Manufactured Parts

Manufactured parts are those manufactured in and by the performing organization's own shops. Usually the decision to manufacture parts in-house has been the result of the evaluation of costs of subcontracting the work or purchasing the parts versus building or manufacturing them in-house. Sometimes however, overriding factors such as time required to go through the procurement cycle, shipping distances and shipping time delays, in-house availability of personnel and proved techniques, and union disputes have resulted in a decision to use manufactured rather than purchased parts. In general it is better to manufacture parts in-house if small quantities are needed, if lead times are short, and if the materials and skills required are available.

It is usually easier to estimate the costs of an in-house manufacturing activity because of familiarity with the personnel, equipment, facilities, and manufacturing methods that will be used.

Purchased Parts or Materials

When larger quantities of parts or materials are required and expert organizations capable of producing these items are available, responsive, and economical, it is better to procure them through another organization. The specialization of American business has made it desirable to procure specialized parts and materials from those most experienced in producing high-quality parts and materials of the type required. The best cost estimate for purchased parts is a firm quotation or bid for the specific type and quantity desired. The next best type of cost estimate is a handbook or catalog price. Handbook or catalog prices are only second best because they are often outdated and often do not reflect the costs of the precise quantities or configurations desired.

Subcontracts

Subcontracts are particularly useful when the required skills or equipment are not readily available to the performing organization or when the work load is sporadic and requires time-phased addition or deletion of effort as a work activity progresses. It is usually profitable to go to the expert if a specific skill or service is desired, and it is desirable to issue a request for quotation and receive a firm bid from the subcontracting organization. Where sufficient time is available, it is desirable to solicit bids from several companies to obtain the best job at the lowest cost. Many organizations have excelled in their fields with little more than good management and administration through the skillful use of multiple subcontracts.

Tooling

Tooling is usually separated from equipment, facilities, materials, and purchased or manufactured parts because it is of a special nature, being designed and manufactured to produce a specific product. Tooling is usually considered a major element of the nonrecurring costs of producing an item, and the tooling sometimes (but not always) can be modified or used for manufacturing or producing another product. Tooling is usually subdivided or categorized into "soft" tooling and "hard" tooling. Soft tooling is less specialized, less permanent, and more flexibly adaptable to changes in configuration of the manufactured or produced item. Hard tooling is built to withstand long production runs, is less adaptable to changes, and is specialized. There are various degrees of softness and hardness, depending primarily on the length of the production run. Harder tooling usually permits a higher production rate but usually is more expensive.

BUILDING IN COST-EFFECTIVENESS

There are various steps that can be taken in developing a cost estimate to build in cost-effectiveness. If these steps are taken at the outset, the chances of producing a credible, accurate, and achievable cost are much greater than if these steps are taken later in the estimating process. The science of cost estimating or, more properly, the art of cost estimating is still progressing to a point where the average businessperson understands why costs are what they are. And usually once a cost estimate is developed, the tendency is to stick to that estimate despite any contrary evidence that the estimate should be higher or lower. This phenomenon is an aspect of human nature that has not yet been overcome by the development and proof of infallible means of estimating costs—and is not likely to change until even more methodical and systematic methods are universally applied.

Choose the Right Make-or-Buy Structure

For a given work output to be provided by a given business, industrial, or governmental organization, there is undoubtedly an optimally cost-effective make-or-buy structure. The key to cost-effectiveness is to come as close as possible to this optimum in the original estimate and to stay with it as closely as practicable during performance of the work. Changes in make-or-buy arrangements during the progress of work activity, unless tied to newly discovered cost efficiencies, can have a disastrous effect on costs and schedules owing to the need for training a new organization or team to do the work. The best rule to apply is to make best use of your own work force and then to add subcontract skills and services that do not exist in your own organization. Subcontracts can also be used to handle peak work loads, resulting in greater stability of employment for full-time career employees.

Choose the Best Location

With continuing uncertainty in energy, transportation, and travel costs, it is becoming increasingly important to choose the appropriate geographical location for performance of the work. Some companies are establishing new divisions or locating new subsidiaries near the customer to reduce transportation and travel costs for goods and personnel. The move to geographical areas with low-cost energy and transportation has become a necessary and even essential practice in many instances in order to keep pace with increasing competition from abroad.

Balance and Time Phase the Skill Mix and Skill Levels

One often overlooked method of cutting costs while still providing an achievable performance target is skillfully and carefully balancing and time phasing the mix and level of skills employed in the work activity. Higher skill levels are usually needed at the beginning of a new work activity because innovation and flexibility born of experience are needed to adapt an organization to a new work effort. Once the initial learning experience has been encountered and successfully met, however, lower-level skills should immediately replace higher-level skills wherever possible to reduce costs commensurate with product maturity. Also, the mixture of skills used on a job should be appropriately adjusted as the work progresses to prevent dead time for those skills not required during subsequent phases of the work.[1] Ideally, multiple work outputs being provided by any organization should be time phased and interrelated to provide maximum utilization of each employed skill category and skill level. This integration of multiple work activities is a master planning activity that most companies and businesses employ, but many performing organizations fail to make maximum use of an overview knowledge of multiple work activities to off-load higher-paid personnel effectively and responsively from mature projects to new work activities that need these higher-skill levels. A judicious use and time phasing of skill categories and skill levels among several work activities can result in highly competitive cost estimates.

Team with the Experts

The old saying that nothing succeeds like success is well worn but nevertheless paramount in cost estimating just as it is in any other field of endeavor. When seeking a good cost estimator, you should look to those who have had a history of making accurate and credible cost estimates. The person who is successful as a performer usually knows how well he or she performs and is usually the best able to estimate how well he or she will or can expect to perform the next time. The experience and wisdom of a successful employee or organization cannot be replaced by cost models, formulas, or computer programs.

Beware of Bureaucracy from Within

A key pitfall to avoid when defining the work output and getting ready to make a cost estimate is the expansion of requirements or resources brought about by the self-interests of the individuals or groups preparing the estimate. Salary structures and fringe benefits of supervisors and managers are structured according to the extent, scope, size, and budget of the subunit or element of the organization being supervised or managed. For this reason, an element of an organization may tend to expand, extend, build up, and otherwise magnify or increase the estimates of effort under its control. This tendency for escalation and expansion, caused by purely human motives, must be counteracted by close control and scrutiny of resource estimates if a credible, competitive, and achievable cost estimate is to be derived. It is important that this control be exercised at the beginning of the definition process, since work activity definition is a principal driver of work activity costs.

NOTE

1. See the concepts of static, dynamic, and dynamically adjusted skill mixes in Rodney D. Stewart and Richard M. Wyskida, eds., *Cost Estimator's Reference Manual* (New York: Wiley, 1987), chap. 1.

QUESTIONS

3.1. A Statement of Work (select one):

    a. Lists the agreements between the contractor and his or her employees.

    b. Ensures that no strikes will take place during the contract period.

    c. States the confines of the contractual work to be accomplished.

    d. None of the above.

3.2. You have been given the responsibility for preparing a technical specification package for a hardware development program. List five typical parameters you would define and provide in your technical specification.

3.3. In defining a total program, list the following in order of importance:

    a. Statement of work.

    b. Technical specifications.

    c. Work breakdown structure.

    d. Delivery schedule.

3.4. The statement of work is the key element in program definition because (select one):

    a. It states what is to be done.

    b. It establishes a baseline for estimating and pricing.

    c. It informs the customer of organizational arrangements.

    d. It justifies the price.

3.5. Of the following, select the one category that would not be usual program definition data.

    a. Statement of work.

    b. Financial statements.

    c. Schedules.

    d. Equipment list.

    e. Make-or-buy plan.

4
THE TOOLS REQUIRED FOR ESTIMATING

And behold, there was a wall on the outside of the temple all around, and in the man's hand was a measuring rod of six cubits, each of which was a cubit and a handbreadth. So he measured the thickness of the wall, one rod; and the height, one rod.

Ezekiel 40:5

FOUR BASIC TOOLS

Information

Every cost estimate must be based on complete, thorough, and current information concerning the process, product, project, or service being estimated. The information takes many forms, among them drawings, specifications, production schedules, manufacturing plans, actual production labor-hour and cost records, handbooks, professional and reference books, personal knowledge of the shop or office operation, and market or industrial surveys. A credible and usable cost estimate can be formulated by selecting the appropriate information from among this vast store of knowledge and synthesizing the information as inputs to the cost estimate.

Methods

Before starting to develop a cost estimate, a decision must be made concerning the estimating method or combination of methods to be used. The method chosen depends principally on the time allotted to prepare the estimate and the accuracy and depth of penetration of rationale required.

Schedule

A vital tool required for the development of a good cost estimate is a schedule for the estimating activity itself. For simple cost estimates a completion date may be all that is required. An in-depth detailed cost estimating or cost proposal activity, however, must be supported by an estimating schedule that shows all phases of the estimating cycle.

Skills

A number of different skills are needed in the preparation of a cost estimate. Whether these skills are possessed by one person or by an organization, it is necessary to arrange for their availability and application to the cost estimating process during the appropriate time phase of the estimating activity.

INFORMATION TO BE COLLECTED BEFORE STARTING AN ESTIMATE

Recent Experience in Similar Work

One of the most valuable categories of information used for cost estimating is actual data concerning the resources used in recently performing similar or identical work. This information can be obtained from periodic personnel and financial reports or from records of actual on-site observations of work processes.

There are several pitfalls to avoid in using actual performance data from past or current activities. One is the possibility of ignoring or failing to discover inefficiencies in the past or current work. If inherent inefficiencies in performing a specific task are not eliminated, the estimate will have a built-in bias that will make the estimate excessively high and could cause loss of business to the competition. Another pitfall is the failure to adjust the data to the specific ground rules of the work being estimated. Unmodified resource data from an activity cannot be used for estimating another activity unless the activities are identical. Any changes in complexity, quantity, environment, location, and delivery schedule could cause significant differences in costs.

An important part of any cost estimating organization's activities is the documentation, collection, summarization, and storage of previously estimated or performed work. This information, if complete and well-organized, can be an indispensable asset in cost estimating. When collecting and storing actual and/or estimated resource data from previous work activities, keep in mind that it must have enough "granularity," or visibility into the depth of the activity, to be useful in producing estimates of similar depth.

Professional and Reference Material

The Bibliography to this book contains a list of publications that can be used as reference material for supporting the various aspects of cost estimating, and there are many more such references than those included here. Useful reference books to support cost estimating activities can usually be found under the headings of accounting, cost control, construction estimating, economics, engineering economics, learning curves, management, statistics, and wages and salaries, among others. These books, as well as appropriate periodicals, reports, theses, surveys, and bibliographies, can be found in corporate libraries, university libraries, public libraries, and government agencies, as well as in libraries and book or periodical collections of individual cost estimators, accountants, engineers, managers, professional engineers, architects, and contractors. In preparing a cost estimate, it is important to do sufficient library research to assure yourself that you have the most up-to-date information on the resources required to accomplish the job.

Knowledge of Shop or Office Operation

Before starting the cost estimating process, the estimator must become familiar with the facilities, equipment, and personnel who will perform the work. Recent shop records, production records, labor reports, material reports, and time-and-motion surveys are helpful. In software development or maintenance, the estimator must become familiar with the user's requirements, the organization that will be performing the development or maintenance, and the tools that will be used to assist in the software production work. Because of the complexity of most current high-technology tasks, it is particularly important to have direct access to the judgment and knowledge of individuals who have been performing the work. The person who will do the work is not only more qualified to provide accurate estimate data but is also motivated to provide a realistic estimate because the consequences of over-estimating or underestimating can be severe. For instance, a company proposal that is over- or underestimated may mean the loss of a contract due to insufficient resources. Knowledge of the shop or office facilities, equipment, and personnel includes the projected or expected upgrading, modification, or replacement of equipment or facilities and the potential future loss or gain of personnel skills and capabilities.

Market and Industrial Surveys

An essential part of the information that is needed to start the development of a credible, accurate, and competitive cost estimate is a market or industrial survey that shows the demand, the potential supply of the work output, and competitive forces that may affect the supply, demand, or price of an item (see Chapter 8). This all-important information will be used to establish cost targets and pricing objectives and could very well affect the schedule, quantities, or specifications of the selected work output.

These market and industrial surveys can best be performed by the organization doing the estimating. Although consultants, marketing firms, public relations firms, and advertising agencies are available to assist in the estimating, these outside individuals and/or firms tend to be overly optimistic and often do not take into consideration the possible pitfalls of a venture. This is principally because they obtain their fee even if the operation fails, and they have little to lose as an entity.

The best advice in deriving marketing objectives and goals is to involve the part of the organization that will perform the work. This will provide sufficient realism and credibility to counteract the optimism of the marketing department or sales representatives.

METHODS USED IN THE ESTIMATING PROCESS

Detailed Estimating

Detailed estimating involves the synthesis of a cost estimate from resource estimates made at the lowest possible level in the work breakdown structure. Detailed estimating presumes that a detailed design of the product or project is available and that a detailed manufacturing, assembly, testing, and delivery schedule is available for the work. This type of estimating assumes that skills, labor-hours, and materials can be identified for each work element through one or more of the methods that follow. A detailed estimate is usually developed through a synthesis of work element estimates developed by various methods.

Direct Estimating

A direct estimate is a judgmental estimate made in a "direct" method by an estimator or performer who is familiar with the task being estimated. The estimator will observe and study the task to be performed and then quote the estimate in terms of labor-hours, materials, and/or dollars. For example, a direct estimate could be quoted as "so many dollars." Many expert estimators can size up and estimate a job with just a little familiarization. One estimator I know can take a fairly complex drawing and, within just a few hours, develop a rough order-of-magnitude estimate of the resources required to build the item. Direct estimating is a skill that comes with experience in both estimating and actually performing the work.

Estimating by Analogy

This method is similar to the direct estimating method in that considerable judgment is required, but an additional feature is the comparison with some existing or past task of similar description. The estimator collects resource information on a similar or analogous task and compares the task to be estimated with the similar or analogous one. He or she would say that "this task should take about twice the time [labor-hours, dollars, materials, etc.] as [the one used as a reference]." This judgmental factor (a factor of 2) would then be multiplied by the resources used for the reference task to develop the estimate for the new task. A significant pitfall in this method of estimating is the potential inability of the estimator to identify subtle differences in the two work activities and, hence, to be estimating the cost of a system based on one that is really not similar or analogous.

Firm Quotes

One of the best methods of estimating the resources required to complete a work element or to perform a work activity is the development of a firm quotation by the supplier or vendor. The two keys to the development of a realistic quotation are (1) the solicitation of bids from at least three sources and (2) the development of a detailed and well-planned request for quotation (RFQ). Years of experience by many organizations in the field of procurement have indicated that three bids are the optimum from a standpoint of achieving the most realistic and reasonable price at a reasonable expenditure of effort. The acquisition of at least three bids provides sufficient check and balance and furnishes realistic bid prices and conditions for comparison, evaluation, and selection. A good RFQ is essential, however, to produce bids that will enable you to evaluate the bids effectively. The RFQ should contain ground rules, schedules, delivery locations and conditions, evaluation criteria, and specifications for the work. It should also state and specify the format required for cost information. A well-prepared RFQ will result in a quotation or proposal that will be easily evaluated, verified, and compared with independent estimates.

Handbook Estimating

Handbooks, catalogs, and reference books containing information on virtually every conceivable type of product, part, supplies, equipment, raw material, and finished material are available in libraries, bookstores, and directly from publishers. Many of these handbooks provide labor estimates for installation or operation, as well as the purchase price of the item. Some catalogs either do not provide price lists or provide price lists as a separate insert to permit periodic updates of prices without changing the basic catalog description. Information services provide on-line databases, updated optical disks, or microfilmed cassettes and viewing devices for access to the descriptions and costs of thousands and even tens of thousands of items.

If you produce a large number of estimates, it may pay to subscribe to an on-line pricing database, accessed through computer modem, an optical storage disk pricing update service, a microfilm catalog and handbook data access system, or, at least, to develop your own library of handbooks and catalogs.

The Learning Curve

The concept of the learning curve first appeared in T. P. Wright's article, "Factors Affecting the Cost of Airplanes," in February 1936.[1] The learning curve is an explanation for the widely observed trend in increased worker efficiency and management innovations associated with repetitive production involving human activity. (This phenomenon is not as observable in automated manufacturing.) The basic concept behind the learning curve is that the dependent variable—either cost or labor hours—decreases in a constant proportion as the independent variable, quantity, is doubled.

The term "learning" was used because it related to the improvement of mental or manual skills observed when an operation is repeated. Learning is also used to describe the reduction in machine time or other improvements seen in modifying the production process or equipment. Areas where improvement or learning can occur include the following ones:

Labor	Materials	Indirect Expenses
Assembly	Scrap rate	Overhead
Fabrication	Spoilage rate	General and
Test	Raw materials	administrative
Engineering	Purchased parts	
Tooling	Subcontracted components and sub-assemblies	

Many factors affect the rate of improvement, including those shown in the following list:

Experience with the item
Product design
Number of modifications and changes to the item
Amount of manual labor
Types of materials and manufacturing processes used
Quantity to be made
Rate of production
Quality and kind of tooling, jigs, and fixtures
Use of power equipment
Purchasing efficiency
Stability of personnel
Shop management

The arithmetic equation for the learning curve is

$$Y = AQ^b,$$

where: Y = cost of the Qth unit,
   A = cost of the first unit,
   Q = quantity (number of the Qth unit)
   b = learning curve exponent.

This same equation can be written in log-linear form as

$$LN\ Y = LN\ A + b\ LN\ Q.$$

Graphically these two equations appear as shown in **Figure 4.1**.

The slope of the learning curve is accounted for in the learning curve exponent. It is the constant proportion by which cost (or labor) decreases as the quantity is doubled. Derived mathematically slope is included in the learning curve exponent as follows:

$$b = \frac{LN\ S}{LN\ 2},$$

where: b = the learning curve exponent in the learning curve equation, and
S = the slope expressed as a percentage, ranging from 70 to 100 percent.

For example, the b factor representing a 90 percent learning curve slope is:

$$b = \frac{LN\ .90}{LN\ 2} = \frac{-0.10536}{0.69315} = -0.15200.$$

Table 4.1 shows representative values for the b factor corresponding to various percentage slopes.

There are two different applications or theories concerning the learning curve: the "Crawford," or unit, theory and the "Wright," or cumulative average, theory. The preceding equations will yield the cumulative average cost of Q units as y if the right theory is used. **Table 4.2** lists advantages and disadvantages of each theory.

It is important to know which theory is to be used when working with learning curves. Generally buyers tend to use the unit theory because it tends to predict lowest costs. Sellers tend to use the cumulative average theory because the weighted effects cause the cost to be higher than that in unit theory.

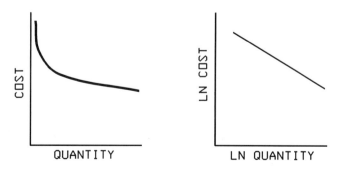

Figure 4.1   Learning curve forms on cartesian and logarithmic coordinates.

TABLE 4.1 Exponent (*b*) Values Corresponding to Slope Percentage

Slope (%)	Exponent (*b*) Value
99	−0.0145
98	−0.0291
97	−0.0439
96	−0.0589
95	−0.0740
94	−0.0893
93	−0.1047
92	−0.1203
91	−0.1361
90	−0.1520
89	−0.1681
88	−0.1844
87	−0.2009
86	−0.2176
85	−0.2345
84	−0.2515
83	−0.2688
82	−0.2863
81	−0.3040
80	−0.3219
79	−0.3401
78	−0.3585
77	−0.3771
76	−0.3959
75	−0.4150
74	−0.4344
73	−0.4540
72	−0.4739
71	−0.4941
70	−0.5146

Put another way, the unit theory is based on the concept that as the total quantity of units produced doubles, the hours required to produce the last unit of this doubled quantity will be reduced by a constant percentage. This means that the hours required to produce unit 2 will be a certain percentage less than the hours required to produce unit 1; the hours required to produce unit 4 will be the same percentage less than the hours required to produce unit 2; the hours required to produce unit 8 will be the same percentage less than unit 4; and this constant percentage of reduction will continue for doubled quantities as long as uninterrupted production of the same item continues. The compliment of this constant percentage of reduction is commonly referred to as the "slope." This means that if the constant percentage of reduction is 10 percent, the slope would be 90 percent. **Table 4.2** gives an example

TABLE 4.2   Advantages and Disadvantages of Learning Curve Theories

	Cumulative Average *(Wright)*	Unit *(Crawford)*
Advantages	Smooths data points Easy to use	Trends readily identified More sensitive to change Usable with missing quantity data

Disadvantages	Conceals major
	    deviations
	May indicate a
	    nonexistent
	    improvement rate
		Requires midpoint
		    calculation
		Very responsive to
		    fluctuations

of a learning curve with 90 percent slope when the number of hours required to produce the first unit is 100.

The reason for using "slope" in naming this reduction will be readily apparent when the learning curve is plotted on coordinates with logarithmic scales on both the *x* and *y* axes (in this instance, the learning "curve" actually becomes a straight line). But first let us plot the learning curve on conventional coordinates. You can see by the plot in **Figure 4.2** that it is truly a curve when plotted on conventional coordinates and that the greater the production quantity is, the smaller is the incremental reduction in labor-hours required from unit to unit.

When the learning curve is plotted on logarithmic coordinates (**Figure 4.3**) it

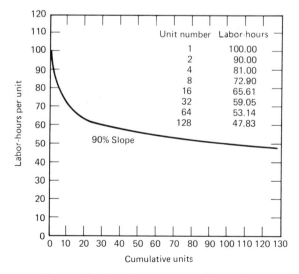

Figure 4.2   Learning curve on a linear plot.

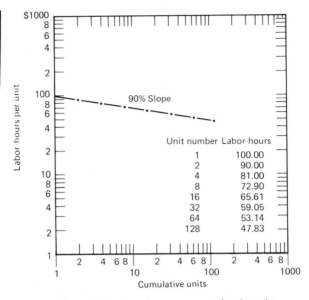

Figure 4.3   Learning curve on a log-log plot.

becomes a straight line. The higher the slope is, the flatter the line is; the lower the slope is, the steeper the line is.

The effects of plotting curves on different slopes can be seen in the chart shown in **Figure 4.4**. This chart shows the effects on labor-hour reductions of doubling the quantities produced 12 times.

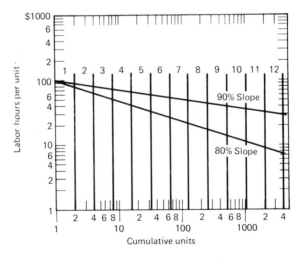

Figure 4.4   Comparison between two learning curves.

Summarized formulas for the unit curve and the cumulative average curve are shown in **Table 4.3**.

Care should be taken in the use of the learning curve to avoid an overly optimistic (low) learning curve slope and to avoid using the curve for too few units in production. Remember also that learning curve theory originated in the 1940s and 1950s when a larger part of design, manufacturing, assembly, and testing was accomplished by hands-on skilled technicians and skilled workers. Although the "learning" curve can also depict overall improvements in efficiency, its use in the era of advancing production automation, robotics, computer-aided design, computer-aided engineering, and test and inspection automation is becoming increasingly inappropriate for selected industries. An increasing number of researchers in the field of cost analysis are advocating the use of multiple step functions, each with very steep learning curve functions within themselves, to depict the effect of technology step improvements. For the lack of a better term at present, we will call this the technology improvement function (TIF).

The Technology Improvement Function

Technology step improvements can be shown as a series of steps with very steep learning curves that occur at levels and time increments determined by the nature and timing of the improvement related to each technology step function (**Figure 4.5**). These steps do not necessarily occur at regular intervals as shown in the figure but occur when new technologies are introduced into the workplace. Experience has shown that very steep learning curves can be achieved with new technology that has

TABLE 4.3   Learning Curve Formulas: Summary

Unit curve $Y = AQ^b$

where

$Y =$	cost or number of direct labor hours required to produce the Xth unit
$A =$	cost or number of direct labor hours required to produce the first unit
$Q =$	number of units produced

and

$$b = \frac{LN\ S}{LN\ 2}$$

where

$S =$ slope of curve expressed in positive hundredths (e.g., $n = 0.80$ for an 80% curve)

cumulative average curve

$$V_x = \frac{A}{x\ (1+b)} * [\ (x + 0.5)^{(1+b)} - (0.5)^{(1-b)}]$$

where $V_x =$ the cumulative average number of direct labor hours required to produce x units

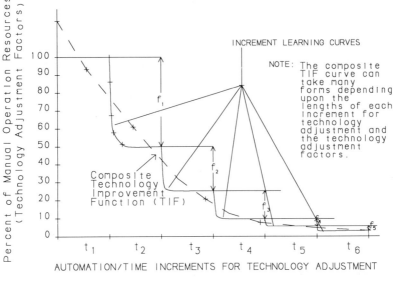

Figure 4.5   Technology improvement function.

built-in "worker friendliness" and ease of operation. Learning is reduced to a short period at the front end of each step through the provision of predebugged instructions, menus, help functions, and preengineered user interfaces that reduce training and initial start-up times. The repetitive hours formerly spent by each employee, technician, operator, designer, or system user is now preprogrammed into the computer-aided design (CAD), computer-aided manufacturing (CAM), computer-aided software engineering (CASE), simulation, testing, inspection, or production tool by the designers of the productivity tool. Hence, astonishingly quick "learning" is achieved by the operator. "Learning" curve values of less than 50 percent for each step are now not uncommon in adopting new high-technology tools. The first operation usually takes much longer than manual operation, but the second is accomplished in less than half that of the first, and subsequent doubling of quantities sees similar improvements until the automated function is producing unit and cumulative average labor values at only a fraction of those of the old manual learning curve of 85 to 95 percent.

The TIF is more complex to use since the estimator is required to estimate the time or cost reduction, adoption learning slope, and calendar time of adoption for each technology improvement step before constructing a composite TIF curve. The TIF curve can take many forms, depending on the lengths of each time increment for technology adjustment (t_i) and the technology adjustment factor (f_i). The calendar time (T_c) to any level of performance is:

$$T_c = t_1 + t_2 + t_3 + \ldots + f_n.$$

The resource reduction (R_c) at that calendar time (T_c) is:

$$R_c = f_1 + f_2 + f_3 + \ldots + f_n$$

The TIF curve, generated by a least-squares regression method or through the rigors of integral calculus, is a best-fit curve that depicts the composite effects of all technology improvement steps.

For industries where large steps are being made and are expected to continue, a TIF method should be adopted to predict the behavior of future resource requirements.

Staffing Methods

One of the most straightforward methods of estimating resources or labor-hours required to accomplish a task is the staffing, or shop-loading, method. This estimating technique is based on the fact that an experienced participant or manager of any activity can usually perceive, through judgment and knowledge of the activity being estimated, the number of individuals of various skills needed to accomplish a task. The shop-loading method is similar in that the estimator can usually predict the portion of an office or shop's capacity that will be occupied by a given job. This percentage shop-loading factor can be used to compute labor-hours or resources if the total shop labor or total shop operation costs are known. Examples of the staffing and shop-loading methods based on 1986 labor-hours per labor-year are shown in **Table 4.4**.

Statistical and Parametric Estimating

Statistical and parametric estimating involve collecting and organizing historical information through mathematical techniques and relating this information to the work output being estimated. A number of methods can be used to correlate historical cost and manpower information; the choice depends principally on the mathematical skills and imagination of the estimator and access to data. These mathematical and statistical techniques provide some analytical relationship between the process, product, project, or service being estimated and its physical or performance characteristics. The format most commonly used for statistical and parametric estimating is the estimating relationship, which relates some physical characteristic of the work output (weight, power requirements, size, or volume) with the cost or labor-hours required to produce it. These relationships involving cost are known as cost estimating relationships (CERs). The most widely used estimating relationship is linear. That is, the mathematical equation representing the relationship is a linear equation, and the relationship can be depicted by a straight line when plotted on a graph with conventional linear coordinates for both the x (horizontal) and y (vertical) axes. Other forms of estimating relationships can be derived based on the curve-fitting techniques presented in any standard textbook on statistics.[2] For the purpose of simplicity and to illustrate the technique of developing an estimating relationship, study the following linear estimating relationship example.

Suppose that 10 historical data points exist pertaining to the number of labor-

TABLE 4.4 Staffing and Shop-Loading Methods

	Time Increment (year)						
	1	2	3	4	5	6	7
Staffing method							
Engineers	1	1	1	2	1	0	0
Hours	1,896	1,896	1,896	3,792	1,896	0	0
Technicians	3	4	4	6	2	1	0
Hours	5,688	7,584	7,584	11,376	3,792	1,896	0
Draftsmen	0	0	1	3	6	4	2
Hours	0	0	1,896	5,688	11,376	7,584	3,792
Shop-loading method							
Electrical shop (5 workers)	10%	15%	50%	50%	5%	0%	0%
Hours	948	1,422	4,740	4,740	474	0	0
Mechanical shop (10 workers)	5%	5%	10%	80%	60%	10%	5%
Hours	948	948	1,896	15,168	11,376	1,896	948

hours required to produce various quantities (pounds) or "lots" of a product. To develop the mathematical equation for an estimating relationship that best represents the aggregate of these data points, the method of least squares is used. The least-squares method defines a straight line through the data points such that the sum of the squared deviations or distances from the line is smaller than it would be for any other straight line. The resulting straight line goes through the overall "mean" of the data. When the data points represent a random sample from a larger population of data, the least-squares line is a best estimate of the relationship for the total population. The equation of the straight line to be defined is

$$y = mx + b$$

where m is the slope of the line
b = the point where the line intercepts the y axis.

If n is the number of data points and x_i and y_i are the coordinates of specific data points, the two equations shown in **Table 4.5** can be solved simultaneously to define the line that best fits the data.

The data points are shown in **Table 4.6**, and derived values of the expressions contained in the equations are shown in **Figure 4.6**. Substituting the appropriate values from Table 4.6 into the equations shown on Table 4.5, we get the following two simultaneous equations:

$$165.2 = 10b + 860m$$

$$18,469 = 860b + 98,800m$$

By multiplying the first equation by -1 and dividing the second equation by 86, we can add the two equations as follows:

$$
\begin{array}{rl}
-165.20 = & -106 - 860m \\
\underline{214.76 = } & \underline{\;\;106 + 1148.84m} \\
49.56 = & \qquad\quad 288.84m
\end{array}
$$

$$m = \frac{49.56}{288.84} = 0.172$$

TABLE 4.5   Sample Estimating Formulas

1. $\displaystyle\sum_{i=1}^{n} v_i = nb + m\sum_{i=1}^{n} x_i$

2. $\displaystyle\sum_{i=1}^{n} y_i x_i = b\sum_{i=1}^{n} x_i + m\sum_{i=1}^{n} (x_i)^2$

TABLE 4.6   Sample Estimating Chart

Lot	x_i (pounds)	y_i (staffing)	$(x_i)^2$	(x_iy_i)
1	20	3.5	400	70
2	30	7.4	900	222
3	40	7.1	1,600	284
4	60	15.6	3,600	936
5	70	11.1	4,900	777
6	90	14.9	8,100	1,341
7	100	23.5	10,000	2,350
8	120	27.1	14,400	3,252
9	150	22.1	22,500	3,315
10	180	32.9	32,400	5,922
	$\Sigma x_i =$ 860	$\Sigma y_i =$ 165.2	$\Sigma(x_i)^2 =$ 98,800	$\Sigma(x_iy_i) =$ 18,469

Therefore $b = 1.728$. The equation for the "best-fit line," then, can be expressed as $y = mx + b$ or labor-hours $= (0.172 \times \text{pounds}) + 1.728$.

The equation that was developed addressed the cost estimating relationship (CER). Estimating relationships, whether based on a linear best-fit curve such as the one shown or on some other statistical averaging technique, have certain advantages but certain distinct limitations. They have the advantage of providing a quick estimate even though very little is known about the work output except its physical characteristics. They correlate the present estimate with past history of resource utilization on similar items, and their use simplifies the estimating process. They require the use of statistical or mathematical skills rather than detailed estimating skills, which may be an advantage if detailed estimating skills are not available to the estimating organization.

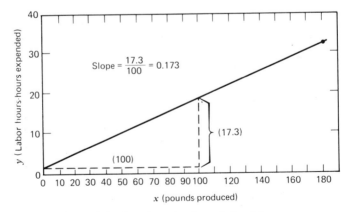

Figure 4.6   Sample estimating relationships.

On the other hand, because of their dependence on past (historical) data, they may erroneously indicate cost trends. Some products, such as mass-produced electronics, are providing more capability per pound and lower costs per pound, volume, or component count every year. Basing electronics costs on past history may therefore result in noncompetitively high estimates. History should not be repeated if it contains detrimental inefficiencies, duplications, unnecessary redundancies, rework, or overestimates. It is important to determine what part of historical data should be used to reflect future resource requirements accurately. CERs will yield reliable costs only within the limits of the spread of independent variables represented in the data.

Finally, the parametric or statistical estimate, unless used at a very low level in the estimating process, provides only limited in-depth visibility and permits no determination of cost effects from subtle changes in schedule, performance, or design requirements. The way to use the statistical or parametric estimate most effectively is to subdivide the work into the smallest possible elements and then to use statistical or parametric methods to derive the resources required for these small elements.

There are several parametric cost estimating models that are used generally. Three aerospace-oriented hardware models are commercially available: General Electric PRICE (Programmed Review of Information for Costing and Evaluation), the John M. Cockerham and Associates CAAMS (Cost Analysis and Management System), and the Freiman Parametric Systems FAST (Freiman Analysis of Systems Technique) models. The General Electric and Freiman systems operate out of Cherry Hill, New Jersey, and John M. Cockerham and Associates is headquartered in Huntsville, Alabama. There are also many software systems parametric models available publicly. An organization of professional parametric model developers and users is the International Society of Parametric Analysts (ISPA), headquartered in McLean, Virginia. The use of these models grew in the 1980s, but their use as the primary means for developing a detailed competitive cost proposal is not recommended because of their lack of traceability of their equations to underlying data. The generic nature of these models makes them very appropriate, however, for calculating comparative cost assessments of alternate approaches and providing a cross-check to other estimating methods.

ESTABLISHING AN ESTIMATE SCHEDULE

For short-term "existing technology" estimates, there may be little need to establish a cost estimating schedule, but where the estimating cycle is expected to take several weeks and inputs will be required from various organizations and/or disciplines, an estimating schedule is essential. The minimum key milestones in a cost estimating schedule are (1) a "kickoff" meeting, (2) a "review of ground rules" meeting, (3) "resources input and review" meeting, and (4) summary meetings and presentations.

Kickoff Meeting

The first formal milestone in an estimate schedule is the estimate kickoff meeting, attended by all those who are expected to have an input to the cost estimate. It usually includes individuals who are proficient in technical disciplines in the work to be estimated, business-oriented individuals who are aware of the financial factors to be considered in making the estimate, project-oriented individuals who are familiar with the project ground rules and constraints, and the cost estimator or cost estimating team.

Sufficient time should be allowed in the kickoff meeting to describe all project ground rules, constraints, and assumptions; to hand out and explain technical specifications, drawings, schedules, and work element descriptions and resource estimating forms; and to discuss these items and answer questions. It is also an appropriate time to clarify estimating assignments among the various disciplines represented in the event that organizational charters are not clear as to who should support which part of the estimate. This kickoff meeting will be held six weeks to three months prior to the estimate completion date to allow sufficient time for the process. If the estimate is being made in response to a request for quotation or request for bid, copies of the request for quotation document will be distributed and its salient points discussed.

Review of Ground Rules Meeting

Several days after the estimate kickoff meeting, when the participants have had the opportunity to study the material, a review of ground rules meeting should be conducted. In this meeting the estimate manager answers questions regarding the conduct of the cost estimate, assumptions, ground rules, and estimating assignments. If the members of the estimating team are experienced in developing resource estimates for their respective disciplines, very little discussion may be needed. However, if this is the first estimating cycle for one or more of the team members, it may be necessary to provide them with additional information, guidance, and instruction on estimating tools and methods. Where individuals who will actually perform the work are doing the estimating, they will require more assistance than will experienced estimators.

The Resources Input and Review Meeting

Several weeks after the kickoff and review of ground rules meetings, each team member who has a resources (labor-hours and/or materials) input is asked to present the information before the entire estimating team. This is one of the most valuable parts of the estimating process: the interaction of team members to reduce duplications, overlaps, and omissions in resource data.

The most valuable aspect of a team estimate is the synergistic effect of team interaction. In any multidisciplinary activity, it is the synthesis of information and actions that produces wise decisions rather than the mere volume of data. In this review meeting, the estimator of each discipline area has the opportunity to justify and explain the rationale for the estimates to colleagues, an activity that tends to iron out inconsistencies, overstatements, and incompatibilities in resources estimates. Occasionally inconsistencies, overlaps, duplications, and omissions will be so significant that a second input and review meeting will be required in order to collect and synthesize all inputs for an estimate.

Summary Meetings and Presentations

Once the resource inputs have been collected, adjusted, and priced or costed, the cost estimate is presented to the estimating team as a dry run for the final presentation to the company's management or the requesting organization. This dry run can uncover other inconsistencies or errors that have crept into the estimate during the process of consolidation and reconciliation. The final review with the requesting organization or with the company's management could also bring about some changes in the estimate due to last-minute changes in ground rules or budget-imposed cost ceilings.

NEEDED ESTIMATING SKILLS

The quality of the mix of skill types and the skill levels used to develop cost estimates has a great bearing on the overall credibility, accuracy, and completeness of the resulting cost estimate. A few of the generic skills used in cost estimating follow, along with a description of the functions performed by these skill types and an indication of the skill levels required for credibility in estimating.

Business and Finance Skills

In many organizations there is an erroneous and prevalent concept that estimating is solely an engineering or technical function. Although engineering and technical skills are vital to the estimating process, these skills alone cannot produce consistently competitive and realistic cost estimates. The reason is the continually evolving and changing financial environment that exists in a dynamic and growing society. Growth implies change. Technological and social progress has resulted in changing economics and business policies, practices, and procedures, as well as in such widely fluctuating economic indicators as inflation and interest rates. Business and finance skills are essential to the estimating process; a knowledge of accounting procedures and techniques is needed to convert labor-hour and material estimates into a complete, consolidated cost estimate.

A person with knowledge of business and financial methods and techniques will have a full appreciation for many of the "hidden costs" included in any estimate, such as direct charges that are added to basic direct costs by "factoring," (multiplying the base costs by a factor or percentage) overhead costs, general and administrative costs, and profit or fee. To the engineer these costs are unnecessary and superfluous; to the businessperson, consideration of these other costs is vital to the process of staying in business.

In the past, small businesspeople (notably home construction contractors) have occasionally developed estimates merely by adding up the labor and materials required to do the job. Although they may make a small profit on the sale of the materials, this is not enough to pay for overhead costs and other unforeseen direct material costs. Seldom does this sum include enough money for overall business profit. Hence these small businesspeople have denied themselves a profit, and they are paying themselves nothing for staying in business. (In fact, many are not even covering their basic overhead expenses.) Assuming that the purpose of a business is to provide a livelihood for its owners, the estimate must be constructed so that it will do more than merely recover the costs of labor and materials. Business and finance skills are mandatory to understand this fact and to convert the basic direct costs into a competitive estimate that will cover all costs of the work output with sufficient allowance for profit.

Engineering and Technical Skills

Engineering and technical skills, reflected in on-the-job experience, are the basis for a sound, competitive, and realistic estimate. These skills are just as necessary as business and finance skills in making an estimate. A completed cost estimate must be based on a practical knowledge of the work output as well as the theory of design of the process, product, project, or service. Although educational background and knowledge of theory are important in estimating the resource elements and levels needed to accomplish a task, this book knowledge must be supplemented by actual hands-on experience in producing a similar or identical work output. Of course, the engineering, technical, and operational skills of the work force are a vital factor in producing a work output that is of sufficient quality, utility, and serviceability to hold a consumer market, to keep sales at an acceptable level, and to expand into other markets where feasible.

Manufacturing and Assembly Skills

For products and processes that involve manufacturing and assembly operations, detailed knowledge of each manufacturing, assembly, test, and/or inspection function is essential. This knowledge comes from people who have had experience in the manufacturing and assembly operations. They have the ability to envision and review the proposed work output and identify gaps, overlaps, and duplications in the proposed effort. The most common fault in manufacturing estimating is the omission of essential steps in the process—for example, receiving and unpacking raw materials or parts, inspection of incoming parts, in-process inspection, attaching labels and markings, and packaging and shipping of the final product. A skilled planner can readily spot these oversights because he or she will not immediately assume that the labor-hours and materials estimated to do the job are accurate.

Marketing and Management Skills

Part of any estimating team's expertise must consist of marketing and management skills. These two areas are tied together because the management of any enterprise must be closely related to and even inextricably entwined with the marketing or sales of its work output. The success of any venture depends on two factors: (1) its ability to schedule, plan, and estimate an activity that fills a need and (2) to produce, manufacture, develop, and market its work output effectively, efficiently, and economically. The ultimate success of a company depends on its ability to provide its service or product at an overall profit consistently. Marketing and management skills are essential in the estimating process because one element to be estimated in any activity is the cost of management itself.

Mathematical and Statistical Skills

Higher mathematics and the application of statistics are not always required in the development of a credible and supportable cost estimate. In estimating high-technology, multidisciplinary projects and products, however, these skills are becoming more and more important. When new products are designed and new services envisioned, it is always best to verify their cost projections by use of mathematical and statistical techniques. Statistical and parametric estimating usually require a higher form of mathematics than that required by ground-up or detailed industrial engineering labor-hour and material-based estimating. Often cost estimating requires only simple and straightforward arithmetic to add and subtract resource estimates and to multiply labor-hours and costs by the approximate labor rates and factors. But a knowledge of higher-level mathematical techniques will provide an appreciation for other techniques available in estimating.

Production Planning and Industrial Engineering Skills

Production planning and industrial engineering skills are closely related to manufacturing and assembly skills but are usually learned and applied at a higher organizational level. Where the manufacturing and assembly skills used in estimating are derived from hands-on experience by workers or their immediate supervisors, production planning and industrial engineering skills are based on an overall knowledge of the work load and work flow in an office, factory, or processing plant. The industrial engineering discipline is one that is most closely related to the emerging estimating profession because it involves most of the skills previously discussed. As educational institutions become more fully aware of the pressing need for estimating, more business and finance skills will be added to the industrial engineer's capabilities to balance engineering knowledge and engineering approach. Production planning and industrial engineering skills are particularly important for work outputs that involve higher rates or larger quantities of production; knowledge of automation and labor-saving techniques in the shop, factory, or office becomes important in these applications.

Now that we have looked at the basics, defined the work, and defined the tools, it is time to get down to the task of estimating by formulating the schedule, estimate elements, and ground rules.

NOTES

1. T. P. Wright, "Factors Affecting the Cost of Airplanes," *Journal of Aeronautical Sciences* **Vol. 3 No. 4 (February 1936): p.122.
2. One such textbook is Irwin Miller and John E. Freund, *Probability and Statistics for Engineers,* 3d ed. (Englewood Cliffs, N.J.: Prentice-Hall, 1985).

QUESTIONS

4.1. If the value of the first unit on an 85 percent unit curve is 1000 and the value of the first unit on a 90 percent unit curve is 750, at what unit value do the curves cross each other?

4.2. Given a 90 percent unit curve and a theoretical first unit value of 2000,

    a. What is the unit value of unit 1024?

    b. If the value at unit 1024 is 100 percent efficient (at standard), what is the efficiency of unit 1?

    c. What is the value of unit 8?

4.3. Using the method of least squares:

$$y = a + bx$$

$$a = \bar{y} - b\bar{x}$$

$$b = \frac{\Sigma\,(xy) - x\Sigma y}{\Sigma\,x^2 - x\Sigma x}$$

    a. Find the cost of 460 units from the information listed below:

Lot	x Units	y Lot Cost
1	400	900
2	350	750
3	600	1,400
4	650	1,350
	2,000	4,400

    b. What is the average cost of each lot?

    c. What is the average cost of all lots?

d. What is the weighted average cost?

e. What would the cost of 460 units be using the answer to *c?*

4.4. When reading a log-log graph displaying learning curve data on a straight line unit basis, the average cost for the cumulative quantity occurs: (Hint: construct a learning curve on log-log paper showing both unit and cumulative average values for the same learning curve percentage. For convenience, use 100 as the number of units.)

    a. At half the unit quantity.

    b. At one-third the unit quantity.

    c. At the unit quantity.

    d. At three-quarters of the unit quantity.

    e. None of the above.

4.5. Select the most accurate description of learning curve theory:

    a. Employees continuously get smarter and more efficient.

    b. Employee labor costs decrease as the square of the number of units produced.

    c. Better supervision results in lower costs

    d. An increase in cumulative quantity of articles produced results in progressively higher unit cost.

    e. Unit cost decreases as quantity increases.

    f. The more times a job is done, the fewer mistakes are made.

4.6. What is the primary limitation of a cost estimating relationship (CER)?

    a. The data points may all be in different year dollars.

    b. CERs will yield reliable costs only within the limits of the spread of independent variables represented in the data.

    c. Statistical techniques used to construct the CER are not accurate enough for cost estimating.

    d. There are many CERs that yield conflicting cost projections based on the same data.

4.7. The Crawford Improvement curve theory assumes that unit production labor-hours decrease by a constant percentage each time the quantity of units:

    a. Doubles.

    b. Triples.

    c. Is squared.

4.8. Productivity affects improvement curves.   T   F

4.9. Improvement curves are used only for estimating manufacturing labor.   T   F

5

FORMULATING THE SCHEDULE, ESTIMATE ELEMENTS, AND GROUND RULES

There is an appointed time for everything. And there is a time for every event under heaven.

Ecclesiastes 3:1

TIMING: KEY TO A COST-COMPETITIVE OUTPUT

The key to providing the best possible work output with a given amount of resources is timing the work activities to have as little waste, duplication, overlap, and redundancy of effort and materials as possible. In mass production, a delay in the delivery of a material or part into the process flow or assembly line can hold up the entire work activity. Delays in production can cause product costs to escalate rapidly because many overhead and direct labor costs are constant despite fluctuating work output levels. Too-early delivery of a material or part to a process or assembly line can also cause inefficiencies because the yet-to-be-processed material needs to be stored and handled. In multidisciplined activities or large projects, the timing of application of each unit of resource, whether a unit of labor or material, is important because it usually affects another work activity. For example, labor-hours cannot be expended on material until the material arrives; manufacturing labor cannot be expended before engineering labor is expended to design the hardware; assembly cannot be completed until the manufacturing is complete; and so on. In software cost estimating, scheduling of human resources must coincide with the acquisition of computer tools and software productivity programs such as computer-aided software engineering (CASE) tools. Skills must be in place at the proper time to prepare software documentation and to provide software maintenance and software configuration management once the product is completed.

These interrelationships of resource elements make timing of work activities an important factor in the overall development of a competitive cost estimate.

DELIVERY OR AVAILABILITY KEYED TO NEED DATES

The most important factor to observe in formulating a schedule of any work activity is to provide the work output on the date(s) and at the rate(s) required by the market. The scheduler should have the results of a marketing or planning analysis and a customer request for proposal (RFP) to show (1) the goals and objectives of the work activity, (2) the plan for supplying the work output, (3) the requirements of the delivered product or service, (4) and the work elements that make up the overall work activity. This marketing or planning analysis will identify the delivery dates and rates that project the most probable future market needs. The scheduler will use the future date of delivery of the work output as an end point and work back in time to the present to develop a detailed milestone schedule.

DEVELOPING A SCHEDULE

Schedule elements are time-related groupings of work activities that are placed in sequence to accomplish an overall desired objective. Schedule elements for a process can be represented by very small (minutes, hours, or days) time periods. The scheduling of a process is represented by the time the raw material takes during each step to travel through the process. The schedule for manufacturing a product or delivery of a service is, similarly, a time flow of the various components or actions into a completed item or activity.

A project (the construction or development of a fairly large, complex, or multi-disciplinary tangible work output) contains distinct schedule elements called "milestones," those dates or events in the schedule that indicate the start or completion of tasks or activities. These milestones are encountered in one form or another in almost all projects: (1) study and analysis, (2) design, (3) procurement of raw materials and purchased parts, (4) fabrication or manufacturing of components and subsystems, (5) assembly of the components and subsystems, (6) testing of the combined system to qualify the unit for operation in its intended environment, (7) acceptance testing, preparation, packaging, shipping, and delivery of the item, and (8) operation of the item.

TECHNIQUES USED IN SCHEDULE PLANNING

A number of analytical techniques are available for developing an overall schedule of a work activity that help to ensure the correct allocation and sequencing of schedule elements: precedence and dependency networks, arrow diagrams, critical path bar charts, and program evaluation and review technique (PERT).[1] PERT analysis of a program is one of the more commonly used techniques in schedule planning. Scheduling techniques use graphical and mathematical methods to develop the best schedule based on sequencing in such a way that each activity is performed only when the required predecessor activities are accomplished. "Milestone" is the term used to signify the date or event that coincides with either the start or completion of a task, work item, or activity. A simple example of how these techniques work is shown in **Figure 5.1**. Eight schedule elements have been chosen, the length of each schedule activity has been designated, and a relationship has been established between each activity and its predecessor activity as in **Table 5.1**.

Notice several things about the precedence relationships: (1) some activities can be started before their predecessor activities are completed, (2) some activities must be fully completed before their follow-on activities can be started, (3) and some activities cannot be started until a specified number of months after the 100 percent completion date of a predecessor activity. Once these schedule interrelationships are established, a total program schedule can be laid out by starting either from a selected beginning point and working forward in time until the completion date is reached or by starting from a desired completion date and working backward in time to derive the required schedule starting date. Often both the start and completion dates are given. In that case, the length of schedule elements and their interrelationships must be established through an iterative process to develop a schedule that accomplishes a job in the required time. If all schedule activities are started as soon as their prerequisites are met, the result is the shortest possible time schedule to perform the work. Milestones that are set are useful in determining the status of important work events.

Most complex work activities have multiple paths of activity that must be accomplished parallel with each other. The longest of these paths is called a "critical

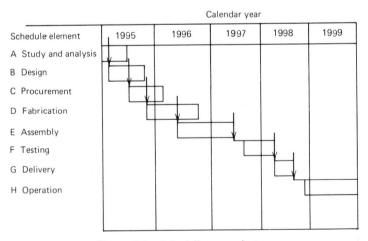

Figure 5.1   Scheduling a project.

TABLE 5.1   Schedule Relationships

Schedule Element	Title of Schedule Element	Time Required for Completion	Percentage Completion Required[a]
A	Study and analysis	6 months	33 1/3
B	Design	8 months	50
C	Procurement	8 months	50
D	Fabrication	12 months	66 2/3
E	Assembly	12 months	100 plus 2 months
F	Testing	8 months	100
G	Delivery	4 months	100 plus 4 months
H	Operation	36 months	100

[a]Percentage completion required before subsequent activity can be accomplished.

path," and the schedule critical path is developed by connecting all of the schedule activity critical paths. Construction of a schedule such as that shown in Figure 5.1 brings to the light a number of other questions. The first is, "How do I establish the length of each activity?" This question strikes at the heart of the overall estimating process itself since many costs are incurred by the passage of time. Costs of an existing work force, overhead (insurance, rental, and utilities), and material handling and storage continue to pile up in an organization whether there is a productive output or not. Hence it is important to develop the shortest possible overall schedule to accomplish a job and each schedule element in the shortest time and the most efficient method possible. The length of each schedule activity is established by an analysis of that activity and the human and material resources available and required to accomplish it. The staffing and material estimating techniques examined shown in Chapter 6 are used extensively by the estimator in establishing the time required to accomplish a schedule activity, as well as the labor-hours and materials required for its completion.

A second question is, "What do I do if there are other influences on the schedule, such as availability of facilities, equipment, and staffing?" This is a factor that arises in most estimating situations. There are definite schedule interactions in any multiple-output organization that must be considered in planning a single work activity. Overall corporate planning must take into account these schedule interactions in its own critical path chart to ensure that facilities, personnel, and funds are available to accomplish all work activities effectively and efficiently.

A final question is, "How do I establish a credible 'percentage complete' figure for each predecessor work activity?" This is accomplished by breaking each activity into subactivities. For instance, design can be subdivided into conceptual design, preliminary design, and final design. If the start of the procurement activity is to be keyed to the completion of preliminary design, then the time that the preliminary design is complete determines the percentage of time and corresponding design activity that must be completed prior to the initiation of procurement.

TIME PHASING OF SKILLS, A VITAL CONCEPT

A vital concept in the formulation of ground rules for a competitive estimate or proposal is the time phasing of acquisition and utilization of skills for performing a work activity. Chapter 3 describes the need for balancing and time phasing of skill categories and skill levels. Four factors determine the optimum time phasing of skills for any given work activity: (1) the attrition or "turnover" rate for each skill category, (2) the overall company or shop growth rate in numbers of personnel, (3) the merit salary increases (above inflation or cost of living increases), and (4) the initial and final mixture of skill categories and skill levels. A company with a high attrition rate or a high overall growth rate will have ample opportunity to add skills at lower salary levels to keep its labor costs low despite inflation, and it can provide room for advancement of its total work force through merit salary increases and promotions. A relatively static organization with a stable work force and continuous merit increases and promotions will find it difficult to stay competitive because of "salary creep" and "skill-level creep." The only solution to staying competitive in this environment is to seek out other complex and difficult tasks that can be accomplished by a highly skilled, competent, and mature work force.

SCHEDULE AND SKILL INTERACTIONS WITHIN A MULTIOUTPUT ORGANIZATION

Any organization that is preparing a cost estimate must observe and consider the interactions of the job being estimated with other jobs that are in various stages of completion. Optimum planning and scheduling of work activities within an organization will result in full utilization of all available personnel. As the more difficult early phases of a project are completed, it is desirable to off-load experienced and highly paid staff to other projects that are just entering their early phases. This "macroscopic" view of an organization's work load must continue to be considered when planning, scheduling, and estimating new work activities. The following steps are required to develop a cost-effective and competitive skill mix throughout the lifetime of a project:

1. Identify the skill categories (engineering, analysis, design, manufacturing, testing, programming, etc.) required to perform the task.
2. Identify the required skill levels (senior, associate, junior, apprentice) in each skill category.
3. Time-phase skill levels to take advantage of learning and on-the-job training; and to take advantage of the potential of moving personnel between tasks.
4. Adjust skill levels to closely match available or acquirable personnel.

TREATMENT OF LONG LEAD-TIME ITEMS

Because of reduced raw material availability, long transportation times, and occasional monopolistic practices by suppliers and vendors, it is sometimes necessary to place orders for materials, parts, and supplies long before the appropriate predecessor activity is completed. Often a company must take a calculated risk that the material, parts, or supplies possess the right composition, shape, size, and performance to meet the job specifications suitably, and it has to order these items far in advance of expected delivery to ensure that the subsequent milestones can be met. It usually pays to have a stock of scarce materials and parts on hand to avoid undue delays. The estimate schedule should take into account the use of existing material stocks as well as the lead times required for their procurement and replenishment.

MAKE-OR-BUY DECISIONS

When formulating the schedule and ground rules for a cost estimate, it is necessary to determine which items will be built in-house by the company's operational arm (make) and which items will be purchased or subcontracted (buy). The best way to arrive at the make-or-buy structure is to (1) do a cursory analysis of the in-house work load, (2) compare purchase costs with equivalent in-house manufacturing costs, and (3) select the most cost-effective alternative.

The amount of work a company subcontracts is a function of its expertise and skill in the required disciplines, its work load, and its overall company policy regarding subcontracted work. Generally it is not cost-effective to subcontract more than 60 percent of an organization's work because fee and administrative expenses must be charged to both the prime contractor and the subcontractor. The development of a make-or-buy structure usually involves the listing of all work elements and a designation of or decision on each work element as to whether it will be done by the prime contracting organization or by a contractor. This step must be taken as a part of the establishment of cost estimating ground rules because the estimating methodology to be employed depends on whether the work element is a make item or a buy item. Make items are usually estimated using standard industrial engineering labor-hour and material estimates; buy items are priced by obtaining quotations from vendors. Vendor quotations can be cross-checked or verified by an independent ground-up estimate made by the procuring organization. The make-or-buy plan does not necessarily determine the ratio of purchasing to operational skills required to develop a cost estimate.

PRODUCT DEVELOPMENT AND PRODUCTION SCHEDULES

The development of a new process, product, project, or service is usually funded in a way different from its production. Development involves some risk and uncertainty and is funded from the profits of production, from venture capital, or from public funds. Product development schedules must include sufficient time for replanning, rescheduling, redesigning, and reestimating of the work output; and these schedules should allow time for pilot or trial runs of the production cycle. Product development is usually labor intensive rather than materials intensive because a large number of labor-hours goes into analysis, design, engineering, planning, and testing of the new work output.

Once a work output has proceeded to production, a better schedule estimate can be made because there are fewer unknown factors. Materials costs become a larger part of the total costs, and there are more opportunities for cost savings because lower skill levels can be used, greater reliance can be placed on machine labor and automation, and allowances for rework, scrappage, and in-process testing can be reduced.

ESTABLISHING THE ESTIMATE ELEMENTS

Three categories of estimate elements should be derived as part of the ground rules for a cost estimate: schedule, cost, and work elements. The composition and description of each of these categories vary widely depending on the type of work output being estimated. Occasionally the schedule elements and work elements coincide, and cost elements often coincide with either. In the example described here, the three categories of estimate elements contain different element titles.

Schedule Elements

If the overall milestone schedule for a work activity is considered as a level 1 schedule, the schedule elements listed earlier in this chapter (study and analysis, design, procurement, fabrication, assembly, testing, delivery, and operation) can be considered as level 2 schedule elements. These level 2 schedule elements can be further subdivided.

Study and Analysis. Establishing even the simplest business operation will require some study, planning, analysis, scheduling, and estimating before the activity is started. The act of putting into practice the principles described in this book will take time, labor-hours, and some materials. Travel costs, computer costs, subcontracts, and other direct costs could also be incurred in study and analysis. It is during this initial phase of a schedule that the architect, industrial engineer, marketing specialist, or entrepreneur studies the basic requirements of the work output, analyzes alternative approaches for accomplishing the objectives of the work, and selects the most cost-effective approach that will accomplish its objectives. This study and analysis phase includes definition of the technical, schedule, and cost aspects of the work and, usually, development of a preliminary concept of the process, product, project, or service. The preliminary concept could be represented by a block or flow diagram, sketches or artist's concepts, listings of requirements, preliminary specifications, and process or service plans. Each of these schedule subelements (which could also be duplicated as work elements or cost elements) represents a level 3 schedule element and can be depicted on a bar chart.

Design. The second element of a schedule is usually the design of the process, product, process, or service. Design typically is subdivided into conceptual, preliminary, and final design. In large projects these subelements are distinctly separated and usually interposed with design reviews at the end of each phase. In smaller projects the subdivision is less clear yet present. Conceptual design usually starts during the study and analysis phase, and completion of preliminary design is usually when orders can be placed for long lead time raw materials. Initiation of fabrication activities (if a product or project is being estimated) must usually await the completion of the detailed design phase.

Procurement. Planning the procurement cycle is an important part of schedule formulation because the costs of materials and subcontracts may well depend on whether competitive bidding is employed and on the selection of the most cost-effective bid. The request for quotation or bid is an effective tool, if used properly, to develop a credible cost estimate. The time to prepare requests for proposal, the time required for potential subcontractors to prepare their bids, and the time to accomplish an effective cost evaluation are schedule subelements under procurement. Once a supplier or subcontractor is selected, sufficient time should be allowed for negotiation or award of an acceptable contract. If a work activity contains a large number of buy items, considerable time must be spent in defining and laying out the procurement schedule.

Fabrication, Construction, and Assembly. Fabrication, construction, manufacturing, and assembly of tools, parts, components, structures, and subsystems must start in time to have the appropriate hardware elements ready for testing and subsequent delivery. Part of the scheduler's task is to determine the optimum time to initiate fabrication, construction, or manufacturing and assembly of each hardware or facility item. The scheduler must also plan the best use of company facilities, equipment, and personnel in establishing a fabrication schedule.

The key to fabrication planning is the development of a process plan or operations sheet for each part depicting the sequence for all fabrication operations. It shows the materials, machines, and functions required for each step of the fabrication process and will be used later as a basis for the development of the labor-hour and materials cost estimates.

Typical functions in the fabrication process are annealing, coating, coil winding, cutting, deburring, drilling, encapsulating, forming, heat treating, grinding, notching, milling, printing, plating, processing, punching, riveting, sawing, silk screening, soldering, turning, welding, and wiring. In the chemical process industries, typical operations are atomization, baking, blending, coagulating, condensing, cleaning, diluting, distilling, evaporating, fermenting, filtering, freeze-drying, gasifying, polymerizing, precipitating, pumping, purifying, separating, and settling.

In the processing of a substance, the fabrication of a product, the conduct of a project, or the delivery of a service, each appropriate work operation or work function must be listed in sequence for later application of labor-hour and material estimates. Operations sheets for any work activity should consider the flow of materials and parts into the fabrication process, the need for standard and special tooling, and the adaptability of the process or operations sheet to the later application of "standard time" data. (Standard time is that which is computed using motion and time methods; see Chapter 2.)

Scheduling of the assembly process for fabricated items or parts is similar to the scheduling of the fabrication process. Operations or planning sheets should be developed for each assembly. Where multiple outputs are planned, it is wise to build a sample unit to verify the operations and times required to assemble the item. In the planning of the assembly process, the assembly sequence should be itemized in detail, noting the location and method of attaching each part or subassembly and the requirement for design and construction of special jigs, fixtures, tools, and assembly aids. Time cycles of final assembly line workstations should be balanced to provide economical, effective, and efficient flow of the product through each assembly operation. Assembly planning sheets should be constructed to allow easy application of standard time data.

Testing and Inspection. The quality and acceptability of any work output depends not only on the care and precision with which the total job is performed but also will be assured and verified through some type of testing and inspection activity. Simple products, processes, or services may require only a sampling inspection to verify the quality of the work output. More complex work activities, such as high-technology products or projects, require the planning of several steps or phases in the testing and inspection activity. The three key steps in the testing process are (1) performance or development testing, (2) qualification testing, and (3) acceptance testing.

Performance or development testing is done during the early phases of the life cycle of many new products or projects to prove that the item will fulfill its intended function. Often this development testing is repetitive and interspersed with design and manufacturing changes that make the item work better, perform more efficiently, require less maintenance, or cost less to produce. Once the iterative cycle of testing and design is completed, the item is subject to a qualification test program. The final product design is subjected to a prespecified test sequence in which various conditions are imposed on the item to prove that it will work under a wide variety of environments and operational conditions. Qualification testing usually subjects the item to more severe environments than does the next step, acceptance testing.

Once the qualification tests are completed, the end item production is started. As units are completed, they are subjected to acceptance tests to verify that each unit will perform as advertised. Where qualification testing qualifies the design of an item and proves that it will operate under more severe conditions than those expected to be encountered normally, acceptance testing proves that a particular end item will perform at nominal conditions.

In planning any of the categories of testing, it is important first to determine the best overall testing method to demonstrate performance capabilities. It is in test planning that cost targets first come strongly into play because the actual verification of many design parameters or goals is often time-consuming and expensive. Examples are lifetime testing and reliability testing. It is often not practical or cost-effective to test an item for two years to demonstrate a two-year lifetime. Methods of accelerated testing and sampling must be used to make this type of testing practicable.

Proving the reliability of an item through testing can also become exceedingly expensive. Statisticians tell us that to prove or demonstrate a high reliability at a relatively high confidence level requires thousands of tests. Compromises in this area are mandatory for a cost-effective test program. Once the overall testing has been established, the test cycle should be subdivided into test positions by test functions, and the desired testing time cycle at each position should be indicated. Test equipment lists and test setup schematics and drawings must be prepared for each position. Time must be allowed for test equipment design, construction of special test fixtures, and acquisition of special test equipment. Step-by-step procedures should be developed for each test position just as was done for the fabrication and assembly functions. Time should also be allowed for setting up and checking out test positions and for instruction of a test operator.

Delivery and Operation. An often overlooked schedule element during initial schedule planning is the delivery schedule. The importance of packaging, preserving, shipping, storing, handling, and supplying parts, materials, and end items has been recognized by the emergence of a whole new profession called "logistics," which is devoted to these activities. Considerable difficulty can be avoided with adequate logistics planning. There have been many instances of delay, damage, and equipment malfunction brought about by a failure to consider the logistics during the delivery and operation phase of a work activity. The best way to avoid these problems is to consult a qualified logistician when developing the delivery and operations phase of any work activity. Using the appropriate expertise in this area will cause the estimator to avoid the possibility of unforeseen costs and delays brought about by inadequately considering the logistic aspects of a job.[2]

Cost Elements

The major cost elements of a cost estimate can vary considerably and depend on the work activity being estimated. Generally, however, the costs for any activity can be subdivided into labor costs, labor overhead costs, subcontract costs, material and material overhead costs, travel costs, computer costs, other direct costs, general and administrative expenses, and profit or fee. Labor cost elements are derived by estimating labor-hours and multiplying the labor rates for each skill by the hours for each skill. Because the overhead of a company depends to some extent on the proportions of each skill category required to do a total job, most companies develop overhead "pools" that entail the use of different overhead rates for each major skill category. For example, an engineering overhead pool includes the overhead costs for a category that includes a predetermined mix of engineering skill levels (i.e., senior engineer, engineer, junior engineer, technician, draftsman). Along with an overhead pool, a composite engineering labor rate can be developed based on the same mix of skill levels. Hence the cost estimates can be reduced to estimates of the hours required by several major skill categories, and labor costs can be computed using a composite labor rate for that skill category. The overhead costs for that skill category can then be computed by using the overhead rate that corresponds to that skill category.

Labor Costs. One set of skill or labor categories that can be used for estimate development is as follows: engineering; manufacturing; tooling; quality, reliability, and safety; and testing. Another category, labeled "other," provides a means for costing labor-hours that do not fall into any of these categories. The six skill categories are described in the following sections.

Engineering Labor. Engineering labor includes the study, analysis, design, development, evaluation, and redesign for specified subdivisions of work. This skill includes the preparation of specifications, drawings, parts lists, and wiring diagrams; technical coordination between engineering and manufacturing; vendor coordination; test planning and scheduling; analysis of test results; software engineering; data reduction; and engineering report preparation.

Manufacturing Labor. Manufacturing (or manufacturing and assembly) labor includes such operations as fabrication, processing, subassembly, final assembly, reworking, modification, experimental production, and installation of parts and equipment. Included is the preparation and processing of material of any kind (metal, plastic, glass, cloth, etc.). Preparation and processing includes but is not limited to flashing operations, annealing, heat treating, baking, refrigeration, anodizing, plating, painting, and production services. Fabrication (the construction of detail parts from raw materials) includes the hours expended in the cutting, molding, forming, stretching, and blanking operations performed on materials of any kind (metal, wood, plastic, cloth, tubing) to make individual parts. Hours spent in the construction of mock-up models, test articles, testing, and reworking during the test program should be considered direct manufacturing labor-hours, as should machine setup time when performed by the operator of the machine.

Tooling Labor. Tooling labor includes planning, design, fabrication, assembly, installation, modification, maintenance, and rework of all tools, dies, jigs, fixtures, gauges, handling equipment, work platforms, test equipment, and special test equipment in support of the manufacturing process. This skill includes effort expended in the determination of tool and equipment requirements, planning of fabrication and assembly operations, maintaining tool and equipment records, establishing make-or-buy plans and manufacturing plans on tooling components and equipment, scheduling and controlling tool and equipment orders, and programming and preparation of tapes for numerically controlled machine parts. It also includes preparation of templates and patterns.

Quality, Reliability, and Safety Labor. Quality, reliability, and safety labor includes the development of quality assurance, reliability assurance, and safety assurance plans; receiving inspection, in-process inspection, and final inspection of raw materials, tools, parts, subassemblies, and assemblies; and reliability testing and failure report reviewing. It includes the participation of quality, reliability, and safety engineers in design reviews and final acceptance reviews.

Testing Labor. Testing labor includes the skills expended in the performance of tests on all components, assemblies, subsystems, and systems to determine and unify operational characteristics and compatibility with the overall system and its intended environment. Such tests include design feasibility tests, design verification tests, development tests, qualification tests, acceptance tests, reliability tests, and tests on parts, systems, and integrated systems to verify the suitability in meeting the criteria for intended usage. These tests are conducted on hardware or final designs that have been produced, inspected, and assembled by established methods. Skills expended in test planning and scheduling, data reduction, and report preparation are also included in this category.

Other Labor Costs. Other labor costs include categories of labor and skills not included in the previous five categories, such as direct supervision and management, direct clerical costs, and miscellaneous direct labor activities.

Materials and Subcontract Costs. Where there are a large number of buy items (items or services to be procured from outside organizations), the "subcontracts" cost element is usually subdivided into major subcontracts and other subcontracts. Major contracts are usually established by setting up a cost value above which the contract is considered a "major subcontract." The reason that major subcontractors are singled out is that their performance has a significant effect on the conduct of the overall primary work activity. Cost and financial reporting, schedule reporting, and performance reporting are usually required to a higher degree from major subcontractors than from other contractors. This greater depth of reporting and visibility into the work of major subcontractors gives the primary performing organization better management control of the work progress.

The "materials" cost element includes tangible raw materials, parts, tools, components, subsystems, and assemblies needed to perform the work. Service contracts are not usually covered under materials, but there are gray areas in the definitions of materials and subcontracts that result in some overlap. An organization's accounting system normally will specify clearly under which category each procurement falls.

Work Elements

To subdivide the work into small segments that can be easily estimated, it is necessary to develop a hierarchical work breakdown structure consisting of functional and physical work elements, or both.

Work elements are chosen for a work activity in a way that will make it easy to assign the primary responsibility for each one to a segment of the organization that will do the work. The work elements conceivably could be identical to the schedule elements. This poses the difficulty that a work element for, say, procurement would have very little interaction with other parts of the schedule despite the fact that the purpose of the procurement function is to support multiple functions (more than one schedule element). Work elements identical to the cost elements are also possible. If a structure containing only cost elements were used, there would be no check and balance between cost categories. Each cost center would be vying for its share of the budget rather than helping to ensure that the whole job is done on schedule and within the overall budget.

The interplay of the three factors of schedule, cost, and performance is paralleled by the interplay of schedule, cost, and work elements. This interplay can be maximized by what is known as a "matrix" of responsibilities. Effectively, the choice of different schedule, cost, and work elements creates a matrix situation that forces equal attention to all three of these important program factors. Therefore, particularly in a large high-technology project, it is desirable to define the elements of schedule, cost, and work separately and to have them interact with each other in the form of a three-dimensional matrix.

An infinite number of combinations of work elements can be established for almost every work activity. One work element list, a mixture of functional and physical elements, has proved successful for a large number of projects:

Project management.
Systems engineering and integration.
Subsystems development or acquisition.
Manufacturing, assembly, and verification.
Operations, support, and logistics.

Notice that these work elements can be easily aligned with an organizational structure. For example, the project management activity can be accomplished by the project management organization, the systems engineering and integration can be performed by the systems engineering and integration organization, the subsystems development or acquisition can be performed by the subsystem development or procurement organizations, and so forth. Assignment of work elements to more than one organization is possible but is not good practice unless a lead organization is chosen. Choice of a lead organization for performing a work element provides greater management control of schedule, cost, and performance factors for that work element.

ANALYSIS OF A REQUEST FOR PROPOSAL

When analyzing the reasonableness of a schedule included in an RFP, the analyst should:

- Identify and understand all tasks from the Statement of Work.
- Know the types and quantities of deliverable hardware, software, and deliverable data items; the overall program schedule and delivery dates; and specifications called out in the RFP.
- Review the proposed schedule for events that require customer approval before continuing work and key milestones that address decision points, deliveries, or commitments to ordering material or committing labor.
- Understand the proposed period of performance of the schedule and determine if all proposed activities can be accomplished in that period. This analysis can be done effectively by laying out a schedule of start and stop dates for all work elements, ensuring that all requirements of the RFP are met.
- Review the manufacturing activities for time phasing to the proposed schedule and the RFP requirements.
- Check engineering labor to ensure that the time-phased labor requirements are reasonable and logical. Tasks may be mistimed and cause inefficient use of labor skills.
- Check for reasonableness of delivery of items from vendors, especially when advanced technologies are proposed. These items may not be available in the appropriate quantities to meet the schedule, especially if they push the state of the art and have not been fully developed by the time the RFP is released.
- Analyze the responsibilities and relationships of the functional organizations, clarifying or modifying any tasks that overlap or are out of sequence.

WORK BREAKDOWN STRUCTURE DICTIONARY

Another vital step in the formulation of schedules, ground rules, and estimate elements for any cost estimate is the development of a well-defined work breakdown structure (WBS) dictionary. The amount of detail in this dictionary will vary widely depending on the type of process, product, project, or service being estimated. The credibility, accuracy, and supportability of the cost estimate for any work output or activity will depend to a large degree on the care, knowledge, and time spent on developing a detailed WBS dictionary. Each element in the structure must be fully described to allow the specialist in that area to estimate accurately the resources required to do the job. To avoid duplications, overlaps, or omissions, it is important to identify exactly what is included in and excluded from each work element. If there is a possibility of overlap or duplication, the person developing the WBS dictionary should cross-reference WBS elements to show their interrelationships and should show where interfacing elements fit into the element being described.

A typical work element dictionary for a space vehicle, reproduced as Appendix III, illustrates the basic principles required in developing a work breakdown structure dictionary:

1. Attention to detail.
2. The ability to envision and anticipate potential overlaps, duplications, and ambiguities and to state clearly where various efforts are to be placed.
3. The need to envision all effort required to perform a project and to describe that effort clearly and concisely.

The example WBS dictionary in the appendix shows the typical elements required for the development of a high-technology, multidisciplinary project. This dictionary was prepared with meticulous attention to detail and with the objective of including and defining as much of the job as possible. Work activities or work outputs with fewer elements will result in a much simpler dictionary. No matter what the job is, however, it is beneficial to describe each of the elements in such a thorough manner that the possibility of misinterpretation is remote.

TREATMENT OF OTHER NECESSARY GROUND RULES

While you are developing the time schedule for your work output, the estimate elements, and element descriptions, you should be recording and defining other ground rules and assumptions that will affect the resources required to do the job. These ground rules and assumptions can include areas such as the policy for providing spares, spare parts, warranties, maintenance manuals, repair manuals, optional equipment and services, and customer services. The ever-present areas of scrap, waste, and human error allowances can cause large errors in estimating and must not be overlooked when formulating estimates of each work element.

Spares and Spare Parts

In the manufacture or development of a product or project, it is important to determine the degree of manufacture, distribution, stocking, warehousing, and sales of spare parts. Virtually every product manufactured has certain subsystems, components, or parts with a limited lifetime. Items such as batteries, gaskets and seals, drive belts, and illumination devices invariably have to be replaced before the useful lifetime of the overall product is expended. These so-called expendable items must be periodically replaced by the owner or user and must be readily available to keep the product operational. The business organization that is interested in maintaining growth or expansion through satisfied customers must include the logistics system to provide these spare parts. Similarly nonexpendable parts must also be stocked to replace those that wear out, malfunction, or are misused.

The best procedure for developing an initial spare parts list is to review the complete list of parts, assemblies, and subassemblies and to make decisions concerning the spares level for each based on an anticipated or assumed failure or use rate. The estimator can use this completed spares list in developing the total quantities needed, the manufacturing rate, and the resulting resource estimate.

Maintenance and Repair Manuals

Virtually every work activity or work output is accompanied by some sort of assembly, maintenance, repair, or instruction manual. These manuals usually take a significant amount of time and effort to develop because their content must be extracted, condensed, simplified, and clearly described based on more complex engineering and manufacturing documentation. In establishing initial estimate ground rules, then, specific assumptions must be made as to the quantity, quality, number of pages, types of illustrations and artwork, and distribution of these instructions and manuals.

Optional Equipment and Services

In industries where products are standardized to reduce production costs and to increase the benefits of mass production, there are few options provided, but the trend toward customization, individuality, and adaptability of a work output to a specific individual's or company's taste or circumstances has resulted in numerous products that have optional extra equipment or services. In some products the list of options is even longer than the list of parts in the original item. For this reason it is important to consider carefully what optional equipment and services are to be included in the inventory and to develop a resources policy for these items and services.

Scrap, Waste, and Human Error

As we delve into the processes of estimating labor and material in later chapters, we discuss the methods of making allowances for inefficiencies that are inevitable in any work activity. The ground rules of the estimate, however, should state if these normal inefficiencies should be included within the basic detailed resources estimates or added as an overall allowance for cost growth.

Once the schedule, estimate elements, and ground rules are established, the estimation of direct materials and labor-hours can proceed.

NOTES

1. Joseph J. Moder, et al., *Project Management with CPM, PERT, and Precedence Diagramming* (New York: Van Nostrand Reinhold, 1983).
2. See Linda Green, *New Dimensions in Logistics* (New York: Wiley, 1991).

QUESTIONS

5.1. PERT analysis of a program is one of the more commonly used techniques in schedule planning.   T   F

5.2. "Milestone" is the term used to signify the date or event that coincides with:

    a. The start . . .

    b. The completion . . .

    c. Either the start or completion . . .

             of a task, work item or activity.

5.3. List the four key steps an analyst should take in developing a cost-effective skill mix.

5.4. Your company is responding to a request for proposal that encompasses development and production of hardware. You have been assigned overall responsibility for coordinating, compiling, and evaluating the cost proposal and preparing the cost document.

    The functional departments within your company that will ultimately perform the contract tasks will prepare estimates for their areas as you direct.

    List and briefly discuss 10 subjects you must cover in writing estimating instructions to the functional departments that will support you in preparing this proposal. (Develop some ideas not included in this chapter.)

5.5. Cost elements can reflect actual, estimated, allocated, and/or fixed costs.   T   F

5.6. Which of the following is not generally considered an element of cost?

    a. Labor-hours.

    b. Labor rates.

    c. Purchased equipment.

    d. Engineering management.

5.7. A make-or-buy list defines responsibility between purchasing and operational organizations in the company.   T   F

5.8. The make-or-buy plan determines the ratio of operational to purchasing talent needed to develop the estimate.   T   F

6
ESTIMATING DIRECT MATERIAL COSTS AND LABOR-HOURS

A measure of fine flour shall be sold for a shekel, and two measures of barley for a shekel.

2 Kings 7:1

Since overhead costs, general and administrative expenses, and profit are usually added to costs as a percentage of direct labor and material costs, it is imperative that estimate accuracy begin with precise estimates of the materials and labor-hours required to do the job. In many organizations, the materials and hands-on labor are estimated before any other peripheral costs are estimated, although these peripheral costs frequently exceed the original hardware costs. This chapter describes the methods used to determine material quantities and costs, labor-hours, factors that are used to adjust these material and labor costs, and direct costs other than those that are normally classified as material and labor costs.

ESTIMATING BASIC MATERIAL COSTS

The first step in estimating direct material costs is the determination of the material quantities required to do the job. The pounds, cubic or square yards, board feet, square feet, gallons, or linear feet of the required materials are usually obtained by determining or computing quantities directly from a "bill of materials" or parts list or from detailed drawings and specifications of the completed item with added sufficient allowance for waste or scrap. The next step is to apply the appropriate material unit price or cost to this quantity to develop the final material costs. The costs of procuring, handling, storing, and maintaining materials stocks and supplies can be included in the material costs or may be included in material overhead costs, described in Chapter 7. Usually materials are classed (together with another category of effort to be described later: subcontracts) as those items purchased rather than made by an organization.

Drawing Takeoff

The best means of determining the actual quantity of materials required to do a job is to extract or calculate material quantities from drawings of the item or specifications for the process or service. Calculation of material quantities involves such considerations as the anticipated method of manufacturing the item, conducting the process, or delivering the service; the size or quantity of uniform purchase lots; and the anticipated scrap, waste, boil-off, or leakage. Since the term "materials" covers a wide range of substances, varying from raw materials to completed parts, there is often a delicate balance between the type, shape, and kind of material purchased and the labor to be performed on it after it is purchased.

Careful analysis of the drawings and specifications of the work output is required to determine (1) the best state or condition in which to purchase the material, (2) the optimum size or quantity of material bought, (3) the method of fabrication that will best use the full quantity of purchased material, and (4) the expected quantity of scrap or waste resulting from successful manufacture of the product. The word "successful" is used here because we have not yet considered the effects of accidents or mistakes on material scrap or waste. A certain amount of waste can be expected from even a successful manufacturing process because the material sizes do not always conform to the shape of the completed part. Good manufacturing design, however, will take maximum advantage of available material sizes and shapes to minimize waste.

Material Handbooks and Supplier Catalogs

Once material quantities have been developed from drawings, specifications, and parts lists, costs can be derived from material handbooks, supplier catalogs, or supplier quotes. The most highly refined catalogs and handbooks are available for architectural building construction, but ample catalogs are available for the manufacturing and process industries, and catalogs and handbooks are becoming available for high-technology industries such as electronics, microprocessors, electrooptics, sensors, composites, and other advanced materials and parts. With constantly changing prices and markets, it is always desirable to use the latest available catalog prices.

Some available catalogs and sources of pricing information are as follows:

Sweet's Division [construction]
McGraw-Hill Information Systems Company
1221 Avenue of the Americas
New York, NY 10030
  Architectural Catalog File
  Interior Design File
  Samples File
  Showroom Guide
  Light Construction Catalog File

Industrial Construction and Renovation Catalog File
Dodge Building Cost Calculator and Valuation Guide
Dodge Digest of Building Costs and Specifications
Dodge Manual for Building Construction Pricing and Scheduling
Dodge Guide for Estimating Public Works Construction Costs
Dodge Construction System Costs

Thomas Register—14 volumes [construction and manufacturing]
Thomas Publishing Company
One Penn Plaza
New York, NY 10001

Information Handling Services [construction, manufacturing, aerospace]
381 5 N.E. Expressway
Suite 102
Atlanta, GA 30340

R. S. Means Co., Inc. [construction, architecture]
150 Construction Plaza
Duxbury, MA 02332

Richardson Engineering Services, Inc.
P.O. Box 370
Solana Beach, CA 92075

Craftsman Book Company
6058 Corte del Cedro
P.O. Box 6500
Carlsbad, CA 92008

  Construction Estimating Reference Data
  Building Cost Manual
  Berger Building Cost File
  Estimating Tables for Home Building
  Electrical Construction Estimator
  Estimating Home Building Costs
  Cost Records for Construction Estimating
  Carpentry Estimating
  Estimating Plumbing Costs
  Concrete Construction and Estimating
  Masonry Estimating
  Estimating Electrical Construction

Many of these catalogs and handbooks contain both materials and labor costs. Some are published yearly with quarterly updates; some are updated continually as prices change. A good estimator will obtain and keep a complete file of catalogs and handbooks containing descriptions and prices of materials, parts, supplies, and subsystems and components of the major product or products he or she is estimating. Often the material is so voluminous that microfilm or microfiche files are required to save space and to allow easy and quick access and viewing. It is common practice in the insurance adjusting business, particularly for automobiles, to retain and keep current a complete microfilm parts list and labor estimate for all major repair and replacement items for all late model cars.

Quantity Buy and Inventory Considerations

The quantity or number of supplies or parts purchased or stocked strongly affects the materials costs. The study of materials, supplies, and goods and their handling, transportation, packaging, shipping, and storage is called logistics. To stock the right quantity of materials or supplies, a logistics study must be done of the economics of inventory systems.[1]

The basic decision that faces a company concerning materials costs is whether to take advantage of the lower costs made possible by buying materials in large quantities and saving these materials until they are needed or whether to wait until the materials are needed before purchasing them. The benefits of buying materials in large quantities are fourfold.

First, suppliers and producers can offer their materials at lower prices when larger quantities are purchased because their cost per unit is lower for higher production rates. A vendor that provides large quantities of an item or substance to one customer has costs that are less per unit than when providing small quantities to many customers because handling, shipping, marketing, and administrative costs are lower for a single customer.

Second, by purchasing large quantities of a needed material, the buyer avoids future cost or price increases for that product. In commodity areas where prices are rapidly rising due to inflation, escalation, shortages in supply, or decreasing production capability, stockpiling of needed materials is often cost-effective.

Third, the ready availability of vital materials will often serve as a cost avoidance in producing a work output where there is a fluctuating demand. The investment in material to be available on short notice is usually prudent because it is then available when the labor or equipment is ready to convert it into the final product. The law of supply and demand will assist the stockpiler of needed materials because there is a price for ready availability that adds to the basic cost of the material itself.

Fourth, the cost incurred by a buyer's purchasing and inventory system in making procurements usually depends on the number of individual procurements rather than the size of the procurement. These costs are usually independent of the quantity as opposed to storage costs, which are quantity dependent. Purchasing larger quantities of needed materials at one time rather than in separate lots reduces the procurement cost per unit of material.

These four benefits of buying and stockpiling quantities of materials larger than those needed immediately for the work activity are counteracted by costs associated with the storage, maintenance, handling, and use of the larger quantities of materials and by the opportunity cost of having capital tied up in inventory. The real out-of-pocket costs of carrying an inventory include insurance and taxes on the stock-piled material and the land or building it is stored in; breakage, deterioration, and pilferage of the material; and heating, light, and security for the warehouse or storage area. The opportunity cost that is lost through the purchase of large quantities of materials is equal to the largest rate of return that could be obtained through alternate investments. (Chapters 7, 8, and 9 discuss of rate of return.)

It is important to analyze the costs associated with material purchases before choosing a specific procurement and inventory plan for a given material or supply item because there are so many variables involved in the costs of materials systems, among them floor or shelf space available for storage of materials, procurement lead time, usage rate and standard deviation of usage rate of the material, the number of different materials to be stocked, the number of stocking locations, budget and cash flow constraints, and the value or scarcity of the materials. A careful analysis of these variables should be carried out to reveal optimum order dates, lot sizes, reorder frequencies, and inventory levels.

The costs of ordering the material and carrying it in inventory until use must be considered. The cost of ordering materials is also known as the procurement cost. It is basically the cost of processing the purchase requisitions, purchase orders, and other administrative paperwork. Normally this cost is fixed regardless of the quantity of materials ordered because it costs the firm the same to process paperwork for 100 or 100,000 units of the same item. This cost is unique for each firm, and it should be computed by collecting time and materials used in processing a typical procurement action. Some firms use a high-level calculation where the total annual procurement department expenses are divided by the number of requisitions processed annually. Often material procurement costs are included as part of a "material burden" or "material overhead" (see Chapter 7).

The second material-related cost, besides the cost of the materials themselves, is the inventory carrying cost. It is a function of the amount of inventory stored and the length of time the material is stored. This cost needs to include the following categories:

Cost of insurance and taxes covering the inventory

Cost of obsolescence, spoilage, or loss

Cost of storage space

Cost of material handling equipment

Opportunity cost of capital tied up in the inventory.

There are several excellent managerial economic textbooks listed in the Bibliography that thoroughly cover how these costs are computed.

Organizations that are involved with a continuing work activity will find that it is economically desirable to have goods arrive precisely when the demand occurs. To help accomplish this task, costs of an inventory or "just-in-time" system must be included in the cost estimate. This cost can be added as a direct cost to a work activity or included in material overhead (discussed in Chapter 7).

Advance material handling systems have significantly reduced the cost and time required for storage and retrieval of stockpiles. Storage and retrieval machines, some consisting of rack and storage structures over 100 feet tall, are often used as part of the storage building or warehouse structure. Use of integral automated storage and retrieval systems with handling speeds in excess of 500 feet per minute and hoisting speeds of up to 150 feet per minute are available. The U.S. Internal Revenue Service has ruled that these special-purpose structures can, for tax purposes, be depreciated as equipment rather than regarded as part of the building and therefore may qualify for investment credit and sales tax exemption. Some companies have realized savings of more than 20 percent by using integral storage systems. In addition, savings in time and improvements in efficiency are brought about by the use of high-speed, automated, computerized systems.

Space is also saved by automated handling systems because aisle space need be only inches wider than the load itself. The following companies can provide cost estimates and cost savings realized through the use of automated storage and retrieval systems: Harnisch Feger Corporation (Milwaukee, Wisconsin), Webb Systems Group (Farmington Hills, Michigan), Rapistan Division of Lear Siegler, Inc. (Grand Rapids, Michigan), Litton Unit Handling Systems (Florence, Kentucky), EATON Automated Systems (Salt Lake City, Utah), S. I. Handling Systems, Inc. (Easton, Pennsylvania), and Munck Systems (Hampton, Virginia).

Scrap and Waste Considerations

Scrap and waste in material estimating must not be forgotten or omitted in the analysis of the job to be done. A normal amount of waste or scrap occurs in almost every manufacturing or production process because materials must be changed in form, shape, or volume in some manner to arrive at a final product. In this process of converting the shape or form of a material, scrap material is produced by the machining process, by-products are formed, and the inspection process will result in a certain percentage of rejected work. Another category of scrap or waste is caused by poor design, the use of unskilled personnel, or the use of defective equipment.

Designers should endeavor to use standard sizes or quantities of material to reduce waste, and manufacturing plants should be staffed with skilled personnel and well-maintained equipment to reduce or eliminate inadvertent waste. When scrap, waste, or by-products regularly result from a work activity, some method of reclamation of the waste or scrap material should be considered. Many product lines have been developed through the practical application of a scrap or waste material to a known need. In some instances the by-product or waste material has become the principal product of a company, while the initial product has become a secondary income producer. Examples are the production of rock-wool insulation from slag and the discovery of Teflon and Eastman 910 adhesive from by-products of another process.

The estimation of scrap and waste factors can be done most effectively by reviewing the actual manufacturing or production process, observing actual scrap and waste factors on previous projects, and judiciously applying these factors to the activity being estimated.

Bills of Material

When a product is designed, a key part of the design documentation is a bill of material. A bill of material or parts list, which is an itemized listing of the parts with quantities of each specified, is usually included in or with the initial detailed design drawings of an item and is updated as the design changes. This bill of material is a valuable source of material quantity information for the estimator. If it is not available, the estimator must be able to read and interpret drawings with sufficient skill to be able to envision and interpret the size, type, and quantity of material required based on measuring dimensions and interpreting notes from the drawing itself. Since there may be a number of different ways that materials can be applied to a design, it is always desirable for the designer or draftsman to specify the bill of materials rather than to rely on the estimator or the machinist to develop this information directly from the drawing. Material quantities are developed directly from a bill of material by adding scrap and waste allowances and by combining identical materials into a lot or quantity purchase.

Subcontracts

In defining an overall category of purchased items for a given work activity, the term "materials" often includes the use of subcontracts to produce partially finished materials, parts, or components. Since subcontracts and materials are procured items, they are usually categorized together in a cost estimate. The reason for this is that there is a gray area in the definition of what is a material and what is a subcontract. One type of subcontract that is not materials in the strictest sense is a service or support contract that provides labor that contributes to the overall work activity. This labor can alter or modify the shape or configuration of a material or part or can be used to provide an overall direct service to the factory itself. Often a distinction between materials and subcontracts can be made by determining the degree of completion of the delivered item. In general, however, they are categorized together.

ESTIMATING ENGINEERING ACTIVITIES

The National Society of Professional Engineers has developed position descriptions and recommended annual salaries for nine levels of engineers. (These skill levels are reproduced in **Figure 6.1**, which appears on the front inside cover, by permission of the National Society of Professional Engineers.) These skill levels are broad enough in description to cover a wide variety of engineering activities. The principal activities performed by engineers are described in the following sections.

Design

The design activity for any enterprise encompasses conceptual design, preliminary design, final design, and design changes. The design engineer must design prototypes, components for development or preproduction testing, special test equipment used in development or preproduction testing, support equipment, software, and production hardware. Increasingly complex and sophisticated processes, products, projects, and services require systems engineering and integration to coordinate and meld all engineering efforts together. Software engineering and analysis is required to perform the software design function. Since design effort is dependent on the specific work output description, design hours must be estimated by a professional experienced in the area being estimated.

Analysis

Analysis goes hand in hand with design and employs the same general skill level as design engineering. Categories of analysis that support, augment, or precede design are thermal analysis, stress analysis, failure analysis, dynamics analysis, manufacturing analysis, safety analysis, software analysis, and maintainability analysis. Analysis is estimated by professionals skilled in analytical techniques. It usually includes computer programming time, sensitivity studies, trade studies, data reduction, and engineering labor-hours.

Drafting, Writing, and Coding

Drafting, writing, and coding are areas in the engineering disciplines where labor-hours can be correlated to a product: the completed engineering drawing, specification, or computer program. Labor-hour estimates must still be quoted in ranges, however, because the labor-hours required for these engineering activities will vary considerably depending on the complexity of the item and whether computer-aided design (CAD) systems or computer-aided software engineering (CASE) systems are used.

As an example the drafting times shown in Table 6.1 are approximations for manual production of Class A drawings of nonelectronic (mechanical) parts where all the design information is available and where the numbers represent "board time," that is, the actual time that the drafter is working on the drawing plus its supporting documentation (parts lists). A Class A drawing is one that is fully dimensioned and has full supporting documentation. An additional time allotment is usually required to obtain approval and sign-offs of stress, thermal, supervisors, and drawing release system personnel. If a shop drawing is all that is required (only sufficient information for manufacture of the part with some informal assistance from the designer and/or drafter), the board time labor-hours required would be approximately 50 percent of that listed in **Table 6.1**. Note that CAD drawings take about two-thirds of the time to generate than manual drawings but can be revised in one-fourth of the time on the average.

MANUFACTURING/PRODUCTION ENGINEERING

The manufacturing/production engineering activity required to support a work activity is preproduction planning and operations analysis. This differs from the gener-

TABLE 6.1   Engineering Drafting Times

Drawing Letter Designation	Size	Approximate Manual Board Time Hours for Drafting of Class A Drawings	Approximate CAD System Generation Time
A	8½ × 11	1–4 hr.	40 min.–2 hr.
B	11 × 17	2–8 hr.	1–5 hr.
C	17 × 22	4–12 hr.	2–8 hr.
D	22 × 34	8–16 hr.	5–10 hr.
E and F	34 × 44 and 28 × 40	16–40 hr.	11–27 hr.
J	34 × 48 and larger	40–80 hr.	27–54 hr.
Revision time		Multiply by 0.20	Multiply by 0.05

al type of production engineering wherein overall manufacturing techniques, facilities, and processes are developed. Excluded from this categorization is the design time of production engineers who redesign a prototype unit to conform to manufacturing or consumer requirements, as well as time for designing special tooling and special test equipment. A listing of some typical functions of manufacturing engineering follows:

1. Fabrication planning

   Prepare operations sheets for each part.

   List operational sequence for materials, machines, and functions.

   Recommend standard and special tooling.

   Make up tool order for design and construction of special tooling.

   Develop standard time data for operations sheets.

   Conduct liaison with production and design engineers.

2. Assembly planning

   Develop operations sheets for each part.

   Build first sample unit.

   Itemize assembly sequence and location of parts.

   Order design and construction of special jigs and fixtures.

   Develop exact component dimensions.

   Build any special manufacturing aids, such as wiring harness jig boards.

   Apply standard time data to operations sheet.

   Balance time cycles of final assembly line workstations.

   Effect liaison with production and design engineers.

   Set up material and layout of each workstation in accordance with operations sheet.

Instruct mechanics in construction of the first unit.

3. Test planning

   Determine overall test method to meet performance and acceptance specifications.

   Break total test effort into positions by function and desired time cycle.

   Prepare test equipment list and schematic for each position.

   Prepare test equipment design order for design and construction of special-purpose test fixtures.

   Prepare a step-by-step procedure for each position.

   Effect liaison with production and design engineers.

   Set up test positions and check out.

   Instruct test operator on first unit.

4. Sustaining manufacturing engineering

   Debug, as required, engineering design data.

   Debug, as required, manufacturing methods and processes.

   Recommend more efficient manufacturing methods throughout the life of production.

The following formula may be helpful in deriving manufacturing engineering labor-hour estimates for high production rates:

1. Total fabrication and assembly labor-hours, divided by the number of units to be produced, multiplied by 20 gives manufacturing engineering start-up costs.
2. For sustaining manufacturing engineering, take the unit fabrication and assembly labor-hours and multiply by 0.07. (These factors are suggested for quantities up to 100 units.)

Engineering Documentation

A large part of an engineer's time is spent in writing specifications, reports, manuals, handbooks, and engineering orders. The complexity of the engineering activity and the specific document requirements are important determining factors in estimating the engineering labor-hours required to prepare engineering documentation.

The hours required for engineering documentation (technical reports, specifications, and technical manuals) will vary considerably depending on the complexity of the work output; however, average labor-hours for origination and revision of engineering documentation have been derived for both manually generated and computer-generated documentation based on experience, and these figures can be used as average labor-hours per page of documentation. (See **Tables 6.2 and 6.3.**)

TABLE 6.2 New Documentation

Function	Manual Labor-Hours per Page	Computer-generated Labor-Hours per Page
Research, liaison, technical writing, editing, and supervision	5.7	3.8
Typing and quality control	0.6	0.3
Illustrations	4.3	2.8
Engineering	0.7	0.7
Coordination	0.2	0.2
Total	11.5	7.8

TABLE 6.3 Revised Documentation

Function	Manual Labor-Hours per Page	Computer-generated Labor-Hours per Page
Research, liaison, technical writing, editing, and supervision	4.00	2.66
Typing and quality control	0.60	0.16
Illustrations	0.75	0.18
Engineering	0.60	0.60
Coordination	0.20	0.20
Total	6.15	3.80

ESTIMATING MANUFACTURING/PRODUCTION, ASSEMBLY, AND CONSTRUCTION ACTIVITIES

The Process Plan

A key to successful estimating of manufacturing or construction activities is the process plan, a listing of all operations that must be performed to manufacture a product or to complete a project, along with the labor-hours required to perform each operation. The process plan is usually prepared by an experienced supervisor, engineer, or technician who knows the company's equipment, personnel, and capabilities or by a process planning department chartered to do all of the process planning. The process planner envisions the equipment, workstation, and environment; estimates the number of persons required; and estimates how long it will take to perform each step. The labor-hours required are derived from this information. Process steps are numbered, and space is left between operations listed to allow easy insertion or omission of operations or activities as the process is modified. A typical process plan for a welded cylinder assembly is given in **Table 6.4**.

The process plan is used not only to plan and estimate a manufacturing or construction process but also as part of the manufacturing or construction work order itself. As such, it shows the shop or construction personnel each step to take in the completion of the work activity. Fabrication of items from metals, plastics, or other materials in a shop is usually called "manufacturing," and fabrication of buildings, structures, bridges, dams, and public facilities on site is usually called "construction." Different types of standards and estimating factors are used for each of these categories of work.

Developing Labor-Hour Estimates Based on Time Standards

The process plan described can be based on the judgment of the estimator using staffing or shop-loading techniques, or it can be developed using time standards developed by industrial engineering time or job analysis techniques. Predominant among organizations that specialize in study, publication, and training in the development and use of time standards is the MTM Association for Standards and Research in Fair Lawn, New Jersey.

Detailed time standards developed through job analysis usually involve the subdivision of a task into each human body movement required to perform a job. These movements, such as "pickup, place, or position," are accomplished in very small increments, usually 0.001 to 0.0001 minute. Because it is impractical for the estimator to break work activities into increments this small, aggregate time standards rather than detailed standards can be used. These aggregate standards are developed through a synthesis of a number of small body movements into an overall body motion or work increment that ranges in time from 0.05 minute to 0.50 minute. The use of aggregate standards takes more estimating time to accomplish than the staffing or shop-loading method, but there are certain advantages to using time standards: (1) they can be used by persons who do not have an intimate familiarity with the job being estimated, (2) they promote consistency between estimates, and (3) resulting estimates are less likely to vary with the estimator because they are based on work content rather than judgment or opinion. Time standards are used extensively in estimating labor-hours required for manufacturing activities. Some samples are shown in Tables 6.5 through 6.9.

MANUFACTURING ACTIVITIES

Manufacturing activities are subdivided into various categories of effort such as metal working and forming; welding, brazing, and soldering; application of fas-

TABLE 6.4   Process Plan for Welded Cylinder Assembly

Drawing No. D21216   Part No. 1D21254
Title: Cylinder Assembly (Welded)

Operation Number	Labor-Hours	Description
010	—	Receive and inspect material (skins and forgings)
020	24	Roll form skin segments
030	60	Mask and chem-mill recessed pattern in skins
040	—	Inspect
050	36	Trim to design dimension and prepare in welding skin segments into cylinders (two)
060	16	Locate segments on automatic seam welder tooling fixture and weld per specification (longitudinal weld)
070	2	Remove from automatic welding fixture
080	18	Shave welds on inside diameter
090	16	Establish trim lines (surface plate)
100	18	Install in special fixture and trim to length
110	8	Remove from special fixture
120	56	Install center mandrel—center ring, forward and aft sections (cylinders)—forward and aft mandrel—forward and aft rings—and complete special feature setup
130	—	Inspect
140	24	But weld (4 places)
150	8	Remove from special fixture and remove mandrels
160	59	Radiograph and dye penetrant inspect
170	—	Inspect dimensionally
180	6	Reinstall mandrels in preparation for final machining
190	14	Finish OD—aft
	10	Finish OD—center
	224	Finish OD—forward
200	40	Program for forward ring
220	30	Handwork (3 rings)
230	2	Reinstall cylinder assembly with mandrels still in place, or on the special fixture
240	16	Clock and drill index holes
250	—	Inspect
260	8	Remove cylinder from special fixture; remove mandrel
270	1	Install in holding cradle
280	70	Locate drill jig on forward end and hand drill leak check vein (drill and tap) and hole pattern
290	64	Locate drill jig on aft ring and hand drill hole pattern
300	—	Inspect forward and aft rings
310	8	Install protective covers on each end of cylinder
320	—	Transfer to surface treat
340	24	Remove covers and alodine
350	—	Inspect
360	8	Reinstall protective covers and return to assembly area

TABLE 6.5   Raw Material Cutting Standards

	Soft material	Hard Material
Setup on band saw or power hacksaw: 0.1 hour		
Pick up material, position to saw, take out of saw		
(Part size = 1 in. to 2 ft.) 0.05–0.50 min.		
Weld blade for internal cut (band saw)		
Open saw guard, break blade, remove slide, put blade through, grind ends of saw blade, clamp blade in weld fixture, weld, anneal, unclamp smooth weld, put saw on pulleys and guides, adjust saw, close guard 3.50 min		
	Minutes per Inch	

	Soft material	Hard Material
Time required to cut 1 in. of metal (band saw)		
⅛-in. thick stock	0.02	0.50
Time required to cut 1 in. of metal (power hack saw)		
1-in. thick stock	0.30	1.15
3-in. thick stock	2.55	10.50
6-in. thick stock	10.40	42.50

teners; plating, printing, surface treating, and heat treating; and manufacture of electronic components (a special category). The most common method of estimating the time and cost required for manufacturing activities is the industrial engineering approach whereby standards or target values are established for various operations. The term "standards" is used to indicate standard time data. All possible elements of work are measured, assigned a standard time for performance, and documented. When a particular job is to be estimated, all of the applicable standards for all related operations are added together to determine the total time.

The use of standards produces more accurate and more easily justifiable estimates. Standards also promote consistency between estimates as well as among estimators. Where standards are used, personal experience is desirable or beneficial but not mandatory. Standards have been developed over a number of years through the use of time studies and synthesis of methods analysis. They are based on the level of efficiency that could be attained by a job shop producing up to 100 units of any specific work output. Standards are actually synoptical values of more detailed times. They are adaptations, extracts, or benchmark time values for each type of operation. The loss of accuracy occasioned by summarization and/or averaging is acceptable when the total time for a system is being developed. If standard values are used with judgment and interpolations for varying stock sizes, reasonably accurate results can be obtained. Examples of standards for machining operations are included in this chapter to familiarize readers with their format and use. Standards for values of other manufacturing, metal treating, and electrical and electronic work are included in Appendix I.

Machining operations make up a large part of the manufacturing costs of many products and projects. They are usually divided into setup times and run times. Setup time is the time required to establish and adjust the tooling, to set speeds and feeds on the metal removal machine, and to program for the manufacture of one or more identical or similar parts. Run time is the time required to complete each part. It consists of certain fixed positioning times for each item being machined as well as the actual metal removal and cleanup time for each item. Values listed are for "soft" and "hard" materials. Soft values are for aluminum, magnesium, and plastics. Hard values are for stainless steel, tool steel, and beryllium. Between these two times are standard values for brass, bronze, and medium steel. Standard times for setup and run of several common manufacturing operations (cutting, turning, milling, drilling, and manual production of printed circuit boards follow in **Tables 6.5–6.9.**

TABLE 6.6   Cutting/Turning on a Lathe (Warner Swasey, Type 3)

	Minutes per Job
Setup Times	
Fill in time slip, check in, and analyze job from blueprint	2.00
Trip to tool crib and return	5.00
Set up measuring instruments—average 3 (0.70 min. each)	2.10
Install collet or chuck	2.00
Install and square-off stock	3.00
Deliver first part to inspection	0.70
Teardown Times	
Remove collet or chuck	1.50
Clean and store measuring tools	1.00
Total	17.3
Add per Cutting Tool	
Install hex turret tools—average 6 (3 min. each)	18.00
Install cross slide tools—average 2 (5 min. each)	10.00
Tear down, clean, store—average 8 (2 min. each)	16.00
Total	44.00
Runtime handling Time per Part	
(1-in. diameter stock)	
Release collet, chuck advance bar to stop	0.105
Tighten collet chuck	0.02
Start machine	0.05
Position coolant	0.05
Change spindle speed	0.10
Cut off, remove part, and set aside	0.0325
Check part	0.04
Total	0.35

	Minutes per Inch	
	Soft Material	Hard Material
Turn on bore (1-in. diameter stock)[a] back hex terret from work, index to next station, advance tool to work	0.110	0.110

(continued)

TABLE 6.6   (*Continued*)

	Minutes per Inch	
	Soft Material	Hard Material
Turn, bore, etc., 0.0075-in. feed × 0.125 in. depth[b]	0.096	0.700
Total	0.206	0.810

Tap Handling Time

Change to slower spindle speed		0.066
Reverse spindle direction backout		0.031
Change spindle direction to tap		0.026
Brush oil on tap		0.070
Blow tap clean		0.120
Total		0.379

Machine Time

(Noncollapsing taps) (includes backout at 2 × tap): 1/8-in. diameter × NS40 threads per in.		0.240

Thread Handling Time

Change to slower spindle speed		0.066
Change speed back to selected work speed		0.066
Position collect		0.048
Blow die head clean		0.120
Total		0.300
Machine time (based on automatic or self-opening dies:		
1/4-in. diameter × NS32 threads per in.	0.128	0.208
Total threading time	0.428	0.508

Taper Handling Time

Release compound rest, swing to proper angle, secure		0.500
Advance tool to work		0.100
Back tool from work		0.100
Release compound rest, swing back to normal position, secure		0.400
Total		1.100

	Minutes per Inch	
	Soft Material	Hard Material
Machine Time		
0.0075-in. feed × 0.125-in. depth	0.096	0.700

[a]Time to bore or turn 1 linear inch of 1-inch diameter stock may be used as a basic time unit in estimating small machined parts. Used with discretion, it serves as an average time per cut to turn, bore, drill, ream, knurl, form, and cut off.

[b]Feeds for aluminum vary from 0.002 to 0.030 inch and for steel from 0.003 to 0.010 inch. A light rough cut is represented by 0.0075 inch feed. Double the times shown for rough and finish cut.

TABLE 6.7   Milling (Milwaukee No. 2 or Equal Machines)

	Minutes per Job
	Soft or Hard Materials
Setup Times	
Charge time on card and check in	1.00
Analyze drawing	1.00
To tool crib for tools and return tools for previous tasks	5.00
Clean T-slots and table	3.00
Assemble and align vise or holding fixture	5.00
Install cutter to collet	8.00
Adjust table to locate initial cut	2.00
Use various measuring devices; deliver first piece to inspection	3.00
Total	28.00
Handling Time per Part[a]	
Pick up and clamp in vise	0.20
Release after cut	0.05
Check part with micrometer	0.05
Part to tray	0.05
Clean vise for text	0.05
Total	0.40
Operations per Cut	
Start machine and advance work to cutter	0.10
Back work from cutter and stop	0.10
Set table at proper position for work by moving up, down, or in saddle	0.20
Index dividing head	0.15
Total	0.55

	Minutes per Inch	
	Soft Material	Hard Material
Profile or End Mill		
Rough profile, $1/2$-in. deep $\times$ $3/4$-in. wide cutter	0.067	0.260
Finish profile, $1/2$-in. deep $\times$ $3/4$-in. wide cutter	0.033	0.130
Total	0.100	0.390

(*continued*)

TABLE 6.7 (*Continued*)

	Minutes per Inch	
	Soft Material	Hard Material
Surface or Face Mill		
Cutters—plain, helical, slab, or shell end; diameter of cutters = 2½ to 4½ in.; face width of cutters = 2 to 6 in.; ½-in. depth × 6-in. wide cut	0.034	1.000
Side Mill, Straddle Mill, Slotting		
Cutters—stagger tooth, half-side; diameters = 4 to 8 in.; width of face = ¼ to 1 in.; ½-in. depth × 1-in. cutter face	0.067	2.000
Corner, Groove, Slot		
Round corner—⅓-in. radius	0.031	0.527
V-groove or chamfer—½-in. deep × 1-2/in. wide	0.050	0.588
Key slot—½-in. deep × ⅜-in. wide	0.052	0.410

[a]If a complex fixture is used or if alignment of part with a dial indicator is required, double these times.

TABLE 6.8 Drilling

	Minutes per Job
Setup Times	
Fill in job card, check in, and analyze drawing	2.00
Go to tool crib for tools and return	5.00
Handle jigs, fixtures, and vises	1.50
Adjust machine, change speeds and feeds	0.80
Adjust feed stop	0.50
Insert drill bit in spindle	1.75
Deliver first piece to inspection	0.70
Total	13.25

		Minutes per Inch	
	Constant Time[a]	Soft Material	Hard Material
Operation			
General-purpose (spindle RPM = 500–2000) drill ⅛-in. diameter hole	0.05	0.140	0.556
Tap ⅛ in. × NS40	0.05	0.119	0.240
Countersink ⅛ in. × 1/16 in. deep	0.05	0.009	0.009
Heavy duty press (spindle RPM = 1–1000)			
Drill 2-in. diameter hole	0.05	0.250	1.170
Tap 2 in. × 4½ threads/inch	0.05	0.035	0.555

[a]Constant time is the value for moving the part to align for next hole plus lowering the drill to surface.

TABLE 6.9   Manual Insertion of Components on Printed Circuit Boards

Part/Component Type	Operation Performed	Time (Seconds)
Axial components	Form leads, insert, cut, and clinch leads	17–22
Radial components or can-type ICs	Insert, cut, and clinch leads	9–12, basic time, plus 1.5–3.0 sec. per lead
DIP/DIP sockets, posts, pin-grid arrays, and odd-shaped components	Insert component	4–7, basic time, plus 0.5 to 1.0 sec. per post or lead
SIP/SIP sockets or connectors	Insert component	8–12
Sleeve	Cut and add to one lead	12–18
Heat sink	Add to transistor	25–30
Jumper wire	Cut, strip, and tie leads, insert and solder	50–75
Leads and posts	Hand solder one	5–7
Manual solder	First lead	5–7
	Repetitive leads	4–5
	Clean solder tip	1–3

CONSTRUCTION ACTIVITIES

General

One of the most structured, documented, and well-thought-out activities that es-timators deal with is construction. Almost from the beginning of recorded history, people have had to provide structures for shelter, business, travel, entertainment, worship, and many other varied human needs. Despite a wealth of information on the construction process, there are still evidences of cost overruns and underesti-mates due to factors such as inadequate planning, escalation and inflation, unforeseen natural disasters, and growth in complexity or content of construction projects. The key to avoiding many of these cost growth factors is to take maximum advantage of the structured planning, scheduling, and estimating process. It is important to recognize and to include adequate labor-hours and materials for each step in the construction process and to lay out and identify each construction activity. Because construction activities are usually performed at the site where the structure or public utility is needed, they differ considerably from the manufacturing and assembly activities covered earlier in this chapter.

The need for physical access to the construction element being performed at a given time dictates a general flow of activities for the construction process. The unique feature of an integrated on-site manufacturing and assembly process performed by diverse skills makes it particularly important to lay out the flow sequence of construction as a prerequisite to and an integral part of the estimating of labor-hours and materials. Construction activities consist of four general construction categories: building, public utilities, transportation, and special facilities. Building construction includes the construction of auditoriums, civic centers, churches, factories, homes, hotels and motels, offices, schools, sports arenas, stores, and warehouses. Public utilities construction includes the construction of communications networks and antenna towers, dams and reservoirs, electrical power generation and distribution networks, sewage collection and treatment systems, recreational facilities, and water storage and treatment and distribution systems. Transportation construction includes the construction of airports, bridges, bus terminals, canals, docks, railroads, roads, train terminals, and tunnels. Special facilities construction includes oil drilling rigs and platforms and space launch vehicle facilities. Each construction category and subdivision is accompanied by its own background and experience, a specific labor skill mix, and usually a well-thought-out and experience-proved planning, scheduling, and estimating methodology.

One of the most common types of construction is the single-family residence. Although single-family residences come in an almost infinite variety of shapes, sizes, decor, and floor plans, home construction can be depicted by a fairly standardized sequence of activities. One such flow sequence for a residence is shown in **Figure 6.2**. Note that even in a construction project as simple as home construction there are over 100 major steps. Each step encompasses other smaller steps that can, in turn, be estimated. By using a construction sequence diagram, an estimator can envision each construction step, determine the labor skill and materials required, and estimate the labor-hours required based on the architectural drawings, specifications, and material lists for that particular home. The flow diagram shown, for a one-story brick home, can be easily adapted to many other types of home construction. In estimating materials required for construction, it is also handy to have a checklist for comparison with the structure's requirements. **Figure 6.3** is a checklist provided by the Federal Housing Authority for estimating material requirements for residential construction.

Construction Standards

In the fields of residential and industrial construction alone, there are nearly 3000 categories of material and labor. Many construction labor standards are tied to the item being installed or material being used. Within each category the labor-hours required often vary with the specific type and brand name of the item or material being installed. There are estimating standards for new construction and for remodeling and repair, and there are overall square foot cost relationships available for residential, commercial, industrial, and farm buildings. Construction estimating manuals usually include average wage rates for various construction skills and trades, wage modification factors that adapt these wage rates to various geographical areas, and material and labor costs associated with each construction activity. A sample table from one such estimating manual, the *National Construction Estimator* for 1989, is shown in **Table 6.10**.

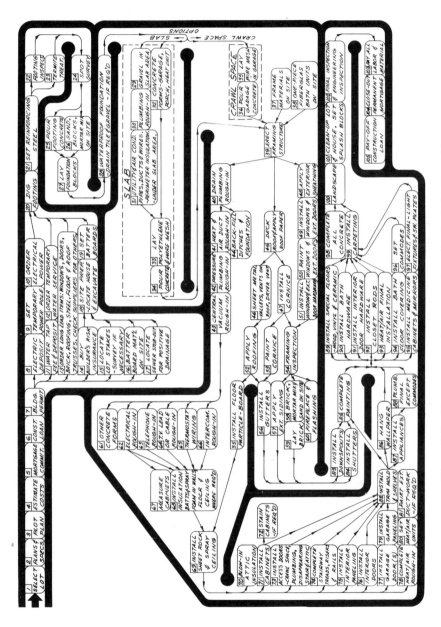

Figure 6.2 Flow sequence for construction of a single-family residence.

FHA Form 2005
VA Form 26–1852
Rev. 3/68

For accurate register of carbon copies, form may be separated along above fold. Staple completed sheets together in original order.

Form approved.
Budget Bureau No. 63–R055.11.

☐ Proposed Construction

DESCRIPTION OF MATERIALS

No. _____
(To be inserted by FHA or VA)

☐ Under Construction

Property address _____ City _____ State _____

Mortgagor or Sponsor _____ _____
(Name)   (Address)

Contractor or Builder _____ _____
(Name)   (Address)

INSTRUCTIONS

1. For additional information on how this form is to be submitted, number of copies, etc., see the instructions applicable to the FHA Application for Mortgage Insurance or VA Request for Determination of Reasonable Value, as the case may be.
2. Describe all materials and equipment to be used, whether or not shown on the drawings, by marking an X in each appropriate check-box and entering the information called for in each space. If space is inadequate, enter "See misc." and describe under item 27 or on an attached sheet.
3. Work not specifically described or shown will not be considered unless

required, then the minimum acceptable will be assumed. Work exceeding minimum requirements cannot be considered unless specifically described.
4. Include no alternates, "or equal" phrases, or contradictory items. (Consideration of a request for acceptance of substitute materials or equipment is not thereby precluded.)
5. Include signatures required at the end of this form.
6. The construction shall be completed in compliance with the related drawings and specifications, as amended during processing. The specifications include this Description of Materials and the applicable Minimum Construction Requirements.

1. EXCAVATION:
Bearing soil, type _____

2. FOUNDATIONS:
Footings: concrete mix _____; strength psi _____ Reinforcing _____
Foundation wall: material _____ Reinforcing _____
Interior foundation wall: material _____ Party foundation wall _____
Columns: material and sizes _____ Piers: material and reinforcing _____
Girders: material and sizes _____ Sills: material _____
Basement entrance areaway _____ Window areaways _____
Waterproofing _____ Footing drains _____
Termite protection _____
Basementless space: ground cover _____; insulation _____; foundation vents _____
Special foundations _____
Additional information: _____

3. CHIMNEYS:
Material _____ Prefabricated (make and size) _____
Flue lining: material _____ Heater flue size _____ Fireplace flue size _____
Vents (material and size): gas or oil heater _____; water heater _____
Additional information: _____

4. FIREPLACES:
Type: ☐ solid fuel; ☐ gas-burning; ☐ circulator (make and size) _____ Ash dump and clean-out _____
Fireplace: facing _____; lining _____; hearth _____; mantel _____
Additional information: _____

5. EXTERIOR WALLS:
Wood frame: wood grade, and species _____ ☐ Corner bracing. Building paper or felt _____
　Sheathing _____; thickness _____; width _____; ☐ solid; ☐ spaced _____" o. c.; ☐ diagonal; _____
　Siding _____; grade _____; type _____; size _____; exposure _____"; fastening _____
　Shingles _____; grade _____; type _____; size _____; exposure _____"; fastening _____
　Stucco _____; thickness _____"; Lath _____; weight _____ lb.
　Masonry veneer _____ Sills _____ Lintels _____ Base flashing _____
Masonry: ☐ solid ☐ faced ☐ stuccoed; total wall thickness _____"; facing thickness _____"; facing material _____
　　Backup material _____; thickness _____"; bonding _____
Door sills _____ Window sills _____ Lintels _____ Base flashing _____
Interior surfaces: dampproofing, _____ coats of _____; furring _____
Additional information: _____
Exterior painting: material _____; number of coats _____
Gable wall construction: ☐ same as main walls; ☐ other construction _____

6. FLOOR FRAMING:
Joists: wood, grade, and species _____; other _____; bridging _____; anchors _____
Concrete slab: ☐ basement floor; ☐ first floor; ☐ ground supported; ☐ self-supporting; mix _____; thickness _____";
　reinforcing _____; insulation _____; membrane _____
Fill under slab: material _____; thickness _____". Additional information: _____

7. SUBFLOORING: (Describe underflooring for special floors under item 21.)
Material: grade and species _____; size _____; type _____
Laid: ☐ first floor; ☐ second floor; ☐ attic _____ sq. ft.; ☐ diagonal; ☐ right angles. Additional information: _____

8. FINISH FLOORING: (Wood only. Describe other finish flooring under item 21.)

LOCATION	ROOMS	GRADE	SPECIES	THICKNESS	WIDTH	BLDG. PAPER	FINISH
First floor __							
Second floor __							
Attic floor __	__ sq. ft.						
Additional information: __							

FHA Form 2005
VA Form 26–1852

I

DESCRIPTION OF MATERIALS

Figure 6.3 Description of materials.

9. PARTITION FRAMING:

Studs: wood, grade, and species _____ size and spacing _____ Other _____

Additional information: _____

10. CEILING FRAMING:

Joists: wood, grade, and species _____ Other _____ Bridging _____

Additional information: _____

11. ROOF FRAMING:

Rafters: wood, grade, and species _____ Roof trusses (see detail): grade and species _____

Additional information: _____

12. ROOFING:

Sheathing: wood, grade, and species _____ ; ☐ solid; ☐ spaced _____ " o.c.

Roofing _____ ; grade _____ ; size _____ ; type _____

Underlay _____ ; weight or thickness _____ ; size _____ ; fastening _____

Built-up roofing _____ ; number of plies _____ ; surfacing material _____

Flashing: material _____ ; gage or weight _____ ; ☐ gravel stops; ☐ snow guards

Additional information: _____

13. GUTTERS AND DOWNSPOUTS:

Gutters: material _____ ; gage or weight _____ ; size _____ ; shape _____

Downspouts: material _____ ; gage or weight _____ ; size _____ ; shape _____ ; number _____

Downspouts connected to: ☐ Storm sewer; ☐ sanitary sewer; ☐ dry-well. ☐ Splash blocks: material and size _____

Additional information: _____

14. LATH AND PLASTER

Lath ☐ walls, ☐ ceilings: material _____ ; weight or thickness _____ Plaster: coats _____ ; finish _____

Dry-wall ☐ walls, ☐ ceilings: material _____ ; thickness _____ ; finish _____ ;

Joint treatment _____

15. DECORATING: *(Paint, wallpaper, etc.)*

Rooms	Wall Finish Material and Application	Ceiling Finish Material and Application
Kitchen _____		
Bath _____		
Other _____		

Additional information: _____

16. INTERIOR DOORS AND TRIM:

Doors: type _____ ; material _____ ; thickness _____

Door trim: type _____ ; material _____ Base: type _____ ; material _____ ; size _____

Finish: doors _____ ; trim _____

Other trim *(item, type and location)* _____

Additional information: _____

17. WINDOWS:

Windows: type _____ ; make _____ ; material _____ ; sash thickness _____

Glass: grade _____ ; ☐ sash weights; ☐ balances, type _____ ; head flashing _____

Trim: type _____ ; material _____ Paint _____ ; number coats _____

Weatherstripping: type _____ ; material _____ Storm sash, number _____

Screens: ☐ full; ☐ half; type _____ ; number _____ ; screen cloth material _____

Basement windows: type _____ ; material _____ ; screens, number _____ ; Storm sash, number _____

Special windows _____

Additional information: _____

18. ENTRANCES AND EXTERIOR DETAIL:

Main entrance door: material _____ ; width _____ ; thickness _____ ". Frame: material _____ ; thickness _____ "

Other entrance doors: material _____ ; width _____ ; thickness _____ ". Frame: material _____ ; thickness _____ "

Head flashing _____ Weatherstripping: type _____ ; saddles _____

Screen doors: thickness _____ "; number _____ ; screen cloth material _____ Storm doors: thickness _____ "; number _____

Combination storm and screen doors: thickness _____ "; number _____ ; screen cloth material _____

Shutters: ☐ hinged; ☐ fixed. Railings _____ , Attic louvers _____

Exterior millwork: grade and species _____ Paint _____ ; number coats _____

Additional information: _____

19. CABINETS AND INTERIOR DETAIL:

Kitchen cabinets, wall units: material _____ ; lineal feet of shelves _____ ; shelf width _____

Base units: material _____ ; counter top _____ ; edging _____

Back and end splash _____ Finish of cabinets _____ ; number coats _____

Medicine cabinets: make _____ ; model _____

Other cabinets and built-in furniture _____

Additional information: _____

20. STAIRS:

Stair	Treads		Risers		Strings		Handrail		Balusters	
	Material	Thickness	Material	Thickness	Material	Size	Material	Size	Material	Size
Basement _____										
Main _____										
Attic _____										

Disappearing: make and model number _____

Additional information: _____

2

Figure 6.3 *(Continued)*

21. SPECIAL FLOORS AND WAINSCOT:

	Location	Material, Color, Border, Sizes, Gage, Etc.	Threshold Material	Wall Base Material	Underfloor Material
FLOORS	Kitchen				
	Bath				

	Location	Material, Color, Border, Cap. Sizes, Gage, Etc.	Height	Height Over Tub	Height in Showers (From Floor)
WAINSCOT	Bath				

Bathroom accessories: ☐ Recessed; material _____; number _____; ☐ Attached; material _____; number _____
Additional information: _____

22. PLUMBING:

Fixture	Number	Location	Make	Mfr's Fixture Identification No.	Size	Color
Sink						
Lavatory						
Water closet						
Bathtub						
Shower over tub△						
Stall shower△						
Laundry trays						

△☐ Curtain rod   △☐ Door   ☐ Shower pan: material _____
Water supply: ☐ public; ☐ community system; ☐ individual (private) system.★
Sewage disposal: ☐ public; ☐ community system; ☐ individual (private) system.★
   ★*Show and describe individual system in complete detail in separate drawings and specifications according to requirements.*
House drain (inside): ☐ cast iron; ☐ tile; ☐ other _____   House sewer (outside): ☐ cast iron; ☐ tile; ☐ other _____
Water piping: ☐ galvanized steel; ☐ copper tubing; ☐ other _____   Sill cocks, number _____
Domestic water heater: type _____; make and model _____; heating capacity _____
_____ gph. 100° rise. Storage tank: material _____; capacity _____ gallons.
Gas service: ☐ utility company; ☐ liq. pet. gas; ☐ other _____   Gas piping: ☐ cooking; ☐ house heating.
Footing drains connected to: ☐ storm sewer; ☐ sanitary sewer; ☐ dry well. Sump pump; make and model _____
_____; capacity _____; discharges into _____

23. HEATING:
☐ Hot water. ☐ Steam. ☐ Vapor. ☐ One-pipe system. ☐ Two-pipe system.
   ☐ Radiators. ☐ Convectors. ☐ Baseboard radiation. Make and model _____
   Radiant panel: ☐ floor; ☐ wall; ☐ ceiling. Panel coil: material _____
   ☐ Circulator. ☐ Return pump. Make and model _____; capacity _____ gpm.
   Boiler: make and model _____   Output _____ Btuh.; net rating _____ Btuh.
Additional information: _____
Warm air: ☐ Gravity. ☐ Forced. Type of system _____
   Duct material: supply _____; return _____   Insulation _____, thickness _____ ☐ Outside air intake.
   Furnace: make and model _____   Input _____ Btuh.; output _____ Btuh.
   Additional information: _____
☐ Space heater; ☐ floor furnace; ☐ wall heater. Input _____ Btuh.; output _____ Btuh.; number units _____
   Make, model _____   Additional information: _____
Controls: make and types _____
Additional information: _____
Fuel: ☐ Coal; ☐ oil; ☐ gas; ☐ liq. pet. gas; ☐ electric; ☐ other _____; storage capacity _____
   Additional information: _____
Firing equipment furnished separately: ☐ Gas burner, conversion type. ☐ Stoker: hopper feed ☐; bin feed ☐
   Oil burner: ☐ pressure atomizing; ☐ vaporizing _____
   Make and model _____   Control _____
   Additional information: _____
Electric heating system: type _____   Input _____ watts; @ _____ volts; output _____ Btuh.
   Additional information: _____
Ventilating equipment: attic fan, make and model _____; capacity _____ cfm.
   kitchen exhaust fan, make and model _____
Other heating, ventilating. or cooling equipment _____

24. ELECTRIC WIRING:
Service: ☐ overhead; ☐ underground. Panel: ☐ fuse box; ☐ circuit-breaker; make _____ AMP's _____ No. circuits _____
Wiring: ☐ conduit; ☐ armored cable; ☐ nonmetallic cable; ☐ knob and tube; ☐ other _____
Special outlets: ☐ range; ☐ water heater; ☐ other _____
☐ Doorbell. ☐ Chimes. Push-button locations _____   Additional information: _____

25. LIGHTING FIXTURES:
Total number of fixtures _____   Total allowance for fixtures, typical installation, $ _____
Nontypical installation _____
Additional information: _____

DESCRIPTION OF MATERIALS

Figure 6.3 (*Continued*)

DESCRIPTION OF MATERIALS

26. INSULATION:

LOCATION	THICKNESS	MATERIAL, TYPE, AND METHOD OF INSTALLATION	VAPOR BARRIER
Roof ___			
Ceiling ___			
Wall ___			
Floor ___			

HARDWARE: *(make, material, and finish.)* _____

SPECIAL EQUIPMENT: *(State material or make, model and quantity.   Include only equipment and appliances which are acceptable by local law, custom and applicable FHA standards.   Do not include items which, by established custom, are supplied by occupant and removed when he vacates premises or chattels prohibited by law from becoming realty.)*_____

27. MISCELLANEOUS: *(Describe any main dwelling materials, equipment, or construction items not shown elsewhere; or use to provide additional information where the space provided was inadequate.   Always reference by item number to correspond to numbering used on this form.)* _____

PORCHES:

TERRACES:

GARAGES:

WALKS AND DRIVEWAYS:

Driveway: width _____ ; base material _____ ; thickness _____"; surfacing material _____ ; thickness _____ "

Front walk: width _____ ; material _____ ; thickness _____". Service walk: width _____ ; material _____ ; thickness _____ "

Steps: material _____ ; treads _____"; risers _____".   Cheek walls _____

OTHER ONSITE IMPROVEMENTS:

(Specify all exterior onsite improvements not described elsewhere, including items such as unusual grading, drainage structures, retaining walls, fence, railings, and accessory structures.)

LANDSCAPING, PLANTING, AND FINISH GRADING:

Topsoil_____" thick: ☐ front yard; ☐ side yards; ☐ rear yard to _____ feet behind main building.

Lawns *(seeded, sodded, or sprigged)*: ☐ front yard _____ ; ☐ side yards _____ ; ☐ rear yard_____

Planting: ☐ as specified and shown on drawings; ☐ as follows:

_____ Shade trees, deciduous, _____" caliper.	_____ Evergreen trees. _____' to _____', B & B.
_____ Low flowering trees, deciduous, _____' to _____'	_____ Evergreen shrubs. _____' to _____', B & B.
_____ High-growing shrubs, deciduous, _____' to _____'	_____ Vines, 2-year _____
_____ Medium-growing shrubs, deciduous, _____' to _____'	
_____ Low-growing shrubs, deciduous, _____' to _____'	

IDENTIFICATION.—This exhibit shall be identified by the signature of the builder, or sponsor, and/or the proposed mortgagor if the latter is known at the time of application.

Date_____   Signature _____

Signature _____

FHA Form 2005
VA Form 26–1852

GPO 1968 o48—16—80081-1 298-152

Figure 6.3   *(Continued)*

TABLE 6.10   Typical Handbook Values

Item	Unit	Material	Labor	Total
Rafters. Flat, shed, or gable roofs, up to 5 in 12 slope (5/24 pitch), maximum 25′ span. Figures in parentheses indicate board feet per SF of actual roof surface area (not roof plan area), including rafters, ridge boards, collar beams and normal waste, but no blocking, bracing, purlins, curbs, or gable walls				
2″ × 4″ (at $370 per MBF), Std & Btr				
12″ center (.89 BF per SF)	SF	.33	.40	.73
16″ center (.71 BF per SF)	SF	.26	.32	.58
24″ center (.53 BF per SF)	SF	.20	.24	.44
2″ × 6″ (at $355 per MBF), #2 & Btr				
12″ center (1.29 BF per SF)	SF	.46	.52	.98
16″ center (1.02 BF per SF)	SF	.36	.42	.78
24″ center (.75 BF per SF)	SF	.27	.31	.58
2″ × 8″ (at $340 per MBF), #2 & Btr				
12″ center (1.71 BF per SF)	SF	.58	.68	1.26
16″ center (1.34 BF per SF)	SF	.46	.53	.99
24″ center (1.12 BF per SF)	SF	.38	.44	.82
2″ × 10″ (at $415 per MBF), #2 & Btr				
12″ center (2.12 BF per SF)	SF	.88	.82	1.70
16″ center (1.97 BF per SF)	SF	.82	.76	1.58
24″ center (1.21 BF per SF)	SF	.50	.47	.97
2″ × 12″ (at $420 per MBF), #2 & Btr				
12″ center (2.52 BF per SF)	SF	1.06	.94	2.00
16″ center (1.97 BF per SF)	SF	.83	.74	1.57
24″ center (1.43 BF per SF)	SF	.60	.53	1.13
Add for hip roof	%	—	15.0	—
Add for cut-up roof	%	5.0	35.0	—
Add for slope over 5 in 12	%	—	25.0	—
Deduct for small or no overhang	%	—	10.0	—
Ribbons (ribbands), let-in to wall framing. See also Ledgers in this section. Figures in parentheses indicate board feet per LF including 10% waste				
1″ × 3″, Std & Btr (.28 BF per LF) (at $440. per MBF)	LF	.12	.38	.50
1″ × 4″, Std & Btr (.37 BF per LF) (at $440. per MBF)	LF	.16	.38	.54
1″ × 6″, Std & Btr (.55 BF per LF) (at $440. per MBF)	LF	.24	.56	.80
2″ × 3″, Std & Btr (.55 BF per LF) (at $390. per MBF)	LF	.21	.76	.97
2″ × 4″, Std & Btr (.73 BF per LF) (at $370. per MBF)	LF	.27	.76	1.03
2″ × 6″, #2 & Btr (1.10 BF per LF) (at $355. per MBF)	LF	.39	.83	1.22
2″ × 8″, #2 & Btr (1.47 BF per LF) (at $340. per MBF)	LF	.50	.83	1.33

(continued)

TABLE 6.10   (*Continued*)

Item	Unit	Material	Labor	Total
Roof decking. See also Sheathing in this section. Flat, shed, or gable roofs to 5 in 12 slope (5/24 pitch). Figures in parentheses indicate board feet per SF of actual roof area (not roof plan area), including 5% waste. These material costs are based on T&G fir, commercial grade. See Lumber section (Roof decking) for other species and grades.				
2″ × 6″ (2.28 BF per SF, $480. per MBF)	SF	1.09	.80	1.89
2″ × 8″ (2.25 BF per SF, $480. per MBF)	SF	1.08	.80	1.88
3″ × 6″ (3.43 BF per SF, $685. per MBF)	SF	2.35	.88	3.23
Add for steep pitch roof	%	—	40.0	—

The following types of construction activities are estimated using handbook values:

- General requirements (including construction estimating),
- Site work,
- Concrete work,
- Masonry work,
- Metal construction,
- Wood and plastic construction,
- Thermal and moisture protection,
- Doors and windows,
- Finishes,
- Specialties,
- Equipment,
- Furnishings,
- Conveying systems,
- Mechanical work, and
- Electrical work.

The handbook values are used in conjunction with detailed construction drawings and materials lists to develop costs of all parts of a structure and all related construction activities. For a simpler and quicker method of estimating building costs, dollar per square foot values can be used. These values are empirical in nature and must be modified to conform to the prevailing costs in a given geographical area and the quality of the structure.

Tables 6.11—6.14 are examples of dollar per square foot estimating values and their appropriate modification factors for masonry or concrete office buildings. Notice in **Table 6.11** that the costs per square foot vary with the size of the building and that the second and higher stories cost less per square foot than the first floor. Costs per square foot vary considerably with quality, ranging downward from

TABLE 6.11 Dollar per Square Foot Cost for Masonry or Concrete Office Buildings

Quality Class	Square Foot Area										
	1,000	1,500	2,000	2,500	3,000	4,000	5,000	7,500	10,000	15,000	20,000
First story											
Exceptional	111.69	102.50	97.22	93.70	91.14	87.61	85.25	81.64	79.52	77.05	75.59
1, Best	101.53	93.18	88.38	85.18	82.86	79.65	77.50	74.21	72.29	70.04	68.72
1 and 2	91.30	83.79	79.47	76.60	74.50	71.62	69.69	66.73	65.00	62.98	61.79
2, Good	81.84	75.11	71.24	68.66	66.79	64.20	62.47	59.82	58.27	56.46	55.39
2 and 3	74.27	68.17	64.65	62.31	60.61	58.26	56.69	54.29	52.88	51.24	50.27
3, Average	66.65	61.17	58.02	55.91	54.39	52.28	50.87	48.71	47.45	45.98	45.11
3 and 4	59.66	54.75	51.93	50.05	48.68	46.80	45.54	43.61	42.48	41.16	40.38
4, Low	52.53	48.21	45.73	44.07	42.87	41.21	40.10	38.40	37.40	36.24	35.56
Second and higher stories											
Exceptional	103.26	95.35	90.73	87.62	85.35	82.18	80.04	76.75	74.80	72.51	71.16
1, Best	93.77	86.59	82.39	79.56	77.50	74.62	72.68	69.69	67.92	65.84	64.61
1 and 2	84.83	78.34	74.54	71.98	70.11	67.51	65.76	63.05	61.45	59.57	58.46
2, Good	76.59	70.73	67.30	64.99	63.30	60.95	59.37	56.92	55.48	53.78	52.78
2 and 3	69.23	63.93	60.83	58.75	57.22	55.10	53.66	51.46	50.15	48.62	47.71
3, Average	61.66	56.94	54.18	52.32	50.96	49.07	47.79	45.82	44.66	43.30	42.49
3 and 4	54.64	50.45	48.01	46.36	45.16	43.48	42.35	40.61	39.58	38.36	37.65
4, Low	48.39	44.68	42.52	41.06	39.99	38.51	37.50	35.96	35.05	33.98	33.34

Source: National Construction Estimator, 1989 ed., and *Building Cost Manual*, 1989 ed. Copyright by Craftsman Book Company.

Note: Square foot costs include the following components: Foundations as required for normal soil conditions; floor, wall, and roof structures; interior floor, wall, and ceiling finishes; exterior wall finish and roof cover; interior partitions; cabinets, doors, and windows; basic electrical systems and lighting fixtures; rough plumbing and fixtures; permits and fees; contractors' mark-up.

TABLE 6.12 Description of Quality Classes for Masonry or Concrete Office Buildings

	Class 1: Best Quality	Class 2: Good Quality	Class 3: Average Quality	Class 4: Low Quality
Foundation	Reinforced concrete	Reinforced concrete	Reinforced concrete	Reinforced concrete
First floor structure	Reinforced concrete slab on grade or standard wood frame.	Reinforced concrete slab on grade or standard wood frame	Reinforced concrete slab on grade or 4″ × 6″ girders with plywood sheathing	Reinforced concrete slab on grade
Upper floor structure	Standard wood frame, plywood and 1½″ light-weight concrete subfloor	Standard wood frame, plywood and 1½″ light-weight concrete subfloor	Standard wood frame, 5/8″ plywood subfloor	Standard wood frame, 5/8″ plywood subfloor
Walls	8″ decorative concrete block or 6″ concrete tilt-up	8″ decorative concrete block or 6″ concrete tilt-up	8″ reinforced concrete block or 8″ reinforced brick or 8″ clay tile	8″ reinforced concrete block or 8″ clay tile
Roof structure	Standard wood frame, flat or low pitch	Standard wood frame, flat or low pitch	Standard wood frame, flat or low pitch	Standard wood frame, flat or low pitch
Exterior finish Walls	Decorative block or large rock imbedded in tilt-up panels with 10–20% brick or stone veneer	Decorative block or exposed aggregate and 10–20% brick or stone veneer	Stucco or colored concrete block	Painted concrete block or tile

(*continued*)

115

TABLE 6.12 (*Continued*)

	Class 1: Best Quality	Class 2: Good Quality	Class 3: Average Quality	Class 4: Low Quality
Windows	Average number in good aluminum frame; fixed plate glass in good frame on front side	Average number in good aluminum frame; some fixed plate glass in front	Average number of average aluminum sliding type	Average number of low-cost aluminum sliding type
Roof/Cover	5 ply built-up roofing on flat roofs; heavy shake or tile on sloping roofs	5 ply built-up roofing on flat roofs; average shake or composition, tar and large rock on sloping roofs	4 ply built-up roofing on flat roofs; wood shingle or composition, tar and pea gravel on sloping roofs	3 ply built-up roofing on flat roofs; composition shingle on sloping roofs
Overhang	3' closed overhang, fully guttered	2' closed overhang, fully guttered	None on flat roofs; 18" open on sloping roofs; fully guttered	None on flat roofs; 12" to 16" open on sloping roofs; gutters over entrances
Floor finish				
Offices	Very good carpet	Good carpet	Average grade carpet	Minimum tile
Corridors	Solid vinyl tile or carpet	Vinyl asbestos tile	Vinyl asbestos tile	Minimum tile
Bathrooms	Sheet vinyl or ceramic tile	Sheet vinyl or ceramic tile	Vinyl asbestos tile	Minimum tile

116

Interior wall finish				
Offices	Good hardwood veneer	Hardwood veneer paneling or vinyl wall cover	Gypsum wallboard, texture and paint	Gypsum wallboard, texture and paint
Corridors	Good hardwood veneer	Gypsum wallboard and vinyl wall cover	Gypsum wallboard, texture and paint	Gypsum wallboard, texture and paint
Bathrooms	Gypsum wallboard and enamel with ceramic tile wainscot	Gypsum wallboard and enamel or vinyl wall covering	Gypsum wallboard and enamel	Gypsum wallboard, texture and paint
Ceiling finish	Suspended "T" bar and acoustical tile	Gypsum wallboard and acoustical tile.	Gypsum wallboard and acoustical texture.	Gypsum wallboard and paint.
Utilities				
Plumbing	Copper tubing and top-quality fixtures	Copper tubing and good fixtures	Copper tubing and standard fixtures	Copper tubing and economy fixtures
Lighting	Conduit wiring, good fixtures	Conduit wiring, good fixtures	Romex or conduit wiring, average fixtures	Romex wiring, economy fixtures

Source: National Construction Estimator, 1989 ed., and *Building Cost Manual*, 1989 ed. Copyright by Craftsman Book Company.

TABLE 6.13   Geographical Factors for Construction Costs

Alabama	0.77
Alaska	2.99
Arizona	1.01
Arkansas	0.83
California	1.21
Colorado	1.07
Connecticut	1.08
Delaware	1.03
District of Columbia	1.30
Florida	0.90
Georgia	0.79
Guam	1.51
Hawaii	1.61
Idaho	1.03
Illinois	1.06
Indiana	0.92
Iowa	0.92
Kansas	0.86
Kentucky	0.91
Louisiana	0.85
Maine	1.05
Maryland	0.95
Massachusetts	1.19
Michigan	0.99
Minnesota	1.01
Mississippi	0.78
Missouri	0.97

(continued)

"exceptional" through the four quality classes shown in **Table 6.12**. Dollar per square foot values must be modified for location by multiplying them by the geographical location factors shown in **Table 6.13**. The square foot costs shown are based on a wall height of 10 feet for the first floor and 9 feet for upper floors. If the wall heights vary from these values, they are modified by the wall adjustment factors shown in **Table 6.14**. Similar adjustments can be made for common walls or lack of exterior finish using Table 6.14. The costs shown do not include heating and air-conditioning systems, elevators, fire sprinklers, exterior signs, paving and curbing, miscellaneous yard improvements, covered porches, and garages. The costs shown are for calendar year 1989; costs for subsequent years should be estimated by using an appropriate inflation factor for that year. Tables 6.11–6.14 are based on the 1989 editions of the *National Construction Estimator and Building Cost Manual*. Other types of buildings (single and multifamily residences, urban stores, suburban stores, supermarkets, small food stores, discount houses, banks and savings offices,

TABLE 6.13   *(Continued)*

Montana	0.98
Nebraska	0.91
Nevada	1.21
New Hampshire	1.06
New Jersey	1.17
New Mexico	0.86
New York	1.13
North Carolina	0.79
North Dakota	0.97
Ohio	1.10
Oklahoma	0.86
Oregon	1.04
Pennsylvania	1.07
Puerto Rico	0.86
Rhode Island	1.05
South Carolina	0.78
South Dakota	1.01
Tennessee	0.78
Texas	0.81
Utah	1.00
Vermont	1.09
Virginia	0.92
Virgin Islands	1.19
Washington	1.07
West Virginia	1.01
Wisconsin	1.01
Wyoming	1.00

department stores, medical and dental buildings, hospitals, funeral homes, restaurants, theaters, mobile home parks, service stations, warehouses, light industrial buildings, and factories are also included in the *Building Cost Manual.*

IN-PROCESS INSPECTION

The amount of in-process inspection performed on any process, product, project, or service will depend on the degree of reliability required for the final work output. In high-rate production of relatively inexpensive items, it is often economically desirable to forgo in-process inspection entirely in favor of scrapping any parts that fail a simple go, no-go inspection at the end of the production line. On the other hand, expensive and sophisticated precision-manufactured parts may require nearly 100 percent inspection. A good rule of thumb is to add 10 percent of the manufacturing and assembly hours for in-process inspection. This in-process inspection does not include in-process testing, covered in the following section.

TABLE 6.14 Wall Adjustment Factors for Masonry or Concrete Office Buildings

Wall Height Adjustment[a]

Quality Class	Square Foot Area										
	1,000	1,500	2,000	3,000	4,000	5,000	7,500	10,000	15,000	20,000	40,000
1, Best	2.96	2.32	1.96	1.55	1.32	1.17	.94	.81	.66	.57	.40
2, Good	2.47	1.94	1.64	1.30	1.10	.98	.79	.67	.55	.47	.34
3, Average	2.09	1.64	1.38	1.10	.93	.83	.66	.57	.46	.40	.28
4, Low	1.82	1.42	1.20	.95	.81	.72	.58	.50	.40	.35	.25

Perimeter Wall Adjustment[b]

Class	For a Common Wall, Deduct per Linear Foot	For No Wall Ownership, Deduct per Linear Foot	For Lack of Exterior Finish, Deduct per Linear Foot
First Story			
1	$155.40	$241.30	$117.90
2	123.30	198.40	73.00
3	92.20	171.60	42.10
4	70.80	150.10	24.30
Second and Higher Stories			
1	$150.10	$203.70	$117.80
2	123.30	182.30	74.00
3	93.30	166.30	42.10
4	85.80	150.10	25.50

Source: National Construction Estimator, 1989 ed., and Building Cost Manual, 1989 ed. Copyright by Craftsman Book Company.

[a]The square foot costs for general offices are based on the wall heights of 10 feet for first floors and 9 feet for higher floors. The main or first floor height is the distance from the bottom of the floor slab or joists to the top of the roof slab or ceiling joists. Second and higher floors are measured from the top of the floor slab or floor joists to the top of the roof slab or ceiling joists. Add or subtract the amount listed in this table to the square foot of floor cost for each foot of wall height more or less than 10 feet, if adjusting for a first floor, and 9 feet, if adjusting for upper floors.

[b]A common wall exists when two buildings share one wall. Adjust for common walls by deducting the linear foot cost below from the total structure cost. In some structures one or more walls is not owned at all. In this case, deduct the "no ownership" cost per linear foot of wall not owned. Where a perimeter wall remains unfinished, deduct the "lack of exterior finish" cost.

TESTING

Testing usually falls into three categories: (1) development testing, (2) qualification testing, and (3) production acceptance testing.

Rules of thumb are difficult to come by for estimating development testing because testing varies with the complexity, uncertainty, and technological content of the work activity. The best way to estimate the cost of development testing is to produce a detailed test plan for the specific project and to cost each element of this test plan separately, being careful to consider all skills, facilities, equipment, and material needed in the development test program.

Qualification testing is required in most commercial products and on all military or space projects to demonstrate that the article will operate or serve its intended purpose in environments far more severe than those intended for its actual use. Automobile crash tests are an example. Military products must often undergo severe and prolonged tests under high shock, thermal, and vibration loads as well as heat, humidity, cold, and salt spray environments These tests must be meticulously planned and scheduled before a reasonable estimate of their costs can be generated.

Receiving inspection, production testing, and acceptance testing, all forms of nondestructive testing, can be estimated using experience factors and ratios available from previous similar work activities. Receiving tests are tests performed on purchased components, parts, and/or subassemblies prior to acceptance by the receiving department. Production tests are tests of subassemblies, units, subsystems, and systems during and after assembly. Experience has shown that test labor generally varies directly with the amount of fabrication and assembly labor. The ratio of test labor to other production labor will depend on the complexity of the item being tested. **Table 6.15** gives the test labor percentage of direct fabrication and assembly labor for simple, average, and complex items.

Special Tooling and Test Equipment

Special-purpose tooling and special-purpose test equipment are important items of cost because they are used only for a particular job; therefore, that job must bear the

TABLE 6.15   Test Estimating Ratios

	Percentage of Direct Labor		
	Simple	Average	Complex
Fabrication and Assembly Labor Base			
Receiving test	1	2	4
Production test	9	18	36
Total	10	20	40
Assembly Labor Base			
Receiving test	2	3	7
Production test	15	32	63
Total	17	35	70

TABLE 6.16   Manufacturing Startup Ratios

Cost Element	Degree of Precision and Complexity	Percentage of Recurring Manufacturing Costs Lot Quantity			
		10	100	1,000	10,000
Production planning	High	20	6	1.7	0.5
	Medium	10	3	0.8	0.25
	Low	5	1.5	0.4	0.12
Special tooling	High	10	6	3.5	2
	Medium	5	3	2	1
	Low	3	1.5	1	—
Special test equipment	High	10	6	3.5	2
	Medium	6	3	2	1
	Low	3	1.5	1	0.5
Composite total	High	40	18	8.7	4.5
	Medium	21	9	4.8	2.25
	Low	11	4.5	2.4	1.12

full cost of the tool or test fixture. In contrast to the special items, general-purpose tooling or test equipment is purchased as capital equipment, and costs are spread over many jobs. Estimates for tooling and test equipment are included in overall manufacturing start-up ratios shown in **Table 6.16**. Under "degree of precision and complexity," "high" means high-precision multidisciplinary systems, products, or subsystems, "medium" means moderately complex subsystems or components, and "low" means simple, straightforward designs of components or individual parts. Manual design hours required for test equipment are shown in **Table 6.17**. CAD system hours will be approximately two-thirds of the values shown.

TABLE 6.17   Design Hours for Test Equipment

Type Design	Hours per Square Foot	Standard Drawing Size	Square Feet per Drawing	Hours per Drawing
Original	15	C	2.5	38
concept		D	5.0	75
		H	9.0	135
		J	11.0	165
Layout	10	B	1.0	10
		C	2.5	25
		D	5.0	50
		H	9.0	90
		J	11.0	110
Detail or	3	A	0.7	2.1
copy		B	1.0	3.0
		C	2.5	7.5
		D	5.0	15.0
		H	9.0	27.0
		J	11.0	33.0

COMPUTER SOFTWARE COST ESTIMATING

Chapter 13 provides a complete description of software cost estimating in today's evolving software environment.

LABOR ALLOWANCES

The "standard times" shown in this chapter and in Appendix I assume that the worker is well trained and experienced in the job, applies himself or herself to the job 100 percent of the time, and never makes a mistake, takes a break, loses efficiency, or deviates from the task for any reason—all unreasonable assumptions because there are legitimate and numerous unplanned work interruptions that occur with regularity in any work activity. Therefore, labor allowances must be added to any estimate made up of an accumulation of standard times. These labor allowances can accumulate to a factor of 1.5 to 2.5. The total standard time for a given work activity will depend on the nature of the task. Labor allowances are made up of a number of factors described in the following sections.

Variance from Measured Labor-Hours

Standard hours vary from actual measured labor-hours because workers often deviate from the standard method or technique used or planned for a given operation. This deviation can be caused by a number of factors ranging from the training, motivation, or disposition of the operator to the use of faulty tools, fixtures, or machines. Sometimes shortages of materials or lack of adequate supervision are causes of deviations from standard values. These variances can add 5 to 20 percent to standard time values.

Personal, Fatigue, and Delay (PFD) Time

Personal times are for personal activities such as coffee breaks, trips to the restroom or water fountain, unforeseen interruptions, or emergency telephone calls. Fatigue time is allocated because a worker cannot produce at the same pace all day; operator efficiency decreases as the job time increases. Delays include unavoidable work interruptions caused by the need for obtaining supervisory instructions, equipment breakdown, power outages or operator illness. PFD time can add 10 to 20 percent to standard time values.

Tooling and Equipment Maintenance

Although normal or routine equipment maintenance can be done during other than operating shifts, usually some operator-performed machine maintenance activity must be performed during the machine duty cycle. These activities include adjusting tools, sharpening tools, and periodically cleaning and oiling machines. In electroplating and processing operations, the operator maintains solutions and compounds and handles and maintains racks and fixtures. Tooling and equipment maintenance can account for 5 to 12 percent of standard time values.

Normal Rework and Repair

The overall direct labor-hours derived from the application of the preceding three allowance factors to standard times must be increased by additional amounts to account for normal rework and repair. Labor values must be allocated for rework of defective purchased materials, rework of in-process rejects, final test rejects, and addition of minor engineering changes. Units damaged on receipt or during handling must also be repaired. This factor can add 10 to 20 percent direct labor-hours to those previously estimated.

Engineering Change Allowance

For projects where design stability is poor, production is initiated prior to final design release, and field-testing is being performed concurrently with production, an engineering change allowance should be added of up to 10 percent of direct labor-hours. Change allowances vary widely for different types of work activities. Even fairly well-defined projects, however, should contain a change allowance.

Engineering Prototype Allowance

The labor-hours required to produce an engineering prototype are greater than those required to produce the first production model. Reworks are more frequent, and work is performed from sketches or unreleased drawings rather than production drawings. An increase over first production unit labor of 15 to 25 percent should be included for each engineering prototype.

Design Growth Allowance

Where estimates are based on incomplete drawings, or where concepts only or early breadboards only are available prior to the development of a cost estimate, a design growth allowance is added to all other direct labor costs. This design growth allowance is calculated by subtracting the percentage of design completion from 100 percent (**Table 6.18**).

Cost Growth Allowances

Usually a cost estimate will warrant the addition of allowances for cost growth. Cost growth allowances are best added at the lowest level of a cost estimate rather than at the top levels (see the discussion in Chapter 11 on escalation). These allowances include reserves for possible misfortunes, natural disasters, strikes, and other unforeseen circumstances. Reserves should not be used to account for normal design growth. Care should be taken in using reserves in a cost estimate because they are

TABLE 6.18   Design Growth Allowance

Desirable Design Completion Percentage	Percentage of Design Completed	Design Growth Allowance (%)
100	50	50
100	75	25
100	80	20
100	90	10
100	100	0

usually the first cost elements that come under attack for removal from the cost estimate or budget. Remember that cost growth with an incomplete design is a certainty, not a reserve or contingency. Defend your cost growth allowance, but be prepared to relinquish a reserve if necessary.

ESTIMATING SUPERVISION, DIRECT MANAGEMENT, AND OTHER DIRECT CHARGES

Direct supervision costs will vary with the task and company organization. Management studies have shown that the span of control of a supervisor over a complex activity should not exceed 12 workers. For simple activities, the ratio of supervisors to employees can go down, but the 1-to-12 ratio (8.3 percent) will usually yield best results. Project management for a complex project can add an additional 10 to 14 percent. Other direct charges are those directly attributable to the project being accomplished but not included in direct labor or direct materials: transportation, training, and reproduction costs, as well as special service or support contracts and consultants.

Two cost elements of other direct costs that are becoming increasingly volatile are travel and transportation costs. For this reason, a frequent check on public and private conveyance rates and costs is mandatory. Most companies provide a private vehicle mileage allowance for employees who use their own vehicles in the conduct of company business. Rates differ and depend on whether the private conveyance is being used principally for the benefit of the company or principally for the convenience of the traveler. Regardless of which rate is used, the mileage allowance must be periodically updated to keep pace with actual costs. Many companies purchase or lease vehicles for their employees to use on official business and sometimes personal travel. The decision as to the most cost-effective method of providing business-related employee transportation should be based on one of several types of investment analyses discussed in later chapters.

Per diem travel allowances or reimbursement for lodging, meals, and miscellaneous expenses must also be included in overall travel budgets. These reimbursable expenses include costs of a motel or hotel room; food, tips, and taxes; local transportation and communication; and other costs such as laundry, mailing costs, and on-site clerical services. Transportation costs include the transport of equipment, supplies, and products, as well as personnel, and can include packaging, handling, shipping, postage, and insurance charges.

THE USE OF FACTORS IN ESTIMATING

The practice of using "factors" (e.g., percentages or fractions of a base resource) is becoming increasingly common, particularly in high-technology work activities and work outputs. One company employs the use of an "allocation factor," which allocates miscellaneous labor-oriented functions to specific functions such as fabrication or assembly This company adds 14.4 percent to fabrication hours and 4.1 percent to assembly hours to cover miscellaneous labor-hour expenditures associated with these two functions. It is also common to estimate hours for planning, tooling, quality and inspection, production support, and sustaining engineering based on percentages of manufacturing and/or assembly hours. Tooling, shop materials, and computer supplies are sometimes estimated based on so much cost per labor-hour, and miscellaneous shop hardware (units, bolts, fasteners, cleaning supplies, etc.), otherwise known as "panstock," is estimated at a cost per manufacturing hour.

The disadvantage of the use of such factors is that inefficiencies can become imbedded in the factored allowances and eventually cause cost growth. A much better method of estimating the labor-hours and materials required to accomplish these other direct activities is to determine the specific tasks and materials required to perform the job by staffing, shop-loading, or process planning methods. When the materials, labor-hours, and other direct costs have been estimated, the basic direct resources required to do the job have been identified.

The next step in the estimating process is to determine labor rates, indirect costs, administrative expenses, and profit.

NOTE

1. Many textbooks treat the subject of logistics. Linda Green, *New Dimensions in Logistics* (New York: Wiley, 1991), is a recent logistics reference book.

QUESTIONS

6.1. A software project requires 10,000 lines of code, 40 percent of which are procedural statements written at an average of 30 minutes each and 60 percent of operational software, which takes 1.5 hours per line to write. The costing rate of the programmers is $60 per hour. What is the cost of the project?

6.2. Which of the following are not vendor quote activities?

   a. Look up price in vendor's current catalog.

   b. Call vendor who looks up price in the current catalog and quotes the price verbally.

   c. Call vendor who looks up price in company's current catalog and quotes it verbally with a written confirmation.

   d. Call vendor who works up price based on labor and material and quotes it verbally with or without written confirmation.

   e. Look up price in old vendor catalog and escalate it based on the consumer price index.

   f. None of the above.

   g. All of the above.

6.3. Describe the content of a process plan and its use in estimating.

6.4. An analyst has determined that quality assurance labor-hours are 15 percent of manufacturing labor-hours. For a particular job, manufacturing labor is estimated to be 10,000 hours, tooling labor is estimated to be 2500 hours, and manufacturing engineering labor is 50 percent of quality assurance labor.

   a. What is the total estimate of labor-hours for this job?

   b. What is the percentage of quality assurance labor-hours to total labor-hours?

6.5. "Price breaks" in material costs are influenced by quantity demanded and the scheduled rate of delivery.   T   F

6.6. Direct material used in the manufacturing and assembly of completed products includes:

   a. Raw materials.

   b. Purchased parts.

   c. Subcontracted items.

   d. All of the above.

7

ESTIMATING LABOR RATES, INDIRECT COSTS, AND ADMINISTRATIVE COSTS

And when he had agreed with the laborers for a denarius for the day, he sent them into his vineyard.

Matthew 20:2

LABOR RATES

Chapter 6 discussed the derivation of labor-hours required to do specific tasks and the methods of adding up these labor-hours and applying factors and allowances. Once the total direct labor-hours for each skill category and skill level have been estimated, it is necessary to apply the appropriate labor rate or wage rate in order to develop labor costs. Labor rates can be developed by various methods and can include different costs, depending on their definition. First, there is the hourly, weekly, biweekly, monthly, or yearly compensation the employee receives in dollars. Second, there is the hourly wage rate including benefits. Third, there is the total hourly costs including the employer's labor burden. Fourth, there is the total labor rate with an applied factor for overhead costs. For simplicity in this discussion, we will use the third method of computing labor rates and apply overhead after labor costs are computed by adding a derived overhead percentage.

The labor or wage rate structure in a company, university, or government organization consists of a designation of a specific hourly rate or range of rates for each skill category and a rate or range of rates for various skill levels within that category. Often a composite rate is developed for an entire skill category by selecting a mix of skill levels and computing a weighted average based on this mix. Keeping labor rates reasonable and competitive depends on the company's success in maintaining good distribution of skill levels within a skill category by periodically introducing lower-level skills through new hires. As personnel work their way up through the various skill levels through training, experience, education, and merit pay increases, newer personnel must be added at the lower end of the pay scale to maintain a wide selection of skill levels and commensurate labor rates to be applied to a particular job.

Good company morale and continued high productivity stem from sound compensation practices within a company that are competitive with other companies seeking and performing the same type of work and seeking skilled employees. It is important to be competitive with similar industries, but researchers exploring compensation practices have found that it is more important to employee morale to have internal comparability than to have external comparability of pay scales. Workers are generally more interested in the comparison of their wages with their fellow employees in the same company than with other companies in the same community or same geographical area. Often employees accept a lower pay scale in their company because of fringe benefits or company loyalty, provided that the company's pay scale is equitable and compensates each employee fairly in relation to others from a standpoint of training, experience, and ability.

The use of labor unions in competitive bargaining and negotiations between labor and management has created a trend toward normalization of labor rates and wage rates of skilled and unskilled hourly workers, and the minimum wage laws have established the bottom rung of the pay scale. Still, there is a wide variation of wage rates among hourly workers in various skills and in various locations (**Table 7.1**).

Labor Rate Application

The method of application of labor rates depends to a large degree on the method of estimating labor-hours and the assumptions made by the estimator concerning what is included in an hour of labor. If a detailed estimate of labor-hours has been made through a job analysis, only the actual working hours are included. Actually a worker's time is not available for 8 hours a day, 5 days a week, 52 weeks in the year; workers are allowed paid vacations, paid holidays, paid sick leave, and other forms of paid leave. Depending on company policy, pricing techniques, union agreements, and accounting methods, a company could have a policy of assuming worker availability anywhere from 1850 to 2080 hours per year.

Salaried and hourly workers are sometimes treated differently when actual working hours per year are computed. Labor and burden rates for hourly workers are usually computed based on productive hours of work since hourly workers usually receive no compensation for absences. Paid absences for salaried workers must be figured into a "burdened" labor rate, discussed in the section of this chapter on indirect costs.

Composite Labor Rate Categories

A basic truth about labor rate structures in various companies is that there is very little consistency in structure from one company to another. Some companies have a few simple skill categories, while others have a very complex matrix of skill categories and skill levels within these categories. Many companies use composite labor rate categories that identify with various disciplines. To illustrate a few of the

**TABLE 7.1   Skill Category Total Hourly
Comparisons: Construction**

Trade	Total Hourly Cost Percentage above or below Building Laborer
Bricklayer	+26.4
Bricklayer's tender	− 5.8
Building laborer	00.0
Carpenter	+25.4
Cement mason	+22.3
Drywall installer	+28.1
Drywall taper	+23.4
Electrician	+34.2
Floor layer	+23.4
Glazier	+21.1
Lather	+27.2
Marble setter	+15.5
Millwright	+29.1
Mosaic and terrazzo worker	+17.1
Operating engineer	+37.2
Painter	+21.3
Plasterer	+29.2
Plasterer's helper	− 4.5
Plumber	+37.1
Reinforcing ironworker	+34.1
Roofer (composition)	+38.2
Sheet metal worker	+36.5
Tile layer	+19.7
Truck driver	+11.1

infinite number of ways a company can establish its composite labor rate categories, the labor rate structures of seven companies are examined.

Company A has many skill categories and many skill levels within these categories but uses composite labor rates for the following broad subdivisions of labor when bidding for a job:

Drafting
Engineering
Laboratory support
Manufacturing
Project management
Shop activities

Company B also lumps its labor categories and skill levels into six broad activity areas, but the subdivisions are different from those of company A:

Engineering
Manufacturing
Off-site activities
Other technical services
Quality assurance
Tooling

Company C has four major categories of labor and subdivides several of these into skill levels for bidding purposes:

Skill Category	Skill Levels
Engineering	E-1, E-2, E-3, E-4, E-5
Drafting	D-1, D-2, D-3
Technician	T-1, T-2, T-3, T-4, T-5
Shop activities	(none specified)

Company D uses a labor rate structure based on a broad category of job descriptions that combines both skill category and skill level:

Designer
Engineer
Engineering aide
Engineer, associate
Engineering mathematician
Engineering technician
Member, research staff
Member, technical staff
Research associate
Senior engineer

Company E uses three major labor activity categories with various specialized skills identified within these categories:

Engineering research and development

Advanced design
Development
Engineering
Project management
Quality and reliability assurance
Research

Manufacturing research and development

Finishing and assembly
Inspection
Manufacturing shops
Process control
Raw material preparation
Scheduling

Production

Manufacturing
Process engineering
Project management
Quality assurance

Company F categorizes labor rates into "exempt" and "nonexempt," or salaried and hourly paid employees, respectively. These categories are subdivided into skill categories and skill levels as follows:

Exempt

Administrators (three levels)
Engineer
Managers (two levels)
Member, technical staff (two levels)
Principal engineer
Senior engineer
Senior member, technical staff

Nonexempt

Assembler
Clerical
Draftsman
Graphics
Inspector
Machinist
Planner
Senior technician
Technician

Company G uses a department breakout rather than a skill category and/or skill level subdivision. The following are the department names used:

Design engineering	Process engineering
Development assembly and test	Product engineering
Drafting	Production control
Electrical assembly and test	Program management
Electrical and hydraulic manufacturing	Quality assurance
Engineering staff	Systems engineering
Industrial and production engineering	Tool engineering
Manufacturing engineering	Tool manufacturing
Model shop	

Notice that there seems to be no rhyme or reason to labor skill category and skill level assignments among companies. If other companies were listed, there would likely be other combinations. Although some companies have similar skill matrices, very few are identical. The content of the skill matrix may have developed over a period of years as the company grew and modified its product lines, or the skills may depend on the geographical location or union contract requirements. The main point is that the estimator will have to become familiar with the specific skill matrix of the company to prepare an accurate, detailed, credible cost estimate that properly considers all skill categories and skill levels.

AVAILABLE LABOR RATE INFORMATION

The Department of Labor's Bureau of Labor Statistics (BLS) states in *Employment and Earnings*, that "the Bureau of Labor Statistics' sampling of employment and payrolls is the largest monthly sampling operation in the field of social statistics."[1] BLS publications, which can be obtained at nominal cost from the U.S. Government Printing Office or consulted at many local public libraries, are of considerable value to the cost estimator in determining geographical, seasonal, and occupational wages and variations of labor rates, premium time, employment, hiring, and turnover. The BLS prepares a number of publications available to estimators:

1. *Monthly Labor Review:* Contains articles on employment, labor force, wages, prices, productivity, unit labor costs, collective bargaining, workers' satisfaction, social indicators, and labor developments abroad. Regular features include a review of developments in industrial relations, significant court decisions in labor cases, book reviews, and current labor statistics.

2. *Employment and Earnings:* A monthly publication that contains current labor statistics for the United States as a whole, for individual states, and for more than 200 local areas on employment, hours, earnings, and labor turnover.

3. *Occupational Outlook Handbook:* A biennial publication that contains employment outlook, nature of work, training, requirements for entry, line of advancement, location of jobs, earnings, and working conditions for 700 occupations in 30 major industries.

4. *Occupational Outlook Quarterly:* Contains current information on employment trends and outlook, supplementing and bringing up to date information in the *Occupational Outlook Handbook.*

5. *Current Wage Developments:* A monthly publication that contains wage and benefit changes resulting from collective bargaining settlements and unilateral management decisions, statistical summaries, and special reports on wage trends.

6. *Wholesale Prices and Price Indexes:* A monthly report on price movements at the primary market level, including statistical summary tables and indexes for groups of products and commodities. An annual supplement contains changes in the relative importance of components of the index, revisions in coverage, and annual averages.

7. *Consumer Price Index Detailed Report:* A monthly report that contains detailed data used to measure retail price changes, the purchasing power of the consumer's dollar, and inflation.

8. *Chartbook on Prices, Wages, and Productivity:* A monthly report that presents analytical charts and detailed supporting tables on consumer and wholesale price indexes, hourly compensation, and productivity.

9. *Handbook of Labor Statistics:* An annual publication with historical tables of major series published by the BLS.

INDIRECT COSTS

In most companies the indirect costs of doing business roughly equal the direct costs. For this reason it is extremely important for the cost estimator to know how indirect costs are estimated, budgeted, and controlled. Most companies spend large amounts of money and time in improving established product lines or developing new ones, exerting heavy pressure on the sales force to increase sales, keeping the engineering people continually alert for improvements in design, conducting time studies, making sophisticated machines, and developing techniques for building better and less expensive products while paying only limited attention to the role indirect costs play in influencing the success of these efforts.

Many terms are used to describe indirect costs—"pool expenses," "burden," "overhead," and so on. For simplicity, indirect costs can be defined as those costs that are incurred for the general operation of the business and are not specifically applicable to any one project or product line. Within this definition, many questions arise as to the most effective treatment of these expenses. Indirect costs can be classified in various ways—for example controllable versus noncontrollable, variable versus fixed, and engineered versus managed.

"Controllable" is a definition given to costs that can be controlled by the manager of a specific functional cost center. For example, direct departmental costs are controllable. Indirect labor of the payroll department is controllable by the supervisor of that department; it is a noncontrollable cost in the case of the factory supervisor charged with a prorated amount of the payroll department costs.

Variable indirect costs fluctuate with volume; fixed costs do not. Much indirect cost is semivariable; that is, it will fluctuate with volume but not proportionately.

Engineered costs are those whose dollar amounts can be estimated rather closely based on the amount of work covered by the costs. For example, routine machine maintenance labor can be measured by evaluating the maintenance for each machine in required labor-hours and multiplying by the number of machines. Managed costs are not measurable against volume; thus the amount becomes what the company management determines it will be. Examples of managed costs are research and development, marketing, and many selling type expenses. Managed costs are sometimes defined as discretionary, or as described by E.W. Phillips in *The Internal Auditor,* as "those costs reflecting the corporate standard of living."

A good overall indirect cost management program should provide for:

1. Established indirect budgeting and forecasting techniques.
2. A capability for comparing actual performance with forecasts.
3. Interpretation of variances by responsible managers.
4. A system for readily communicating performance data to appropriate management levels.

As the first requirement with respect to established indirect cost budgets and forecasts, it is usually the responsibility of a budget function within a company to generate budget proposals and negotiate indirect or overhead budgets for applicable elements by organization and department. As a result of the negotiations, recommendations are made to management for acceptance of these results to be used as goals for the company. The budget function must develop overhead projections and related data for inclusion in management budgets, performance reports, and other reports as appropriate. It must deal with the operating organizations' requests for budget revisions and make recommendations to management regarding these revisions and the potential effects on the company's budget goals.

Further, the budget function may include the development of indirect rates to be used for the purpose of pricing the company's products. Too often the indirect rates used in cost estimates are developed with much guesswork and engineered to fit a desired purpose in lieu of having been developed by those most responsible for accuracy and ensured attainment. As a result, the indirect cost rates used for pricing purposes may be so unrealistic as to impair the price competitiveness of a given proposal or product price. Thus, the key to the development of reliable indirect rates is the installation of a rigorous indirect cost budgeting and control program.

The second requirement is to establish indirect cost operating budget benchmarks whereby the budget function must make measurement policy recommendations to management. These take the form of establishing methods of determining budgets and revising these same methods as operations suggest.

The third basic requirement is to furnish indirect cost performance data through compiled reports structured to fit each level of management, most important, departmental management, for the departmental manager has the principal responsibility for controlling the indirect department costs.

An important feature of a sound indirect cost management system should be the methods whereby the disciplines for control are established with the departmental manager. The manager should be held responsible for coordinating his or her requirements with other operating activities and setting the original indirect cost targets of the department. Once a departmental budget is agreed upon, the manager has the continuing responsibility for justifying to top management variances of actual performance to budget objectives. This is a day-to-day responsibility and one that requires continuous interface with company operational elements.

Variances from budget are not uncommon but should not automatically be eliminated by routinely adjusted budgets. They should be thoroughly examined and investigated for cause before embarking on target revisions. If the cause can be corrected by improvement in the department operations, top management should enforce austerity on the operation causing the problem to bring the indirect costs back in line. If the cause of variance is due to major business volume fluctuations, a management-directed overall revision in indirect cost budgets may be necessary.

The purpose of indirect cost variance analysis is to disclose the causes of indirect cost overruns so that corrective action can be taken. To direct that action to the source of the problem, each plant-wide variance must be traced to the specific cost centers where the variance originated.

The goal of department heads and supervisors at lower tiers of the organization is to minimize unfavorable variances in their respective control areas. Hence, a line supervisor should receive performance reports on labor and other significant costs at least weekly and sometimes even daily. Prompt information will enable the supervisor to detect any variances early enough to correct a cost overrun that otherwise might become irreversible. Generally company management will receive overhead reports monthly. Any longer period would not permit timely identification of problem areas, and a shorter period could be considered impracticable.

In normal circumstances there should be no significant business volume variance from predictions over a short period, such as the budget year. Most companies can project production volume realistically from their backlogs and from statistical patterns on such new business as spare parts and components. Anticipated volume on new proposals for major programs or projects cannot be forecasted accurately, but the impact of those potential work activities is often not severe during the first year regardless of a company's success or lack of success in winning them.

The principal impact on the projected volume for a short period comes from the sudden decrease in an ongoing major work activity through partial or total cancellation or deferment of delivery. When that action occurs, all projected costs, both variable and fixed, should be reevaluated. For example, the designation of some administrative staff or supervisory personnel as fixed costs at the previously projected volume range may have been a valid decision for the flexible budget within that range. However, no fixed costs, and especially no staffing costs classified as fixed, should be immune from cost reduction procedures when there is a substantial drop in volume.

Volume variances are useful in disclosing trends. A minor variance during the first quarter that increased in both the second and third quarters would signal a need to reexamine estimates. Fixed costs are not expected to change; neither can all variable costs always be reduced to conform promptly to minor decreases in volume. An unfavorable trend, however, can be observed from the sum of a few minor variances. Company management often will delay taking action in such cases, partially because a decision to lay off staff personnel is not taken lightly.

Spending variances are more likely to become a major problem when volume is increasing. The effect of an increase in the base is a decrease in the overhead rate. That condition may cause a relaxation of controls so that items that are considered nice to have are acquired without an adequate appraisal of the need to have. One serious effect of such relaxation of control could be an increase in fixed assets and administrative staff personnel. After some period of time, the added functions tend to be considered necessary and their costs fixed, even though the volume of production may have declined to its previous level or even below it.

In summary, the operation of a good indirect cost estimating, budgeting, and control program includes several considerations. First, top management must recognize the need for controlling and accurately estimating indirect costs in order to maintain a competitive posture. Without this top management support, the indirect cost estimate becomes meaningless.

Next, the indirect cost control and estimating function must be placed high enough in the company organization to permit effective dealing with all levels of management. It should be part of the finance or comptroller organization, assigned sufficient authority to request and receive account accumulations compatible with an effective program and to make reductions in indirect budgets where appropriate.

The accounts should be clearly segregated to categories that will easily identify the operating responsibility with respect to expenditures. Budgets should be established and then negotiated. Revisions should be made only as changes in volume or overall business trends dictate. Revisions should not be made merely for cosmetic reasons. Each negotiation of the indirect cost budget should seek improvement in criteria and techniques.

After agreement has been reached with respect to indirect cost targets, actual performance should be compared to the target through timely reports that will enable the operating manager to control and the budget function to monitor results easily and effectively. Operating reports should be submitted at least once a month (longer spans such as quarterly are insufficient) and possibly more often. Today's computer systems enable rapid computation and flow of information, permitting timely follow-up action and indirect cost avoidance.

The continual analysis of indirect cost expenditures is essential in estimating for prospective business opportunities. In companies whose indirect cost management functions are cast within the proper framework, a much better competitive posture has evolved. Where primary importance has not been placed on indirect cost, business has usually suffered, and cost performance has been one of cost overruns.

Indirect costs may fall into five general categories, depending on the structure of the company and its products or services offered: engineering overhead, manufacturing overhead, material overhead, general and administrative expenses, and internal research and development and bid and proposal expenses. These indirect costs are normally calculated and used as a percentage of various cost bases. Typically the engineering overhead rate is based on total direct engineering labor, manufacturing overhead on direct manufacturing labor, and material overhead of all materials and subcontracts. General and administrative expenses are based on the sum of direct labor, materials and subcontracts, their respective overhead amounts, and other direct costs such as travel and consultants. Internal research and development and bid and proposal expenses are based on all previous costs including general and administrative expenses and any interdivisional transfers.

Indirect costs are normally forecasted on an annual basis. These forecasted rates can be used by the estimator in accordance with company policy and customer requirements. Firms doing business with the U.S. government need to refer to the Federal Cost Accounting Standards, which are issued by the Cost Accounting Standards Board and are included in the Federal Acquisition Regulations.

Engineering Overhead

The engineering overhead rate is usually calculated by summing the following three areas of indirect costs and division by the total amount of direct engineering labor dollars. The rate is normally expressed as a percentage of direct engineering labor dollars.

1. *Indirect Engineering Salaries and Wages:* Indirect engineering salaries and wages are the sum of the following areas: (1) salaries and wages paid for indirect engineering labor activities; (2) engineering-associated payroll taxes and workmen's compensation fees; (3) engineering costs of pensions, savings, and other employer-provided fringe benefits; and (4) the costs of vacations, holidays, and sick leave associated with engineering labor.

2. *Indirect Engineering Activity Supplies and Expenses:* This typical group of indirect expenses is the sum of the following areas of cost: (1) indirect engineering supplies; (2) photocopying and blueprinting (if not directly charged); (3) engineering equipment depreciation; (4) equipment maintenance; (5) associated insurance and miscellaneous taxes; (6) any indirect perishable engineering tooling or fixturing; (7) facility rent and leasing expenses for engineering use; (8) telephone expenses; (9) training expenses; indirect travel expenses; and (10) utilities expenses.

3. *Allocations:* In large companies, the various operating divisions are allocated expenses associated with the operation of common support functions. This allocation is usually made on the basis of total payroll dollars for each divi-

sion. In this computation the allocation of engineering overhead would be based on the total engineering payroll amount as a percentage of total company payroll.

The formula for computing engineering overhead rates can be expressed in the following way:

Indirect engineering salaries and wages + indirect engineering activity supplies and expenses + allocations = Total indirect engineering expenses.

Total indirect engineering expenses ÷ direct total engineering labor dollars = Engineering overhead percentage.

Manufacturing Overhead

The manufacturing overhead rate is typically calculated by summing three areas similar to those used to compute engineering overhead. The sum of these three areas is divided by the total amount of direct manufacturing labor dollars. The manufacturing overhead rate is normally expressed as a percentage of direct manufacturing labor dollars.

1. *Indirect Manufacturing Salaries and Wages:* Indirect manufacturing salaries and wages are the sum of the following areas: (1) salaries and wages paid for indirect manufacturing labor activities; (2) the manufacturing-associated payroll taxes and workmen's compensation fees; (3) manufacturing costs of pensions, savings, and other employer-provided fringe benefits; and (4) the costs of vacations, holidays, and sick leave associated with manufacturing labor.
2. *Indirect Manufacturing Activity Supplies and Expenses:* The typical indirect expenses that make up this are the following: (1) indirect manufacturing operating expenses; (2) manufacturing equipment depreciation; (3) manufacturing equipment maintenance expenses; (4) manufacturing equipment rental and leasing expenses; (5) associated manufacturing insurance expenses and miscellaneous taxes; (6) perishable manufacturing tooling and fixturing; (7) manufacturing facility tooling and leasing expenses; (8) stationery, printing, and office supplies associated with manufacturing; (9) manufacturing-associated telephone expenses; (10) training expenses; (11) indirect manufacturing travel expenses; (12) utilities; and (13) other indirect manufacturing expenses.
3. *Allocations:* Manufacturing overhead also includes any allocation expenses. This allocation normally uses total manufacturing payroll dollars as the base. It is similar to the allocations in engineering overhead.

The formula for computing manufacturing overhead rates can be expressed in the following way:

Indirect manufacturing salaries and wages + indirect manufacturing activity supplies and expenses + allocations = Total indirect manufacturing expenses.

Total indirect manufacturing expenses ÷ direct total manufacturing labor dollars = Manufacturing overhead percentage.

Material Overhead

The material overhead rate is typically calculated by summing three areas similar to engineering or manufacturing overhead and applying any material-related credits to the sum. Material overhead is normally expressed as a percentage of direct materials and subcontracts costs.

1. *Indirect Materials, Salaries, and Wages:* The salaries and wages of personnel directly involved with procurement, materials receiving and shipping, and subcontracts administration are accounted in this area. Included are other payroll-related costs similar to engineering or manufacturing indirect salaries and wages.
2. *Material Overhead Supplies and Expenses:* The typical indirect expenses associated with material overhead are similar to the ones in engineering or manufacturing overhead. Not all items may be applicable to the materials area, however.
3. *Allocations:* Material overhead also includes any allocation expenses. This allocation normally uses total materials and subcontracts dollar value as the base.
4. *Credits:* These costs are actually negative adjustments to the total amount of materials and subcontracts. It is difficult to predict this amount in advance, but use of historical data could lead to the development of a cost-estimating relationship for use in this situation. Credits may be in the form of scrap and salvage sales proceeds and cash discounts taken if not previously applied to material cost.

The formula for computing material overhead rates can be written as follows:

Indirect materials, salaries, and wages + material overhead supplies and expenses + allocations − credits = Total material overhead expenses.

Total material overhead expenses ÷ total material and subcontract dollars = Material overhead percentage.

OVERHEAD COSTS EXAMINED

Some time ago a young government negotiator took on the corporate financial vice-president of a large company during contract negotiations and questioned the need for overhead costs at all. The negotiator claimed that he did not need any of that overhead; all he needed was the direct labor and materials to do the job, and that was all he was going to pay for! The senior corporate officer carefully pointed out that establishing a labor force of proper skill mix with supplies, materials, equipment, facilities, and appropriate subcontract services brings on many necessary, unavoidable, even essential costs, and that these "overhead" costs represent the primary function that the company performs to produce the work output.

A work output cannot be provided or an organization cannot exist without overhead costs, and the only way to pay these overhead costs is to charge enough for the company's work output to cover them. Overhead costs for engineering functions often reach 100 percent in modern high-technology activities, and manufacturing overheads of up to 150 percent are not uncommon. Overhead cost categories are too numerous to treat exhaustively in a summary such as this because, depending upon the specific industry or business doing the work, numerous cost categories may be included. Some of the major contributors to overhead costs are described briefly here, however, along with some indications of how to go about accurately estimating overhead costs.

Insurance costs represent a large segment of overhead costs for many businesses and industries. Property insurance rates depend on the total investment in facilities, equipment, and supplies in the office or plant, the degree of protection that is available, and the type of activity that is going on in the facility. Insurance companies also consider other factors, such as historical records of claims for similar types of industries, the geographical location, and replacement and construction costs. Liability insurance rates also depend on many of these factors, but they depend principally on the hazard or risk involved to personnel. Because of the large number of factors that must be considered in establishing insurance coverage and rates and their uncertainty, insurance rates tend to fluctuate widely from one geographical location to another and from one period to another. Some believe that the present unprecedented competition in the insurance business is likely to cause insurance rates to plummet during the early 1990s. Many companies will find insurance bargains, but some will insure with companies that will fail because their rates are too low. Some industries have fought off high insurance costs by establishing their own insurance companies. This is not a recommended approach because large capital reserves are required. The best way to estimate insurance costs is to consult with a recognized and established insurance broker who can provide complete and up-to-date information on rates, coverage, and special provisions.

Building Rental

Although the tax benefits for construction of a new building are considerably greater than the tax benefits brought about by lease or rental, it often is necessary to rent temporary office or factory space to meet peak work loads. Rental will range from $10.00 to $40.00 per square foot per year depending on the location, interior layout, and building furnishings and whether certain overhead costs such as utilities and maintenance are included.

Utilities

With the continued high costs of energy, it is vital to understand the effect of utility rates on overhead costs. The utility rate structure in the United States is complex. Natural gas rates and electricity rates are particularly complex because costs per kilowatt hour or cubic foot are calculated based on the amount used, whether the use is commercial or residential, the season of use, and sometimes even the time of day that the energy is used. Just about every city in the United States has its own utility rate structure. The U.S. Department of Energy and other organizations publish exhaustive compilations of utility rate structures in the United States, but these rate structures are constantly changing and must be updated every few months.

Prior to a widespread recognition of the energy shortage, most electricity and gas rates included a minimum charge and a decreasing cost per unit of energy as more energy was used. With a more widespread recognition of the need to conserve energy, an increasing cost rate structure has been adopted by most municipalities and power companies. With increasing costs per amount used, energy conservation is encouraged, and alternate forms of energy, conservation, and energy augmentation with renewable sources such as solar energy appear more attractive. Electricity and natural gas rate pricing steps vary from three to eight, and there is little consistency from city to city in the amounts of energy usage that call for a rate change. This fact requires the estimation of rates for specific localities where and when the work is going to be performed coupled with a careful energy usage analysis.

Whether the energy source to be used is electricity, natural gas, fuel oil, propane, butane, coal, wood, or alcohol (or a combination of these), careful consideration must be given to energy costs and their effects on overhead costs. Other utility costs, such as water, sewage, and waste removal, must also be considered and analyzed as an overall part of overhead costs. Communications cost, sometimes considered a utility cost, can become a major part of overhead cost for some businesses. These costs include telephone, teletype, fax, and computer-based communication costs, and they vary considerably depending on the type of process, product, project, or service being estimated.

Facilities and Equipment Costs

Depreciation or amortization of purchased facilities and equipment is an allowable and a significant part of overhead costs. The cost of any asset purchased to accomplish a job can be recovered by one of several depreciation methods: (1) the straight-line method, (2) the declining-balance method, (3) the sum-of-the-years method, or (4) the sinking-fund method. **Table 7.2** shows an investment of $5000 depreciated by each method. This figure shows the amount of depreciation each year and the value at the end of each year for each method.

The straight-line depreciation method assumes that the value of an asset decreases at a constant rate. Thus, if an asset has a first cost of $5000 and an estimated salvage value of $1000, the total depreciation over its lifetime will be $4000. If the

TABLE 7.2 Sample Methods of Depreciation of Equipment and Facilities

End of Year	Straight-Line Method		Declining-Balance Method (30%)		Sum-of-Years Method		Sinking-Fund Method	
	Depreciation	Value	Depreciation	Value	Depreciation	Value	Depreciation	Value
0	$ 0	$5000	$ 0	$5000	$ 0	$5000	$ 0	$5000
1	$800	$4200	$1500	$3500	$1333	$3667	$710	$4290
2	$800	$3400	$1050	$2450	$1067	$2600	$752	$3538
3	$800	$2600	$ 735	$1715	$ 800	$1800	$797	$2741
4	$800	$1800	$ 515	$1200	$ 533	$1267	$845	$1896
5	$800	$1000	$ 360	$ 840	$ 267	$1000	$896	$1000

estimate lifetime is five years, the depreciation per year will be $4000 ÷ 5 = $800. This is equivalent to 1 ÷ 5, or 20 percent per year.

The declining-balance method of depreciation assumes that an asset decreases in value at a faster rate in the early portion of its service life than in the latter portion of its life. In this method a fixed percentage is multiplied by the book value of the asset at the beginning of the year to determine the depreciation charge for that year. Thus, as the book value of the asset decreases through time, so does the size of the depreciation charge. The depreciation and book values shown in the example in Table 7.2 for a declining-balance method are based on a depreciation percentage rate of 30 percent per year. If the declining-balance method of depreciation is used for income tax purposes, the maximum rate that may be used is double the straight-line rate allowed for the particular asset or group of assets being depreciated. In the example shown in Table 7.2, the maximum rate of depreciation therefore would be 40 percent. This would result in a "double-declining-balance" depreciation schedule showing book values at the end of years 0 through 5 of $5000, $2000, $800, $320, $128, and $51.20.

The sum-of-the-years digits depreciation method assumes that the value of an asset decreases at a decreasing rate. If an asset has an estimated life of five years, the sum of the years will be $1 + 2 + 3 + 4 + 5 = 15$. Thus if the first cost is $5000 and the estimated salvage value is $1000, the depreciation during the first year will be $5/15$ of $4000, or $1333.33. During the second year, the depreciation will be $4/15$ of $4000, or $1066.67.

The sinking-fund depreciation method assumes that the value of an asset decreases at an increasing rate. One of a series of equal amounts is assumed to be deposited into a sinking fund at the end of each year of the asset's life. The sinking fund is ordinarily compounded annually, and at the end of the estimated life of the asset, the amount accumulated equals the total depreciation of the asset. Thus, if an asset has a first cost of $500, an estimated life of five years, and an estimated salvage value of $1000 and if the interest rate is 6 percent, the amount deposited into the sinking fund at the end of each year is $4000 × 0.1774 = $709.60. The value 0.1774 is derived from tables of annual payments for 6 percent at 5 years and can be obtained from textbooks or computed from formulas derived from conventional interest equations.[2]

The accelerated capital recovery system (ACRS) is a method of depreciation that is approved by the Internal Revenue Service (IRS), which seems to change slightly (and to get more complicated) every year. I will provide an overview here as a baseline, but be sure to check the latest tax laws before using these figures for estimating purposes for future years. Currently the IRS recommends ACRS-M, a modified ACRS system using the percentage depreciation for each year for 3-, 5-, 7-, and 10-year depreciation schedules (**Table 7.3**). If more than 40 percent of assets purchased and depreciated are placed in service during the last quarter of the calendar year, different depreciation tables are used depending on the quarter in which the asset is placed in service. These additional tables along with depreciation schedules for 15, 20, 27$1/2$, and 31$1/2$ year plans can be obtained from the IRS.

TABLE 7.3 Depreciation by ACRS-M Method

ACRS-M Depreciation	1	2	3	4	5	6	7	8	9	10	11
3 year	25%	37.50%	25%	12.50%							
5 year	15.00	25.50	17.85	16.66	16.66	8.33%					
7 year	10.70	19.10	15.10	12.25	12.25	12.25	12/25	7.10			
10 year	7.50	13.88	11.79	10.02	8.74	8.74	8.74	8.74	8.74%	8.74%	4.37%

Source: Bara Business Services, Arab, Alabama.

Maintenance Costs

The costs of maintenance, repair, and upkeep of facilities and equipment are often overlooked as part of overhead costs. These costs include supplies and parts required to maintain the work output, as well as the labor required to keep facilities and equipment in top working order. Because repair costs are often sporadic or unpredictable in nature, they are difficult to predict or estimate unless some historical records are available. Many people resort to the use of maintenance or service contracts to even out the costs and to reduce the risks of encountering large unexpected expenditures. It is generally more cost-effective, however (if cash flow is sufficient), to provide maintenance and repair when needed rather than depending on high-cost maintenance contracts.

Effects of OSHA Standards

One factor that has affected the magnitude of overhead costs significantly in recent years is the Occupational Safety and Health Administration standards. These standards call for the investigation and reporting of accidents, maintenance of employee accident and illness records, measurement of a company's safety and health performance, and recognition and control of on-the-job hazards. Some of the measures industry must take to meet these standards involve considerable expense. They include improved housekeeping and maintenance in working areas; marking and guarding hazardous areas and machines; improved lighting, noise control, and atmosphere pollution control; fire and explosion protection; and protective clothing and equipment, such as hard hats, safety shoes, safety glasses, and gloves.

GENERAL AND ADMINISTRATIVE COSTS

Companies also encounter other administrative costs that cannot be legitimately put into the overhead category. For this reason many companies establish a separate cost category called general and administrative expenses (or G&A). These costs include certain administrative functions such as personnel and payroll administration costs, marketing functions such as advertising and public relations, and corporate expenses such as executives' salaries, training costs, and corporate taxes. Administrative costs are those costs that have to do with phases of operations not directly identifiable with the production, sale, or financing of operations. State, local, and federal taxes must be carefully considered in administrative cost estimates. Any costs incurred in connection with policy formation and the overall direction of a business are administrative costs.

BID AND PROPOSAL COSTS AND INDEPENDENT RESEARCH AND DEVELOPMENT COSTS

These two categories of cost are usually paid out of profit if fixed-price contracts or direct sales are the prevalent method of providing a company's work output. Much of a company's future potential and future business will depend on how well these two functions are accomplished. For certain government cost-reimbursable contracts, however, the costs of preparing bids and proposals and the costs of performing independent research and development are allowable overhead costs. The percentage of overhead costs that can be allocated to these two functions is usually a matter of negotiation with the monitoring or responsible government agency.

The G&A expense rate varies widely and depends on the size of the company and number of divisions that must be managed by the corporate or home office. An average range of G&A expenses is from 10 to 20 percent of total costs. It is added to the costs of all labor, material, and indirect costs for bidding purposes prior to the addition of profit or fee. The profit or fee is based on all costs, including G&A expenses.

NOTES

1. Department of Labor, Bureau of Labor Statistics, *Employment and Earnings* (Washington, D.C.: Government Printing Office, 1990),
2. One textbook is J. H. Mize, *Engineering Economy* (Englewood Cliffs, N.J.: Prentice-Hall, 1971).

QUESTIONS

7.1. a. Define "administrative cost," and give at least three examples of the kinds of charges that go into this category.

    b. Define "material overhead," and give another term for this item.

7.2. General and administrative expenses are not usually considered an element of cost.   T   F

7.3. Define five major indirect cost categories and describe how they are computed.

The next three questions refer to the following situation. In preparing a bid for 100 systems, Estimating has received an outside vendor quote on a machined plate of $32.51. One of these plates is required per system. These parts can also be made in-house.

Because of the time frame, these parts are expected to be made in lots of 50 if they are made in-house. The estimated shear time (Fab process) is 0.3 hour for setup and a run time of 25 per hour. The estimated machining time is 2.0 hours for setup and .20 each hour of run time. The Shear requires two operators. The machining would be done on a numerically controlled machine that requires only one operator. The material is estimated to cost $19.68 each.

The direct labor rate is $12.50/hour for fabrication and $14.30/hour for machining. The labor overhead rate for fabrication and for machining is 170 percent. Material overhead is 4 percent of materials costs.

General and administrative costs are approximately 5 percent of material, labor, and overhead costs.

7.4. Should these weldments be made in-house or purchased outside? Tell why.

7.5. For purposes of the bid, would the estimate use the in-house costs or the outside vendor price? Tell why. (Assume that Estimating has the authority to make this decision.)

7.6. If the outside vendor price was $33.00 instead of $32.51, would the decision made in question 7.5 change? Explain your answer.

7.7. You are to prepare a cost estimate for producing 1000 assemblies. Each assembly consists of a cylindrical tube, two identical end covers, and a purchased bracket. The brackets cost $6.25 each. Each tube costs $80 for the casting and requires 2 standard hours of machining. It requires 12 hours to set up the machining operation, and a setup is good for the machining of 500 castings. The end covers are produced on a punch press that requires 0.2 hour per cover of run time and 4.0 hours for press setup. Press setup is good for producing 400 pieces. Material cost per cover is $0.50. The direct labor rate is $14.00 per hour. Manufacturing overhead is 175 percent of direct manufacturing labor. Material overhead is 3 percent of total materials and subcontracts amount. General and administrative costs are 10 percent of labor and material with appropriate overhead.

What is the calculated unit cost through G&A?

8

ESTABLISHING FEE, PROFIT, AND EARNINGS

I am the Lord your God, who teaches you to profit.

Isaiah 48:17

MAXIMIZING PROFITS AS A GOAL

Often the terms "fee," "profit," and "earnings" are used interchangeably, but in reality they have slightly different meanings and connotations. A fee is usually an amount, normally a percentage of the total cost, a company charges to perform a certain task. This fee may or may not include overhead, labor burden, or general and administrative costs. The fee may even cover some or all of the direct labor and materials costs, as in the case of an architect's or consultant's fee. Profit is usually considered to be the income after all expenses of a task have been subtracted. It is the total income minus the total outlay of a venture. "Earnings" is a much more respectable term than "profit" but has essentially the same meaning. "Earnings" indicates that this amount is the wages or salary that a company received for being in business. Every venture has a right to earn a profit. In fact, the potential for making a profit is the strongest motivation for going into any business activity.

There are seven general underlying motivations for prosperity and growth in business and one predominant motivation: (1) organizational survival; (2) growth in sales and employment; (3) security of employment, sales; and profits; (4) freedom from harassment; (5) the desire for public approbation; (6) a desire to contribute to the general welfare; and (7) desire to advance science and technology. The predominant motivation, one that is inextricably entwined with the rest, is maximization of profits. This means not only maximum profit of a single point in time but continued maximization of profits.

It is paradoxical that one of the main problems concerning profit making is that the public, the press, and sometimes even the company itself believe that profit making is evil or shady. Nothing could be further from the truth. The first thing to realize about a profit-making venture is that there is nothing bad about making a

149

profit in business. Most people do not know how to think about profits. Some merely accept profits as an essential ingredient in a capitalist economy; others have a suspicion that profits do not represent a reasonable compensation like wages but in some way constitute an unreasonable windfall by top management or the stockholders. A company that enjoys high profits because of efficiency or inventiveness is often thought of by the public and the press as being exploitive. Here is where public opinion has been in error, and this error has been caused by the way profit increases and decreases have been quoted in the press and in trade and financial publications. If a company's profit increased 40 percent in the third quarter of the most recent fiscal year, some people would misread this as saying the company is making a 40 percent profit. In reality, the profit may have increased only from 5.4 percent to 7.56 percent of sales, a 40 percent increase. Further, in the previous quarter, the profits may have decreased from 7.56 percent to 5.4 percent of sales, a 28.6 percent decrease. Thus a 40 percent increase in the most recent quarter only brought the company back to its prior position. Profit margins are usually used to express a company's profit goals. The profit margin is a percentage above total costs; thus, if the cost to produce an item is $10,000 and the profit margin is 20 percent, the total cost or price is $12,000.

Almost everyone understands the bookkeeping definition of profit: the difference between the total costs and the total receipts of a company. But profit is essentially compensation for the risks of conducting a business. It is an incentive for innovation, which usually involves risk. Without profits, it is impossible to have dynamic economic development. Without the promise of significant reward, there would be little point in an investor's self-exposure to the possibility of loss. The American economy is based on a profit and loss system. Profits are the carrots held out as an incentive to efficiency, and losses are the sticks that penalize the use of inefficient methods or devoting resources to uses not desired by spending consumers. The greater the risk is, the greater is the prospective profit needed to compensate for it. Almost all of the technological advances made in this century—the automobile, the airplane, motion pictures, radio and television, computer systems, and electronic miniaturization—brought large profits to the successful pioneers. Without the pot of gold at the end of the rainbow, they would have had no motive to gamble.

Contrary to a frequently held belief, profits are not excess money or surplus funds over and above a company's needs. Profits are required to provide a return to stockholders for their investment and to provide the company's management with sufficient discretionary funds to permit reinvestment, purchase of new equipment and facilities, development of new product lines, and increasing promotional activities.

THE RELATIONSHIP BETWEEN PROFIT AND RISK

The ultimate success of any business rests on its ability to make a profit on the processes, products, projects, or services offered for sale to the consumer. To provide these work outputs to consumers, the business must commit some of its resources in anticipation of receiving profits some time in the future. The commitment of resources or funds with the expectation of receiving rewards in the future is commonly referred to as a business venture. The process of forecasting or predicting the amount of resources required for the venture and the rate and level of expected rewards is called a "venture analysis". Since the conduct of a venture analysis requires predicting future events that cannot be exactly determined, the comprehensive range of possibilities in both the commitment of resources and level of rewards must be considered if an informed decision on any potential venture is to be made. The range of potential resource requirements is referred to as uncertainty; the range of potential outcomes is designated risk. Risk analysis is the technique by which the decision maker can quantitatively account for the venture's uncertainty and risk.

It is important to know the components of a risk analysis and how they are applied in a value model. A business's value model is a representation of its philosophical, financial, and economic stance toward new investments. It includes, for example, the discount rate, internal rate of return threshold, payback period requirement, philosophy on entering new markets, and product diversification plans. Subsequent to reviewing the financial measures of profitability employed in risk analysis techniques, specific qualitative and quantitative approaches to risk analysis must be employed in determining profit potential and estimating profit.

FINANCIAL MEASURES OF INVESTMENTS

The evaluation of the profit potential of an investment can be performed with a variety of procedures and techniques depending on the objective of the company. In most circumstances the company's primary objective is to maximize profits; however, other objectives, such as securing a larger market, are also included, depending on the company's value model. In order to determine if the profit maximization objective will be met, the company must account for all costs that will be incurred in the venture and all benefits that will be received. The determination of costs and benefits varies across industries and between companies in each industry. This is especially true when defining benefits. For example, benefits can take the form of nonmonetary attributes, such as strengthening the company's reputation within a product line, as well as secondary impacts, such as other new-product spin-offs. Because of the diversity of nonquantitative benefits and the assumption that the secondary impacts of most initiatives are positive, only monetary benefits (returns) can be quantitatively addressed. Therefore the criteria to determine which venture best accomplishes the company's objectives will be the financial measures of profitability.

As a first step in determining investment criteria, the flow of costs and revenues associated with a work output over time must be determined. This flow of expenses and revenues is referred to as the cash flow.

Figure 8.1 is a flow diagram of the components that determine cash flow. The revenue received from the work activity is calculated based on the expected level of

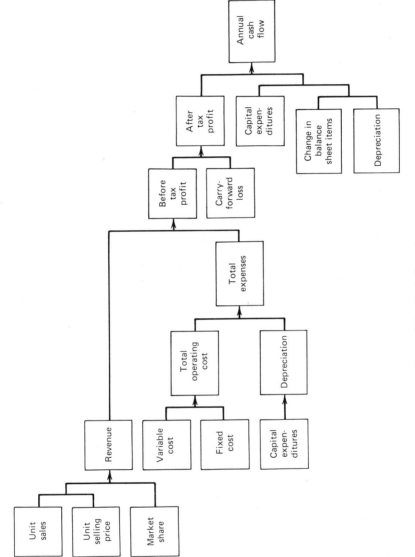

Figure 8.1 Cash flow diagram.

sales (unit sales) in the total market and the estimated price per unit produced (unit selling price). The product of these two items is adjusted by the amount or share of the total available market the company expects to capture for the product or service line. For example, if the company were evaluating the potential of entering the heat pump market, it would multiply the expected price of the heat pump by the total number of heat pumps expected to be purchased in the year under study and adjust this figure to include only that portion of total heat pump sales the company expects to capture.

The expenses incurred in producing a work output are categorized as various types of costs. Variable costs represent those expenses related to the level of production—for example, raw materials used to produce heat pumps. The second component of expenses is fixed costs—those expenditures that remain constant over varying production volumes. Typically these costs, such as insurance, are incurred regardless of the rate of sales. Finally, the costs of plant and equipment, or capital expenditures, must be accounted for when computing expenses. These costs are usually distributed over time (depreciation) until the asset's useful life has expired. Total expenses for any year are the sum of the total operating costs and the depreciation realized from capital expenditures.

The company's profit or loss before taxes is the difference between revenue and expenses less any allowable previous losses. After this step, taxes are subtracted, and the after-tax profit is obtained. Additional changes in the company's assets and liabilities, such as the level of inventory, outstanding receivables, outstanding payables, and so on, are then subtracted from capital expenditures not related to the production of the work output and added to the after-tax profit. The resultant sum is the cash flow for the year under analysis.

The cash flow procedure is repeated for each year of the venture's expected life. For example, if a company contemplating production of a heat pump expected to produce it for 10 years, the procedure would be iterated 10 times. The resultant figures for each year can be plotted to evaluate the cash flow stream. **Figure 8.2** presents an example of such a plot. A negative cash flow represents the amount of funds the venture will require to cover the costs incurred in each year. Once this

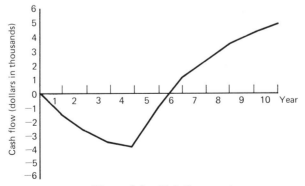

Figure 8.2 Cash flow graph.

curve passes through the horizontal axis, a positive cash flow is realized, and the venture begins to replenish the funds used in the initial years. An additional dimension can be added to this plot to represent the level of indebtedness (**Figure 8.3**). Indebtedness is the cumulative negative cash flow invested in the venture. When this line crosses the horizontal axis, the company has recouped its initial investment.

This explanation of a company's cash flow does not include a provision for the value of money over time, referred to as discounting. Money can be invested in a variety of ways to provide future returns. For example, money deposited in a bank today will accrue interest at the bank's rate until a future time when the money would be withdrawn. If the bank offered 8 percent interest on your money with a promise to pay $10.00 at the end of two years, you would deposit $8.57 today, which is referred to as the present value of your funds at an 8 percent discount rate. The level of the discount rate varies among industries; however, it is usually set at approximately the level of interest a company would have to pay to obtain the funds to make an investment.

The company's cash flow and discount rate(s) are integral inputs to the determination of the values of two of the three most important investment criteria: net present worth and internal rate of return. The third criterion, payback period, does not consider discounting cash flow over time. Many other investment criteria are available, such as the simple rate of return. However, criteria such as the simple rate of return ignore the value of money over time. Application of these simplified criteria would not result in an accurate and comprehensive treatment of the venture.

Payback period is an important investment criterion in a company's value model. The payback period is the amount of time that will elapse before the net revenues from a venture return the costs incurred. Therefore, it can be concluded that a company entering a venture must remain committed to its decision until it has met the payback period requirements. At the end of the payback period, the investor could, theoretically, liquidate the assets of the venture, and the company would not be adversely affected. However, use of the payback period alone as a measure of a venture's profitability can be misleading.

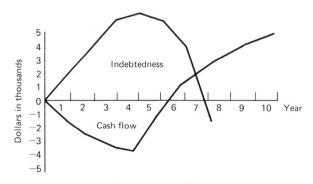

Figure 8.3   Cash flow/debtedness graph.

There are hidden problems associated with the use of the payback period in investment analysis. First, two ventures could display identical payback periods but also have markedly different cash flows. A company with the objective of rapidly recovering its investment to avert a cash flow problem would view the two ventures as equal if only the payback period were employed in the analysis. If the two cash flow streams were examined, one venture may recover 60 to 70 percent of the investment in the first two years of a six-year venture, whereas the other alternative would recover only 15 percent in the first two years. An example of two cash flow streams with identical payback periods is presented in **Table 8.1**. A company ignoring the cash flow stream would view the investments as identical. However, investment option 2 will recover approximately 75 percent of the initial outlay in the first two years, whereas option 1 recovers only 11 percent in the same period. If a company needed to recover investments rapidly to maintain an adequate cash flow chose option 1, that decision could prove disastrous. Clearly reliance on the payback period alone in this hypothetical venture could produce serious cash flow problems.

Application of the payback period as a profitability measure in the company's value model has similar shortcomings. Payback periods do not account for the total useful life of an investment. Thus a firm would not know if one venture would have a similar life span in comparison to another, and it might reject a long-term profitable venture. The establishment of a payback period threshold has several drawbacks analogous to the problems associated with using payback periods as liquidity measures. Rejection of a venture on the premise that the payback period exceeds the company's threshold could result in a loss of long-term profits exceeding those of a comparable venture with a shorter payback period. In spite of these problems, proper use of the payback period in conjunction with the two investment criteria that follow can result in a well-informed investment decision.

Frequently it is advantageous to evaluate an investment employing a single figure of merit. A company that can define its discount rate (cost of capital) can employ an investment criterion known as the net present worth (NPW) of an investment. NPW, which includes the cash flow of the venture over time and the discount rate, is the present value of the summation of net cash flows for each year of the venture, discounted at the company's discount rate. The resultant amount represents the amount of money the company could afford to pay above its investment in the

TABLE 8.1   Payback Period versus Cash Flow

Investment Option	Outlay	Net Cash in Year					Payback Year
		1	2	3	4	5	
1	$85,000	$ 4,500	$ 5,000	$12,000	$21,000	$42,500	5
2	85,000	42,500	21,000	12,000	5,000	4,500	5

venture under consideration and still earn the required rate of interest (discount rate). The following general rules guide investors when interpreting the NPW:

If NPW is greater than 0, undertake the venture.

If NPW is less than 0, reject the venture.

If NPW equals 0, decision is immaterial.

When NPW is 0, the venture will provide a rate of return at the cost of capital and therefore would not have any adverse effect on the company. An NPW less than 0 implies that the venture will not provide returns that will match the company's marginal cost of capital. Thus the company will lose money, and the venture should be rejected. Any NPW above 0 indicates that the company could invest additional funds, up to the value of NPW, and not be adversely affected. Companies employing the NPW as an investment criterion usually seek ventures that will maximize the value of it.

The major drawback encountered when using NPW is the definition of a discount rate. A company must decide the basis for selecting the value of the discount rate from a number of choices, including the average cost of all capital resources, or from an economic viewpoint, the cost of capital. An incorrect discount rate could result in an incorrect investment decision. The discount rate should not be increased to accommodate expected uncertainties in the cost of capital since the values of the cash flows over time could not be realistically interpreted. A venture's NPW is very sensitive to the discount rate. Generally the timing of the cash flow could serve to offset the impact of high discount rates.

Another investment criterion that measures profitability is the internal rate of return (IRR); it establishes the discount rate at the point where the NPW of the investment equals 0. The computational procedure for determining the IRR requires the NPW equation to be iterated, changing the value of the discount rate until the NPW is at 0. If a potential investment produces an IRR equivalent to or greater than the cost of capital available to the company, the venture should be undertaken since the company would be favorably affected. Often a cutoff value is established for acceptance of a venture.

Despite the similarity of the IRR and NPW, they will not result in the same investment decision in all circumstances. Many investment options require commitments of funds beyond the initial outlay in the first year such that the cash flow alternates between positive and negative values over the course of the venture. A situation such as this could produce more than one rate of return.

Naturally many rates of return serve to complicate the investment decision. Comparisons between competing ventures are equally as difficult when using the IRR. If two projects of unequal lifetimes are competing for funds and the project with the shorter life is selected on the basis of a higher rate of return, the company could be rejecting long-term profits. This is true since one assumption underlying the use of the IRR is that the funds remaining at the end of a short lifetime project are reinvested at the same IRR. **Table 8.2** illustrates this characteristic. Project 1, selected on the basis of IRR, would be advantageous in comparison to project 2 only

**TABLE 8.2   Projection Selection Criteria:
IRR versus NPW**

Year	Project 1	Project 2
Initial outlay	($10,000)	($10,000)
1	4,740	2,650
2	4,740	2,650
3	4,740	2,650
4		2,650
5		2,650
6		2,650
Unadjusted net	$ 4,220	$ 5,900
IRR	20% (Best)	15%
NPW (5%)	$ 2,890	$ 3,460 (Best)

if the company could invest the earned funds in another project that would also yield a 20 percent IRR in year 4.

In summary, the application of NPW for investment analysis with profit maximization as a goal is superior to other criteria. However, proper use of each criterion can result in better-informed investment decisions. A summary of profitability measures and their benefits and limitations is presented in **Table 8.3**. These profitability measures and the financial variables employed as inputs to the criteria form the foundation for the majority of quantitative risk analysis methodologies.

THE RELATIONSHIP BETWEEN RISK AND CASH FLOW AND POTENTIAL MARKET

The importance of maintaining an adequate cash flow, especially in a small company embarking on a new venture, cannot be overstated. Access to funds to support new ventures in general, and especially ventures in smaller companies, is a major barrier to innovation. Furthermore, companies recognized as being successful in previous ventures are more likely to obtain the funds required to support future efforts at innovation. Many companies not actively engaged in innovation will therefore have to rely more heavily on internal sources of funds. The drain on internally generated capital places stress on the company's cash flow that could result in financial collapse. Therefore a promising technological innovation could fail strictly because of economic conditions. This element of risk, the timing and fluctuations of the company's cash flow due to venture capital requirements, is of paramount concern to small companies. The second fundamental risk concern of smaller companies is the size of the potential market. Again, a lack of available resources to support a market analysis group eliminates the availability of reliable

TABLE 8.3 Summary of Investment Criteria

Method	Definition	Computation	Advantages	Disadvantages
Payback method	Number of years until investment is recouped	If rate of flow is constant, payback $=$ $\dfrac{\text{investment}}{\text{net cash flow}}$; otherwise, the payback is determined by adding the expected cash inflows until the total equals the initial investment	1. Simple to use and understand 2. Makes allowances for risk attitudes 3. Commonly known and used 4. Useful as a constraint	1. Ignores cash flow beyond payback period 2. Ignores timing within payback period 3. Overemphasizes liquidity as investment criterion
Accounting (or unadjusted) rate of return	Ratio of average annual income after depreciation to the average book value of the investment	$\dfrac{(\text{Average annual cash inflow}) - (\text{Average annual depreciation})}{1/2 \text{ initial investment}}$	1. Easy to compute and understand 2. Commonly known and used	Ignores timing of cash flows

Method	Definition	Formula	Advantages	Disadvantages
Net present worth (NPW)	Difference between cash inflows and outflows discounted to the present at a given interest rate	$\sum_{t=1}^{T} \dfrac{F_t}{(1+i)^t}$ where F_t = net cash flow at time period t i = discount rate T = planning horizon	1. Takes time value of money into account 2. Easier to compute than IRR	1. Requires definition of a discount rate 2. Less intuitive than IRR
ROI/IRR (rate of return on the investment, or internal rate of return)	Discount rate that makes the net present worth of inflows and outflows equal to 0	The IRR is determined by solving the equation $\sum_{t=1}^{T} \dfrac{F_t}{(1+i)^t} = 0$ where i = the rate of return of the investment	1. Takes time value of money into account 2. Does not require definition of a cutoff 3. Intuitively appealing	1. Computationally complex (requires trial and error) 2. Assumes other investment opportunities exist at same IRR 3. Does not consider size of scale of the investment 4. Occasionally provides more than one discount rate, or none

market estimates. This area of exposure could affect production planning and, ultimately, unit price.

For the most part, risk is assessed intuitively by upper management in companies of all sizes. The experiences of the company's executives in similar ventures serve as the risk analysis "model." These qualitative assessments of risk are not, however, conducted without the benefit of any financial criteria. **Table 8.4** illustrates the use made of specific financial criteria by companies according to annual capital budgets.

Among smaller firms, the discounted rate of return and payback period are the dominant financial criteria applied to investment decisions.

QUANTITATIVE APPROACHES TO RISK ANALYSIS

Management's growing concern with respect to the uncertainties associated with new ventures, given the relatively large capital and time commitments required, has produced an expanding variety of quantitative techniques to assess and at least partly account for uncertainty. Efforts in risk analysis have focused on the integration of quantitative measures of uncertainty with qualitative assessments of the decision maker's risk attitudes. There are several techniques employed within the private sector on a routine basis.

Three-Estimate Approach

Perhaps one of the most straightforward approaches to dealing with the range of uncertainty in venture analysis is the use of three estimates representing values of the base case: an optimistic estimate, an average or most likely estimate, and a pessimistic estimate of each investment criterion. The analyst will request three estimates of the data on each of the variables used in the calculation of the financial criteria. Subsequently, three estimates of the NPW of the cash flow stream, IRR, and payback period are produced. Management can then use the values of the extreme estimates as measures of the upper and lower bounds of the investment's potential profitability.

Although this approach is easy to implement and represents an expansion of the data over single figures of profitability, it could inadvertently mislead the decision maker. If the analysts supplying the data failed to note, for example, that there was an 80 percent chance of the pessimistic estimate's prevailing over the others, top management could select the venture based on the most likely case. This approach does not identify to what degree each estimate could vary. An investment with a pessimistic NPW within the corporate threshold value model specifications could be selected. However, if the variance of the pessimistic NPW were known to be large, the venture would be rejected. The value of the three-estimate approach can be considerable, especially when the investment is small in magnitude and if the end user of the information is aware of its limitations.

TABLE 8.4 Financial Criteria Used to Evaluate Capital Investments

Size of Annual Capital Budget	Discounted Rate of Return		Net Present (worth)		Present (worth) Index		Payback Period		Simple Rate of Return		Other	
	Number	Percent	Number	Percent	Number	Percent	Number	Percent	Number	Percent	Number	Period
General Criteria												
Over $100M	45	78	20	34	5	9	42	72	35	60	8	14
$50–100M	23	79	6	21	3	10	18	62	16	55	1	3
$10–50M	42	64	9	14	1	2	45	68	29	44	7	11
$5–10M	9	82	0	—	1	9	6	55	3	27	0	—
Less than $5M	5	50	0	—	0	—	5	50	4	40	0	—
No size indicated	2	67	1	33	0	—	2	67	0	—	1	33
Total business	126	71	36	20	10	6	118	67	87	49	17	10
Primary criteria												
Over $100M	20	34	3	5	0	—	1	2	18	31	4	7
$50–100M	11	38	2	7	1	3	2	7	4	14	0	—
$10–50M	26	39	2	3	0	—	15	23	12	18	3	5
$5–10M	6	55	0	—	1	9	1	9	3	27	0	—
Less than $5M	4	40	0	—	0	—	4	40	2	20	0	—
No size indicated	0	—	0	—	0	—	1	33	0	—	1	33
Total business	67	38	7	4	2	1	24	14	39	22	8	5

Monte Carlo Approach

Application of simulation techniques employing the computer has produced a new dimension in evaluating uncertainty in potential investments. Top management and planning analysts now have the ability to simulate the life of a venture by varying all relevant input parameters to arrive at the potential range of outcomes expressed in terms of probability distributions. Therefore the decision maker can evaluate the mean, standard deviation, and confidence level associated with a number of possible outcomes of a venture. This procedure eliminates many of the detrimental features of single-point and three-estimate analyses. However, the application of this technique requires an understanding of subjective probability and Monte Carlo sampling techniques.

Subjective probability is a derivative of probability theory. Probability theory rests on the assumption that there is an underlying regular pattern of events over a long period of time. True probability estimates are derived using data collected from actual occurrences of the event under study (empirical data) and are repeatable. Since it is not practicable to conduct a venture a large number of times with the venture's characteristics being varied for each unique attempt, subjective probability is employed.

Subjective probability is the quantification of an individual's judgment on the potential of a specific event occurring. For example, a market analyst attempting to define the total heat pump market potential would not express the high level of sales in 19X2 to be 200,000 units; rather the analyst would state that there is a 65 percent chance of the total heat pump market's reaching a sales level of 200,000 units in 19X2. Expressing the characteristics of a venture in this manner enables application of Monte Carlo techniques to simulate the venture.

The use of subjective probability is valuable beyond its application in simulation. It encourages the actors in venture analysis to assess realistically the possible attributes of all financial parameters. Again, borrowing from the heat pump example, the financial analyst requires a cost estimate of unit selling price as an input to the cash flow computation. This detailed estimate or series of estimates will result in maximum and minimum probable costs. Initially, high and low estimates of the heat pump's unit price based on the high and low cost estimates would be requested. If the upper bound was $3560 and the lower limit $3040, a continuum such as the one in **Figure 8.4** would be drawn.

The next step would be to segment this range into intervals. Since five intervals are more easily understood (e.g., a median and two intervals on each side), the range could take the appearance of **Figure 8.5**. It is not necessary to use equal intervals. The interviewee would then be requested to rank the likelihood that the unit price would fall within each interval (**Figure 8.6**).

o--o
$3040 $3560

Figure 8.4   Heat pump unit price range.

o -------------- o --------------- o --------------- o --------------- o --------------- o
$3040 $3144 $3248 $3352 $3456 $3560

Figure 8.5   Intervals of the heat pump unit price range.

This establishes the general shape of the uncertainty profile (skewed right, central, etc.). The likelihood that the unit price will fall into any one of the five intervals is then estimated in relation to the likelihood that it will fall into the other intervals. For example, the relative likelihood, P_2, that the unit price will fall between $3456 and $3560 is equal to $P_1/2$; the chance, P_3, of the unit price's falling in the range of $3248 to $3352 is equal to $P_2/2$, and so on (**Figure 8.7**).

The determination of the likelihood of falling into each interval can be easily derived in quantitative terms (probability estimates). Since the unit price range represents the entire spectrum of uncertainty, the chance of falling within the range of $3040 to $3560 is 1. Therefore the relationships in **Figure 8.7** could be used with those in the equation $P_1 + P_2 + P_3 + P_4 + P_5 = 1$ to solve for the probability estimates. This produces the following values for each interval:

$P_1 = 0.52$
$P_2 = 0.26$
$P_3 = 0.13$
$P_4 = 0.06$
$P_5 = 0.03$

A histogram or probability density function (**Figure 8.8**) can now be drawn with the addition of a vertical axis representing the probability of occurrence. It should be noted that the probability of a given interval in the histogram is indicated by the total area, not height, accounted for by the bar as a fraction of the total area of all the bars. This is particularly important when one is interpreting the graph visually. This procedure would be repeated for each financial parameter employed in the risk analysis.

Since the derivation of the probability distributions is a subjective process, care must be exercised in the selection of data sources. Typically the analyst will solicit data from the departments in an organization that are best qualified to develop the estimates. Therefore potential sales levels, the cost of sales, and marketing costs are obtained from marketing personnel; unit costs, production costs, and maintenance expenditures are derived from the project engineering team. The best approach is to develop a ground-up, industrial engineering labor-hours and materials-based estimate. It is not uncommon, however, to obtain statistical estimates that reflect the

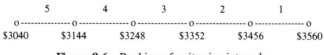

          5   4   3   2   1
o -------------- o --------------- o --------------- o --------------- o --------------- o
$3040 $3144 $3248 $3352 $3456 $3560

Figure 8.6   Ranking of unit price intervals.

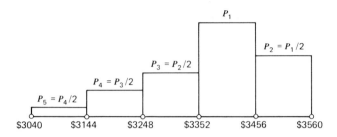

Figure 8.7 Relative likelihood of unit price intervals.

source's individual biases. An engineer with a personal interest in seeing a project advance to the production stage may skew unit costs, for example, to ensure that the project is not cancelled on the basis of its financial attributes. Several procedures to minimize either conscious or unconscious skewing of the data are available. Among the most popular is the delphi technique. This procedure used data collected from a number of individuals knowledgeable in the parameter under examination. Each individual prepares an estimate without the knowledge of what other team members are preparing; then all estimates are compiled and statistical summaries distributed to each member. This procedure is iterated until the group has resolved any data extremes. Although this technique expands the time required to collect data, greater confidence can be placed in the input data and financial figures of merit derived from the analysis.

Once the probabilities associated with the input data have been collected, a financial simulation can be performed employing the Monte Carlo method. The basic financial measures, such as NPW, are calculated a large number of times with the input parameters varying according to the subjective probability distributions.

The number of iterations selected for the Monte Carlo simulation has a direct

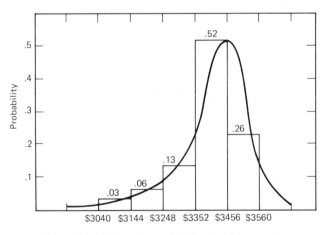

Figure 8.8 Unit price probability density function.

bearing on the accuracy of the model's results. Under normal circumstances approximately 100 iterations will produce results that reflect the majority of possible venture outcomes. A venture characterized by a wide range of values, or a large standard deviation as indicated by the uncertainty profile, for the major uncertainty variables should be iterated 250 to 500 times. This will produce results that portray the impact of a large number of possible outcomes. Furthermore, the number of iterations should be based on the shapes of the probability distributions attached to each uncertainty variable. Uncertainty profiles skewed toward high or low extremes of the range with no pattern across all uncertainty variables are also cause to increase the number of iterations to capture all possible outcomes in the simulation. Under most circumstances, the amount of accuracy gained in simulations with greater than 500 iterations is nominal and not worth the additional data processing costs.

A Monte Carlo simulation of a venture's cash flow would be conducted in the following manner for approximately 100 iterations:

1. The simulation will look at the probability distributions of each variable entered in the cash flow computation. Based on this distribution it will randomly select a value for each input parameter such as unit cost. The selection of a random value is within the confines of the probability distribution. An easy way of visualizing this concept is to develop a "wheel of chance" such as that shown in **Figure 8.9**. Since there is a 52 percent chance that the unit cost will fall in the range of $3352 to $3456, 52 percent of the wheel is devoted to values within that range. Spinning the wheel would result in random values of unit cost to use in the computations. All other probabilistic variables are treated in a similar manner. In order to ensure that the values selected for each variable are consistent from year to year within one scenario, the correlation between years is examined and values interpolated if necessary.

2. At the end of each venture scenario, the risk analysis model stores the rele-

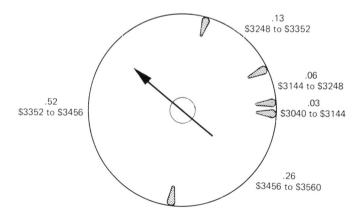

Figure 8.9   Monte Carlo wheel of chance for unit price.

vant figures of merit such as the cash flow stream, net present value, and payback period.

3. Once all iterations are complete, the model calculates statistics on each of the figures of merit to provide the analyst with the mean and standard deviation for each value. Moreover, the frequency at which the values occurred across all iterations is computed to determine the probability of a venture's meeting or exceeding that value.

4. Risk profiles are produced as output from the Monte Carlo simulation for use by the decision maker. Therefore Monte Carlo techniques can simulate one venture under a variety of circumstances to evaluate the merits of the venture under uncertainty.

The output of a Monte Carlo risk analysis provides a clear portrait of the effects of uncertainty. Two examples of the application of Monte Carlo risk analysis results are presented. First, the cash flow over each year of the venture's life can be plotted from the tabular output. Usually the cash flow in each analysis year is listed according to its probability of occurrence. A hypothetical cash flow stream is presented in **Figure 8.10**. The horizontal axis represents each year of the venture's life, and the vertical axis is the actual value of the cash flow in each year. For each level of probability, the cash flow is plotted by the year. Based on the level of risk the decision maker is prepared to assume, the cash flow impact on the company can be assessed. Conservative investors will probably evaluate the cash flow stream at the 80 percent and 100 percent levels. Thus the investor will be reasonably sure of experiencing a cash flow projected at that level. A risk-seeking investor would evaluate the cash flow stream at a lower level of probability. These trade-offs

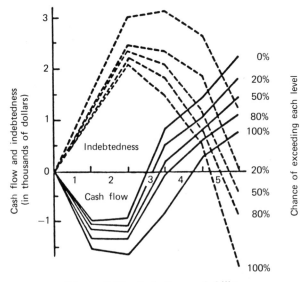

Figure 8.10   Cash flow probability.

complicate the investment decision; however, the magnitude of uncertainty represented in the various levels of cash flow can be explicitly viewed, thereby partially eliminating ambiguity in the process. The availability of a mean and standard deviation value for each financial figure of merit enables an assessment of different investment options within a venture. The average of an investment figure of merit such as NPW is computed as the sum of the NPW produced from each iteration of simulation, divided by the total number of iterations. It represents the average NPW that can be expected from the venture. The standard deviation of each figure of merit measures the dispersion of values about the mean. The lower the standard deviation is for a given distribution of NPW, the more certain a decision maker can be that the actual outcome will approach the mean NPW value. A lower standard deviation implies lower risk for the financial measure under consideration.

By virtue of the Monte Carlo method, most distributions of values (such as NPW) take a normal shape (Gaussian), which produces a graph similar to the one in **Figure 8.11**. In this example, alternatives 1 and 2 have the same level of risk since the standard deviation of the NPW is equivalent. Alternative 2 is preferable, however, since it will realize a higher NPW. The same conclusions could be drawn for alternatives 3 and 4. An investor with the objective of minimizing risk while simultaneously maximizing the NPW (profit) would select Alternative 3 as the best option among the four available. This example shows that the risk premium associated with a project under alternative funding and marketing scenarios can be easily identified. Financial criteria with large standard deviations have a high level of risk. The company's goal is to reduce the standard deviation, increase the mean to offset the high risk, or a combination of both. Financial, marketing, or production changes can be tested in the simulation to determine their effectiveness in reducing risk or providing greater returns to compensate for the risk.

Similar analyses can be performed employing data from a risk analysis based on

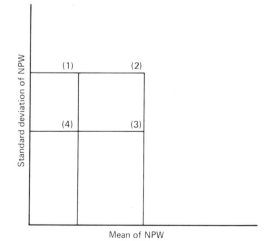

Figure 8.11   NPW risk assessment in standard deviation plane.

the Monte Carlo approach. Other outputs typically obtainable from this approach are risk profiles for the following:

Revenue
Expenses
Capital expenditures
Profit
Cumulative cash flow
Return on assets
Payback period

Some Monte Carlo approaches perform the risk analysis at various discount rates to assist the investor in making a decision when the discount rate or cost of capital cannot be exactly defined, thereby accounting for potential variations in the discount rate.

In summary, Monte Carlo risk analysis approaches provide one of the most comprehensive and explicit means of understanding the uncertainty associated with the venture. It is frequently employed in actual venture analysis in the business community.

DECISION TREE ANALYSIS

An investment decision is usually not confined to options within a single venture but rather is an interrelated decision involving events that are directly or indirectly related to the venture under investigation.

A method of formalizing the relationships between interrelated events, enabling the investor to evaluate the economic consequence of each option, is the decision tree. Decision trees are useful in evaluating potential events related to a venture.

Each decision tree is comprised of two components: decisions, represented by pointers, and chance events, represented by ovals. For illustrative purposes, a hypothetical decision tree relating to the development of building performance standards and the heat pump is used. The developmental process and ultimate commercialization of the heat pump project could benefit from the implementation of performance standards for new buildings. This would be especially important if the commercialization success of the heat pump rested on having an assured level of demand during the first five years in the market. If the performance standards are prepared and successfully adopted and the heat pump is ready for the market, the commercialization risk associated with the heat pump could be reduced.

Figure 8.12 presents a simplified decision tree to aid in the evaluation of the impact of building energy performance standards (BEPS) on the success of the heat pump in terms of the NPW of energy saved under each option. At decision point 1, the options are:

1. Develop and commercialize the heat pump in conjunction with the improvement of building energy performance.
2. Develop the heat pump as a stand-alone effort.
3. Improve building energy performance as a stand-alone effort.

The initial option leads to chance point A, at which time the unit price per British thermal unit (Btu) output of the heat pump will affect future options. The numbers along each branch stemming from chance point A represent hypothetical probabilities of each possible outcome occurring. It is apparent that the evaluating team in this hypothetical situation perceives high or moderate costs per Btu to be more likely to occur. If the high-cost branch is taken, decision point 2 is encountered. At this decision point the course of action taken in improving energy performance effort will affect the commercialization success of the heat pump. Strict adherence to energy performance standards improves the likelihood of achieving a high level of demand and, consequently, a high NPW of energy savings. If minimum energy performance standards are implemented, however, the probability of realizing a low level of initial demand and associated NPW of energy savings will be realized. The

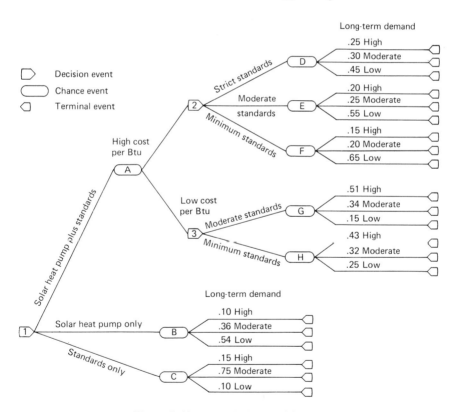

Figure 8.12   Hypothetical decision tree.

consequences of the stand-alone options can be determined by following the tree to the various terminal nodes.

Although this example is only hypothetical, knowledge of the ramifications of each alternative course of action and the critical decision points is clearly beneficial when evaluating investment decisions.

The successful application of decision tree techniques to risk analysis problems requires management to identify the criteria to be employed in determining the course of action at each decision node and the objectives and goals of the problem. Therefore the path through the tree would be based on, for example, selecting the branch from the decision point that has the most attractive cash flow stream with the objective of maximizing the NPW.

Monte Carlo risk analysis and decision tree theory can be complementary tools in evaluating a venture's risk. Monte Carlo risk analysis can supply the requisite figures of merit that can be expected from each alternative path at various levels of probability. Both techniques foster the explicit consideration of the uncertainties associated with a venture, thereby minimizing the likelihood of neglecting a risk factor that might result in failure of the venture.

RISK ANALYSIS IN THE PUBLIC AND UTILITY SECTOR

A public sector entity or a profit-making utility firm operating under a public regulatory body must also consider uncertainty when undertaking a new venture. These entities approach new ventures with goals different from those in the private sector; however, the evaluation tools employed by public entities and regulated utilities are similar to those commonly applied by profit-oriented businesses. An example of such an effort is the demonstration of conversion of waste products into energy. If the technology is proved feasible as a result of a demonstration, "consumers" of the technology would be urban governments and/or regional waste treatment authorities. Adoption of the technology by municipal governments would be based on certain criteria, such as the level of capital required to construct the facility, the presence of a market to purchase the energy produced from the facility, and the level of funds required to maintain the plant. Each of these three concerns contains elements of uncertainty; hence the venture is not risk free.

The major areas of uncertainty mentioned are well suited to the conduct of a financial risk analysis. First, the level of capital expenditures necessary to undertake the venture must be determined. The ability to obtain capital from the sale of bonds and/or internal resources is directly related to the risk associated with the venture. Revenues from operation of the facility must be realized at a level that permits retirement of the principal and interest on the bond. Therefore the cash flow stream of the investment must be computed, which requires consideration of the level of demand for the product (units sales) and anticipated operation and maintenance costs.

Application of the Monte Carlo approach to the problem can produce the information needed to evaluate the impact of uncertainty. Subjective probability distributions based on the experiences gained in the demonstration facility would serve as the input data. This enables ranges of likely costs for plant and equipment, operation and maintenance, and the energy output to be considered. The major deviation from a private sector analysis in this venture analysis is in the evaluation of the results produced from the Monte Carlo approach.

The public sector entity will be more inclined to pursue the venture if the probability of recovering the investment with an NPW equal to 0 is high. Thus the venture can be undertaken at the cost of capital without placing additional resource requirements on the public. In some instances, however, societal benefits may outweigh the costs, at which time an NPW less than 0 may be acceptable. Nevertheless, the projections of revenues and costs alone or as measured in the cash flow stream enable the municipal investment analyst to determine the impact of the venture on the finances of the public entity at various levels of confidence. Therefore if the level of risk associated with the venture is low, the public entity should be able to sell bonds at a rate attractive to both it and the investor.

Within the public sector, accounting practices vary, especially the treatment of depreciation. If the cash flow stream is to be evaluated properly at the federal level to determine the need and level of risk reduction assistance, the venture should be simulated under alternative accounting schemes. This additional effort will foster a more realistic treatment of the venture's risk.

Risk Analysis in a Regulated Environment

The evaluation of a potential venture within a company (such as a utility company) operating under constraints emanating from a public regulatory body complicates the process of risk analysis. Specifically, regulated companies strive to maximize profits; however, the rate of return to the company is limited. This situation can result in a barrier to the adoption of technologies with high risk, since investors normally will accept higher risk only if, simultaneously, a higher rate of return is made available on the investment. For example, consumer attitudes complicate the investment decision process because of increased pressure on government to reduce the frequency and magnitude of utility rate increases, which reduces the utilities' willingness to accept moderate to high risk ventures.

All ventures considered by a regulated company with a limited rate of return are evaluated according to the impact of the venture on the value of the company as a whole. Therefore the normal risk analysis procedure employed outside the regulated environment is reversed. The analyst would start with the allowable rate of return and then determine the likelihood that the different price levels would allow the established rate of return to be achieved. A work output price that would lower the company's rate of return would discourage investors from making the capital available to the company for the venture and/or generate the need for a rate or price increase. Conversely, if the price increased the rate of return above the allowable level, the controlling government agency might either disapprove the venture or reduce the rate structure. The application of traditional financial measures to a potential venture (e.g., cash flow stream, NPW, return on assets, indebtedness) can be employed to assess the impact of the venture on the company. Financial analysis of investments within the utility sector, including risk assessment, is time-consuming and expensive. In addition to the data required for a conventional financial-risk analysis, extensive data on the financial attributes of the company, construction work in progress, and construction projects the company is committed to implement in the future are essential to the analysis. Therefore, any risk analysis model used in the regulated sector would be developed around the unique attributes of one company. Since it is impractical to develop a unique model for each company, the analysis consists of identifying the major risk issues that confront regulated companies in their investment decisions.

Capital information is the major risk obstacle to the introduction of improvements in new technologies. Regulated companies such as utilities are faced at this time with a two-pronged problem. First, they are under obligation to supply adequate levels of their product in spite of the fact that earnings may not be at a level to encourage capital spending. Therefore the regulated industry has only limited discretion in timing its placements of debt and equity issues in an attempt to minimize the cost of capital. The result has been large amounts of debt sold at historically high interest rates. High interest rates reduce debt coverage, which leads to the second prong of the problem: Bond rating companies rate utility bonds as high in risk, which increases the interest rate to compensate investors for their greater risk.

Projects that can be funded with internal funds are more desirable; they represent a lower level of risk because capital costs to the company are reduced. Conventional risk analysis can be effectively applied to determine the likelihood of requiring external financing. Most projects in regulated environments are evaluated on their individual merits, as well as by more rigorous methods incorporating the entire financial position of the company.

U.S. Department of Energy studies have shown that industry perceives technological barriers to be considerably less important to commercialization than market, capital, or regulatory barriers. Thus, merely increasing the extent of research and development funding will not necessarily lead to increased commercialization.

For this reason companies continually reassess the financial characteristics of a venture (including risk analysis) from the point when the idea is conceived to actual introduction in the marketplace. During each stage of the venture's maturation, its financial attributes can be better defined, thereby enabling management to reassess the venture prior to the commitment of the resources required at each stage and to evaluate the degree of fee or profit that must be derived from the venture to compensate for risk and to reward the investment of venture capital.

THE EFFECT OF THE TYPE OF CONTRACT ON PROFIT

Fixed-Price Contracts

Fixed-price or firm-bid contracts offer the greatest potential for abundant profits as well as the greatest potential for significant losses. Bidders for fixed-price work usually add 10 to 20 percent above direct and indirect costs to allow for adequate profit. If the work can be completed more efficiently or quickly at lower cost, the profit can increase significantly. The work must be estimated closely enough to permit slight cost increases without eating into a sizable part of the profits. A thorough market survey, as well as knowledge of the competition and the buyer, could indicate that the job can be won at even higher profits. A company must strive to have several contracts, each maturing and providing income at a different time and profit level to ensure consistency and continuity of business activities. Since a company that desires to be in a steady growth posture must have a continued assurance of operating at a profit, the low- and high-profit ventures must average out to one that creates an acceptable return on the investment on a continuing basis.

Fixed-price contracts are used principally where the process, product, project, or service is reasonably well defined and where historical data are available to support cost and price estimates. Fierce competition for fixed-price contracts will result in a significant lowering of the profit level; hence it is prudent to enter markets where the demand is high but the competition is low. This strategy usually means a continual shifting of markets and work outputs to meet evolving needs. An exception to this is where a highly motivated and competent organization has built up a reputation for high quality and customer satisfaction over a number of years. In these instances customers often prefer good service and high quality to a low bid price. If you desire less control and involvement by the customer, a greater independence of operation, and the opportunity for high gains to reward your top efforts, fixed-price contracts will be the most attractive and profitable.

Cost-Reimbursable Contracts

With the advent of high-technology work outputs, the cost-reimbursable contract has become more prevalent. This type of contract is most often used in government contracting and is usually based on one of the following three fee arrangements.

Cost Plus Fixed Fee (CPFF). The cost-plus-fixed-fee contract is the most prevalent type of cost-reimbursable contract and poses the least risk to the contractor. The fee is based on a percentage of initial negotiated cost (say 10 percent) and is fixed in dollar value unless the scope of work is increased by the procuring agency.

Cost Plus Incentive Fee (CPIF). The cost-plus-incentive-fee contract is based on a percentage of initially negotiated costs (say 5 percent) plus an incentive payment based on performance that could increase the effective fee percentage to that of a CPFF contract or above. Incentive payments can be based on meeting key delivery dates, reaching certain performance goals, or on keeping overall contract costs within a certain limit.

Cost Plus Award Fee (CPAF). The cost-plus-award-fee contract uses a base fee (say 5 percent) computed as a percentage of the initially negotiated price, plus an award fee, which is a cash payment provided by the procuring agency based on a principally subjective evaluation of the contractor's work.

Pitfalls in Cost-Reimbursable Contracts.   Although the potential for profits is good when a cost-reimbursable contract is used (reaching to 12 to 15 percent), there are pitfalls for both buyer and seller. First, because all costs are reimbursable, an extensive cost monitoring system is needed to permit the buyer to verify that what is being charged is cost and not profit. This system often restricts the privacy and adds to the complexity of the contractor's cost accounting and reporting system.

Second, the procurement method government agencies commonly use engenders excessive competitive optimism in the bidding procedure, which frequently causes underestimates and results in cost overruns. Often companies in the posture to perform under a cost-reimbursable contract are not motivated to reduce or limit costs because higher expenditures on a specific contract help to maintain their business base, work force, and opportunity for additional business. The federal, state, and local governments have been struggling with this problem for some time but have not yet found a workable solution to excessive cost growth in government contracts. From a bidder's viewpoint, however, a cost-reimbursable contract is highly attractive because it virtually eliminates the possibility of losses in profit while guaranteeing a fixed-profit amount. If costs increase excessively, however, the venture would not have been as attractive as alternate ventures with higher percentage returns.

EFFECTIVE BIDDING AND MANAGEMENT FOR MAXIMUM PROFIT

Both fixed-price and cost-reimbursable contracts require a good cost estimate and price determination prior to bidding, negotiating, and carrying out a work activity. A company's competitive posture is enhanced most by its ability to propose and use the proper labor skill mix and levels throughout the lifetime of the project. This involves painstaking forethought and planning in the bidding phase, close control and flexibility in the management phase, the use of astute business practices, and the skillful application of a company's knowledge, understanding, and skills in producing a work output. Either contract will yield maximum profits if these principles are followed.

QUESTIONS

8.1. An analyst is told that a supplier uses a 20 percent profit margin. If the total bid price to the customer is $20,000, the profit is:

    a. $4000.

    b. $3333.

    c. $1667.

    d. $3667.

8.2. Financial analysis can be used by management to:

    a. Develop a go, no-go decision involving corporate assets.

    b. Decide if employees should be paid a bonus.

  c. Decide if a company should buy or lease a corporate jet.

  d. All of the above.

8.3. The chart in **Figure 8.13** is a classic portrayal of:

  a. Projected sales.

  b. Projected break-even.

  c. Projected inventory levels.

  d. All of the above

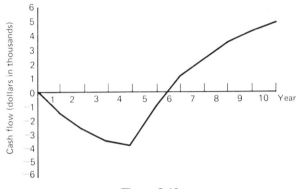

Figure 8.13

8.4. In an analysis of cash flow on a new product, the cash flow measured at the first unit is usually:

  a. Positive.

  b. Break-even.

  c. Negative.

  d. None of the above.

8.5. An analyst is told that a supplier uses a 16 percent profit margin. If the total estimated cost to the customer is $10,000, then the profit is approximately:

  a. $16,000.

  b. $1600.

  c. $1380.

  d. $10,000.

  e. $2560.

8.6. You are to prepare a bid for producing 100 brackets. The brackets are made on a punch press and screen printed with a part number. All screen printing is done at one time, but the brackets are made in batches of 75. Punch press set up time is 2 hours per setup and .05 hour per print. Assume no learning or attrition on either process. Material cost is $.50 per piece. Direct labor rate is $10.00 per hour, and overhead is 150 percent of direct labor. G&A is 20 percent of total material, labor, and overhead cost. A 15 percent profit rate is expected.

What is your bid price for the 100 brackets?

8.7. When a company has had considerable experience in a field, and a fixed, proved design of the product or process is available, the following type of contract would be most appropriate:

a. Cost reimbursable.

b. Incentive contract.

c. Fixed-price contract.

d. Cost plus fixed fee.

e. Any of the above.

9

REVIEWING, PUBLISHING, AND USING THE ESTIMATE

Nor do men light a lamp, and put it under the peck-measure, but on the lamp stand: and it gives light to all who are in the house.

Matthew 5:15

For cost estimates prepared by and for all but the very smallest organizations, the review, publication, and subsequent use of the estimate are the most important phases of the estimating activity. Many key estimators and estimate managers agree that the most significant benefit to be obtained from the estimating process is not necessarily the published estimate itself (although the published estimate is a principal goal) but the improved knowledge imparted to the organization relative to the product definition and resources. This improved knowledge and understanding of the work activity is gained through the review, consolidation, and reconciliation of the estimate, as well as the effective use of the cost estimate after it is published.

Figure 9.1 (which appears on the back inside cover) is an overall summary flow diagram that shows seven basic steps or phases of cost estimating. Previous chapters have discussed the elements that go into the first four of these steps or phases: (1) initiation, (2) formulation, (3) implementation, and (4) estimating. The initiation phase refers to the activity or action that triggers the start of the estimating cycle. The start of the estimating cycle can be triggered by receipt of an invitation to bid, a request for quotation, a management decision to investigate a new product line, or a major change in a work output or work activity. The formulation phase includes the collection and/or synthesis of major programmatic and estimate ground rules. The implementation phase consists of informing major estimate participants of their responsibilities and assignments and familiarizing them with the work activity being estimated. The estimating activity involves the derivation of labor-hours, materials, other direct costs, indirect costs, administrative costs, and profit or fee required to do the job.

This chapter covers the final phases of estimating: review, consolidation and reconciliation, pricing and estimate publication, and the use of the estimate after it has been published.

REVIEWING THE ESTIMATE

The Team Approach

In a cost estimate involving more than one organizational entity, discipline, or technology, it is important to have a team approach to cost estimate review. In a large organization this review is normally done at two levels. The first review is usually done at the departmental or organizational element level. The purpose of the departmental review is to screen all estimates emanating from within the department for accuracy, completeness, credibility, and supportability and to identify any inconsistencies, overlaps, duplications, or omissions within the departmental discipline area. Engineering estimates, for example, would be reviewed by the head of the engineering department, preferably in the presence of principal subordinates. Reviews with all subordinate functions represented are important because each representative can point out inconsistencies in the other discipline areas, thereby exposing duplications and overlaps faster and more effectively than if the supervisor or department head were to be the only one to review the entire estimate. The group or team review is more likely to result in a negotiated value for each estimate rather than an unchallenged value. Since overestimates by department advocates are more likely than underestimates, a principal source of cost excess can be reduced or eliminated by this method.

The identification of gaps or omissions, a far less likely prospect where organizational advocates are involved, must then be carried out by the department head or representing his or her interests. This internal department review and iteration, shown on Figure 9.1 by the slashed lines, within the functions of each responsible functional or organizational element must be done at least once and probably more than once as a result of the next estimate phase: consolidation and reconciliation.

Consolidation and Reconciliation

Once the basic labor-hours, materials, equipment, and facilities estimates have been derived by the responsible functional or organizational elements, these inputs must be consolidated and reconciled with each other at the top level by company management or by an independent organization that represents the interest of company management. This independent organization is usually the estimating department (variously located in the finance department, program resources office, industrial engineering, planning department, or proposal department). It is usually the responsibility of this organizational element, whatever its name, to combine the estimate inputs, reconcile any differences in scope, philosophy, or estimating methodologies, eliminate duplications, identify omissions, and develop a standardized method of presenting the data. The estimating department also adds other resource estimates developed internally or by supporting organizations such as the costs of travel, computer services, and other direct charges.

Either company management or the project engineer or manager responsible for the cost estimate now has the authority and the responsibility to accept or reject the estimate inputs for final estimate pricing and publication. More often than not, this responsible official will reject the estimate and return it to the estimating department and estimating disciplines for one or more of a number of reasons among them incompatibility of the cost estimate total, with the price derived from a market analysis, incompatibility with management cost targets, or inappropriate time phasing of the required funding for initial work activities. It is at this point in the estimating activity that the greatest danger exists in developing an unrealistic cost estimate.

One of the largest pitfalls in cost estimating is the misinterpretation of a management cut in a cost or price estimate. There is definitely a right way and a wrong way to approach a cost estimate reduction, and many ventures have failed because of the use of improper techniques. The wrong way is to impose or legislate an across-the-board cost estimate or budget reduction on all elements of the organization. Many managers use this method in expediency, later regretting it when discovering that an overrun is imminent. The right way and the most successful way of holding costs within a certain target or boundary is intimately related to the consolidation and reconciliation method itself. The most successful method of consolidation and reconciliation of a cost estimate—the team method—also yields the best results when pressures are ultimately brought to bear to reduce the cost estimate. Although the team method takes longer, it yields far more realistic results than do arbitrary across-the-board cuts. The team method of cost estimate consolidation and reconciliation begins with an analysis of the total estimate by a team of estimators and managers through the presentation of cost estimate inputs at an input review meeting.

In this meeting, all participating organizations are required to have key representatives present who can speak for that organization. Then each organization in turn gives a stand-up presentation of the resource inputs and the supporting rationale for them. By this method the reviewing team develops the best possible knowledge and background on the content of the work activity and how the work content relates to the resources requirements. With this in-depth knowledge and background of the project's requirements, activities, and resource needs, the review team is much more capable of suggesting areas where reductions in labor-hours, materials, equipment, or facilities can be made without compromising the quality of work output. If the cost estimate is reduced; specifications, quantities, schedules, and work intent is changed until resource estimates and work content are compatible.

There are several methods of reducing work activity costs without reducing quantity, or quality, or changing the overall project schedule. Brief descriptions of these methods follow.

Combining Work Elements. When a work activity is subdivided into a large number of work elements, estimators tend to load each work element. Since a fraction of an employee is practicable only on paper, full-time personnel are often allocated to what should be part-time activities. Combining work elements that involve the same skill categories and skill levels can reduce costs by allowing effective planning and scheduling of each worker's activities and by reducing wasted labor-hours brought about by isolating single tasks to specific workers.

Relocating Work Areas. Time in transit from one job to another can be reduced and workers can often be used more effectively if they are located adjacent to interfacing work activities. An improved plant layout and modernized handling, storage, and transportation equipment can greatly increase worker productivity and reduce cost without sacrificing work quality or quantity.

Effective Utilization of Skills. In developing cost estimates, as well as in performing any work activity, avoid the practice of using excessively high skill levels in performing the work. Highly skilled workers should be scheduled early in the project, where they are more likely to be needed in ironing out early bugs in the process or developing routine procedures. Skill levels and appropriate salary levels should then be reduced as soon as possible in the schedule and less experienced personnel used to perform more routine functions. *This is vital in developing a competitive cost estimate.*

General Productivity Improvement. **Figure 9.2** shows some general areas of productivity improvement that can increase the competitive nature of any cost estimate. Improved efficiency, economy, and effectiveness in plant or company operation will be accompanied by commensurate cost reductions. The cost estimator, however, must have the full agreement, as well as the participation, of plant management in order to assume in the estimate that any or all of these productivity improvements can and will be made prior to performance of the job being estimated. Automation, the use of microprocessors, and computer-aided design, planning, manufacturing, and monitoring help to provide increased productivity, but company management

- PRODUCT DEVELOPMENT

- COMPUTER-AIDED PLANNING

    - INDIVIDUAL WORK ORDERS
    - OVERALL PROCESS PLANNING (PART FAMILIES)
    - SHOP WORKLOAD VERSUS PRODUCTION CAPABILITY

- INSTALLATION OF INTERACTIVE SENSORS ON MANUFACTURING MACHINE TOOLS

- REDUCTION OF MANUAL PROGRAMMING FOR NUMERICALLY CONTROLLED MACHINES

- AUTOMATED STORAGE AND RETRIEVAL OF RAW MATERIALS

- DEVELOPMENT OF HIGH-SPEED MACHINING TECHNIQUES

    - GREATER MACHINE AUTOMATION
    - IMPROVED CUTTER GEOMETRY AND MATERIALS

- USE OF AUTOMATED EQUIPMENT MONITORING SYSTEMS TO PROVIDE PLANNING INFORMATION TO MANUFACTURING MANAGEMENT TO DETERMINE:

    - ACTUAL MACHINE WORK TIME   - OPERATOR ACTION TIME
    - TOOLING SETUP TIME   - PRODUCTION CONTROL TIME
    - PART LOADING TIME   - OPERATOR AVAILABILITY
    - MAINTENANCE DOWN TIME   - TOOL AVAILABILITY DOWN TIME
    - QUALITY ASSURANCE TIME

- ANALYSIS OF DATA FROM EQUIPMENT MONITORING SYSTEMS TO DETERMINE AREAS FOR IMPROVEMENT (OPTIMUM SHIFT MIX, SKILL MIX, MACHINE MIX)

Figure 9.2 Means of improving productivity.

must be forward thinking and innovative both to recognize and to implement productivity improvements. A number of factors affect worker and employee productivity.

Environmental Factors

Lighting

Heating

Noise

Odors

Vibration

Appearance of work area

Comfort of workstation

Availability of facilities for personal hygiene and refreshment

Safety of operations

Motivational Factors

Performance incentives (monetary and recognition)

Quality of supervision

Personal encouragement

Team pride

Nature of product

Competition

Other Factors

Health of employee and susceptibility to fatigue

Degree of training

Degree of matching skills to job

Factors that affect machine and equipment productivity are the effectiveness of supporting functions such as maintenance, tooling, and quality assurance, the efficiency of overall shop work load planning and resulting machine utilization, and suitability and adaptability of the product design to the machine design. Possible causes for low machine and equipment productivity include poor work load distribution and leveling, low responsiveness of the maintenance and quality assurance organizations, inadequate stocks of standard tools and spare parts, lack of qualified machine operators, and other occurrences such as power failures, strikes, and natural disasters. Although it often appears that little can be done about some of these hindrances to productivity, close management attention to correcting reductions in productivity in this manner can go a long way toward making the cost estimate competitive. Product design itself can have an effect on productivity because some materials and shapes are inherently expensive to manufacture or assemble while others are more suitable for cost-effective production. Human engineering of product design can increase productivity significantly through:

Color coding
Standardization of assembly methods
Interchangeability of parts
Reduction of hardware scrap
Automatic indexing of fit
Ease of inspection
Optimum weight and size of components for handling
Access for assembly, cleaning, and finishing

After all of these factors have been addressed in reducing or reconciling the cost estimate to a lower target cost or price, there are still other measures that can be taken to reduce the cost although not without possible sacrifice of desirable work output characteristics. The use of less expensive materials in the product but without sacrificing quality significantly may be cost-effective in the long run. Cost reductions can be brought about in many ways through changing and altering product or work output specifications. Paramount is the need to avoid cost estimate reductions without reconciling this reduction to a similar decrease in product expectations. It is far better for the long-term health of an enterprise, however, to effect cost estimate reductions through increased efficiency and productivity than through relaxation or reduction of product performance standards.

COMPILING AND PRICING THE ESTIMATE

Once the consolidation and reconciliation phase of estimating has been completed and the resource estimates have been accepted, the estimating team conducts a final review of all resource inputs for accuracy and consistency. Then, both before and after the computation and pricing of the estimate, company management has an opportunity to review the resource and cost numbers, comparing these with estimates derived from other methods of estimating or from independent estimating sources. Since management has participated in the consolidation and reconciliation process, at this time it should be expected to give final approval of the estimated values. Management, of course, has the opportunity and authority to recycle the estimate through any of the previous phases, but if it has been involved in the estimating process, these occurrences should be rare.

Cost estimate resource data are usually compiled and priced for each work element using a format similar to that shown in Figure 9.3. Time-phased labor-hours are entered under the appropriate skill category and fiscal time period. The time period and resources for the work activity can be subdivided into days, weeks, months, quarters, or years. In **Figure 9.3** the time subdivision shown is the fiscal

	Description	FY-	FY-	FY-	FY-	FY-	FY-	FY-	FY-	Total

WBS Number _____   Date _____

WBS Title _____   FY- _____ Fiscal Year

	Description	FY-	FY-	FY-	FY-	FY-	FY-	FY-	FY-	Fiscal Year Total
Labor hours										
	Engineering									
	Manufacturing									
	Tooling									
	Quality									
	Test									
	Other									
	Total hours									
Labor dollars										
	Engineering									
	Manufacturing									
	Tooling									
	Quality									
	Test									
	Other									
	Total labor $									
Overhead dollars										
	Engineering									
	Manufacturing									
	Tooling									
	Quality									
	Test									
	Other									
	Total overhead $									
Materials and subcontract dollars										
Material overhead										
Travel										
Computer										
Other direct										
Subtotal estimated cost										
G&A expense										
Total estimated cost										

Figure 9.3 Sample cost data sheet for computation and consolidation.

year. (Other calendar subdivisions such as calendar year, quarter, month, or week are possible, of course.) Whether the estimate compilation and pricing is done by hand or by automatic data processing techniques, the general format is the same, with the time periods in vertical columns and the resource categories (labor-hours, labor-dollars, overhead dollars, subcontracts, materials, travel, and computer costs) in horizontal rows. The vertical time-oriented columns are summed in a total column at the right.

Labor-hours for each fiscal period and each major skill category (engineering, manufacturing, tooling, quality, test, and other) are summed to obtain total hours and then individually multiplied by their respective labor rates for the appropriate fiscal period. Overhead dollars are computed by multiplying the appropriate overhead factor for each fiscal period and skill category by the labor dollars for that skill category. The estimated cost for the work element is then subtotaled for each fiscal period by adding dollars for labor, overhead, major subcontract, other subcontract, material, material overhead, travel, computer, and other direct dollars. This subtotal is the basis for computation of general and administrative (G&A) expense, which is usually a percentage value. The G&A expense is added to the subtotal costs for the work element to obtain total estimated cost.

Cost data sheets for each work element are summed to the next higher level, using the work breakdown structure as a basis for the summing process. For example, work elements number 1.1.3.1, 1.1.3.2, 1.1.3.3, and 1.1.3.4 are summed to level 1.1.3. The 1.1.3 cost data sheet will be identical in format to subsidiary sheets but will reflect the summation of all elements below it. Then work elements number 1.1.1, 1.1.2, 1.1.3, and 1.1.4 are summed to level 1.1.

This process is repeated until all work elements have been summed into their next higher level according to the work breakdown structure. Once the top-level cost data sheet has been developed in this manner, the fee or profit is added to develop the total estimated cost for the entire work activity.

THE TIME-PHASED SUMMARY OF COST

In preparation for publication of an estimate or cost estimate report, it is important to summarize and display a time-phased summary of cost. Often the timing of expenditures is at least as important as the total costs of the work activity because budgets are usually prepared by fiscal or calendar periods, and expenditures are often considered and allocated one month, one quarter, or one year at a time. This incremental funding is particularly prevalent in federal, state, and local government procurement because government budgets are prepared and approved on a fiscal time period basis. Even in corporate and personal finances, the time phasing of expenditures is important. Estimated expenditures must be weighed against anticipated income to derive the all-important positive cash flow needed for continued business operation and stability. Therefore, an important output of the compiled and priced cost estimate is the bottom-line, time-oriented spread of costs. This fiscal period spread should be summarized and highlighted in the estimate report through a separate chart, table, or graph.

Another summarized cost display that is a useful output of a cost estimate is a depiction of costs for each work element in a matrix of all work elements. In scrutinizing a cost estimate for possible cost reductions and in identifying major cost drivers, it is desirable to have such a work breakdown structure cost summary. Within this type of summarized cost display, other breakouts of cost can be provided, such as summarized labor versus material and subcontract costs, to depict the make-or-buy relationship.

SPECIAL LABOR HOURS AND MATERIAL SUMMARIES

Since estimated labor-hours and material dollars are available to the lowest level in the work breakdown structure, special summary presentations of labor-hours for each skill category and summaries of materials and subcontract costs can be displayed in the estimate report. Some examples of these types of displays are shown in **Figure 9.4**.

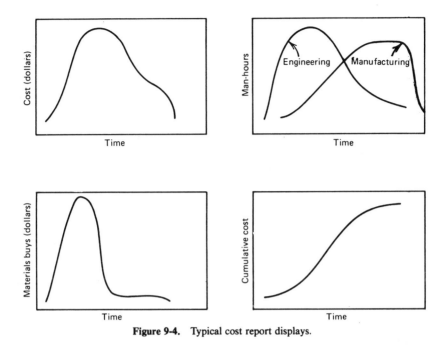

Figure 9-4.   Typical cost report displays.

ORGANIZING THE ESTIMATE ELEMENTS

Completeness

Essential work activities or cost elements must not be omitted from a cost estimate. One of the reasons a rigorous method is used in estimating costs is to assure the estimator and the company management that the estimate is complete, supportable, and credible. A report will not be credible if any areas are overlooked or inadvertently omitted. The purpose of organizing, correlating, and cross-checking all data is to be sure that the estimate is complete. If the estimate is being prepared as a competitive bid for a cost-reimbursable contract, particular attention must be paid to estimate completeness because proposals are usually judged on the proposer's understanding of the requirement and the resources required to accomplish the job. A low bid is of no avail if the proposer is going to be downgraded in the evaluation because of lack of understanding of the requirements and its attendant resources. Omission of an area of cost or failure to address all cost-producing activities, intentional or not, indicates to the evaluation committee a lack of understanding of the requirement.

In fixed-price contracts the consequences of inadvertent omission of a cost element or work activity have less impact on selection to do the job but a sizable impact on the company's ability to perform the work within the bid price.

Most firms have standard proposal sections that include explanations, descriptions, and formats needed to complete any estimate. The estimator combines these standard sections, known as "boilerplate," with the particular cost data to make the complete estimate. U.S. government agencies and some major firms also use boilerplate requests for proposals, changing information about the items or services and schedules to meet specific procurement needs.

Rationale and Backup Data

The recording, preservation, and possible presentation of backup data that support the cost estimate is important to the company in the evaluation, selection, and negotiation process for the initial contract and any changes to it. Retention and traceability of estimate rationale and backup data provide a clear picture of what was actually included in the initial bid and enhance the identification and separate pricing of any new requirements that become apparent during the contract negotiation phase or the performance of the work activity. Retention, traceability, and updating of backup data to reflect actual cost performance are also important to the company in making the next bid or proposal on a similar or identical project. Each cost estimate a company has previously made can be considered a source of information concerning the resources required to perform similar tasks since the labor-hours and material quantities are dimensionless relative to cost and can be applied to other projects on a different time scale provided the same equipment, facilities, and work force are assumed.

Cross-Referencing of Cost Information

Most requests for proposals require the display of cost information in a variety of formats. With a detailed industrial engineering, labor-hour, and material cost estimate sufficient detail is available for almost any required compilation of costs. Care must be taken to cross-reference and cross-check this cost information to prevent inconsistencies and differences in cost information from being displayed in the final estimate report. Small mathematical errors and inconsistencies must be held to a minimum to protect the estimate's credibility.

COMPUTING THE ESTIMATE

The major advantages of computerized systems include standardization of input/output formats, increased responsiveness to staffing and rate fluctuations during the estimating process, compatibility with numerical outputs with desktop publishing systems, consistency of format, and a substantial reduction in staffing and time requirements of the cost estimating process. (This topic is discussed in detail in Chapter 12.) Clerical work is virtually eliminated. Some clients even require the cost estimates to be submitted in disk form for use in automated evaluation and comparison systems.

The total cost estimate report is the principal output of the system (**Figure 9.5**). The report is generated in descending order of the work breakdown structure with

DATE 18 JUL
TITLE X PROJECT
X PROJECT
WBS 1.4

ELEMENTS OF COST		FY - 81	FY - 82	FY - 83	FY - 84	FY - 85	FY -	FY -	FY -	TOTAL
ENGR.	HOURS	394,244	718,037	712,561	427,262	160,498				2,412,602
	LABOR/OH $	11,752,914	21,404,683	21,241,443	12,736,680	4,784,445				71,919,665
MFG	HOURS	20,238	124,483	173,284	89,754	5,042				412,801
	LABOR/OH $	455,962	2,804,602	3,904,089	2,022,158	113,596				9,300,407
TOOLING	HOURS	2,030	48,424	28,357	1,176	1,176				81,163
	LABOR/OH $	43,401	1,035,305	606,273	25,143	25,143				1,735,265
Q * RA	HOURS	88,281	136,154	183,567	144,863	12,574				565,239
	LABOR/OH $	2,368,579	3,653,012	4,925,103	3,881,308	337,360				15,165,362
TEST	HOURS	38,082	127,011	199,028	186,517	80,428				631,066
	LABOR/OH $	998,891	3,331,499	5,220,504	4,892,341	2,109,626				16,552,861
OTHER	HOURS	37,853	63,100	59,412	41,296	64,643				266,304
	LABOR/OH $	1,362,708	2,271,600	2,138,832	1,486,656	2,327,148				9,586,944
TOT LBR	HOURS	580,728	1,217,209	1,356,209	890,668	324,361				4,369,175
	LABOR/OH $	16,981,955	34,500,701	38,036,244	25,044,286	9,697,318				124,260,504
MATERIAL * SUBCON.		10,951,151	28,288,665	34,307,090	5,657,036	2,945,050				82,148,992
MATERIAL OVERHEAD		547,558	1,414,433	1,715,355	282,852	147,253				4,107,451
TRAVEL		17,003	32,312	37,447	30,722	18,159				135,643
OTHER		792,441	1,104,343	1,163,022	1,079,022	568,136				4,706,964
SUBTOTAL EST. COST		29,290,108	65,340,454	75,259,158	32,093,918	13,375,916				215,359,554
G * A EXPENSE		3,514,813	7,840,854	9,031,099	3,851,270	1,605,110				25,843,146
TOTAL EST. COST		32,804,921	73,181,308	84,290,257	35,945,188	14,981,026				241,202,700

Figure 9.5 Computerized cost estimate report.

one page per work breakdown structure level. Each page contains the work element code number, the work element name, and the project name. The fiscal years and cost element totals are arranged in columns, and the cost element labor-hours and labor-overhead dollars are arranged in rows. Subtotal rows for the columns are created, to which is added the G&A expense to result in total estimated costs for each fiscal year. The contractor fee is added to the total estimated cost per fiscal year, giving grand totals per fiscal year.

PUBLISHING THE ESTIMATE

Because cost estimates are usually rather sensitive in nature, large numbers of published copies are unnecessary. It is important, however, that the copies of an estimate document that are reproduced be complete and comprehensive, fully identifying the work activity and its estimated resources. The cost estimate report must contain certain information in addition to cost data:

1. A brief description of the process, product, project, or service that is being estimated.
2. A development or delivery time schedule.
3. A list of ground rules and assumptions that were used in making the cost estimate. This information includes make-or-buy assumptions, work location(s), facilities availability and use, and other programmatic data.
4. A listing of the names and telephone numbers of key individuals who made inputs to the cost estimate and in what discipline areas (optional).
5. Supporting rationale for each of the detailed estimates comprising the overall estimate.

The estimate report should also include the following cost data:

1. Total estimated cost, including fee or profit.
2. Costs for each estimate fiscal period.
3. Costs for each work element.
4. A listing of labor rates, factors, overhead rates, G&A rates, and escalation or inflation rates used in the estimate.
5. Detailed breakouts of cost as appropriate to illustrate the detail available and to allow a more thorough cost evaluation.

The cost estimate report should be published in a handy, easy-to-read format. Cost data in these reports have a tendency to become cumbersome and unwieldy because large double and triple foldouts or extra-large bound volumes are often used to present the data. Computer sheets are sometimes reduced to 50 percent or less of their original size, causing the text to be too small or difficult to read because of poor contrast. The best policy is to use standard size type in an 8½ inch × 11 inch vertical or horizontal page or a single 11 inch × 17 inch foldout. The cost report will be enlivened through the use of figures, graphs, plots, and varying type sizes and treatments. Index tabs on each major subdivision of the work breakdown structure are helpful for quick reference to a desired section. The final, published cost estimate should look something like the volume shown in **Figure 9.6**.

USING THE ESTIMATE

Proposing or Bidding

Cost estimates are most commonly used for proposing or bidding on a job. There may or may not be relationship between the cost estimate and the bid price. A large

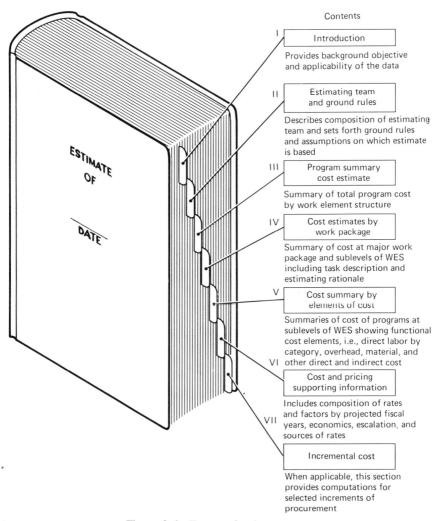

Contents

I   Introduction

Provides background objective and applicability of the data

II   Estimating team and ground rules

Describes composition of estimating team and sets forth ground rules and assumptions on which estimate is based

III   Program summary cost estimate

Summary of total program cost by work element structure

IV   Cost estimates by work package

Summary of cost at major work package and sublevels of WES including task description and estimating rationale

V   Cost summary by elements of cost

Summaries of cost of programs at sublevels of WES showing functional cost elements, i.e., direct labor by category, overhead, material, and VI   other direct and indirect cost

Cost and pricing supporting information

Includes composition of rates and factors by projected fiscal VII   years, economics, escalation, and sources of rates

Incremental cost

When applicable, this section provides computations for selected increments of procurement

Figure 9.6 Format of estimate report.

portion of the cost estimate may never be exposed to the recipient of a bid because the secret to a competitive posture may thereby be revealed. In a cost-reimbursable contract, however, the agency charged with reviewing the bids and managing the contract will take full advantage of any detail presented by the bidder. In these instances the bidder will find that it will be advantageous to be open with the cost estimates and the estimate rationale. To be competitive in the environment of negotiated versus advertised procurements, innovation and cost efficiency are infinitely more successful than obscure pricing and estimating techniques and methods.

Source Evaluation and Selection

Increasingly, independent cost estimates are being used by procuring agencies or companies as a check on vendor- or supplier-submitted bids and proposals. An independent cost estimate, performed by the individual or organization that is procuring a work activity or output, is valuable in ferreting out unrealistically high or low bids. Government agencies use independent government estimates as yardsticks in comparing two or more bidders' proposals. The independent estimate is compared at the lowest work element level to identify areas where the proposer may have over- or underestimated or where an important resource requirement may have been overlooked. If one goes by the philosophy that it is better to pay a little higher price and be sure that the work will get done, elimination of bidders with excessively low estimates may be appropriate. Too often a low bid has been accepted, and the result has been work stoppage because the contractor's cash flow is inadequate or his or her business fails. Independent cost estimates, used to verify vendor bids, can help reduce this possibility.

Cost Control and Work Management

A baseline cost estimate is a valuable tool for cost control and work management. It is a means of checking the performance of the organization and the accuracy of the estimate. It is also a device that can be used for the detailed evaluation of changes to the work activity.

Budgeting

Many organizations use detailed cost estimates successfully as a budgeting tool. Estimates prepared independently without competitive bias tend to be higher in dollar value than those prepared for bid purposes. Higher estimates are desirable when budget figures must be upheld and supported by program advocates and are more likely to include sufficient allowance for cost growth. The estimating process should begin, in fact, with the budgeting process and continue through to project completion. It is the early budget estimates, however, that determine the sufficiency or insufficiency of funds; therefore, careful consideration must be given to independent estimates to support the budgeting process.

QUESTIONS

9.1. Name five purposes or functions of a cost estimate review.

9.2. Name two reasons for changing a cost estimate after it has been developed and passed the review phase.

9.3. Which of the following is the most appropriate method of adjusting an estimate:

    a. Impose a uniform or fixed percentage across-the-board cost estimate reduction for all work elements or all organizational elements?

    b. Impose a budget reduction proportional to the importance of each work element or organizational element?

    c. A team method wherein each organization reviews possible cuts, and reduces costs only commensurate with reductions or changes in specifications, quantities, schedules, and work content?

    d. Reducing the number of personnel assigned to organizations performing the work?

9.4. Name two ways of reducing work activity costs without reducing quantity, quality, or changing the overall project schedule.

9.5. Name five factors that affect worker, employee, or machine productivity.

9.6. Name six types of information that should be contained in a published estimate.

10

LIFE CYCLE COSTING, DESIGN TO COST, AND VALUE ENGINEERING

And they took the thirty pieces of silver, the price of him that was valued.

Matthew 27:9

At the beginning of the twentieth century there was a perception by most businesses, individual consumers, and even some agencies in the small but rapidly growing federal government that resources were plentiful, if not virtually unlimited. The initial cost of major projects was the primary concern at the time; consequently not enough attention was given to the care and feeding of the expanding physical and material assets that were being produced from seemingly inexhaustible natural resources. The full life cycle cost of assets was not foremost in the minds of those who were acquiring new goods, services, products, projects, and systems.

As our knowledge of economics has grown, as labor costs have increased, and as natural resources have begun to appear to have an ultimate limitation, the perception has begun to change from affordability of initial costs to affordability of ownership. As we proceed through the final decade of the twentieth century and into the twenty-first century, cost of ownership will take on even greater importance in economic decisions. The recurring costs for such elements as taxes, insurance, interest, utilities, and labor costs for upgrading, maintaining, repairing, and servicing of the asset to be procured are beginning to make up a large part of the life cycle cost of products acquired by industry, the government, and individuals. The cost of ownership over the asset's lifetime often exceeds the initial acquisition cost. If this cost of ownership is not compensated by a constant or increasing income potential brought about by possession of the asset, higher-initial-cost, low-maintenance-cost alternatives must be considered.

For cost estimators, cost analysts, and economic analysts, the next 100 years will be very different from the largest part of the fading twentieth century because analytically based decisions will be more frequently based on total life cycle cost of ownership rather than initial acquisition cost. The cost of services, which are labor

192

cost driven, will continue to rise just as the service industries have expanded dramatically. A large part of these services are provided to service assets. Therefore, the cost analyst is confronted with new variables of increasing importance in the life cycle cost equation. This chapter addresses some examples of the analysis of life cycle costs, introduces the expanding discipline of design to cost, and reviews the concept and practice of value engineering as it affects the cost estimator and cost analyst.

Researchers have found that much of the life cycle cost potential in large government projects is created in the early years of a program. Conversely cost reduction opportunities are high early in the program and reduce rapidly in its early years. This relationship is shown in **Figure 10.1**, which shows that 70 percent of the life cycle costs are committed in the first year, 85 percent in the second year, and 95 percent in the third year. These commitments are not financial commitments at that time but crucial programmatic and technical decisions that ultimately effect the total life cycle costs. Figure 10.1 emphasizes the need for early detailed analysis and understanding of the effects of early program decisions on life cycle costs.

According to the U.S. comptroller general life cycle costing is a technique for evaluating the total cost of a product over its useful life. Instead of evaluating competing items on initial costs only, life cycle costing considers initial acquisition cost, maintenance, and support costs, and useful life or other measure of utility.[1] The following elements are usually included in life cycle costs:

Initial acquisition costs
Replacement costs
Maintenance costs
Operation costs

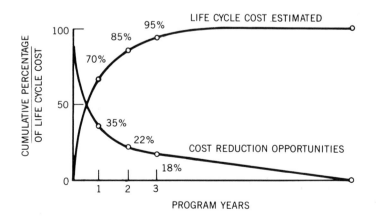

Figure 10.1   Life cycle cost commitment and cost reduction opportunities versus time.

Energy costs

Sales taxes

Property taxes

Income taxes (federal, state, and local)

Insurance costs

Loans and interest costs

Income produced

Salvage value

Disposal costs

Of these elements, only two have the potential for being positive or representing a cash value to the owner: the income produced and the salvage or depreciated value. The rest of the elements are negative or represent expenditures by the owner.

The job of comparing the life cycle costs of projects is made complex by the simple and important but sometimes confusing fact that money changes value with time. The time value of money can be computed with the six equations shown in **Table 10.1**. Equations 1 and 3 are the most commonly used. Equation 1 gives the present worth of a future sum of money, whether it is an income or an expenditure. The net present worth (NPW; see Chapter 8) is the sum of the present worth of all incomes and expenditures for a given venture.

TABLE 10.1   Equations Used in Comparison of Alternatives

Equation

(1)	Present	Single payment present worth factor	$P = F \left[\dfrac{1}{(1 + i)^n} \right]$
(2)	worth		
	comparison	Equal payment series present worth factor	$P = A \left[\dfrac{(1 + i)^n - 1}{i(1 + i)^n} \right]$
(3)	Future	Single payment compound amount factor	$F = P (1 + i)^n$
(4)	worth	Equal payment series compound amount	
	comparison	factor	$F = A \left[\dfrac{(1 - i)^n - 1}{i} \right]$
(5)	Equal	Equal payment series sinking fund factor	$A = F \left[\dfrac{i}{(1 - i)^n - 1} \right]$
(6)	annual		
	payment	Equal payment series capital recovery factor	$A = P \left[\dfrac{i(1 + i)^n}{(1 + i)^i - 1} \right]$
	comparison		

Note: i = annual interest rate, discount rate, or inflation rate; n = number of annual interest periods; P = a present principal sum; A = a single payment in a series of n equal payments, made at the end of each annual interest period; and f = a future sum, n annual interest periods hence; equal to the compound amount of a present principal sum P or equal to the sum of the compound amounts of payments, A in a series.

Dollars expressed in cash flows that are all calculated at a predetermined level of inflation (usually known as a base year) are "constant dollars." The term "current dollars" is used when recording and reporting predicted or historical costs as anticipated or measured at the time. They are escalated at the inflation rate for each year. "Discounted dollars" are nonbudgetary values that are the result of discounting constant dollars cash flows by a discount rate. These dollars are intended to express the future value of constant dollars.

The effects of the time value of money can best be seen by a simple example that uses the sum of $1000 to illustrate various investment strategies. If one invests $1000 in a five-year venture that yields 12 percent per year income I, the future sum F, by use of equation 3 (ignoring inflation), is

$$F = \$1000(1 + 0.12)^5 = \$1762.34.$$

Therefore the venture yields a "profit" of $762.34 after a five-year period. If instead one were instead, merely to hold on to the $1000 for five years, it would still be worth only $1000 after the five-year period. The consequences of failing to invest the money at a 12 percent rate of return or interest rate would effectively be the "loss" of $762.34 over the five-year period. This 12 percent loss due to failure to invest at this return rate is called the "discount rate." Conversely, if there is a prevailing inflation rate of 12 percent per year, the purchasing power of the $1000 will decrease during the five-year period. The future purchasing power can be computed by the same equation used to compute present worth (equation 1):

$$P = 1000 \times \frac{1}{(1.12)^5} = \$567.42.$$

Therefore the strategy of holding on to the money in this instance cost the investor $1000 minus $567.42, or $432.58. By the same reasoning, an investor in a venture with a 12 percent rate of return in an inflationary environment of 12 percent per year will have $1762.34 at the end of five years, but it will be worth only $1000 in today's dollars. That is, the purchasing power of that investment has not changed throughout the five-year period.

If a person were to borrow $1000 at a 12 percent interest rate, at the end of five years he or she would owe the lender $1762.34 (using equation 3). Ignoring inflation, a borrower who reinvested in a venture that yields 12 percent per year would be able to pay off the loan exactly at the end of the five-year period. Obviously, the borrower's goal would be to invest in a venture with a higher rate of return. With the effects of inflation included, the borrower must allow for a return on the investment of nearly 30 percent to do more than break even. The life cycle costs of an acquisition or venture can be computed in present-year dollars (that is, ignoring the effects of inflation) or in real-year dollars (including the effects of inflation).

EXAMPLES OF LIFE CYCLE COST APPLICATIONS

Energy-Consuming Consumer Products

The rising and life cycle costs of electricity, natural gas, and fuel oil made the area of energy-consuming products (such as central heating systems, water heating systems, ranges and ovens, dryers, central air conditioners, room air-conditioners, refrigerators, freezers, and their industrial counterparts) the subject of an in-depth study by the U.S. Department of Energy (DOE) and the industries that supply these products. Recall that the life cycle cost of a consumer product is equal to the first cost or purchase price plus the "discounted" operating and maintenance costs over the lifetime of the product. The first cost may be paid when the product is purchased, or the purchaser may borrow money that is paid back with interest after the purchase is made. For the purpose of this example, the assumption is made that the buyer makes a cash purchase of the product.

The life cycle cost of a consumer product is given by the equation shown in **Table 10.2**. The equation, shown with other economic and marketing criteria, were used by the DOE to determine the economic impact of government-required efficiency improvements in home appliances on consumers, manufacturers, utility

TABLE 10.2   Consumer Product Life Cycle Analysis

$$LCC = P + \sum_{i=1}^{n} \left[(H)_i \times (EC)_i \times \frac{(1 + f)^i}{(1 + r)^i} \right]$$

where P = initial cost of product, in dollars
$(H)_i$ = energy consumption in year i, in millions of British thermal units
$(EC)_i$ = energy costs (fuel price) in year i, in dollars per million British thermal units
n = product lifetime, in years
f = annual fuel escalation rate, in constant dollars
r = discount rate

If a present worth factor (PWF) is defined as follows:

$$PWF = \sum_{i=1}^{n} \left(\frac{1 + f}{1 + r} \right) i$$

then the equation for life cycle cost can be simplifed as follows:

$$LCC = P + [H \times EC \times PWF].$$

companies, and the nation's economy as a whole. Using projected fuel prices, assumed fuel escalation rates, average equipment lifetimes, market coverage percentages, and manufacturers' estimates of cost increases brought about by the increased efficiency requirements, the DOE developed a comprehensive assessment of the economic and energy consumption impact of the efficiency standards.

Congressional legislation requiring increased attention to energy efficiency standards emphasized the need for application of life cycle costing techniques by home owners and businesses alike. A typical finding, for refrigerators and freezers, for example, was that the cost of improving the efficiency of energy-consuming products of this type was more than offset by the savings in energy costs, even if one used relatively conservative (low) assumptions concerning energy costs and escalation rates. A DOE report showed that for classes of refrigerators and freezers that account for 95 percent of sales, the most efficient model will have the lowest life cycle costs. The analysis also showed that the longest payback time for the investment in energy conservation was 10 months. Life cycle cost analyses for clothes dryers, water heaters, ranges and ovens, central air conditioners, and furnaces all show that a life cycle cost improvement can be realized by the consumer through an investment in improvement in their efficiencies.

Industrial Equipment and Machinery

Evaluation of the life cycle cost of industrial equipment and machinery is performed in a manner similar to that shown in the previous consumer product examples, but tax benefits and productivity values are additional economic factors to be considered. An investment tax credit in which a percentage of the total cost of the acquisition is deducted from the company's income tax in the year of purchase is allowed by the federal government for most new acquisitions. Depending on the company's financial and profit situation, the investment tax credit can be of significant benefit in reducing the company's overall taxes. This is one of the life cycle cost benefits of purchasing and owning a piece of equipment.

Newer, more modern, more efficient, updated equipment may also significantly improve productivity. If a new machine produces more than the old one or saves materials or labor, these benefits should be included in the life cycle cost analysis when comparing the new machine with the old machine or in comparing two alternate new acquisitions.

Since most businesspeople think in terms of return on investment, one of the most useful ways of comparing the life cycle cost benefits of an acquisition is to compute the rate of return brought about by it. The computation usually requires the development of a cash flow stream that represents the expenditures and income for each year and a trial and error solution using equations 1 and 2 from Table 10.1. To solve for rate of return, various values of rate of return are assumed, and the resulting NPW value is either plotted on a graph or iterated in numerical form until an interest rate value of the rate of return is found for which the NPW is zero. This interest rate is the rate of return on the investment. This is a handy way to compare equipment and machinery investments with other financial investments because most businesspeople have a return value in mind that they do not want to undershoot when making an investment.

Solar Heating

One of the most complex problems in life cycle costing is computing the life cycle cost savings brought about by the installing solar heating in a residential or commercial structure. This is a complex problem because of the number of variables that must be introduced into the analysis to obtain realistic and credible results. The amount of solar heat that can be used in a building or commercial industrial process depends on the amount of solar energy available each day at the location being analyzed, the weather at that location, the type of solar heating system used and its efficiency, and the heating demand cycle. The savings brought about by the use of solar energy for heating depend on the cost of the solar energy system and the assumed amount and cost of the conventional energy that it is replacing.

A number of computer programs are available to determine the savings made possible by the use of solar energy. Many are published by the government and are available through government assistance programs. One such computer program, termed SHCOST, is briefly described here to illustrate how life cycle costing techniques can be applied to complex problems through the use of computers.

There are some important economic considerations involved in "sizing" a solar heating system, that is, selecting a collector area and determining the resultant percentage of the total annual load carried by the system. A solar installation has both fixed costs—pumps, controls, and ductwork—and variable costs—mainly due to collector area. As the collector area increases, the solar system carries a greater percentage of the load. The characteristic curve of solar system life cycle cost versus collector area is shown in **Figure 10.2**. In low collector areas, not much

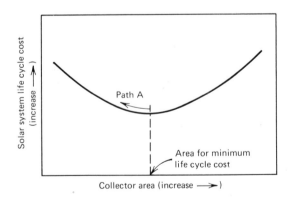

Figure 10.2 Characteristic curves of life cycle cost versus collector area.

sunlight is captured, so little heating value is achieved. A relatively large amount of money has been spent to perform the heating equivalent of a small amount of conventional fuel. At high collector areas, a similar uneconomical phenomenon occurs: Adding collector area, when it is already relatively high, provides a small increase in the percentage of total load carried by the solar system. Hence the added collector area and cost reduce the conventional fuel bill only slightly. There is a collector area on the curve in Figure 10.2 that minimizes life cycle cost; however, this may not be the size of solar system most attractive to the consumer from an economic standpoint. The characteristic curve is relatively flat near the area of minimum life cycle cost. Although reducing collector area has an almost linear effect on reducing system initial cost, a penalty i. paid in terms of increased life cycle cost along path A when collector area is reduced. The important point is that savings in initial cost may be relatively large and attractive to the home owner or businessperson in comparison to the life cycle cost penalty. The sensitivity study and plot features of the computer program allow these alternatives to be studied.

In addition to the plot capability and the computation of life cycle cost savings, the computer program will display the following three measures of cash flow benefits for solar heating systems:

1. *Years to positive cash flow:* The number of years for fuel cost savings to become greater than the extra expenses of the solar system, after taxes.
2. *Years to recover down payment:* The number of years required for accumulated savings to offset initial cash payments and early cash flow losses, after taxes.
3. *Payback period:* The number of years required for accumulated savings to pay for the full cost of the system (or equal the remaining principal on a loan if financed).

Table 10.3 shows the cost elements used in computing solar heating life cycle cost savings. Solar and weather data are provided in SHCOST for 151 cities in the United States. To solve for the life cycle cost savings or to perform a life cycle cost analysis for a specific building in a specific city, a SHCOST user must estimate values for the first four elements listed: acquisition cost, building modification costs, net replacement and repair cost, and maintenance costs (Methods for estimating these costs are discussed in Chapters 2 through 9.) For commercial ventures involving solar energy, added income, if any, expected to be realized through the use of the solar energy system must also be estimated. The remaining cost elements are economic factors that depend on the location of the solar energy application and the method of financing the installation. The SHCOST user then selects one of the 151 cities that is geographically (and economically) nearest the city being investigated.

Selecting values of certain key cost parameters, such as future conventional fuel escalation rates, requires subjective judgment. The program is designed to study a range of values of certain parameters in one run or execution of the program. The

TABLE 10.3 Cost Elements Used in Solar Heating Life Cycle Cost Analysis

Cost Element	Description	Life Cycle Costing Calculation
Acquisition cost	Initial costs incurred by purchase, delivery, installation, and integration	Treated as initial, one-time cost and is not discounted or inflated; a down payment factor may be applied
Building modifications costs	Costs due to structural modifications required for the system	Treated as initial, one-time cost and is not discounted or inflated
Net replacement and repair cost	Yearly cost of replacements and repair to the system	Cost input in year incurred, then inflated and discounted
Maintenance cost	Estimated annual cost for maintenance of the total system	Initial value input for first year, then inflated and discounted
Conventional fuel cost	Annual conventional fuel and energy costs required for system operation	Annual cost for first year input, then inflated by energy escalation factor and discounted
Property taxes	Property taxes paid due to assessed value of the equipment	Same method as for maintenance
Property tax credits	Deductions from income tax due to property taxes paid	Income tax rate times taxes paid
Maintenance expense credits	Reduces commercial taxable income	Income tax rate times expenses
Depreciation credit	Commercial deduction from taxes	Straight line method, no inflation
Added income	Increased rental of solar compared to conventional property due to lower utilities	Income is taxed and discounted
Insurance cost	Cost of insurance on the system	Net annual cost input and discounted, not inflated
Salvage value	Expected value at end of life	Discounted
Loan payments	Annual loan payments on borrowed funds	Loan is amortized and yearly payment computed; yearly interest computed; payment is discounted
Loan interest credits	Tax deduction due to interest paid	Interest from loan computed and discounted
Conventional fuel cost credit	Commercial tax deduction	Annual cost for first year input, then inflated by energy escalation factor

parameters that can be varied are collector area, discount rate, inflation rate, down payment factor, property tax rate, and income tax rate. The program produces graphs of life cycle cost as a function of any of these parameters.

The life cycle cost calculation is formulated for computer solution in the classic work breakdown structure (WBS) format. In this application of the WBS concept, each cost element is a block in the WBS where costs are accumulated from subelements at a lower level and are summed to cost elements at a higher level. A three-level WBS is illustrated in **Figure 10.3**. The highest level block, solar system life cycle cost, is a level 1 block and contains the total life cycle costs of the solar system. There are seven level 2 blocks illustrated from "acquisition" to "loan interest credits." Note that the level 2 block titles are cost elements from Table 10.3. Level 3 is illustrated by showing that "acquisition" has been subdivided into various hardware components (collector, fluid transport, etc.), integration, and installation.

The first step in formulating a user problem is to select from the cost elements for the solar and conventional energy system to be analyzed from Table 10.3. A comparison of life cycle costs for two competing systems needs to consider only cost elements that may be different for the two systems. For example, if no significant difference in property tax is expected between the solar and conventional system, then it is not necessary to include that cost element in the analysis of either system.

The next step is to construct a WBS. The key decisions that the user makes for each WBS block are its proper level, title, WBS number, and block number.

The following additional cost data and problem parameters are required to run SHCOST:

Collector cost	Number of years in the life cycle cost analysis
Discount rate	Starting year
Inflation rate	Collector area
Down payment rate	Liquid or air system
Income tax rate	Commercial or residential application
Total building load	

A SHCOST analysis of a potential residential solar heating system installed in Birmingham, Alabama, with the problem input parameters shown in **Table 10.4** indicates an expected life cycle cost savings of $2915.18, a positive yearly savings in five years, and payoff of the system in nine years. The work breakdown structure used is shown in **Figure 10.4**.

Had the analysis been done for a commercial application, other input parameters, such as maintenance expense credits, depreciation tax credits, added income, and conventional fuel cost credits, would have come into play. The result would be an increased life cycle cost savings from that shown for a residential application.

LIFE CYCLE COSTING AS USED IN LARGE HIGH-TECHNOLOGY PROJECTS

There is considerable emphasis in the federal government, specifically the Department of Defense, on the analysis and exposure of a project's life cycle costs prior to

Figure 10.3 Work breakdown structure for a typical solar system life cycle cost analysis.

202

TABLE 10.4. Sample Input Data for Life Cycle Cost Analysis of a Solar-Heated Home in Birmingham, Alabama

Initial cost of system	$10,000	Collector cost in dollars	$165.70
Down payment	10 percent	Discount rate	10 percent
Mortgage rate	9 percent	Down payment rate	10 percent
Maintenance (percent of initial cost)	1 percent/yr.	Property tax rate	2 percent of initial cost
General inflation rate	6 percent	Income tax rate	30 percent
Fuel inflation rate	10 percent	Number of years in the life cycle cost analysis	20 yr.
Initial fuel cost	10 $/MBtu	Starting year	1992
Load demand	100 MBtu/yr.	Collector area	48.28
Percentage solar	70 percent	Liquid or air system	Liquid
System and mortgage lifetime	20 yr.	Total building load	100 MBtu/yr.[a]
Salvage value	0	Commercial or residential application: Residential	

[a]Millions of Btus per year.

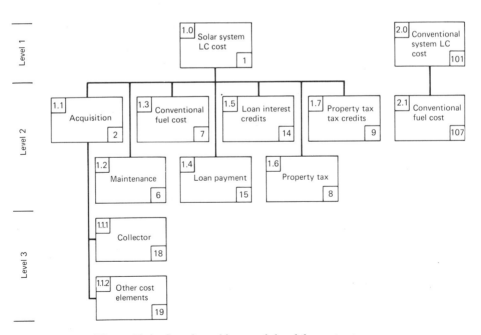

Figure 10.4 Sample problem work breakdown structure.

project approval.[3] This is particularly true in the acquisition of weapon systems for the Department of Defense because these systems must often serve a long lifetime in a peacetime environment. Maintenance, operation, storage, repair, and upkeep of many weapon systems exceed their initial acquisition costs. Further, the U.S. Congress, in its oversight function, is continuing to demand more cost estimating and analysis of total system lifetime cost prior to proceeding with a new project or continuing a current project. The impacts of the study performed by the Packard Blue Ribbon Commission on Defense Management in 1986 and other more recent similar studies are still being felt in the Congress and the executive branch. These studies emphasized the need for estimating the total run-out costs of a project prior to congressional approval and funding the project in multiyear increments.

A circular issued by the Office of Management and Budget[2] states that

each agency acquiring major systems should . . . maintain a capability to

- Predict, review, assess, negotiate, and monitor costs for system development, engineering, design, demonstration, test, production, operation, and support (i.e., life cycle costs).
- Assess acquisition cost, schedule and performance experience against predictions, and provide such assessments for consideration by the agency head at key decision points.
- Make new assessments where significant costs, schedule or performance variances occur.
- Estimate life cycle costs during system design concept evaluation and selection, full-scale development, facility conversion, and production, to ensure appropriate trade-offs among investment costs, ownership costs, schedules, and performance.
- Use independent cost estimates, where feasible, for comparison purposes.

. . . Life cycle cost means the sum total of the direct, indirect, recurring, nonrecurring, and other related costs incurred, or estimated to be incurred, in the design, development, production, operation, maintenance, and support of a major system over its anticipated useful life span.[2]

The reason that thorough consideration must be given to the life cycle cost of major weapon systems is illustrated in **Figure 10.5**. Only 15 percent of the total life cycle cost of typical defense systems is incurred in the validation and development phases, while 85 percent is in the production, operation, and support phases. Historically 50 percent of the total life cycle cost is spent in the operation and support phase.

DESIGN TO COST AND VALUE ENGINEERING

The practice of designing a system to a cost target is closely related to the profession or discipline of value engineering. Design to cost usually involves the design and

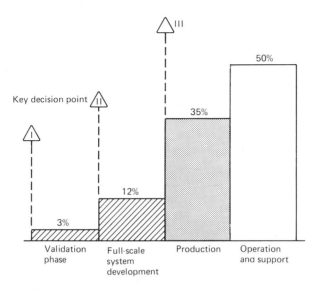

Figure 10.5 Typical defense system cost breakout.

development of an item to meet a cost target or cost range; value engineering is the practice of determining lowest possible cost for a specified process, product, project, or service to reliably accomplish the intended function.

Design to cost, which is an iterative process, can take on various complexions depending on the cost realm addressed. One form of design to cost is design to life cycle cost; here a cost target or range is established for the life cycle cost. Another form of design-to-cost is design to unit production cost; here the target or range of costs is applied to unit production cost.

The first step in the design-to-cost process is to estimate the cost of a system by use of conventional cost estimating techniques. To do this, "point" designs (specific design configurations that will satisfy the performance requirements) are required. The optimum design-to-cost effort includes at least three point designs: (1) a point design representing the *low* end of the performance requirements scale, (2) a point design representing the *middle* of the performance requirements scale, and (3) a point design representing the *high* end of the performance requirements scale. If the cost estimate does not meet the middle design target, the specifications of the work output or activity are changed to increase or decrease the cost to bring the cost estimate in line with the target. If the new estimate is too high or low, the specifications are changed again. This process is repeated until a work output is defined whose cost will equal the cost target or fall within the desired cost range, and a new composite or compromised design is derived to meet the final required target cost.

The goal of the design-to-cost effort is to ensure that the buyer can afford to acquire and own the equipment that is developed. The salient feature of the design-to-cost effort is that the traditional roles of cost and performance are reversed. In this cost-constrained concept, unit production cost or life cycle cost is fixed at an affordable level prior to initiating development. During the design and development, competing contractors seek to demonstrate the best performance possible for this cost. The concept should reduce those unnecessary and unproductive specifications that increase cost without increasing the equipment's operational utility or functional value. To this end, contractors will have full latitude to consider all factors involved in defining performance specifications. Trade-off parameters to be considered will include documentation, special test equipment, installation techniques, maintenance plans, and required training. An advantage of designing to unit production cost rather than to life cycle costs is that reliability and availability requirements will not be reduced but will receive greater attention.

In a design-to-cost exercise, there must be a keen knowledge and awareness of the cost consequences of changing the design or specifications of the work output. This knowledge and awareness must permeate the project organization. For this reason, it is often desirable to locate cost estimators and analysts near or with the design team. This team must have a continuing opportunity for making trades of cost versus performance, must continually reexamine the definition of "acceptable" performance, and must exist in an environment where there is freedom to make decisions. Parochial interests must be eliminated for an effective design-to-cost activity. Minimum formality and maximum flexibility, responsiveness, and team spirit are required to make design-to-cost successful.[3]

Value engineering, on the other hand, is an organized effort directed at (1) identifying the functions of a system, equipment, facilities, procedures, and supplies; (2) establishing a value for those functions; and (3) achieving those functions at the lowest overall cost. It identifies areas of excessive or unnecessary costs and attempts to improve the value of the product. It provides the same or better performance at a lower cost while reducing neither necessary quality, reliability, nor maintainability. Value engineering is a management tool used in conjunction with other management devices, not an isolated technique. It is most effective when applied during the development phase but also useful in the procurement, production, maintenance, modification, and storage phases of a work activity.

A value engineering program is an *organized* set of tasks that support or apply the value engineering discipline to all major elements of a work activity. The word "organized" is significant. Planning, scheduling, measurement, and other control procedures must be applied to ensure an effective value engineering program. The work elements must be stated (and understood) in sufficient detail to be logical entities that can be assigned, labor loaded, costed, and assessed.

In value engineering, the term "value" is used in many different ways and has many different meanings. It is frequently confused with the monetary price or cost of an item. Value to the manufacturer or procurement activity has a meaning different from that of value to the user. Even the user may have different concepts of value, depending on the time, place, and availability of substitute items.

Value is the relationship between the worth or utility of an item (expressed in monetary terms) and its actual monetary cost. The highest value is represented by an item with the essential quality available at the lowest possible overall cost that will reliably perform the required function or service at the desired time and place.

Another way, perhaps more meaningful, to define value is to break it down into four categories:

1. *Cost value:* The summation of the labor, material, overhead, and all other elements of cost required to produce an item or provide a service.
2. *Use value:* The properties and qualities that accomplish a use, work, or service. The use value is equal to the value of the functions performed.
3. *Esteem value:* The properties, features, or attractiveness that create a desire to possess the article but are not necessarily required for functional performance.
4. *Exchange value:* The properties or qualities that will remain attractive enough to permit market resale in the future.

The methodology used for value engineering does not differ significantly from the various methods of cost estimating and cost analysis discussed earlier in this book. The main goal of value engineering is to determine the most cost-effective way of accomplishing a work activity. This is usually done through the comparison of a proposed alternate method of accomplishing a work activity with the existing method.

The following value engineering questions can be posed when examining the value of any work activity or work output:

1. Can it be eliminated without impairing its function or reliability?
2. Does it cost more than it is worth?
3. Does it do more than is required (does it need all of its features)?
4. Is there something better that will to do the job?
5. Can it be made by a less costly method?
6. Can a standard item or specialty product be used?
7. Considering the quantities used, could a less expensive manufacturing technique be used?
8. Considering the quantities to be made, should different tooling be used?
9. Does it cost more than the total of reasonable labor, overhead, material, and profit?
10. Can someone else (a supplier) provide it at less cost without affecting dependability?
11. Is anyone buying this work function or work output at a lower cost?
12. If it were your money, would you buy the item? Why?

A number of value engineering publications and training courses available to both industry and government describe the detailed methodology used to respond to questions and to implement a value engineering program. One of the best sources of information is a course provided by the U.S. Army Management Engineering Training Agency at Rock Island, Illinois. It covers cost estimating and cost modeling, as well as value engineering, and provides many examples of successful application of value engineering techniques. Several large private companies have their own value engineering programs but are understandably reluctant to release extensive details about their programs to potential competitors.

Whether the approach taken to cost-effectiveness comes through a life cycle cost analysis, a design-to-cost program, or a value engineering effort, much more is expected to be heard about the cost evaluation, estimating, and comparison techniques used in all three disciplines during the first years of the new century.

NOTES

1. Life cycle costing for high-technology aerospace and construction projects has been thoroughly treated in Benjamin S. Blanchard, *Design and Manage to Life Cycle Cost* (Portland, Ore.: M/A Press, 1978), and M. Robert Seldon, *Life Cycle Costing: A Better Method of Government Procurement,* Boulder, Colorado, Westview Press, 1979.
2. Office of Management and Budget, *Major System Acquisitions,* circular A-109 (Washington, D.C.: Government Printing Office, April 1976), p. 4, 5.
3. See Jack V. Michaels and William P. Wood, *Design to Cost* (New York: Wiley, 1989).

QUESTIONS

10.1. Costs can be expressed in terms of constant dollars, current dollars, or discounted dollars. Define each of these terms.

10.2. Program life cycle cost reduction can be best achieved by minimizing both acquisition cost and operations and support cost.   T   F

10.3. Generally program decisions commit most of a system total life cycle cost early in program development.   T   F

10.4. To achieve maximum potential program life cycle cost reduction, intensive life cycle cost reduction efforts should start:

    a. During design concept development and performance requirements definition.

    b. At development program contract award.

    c. At preliminary design review.

    d. At final design review.

10.5. Life cycle cost considers all costs incurred during the projected life of the system, subsystem, or component. Match the program elements to the appropriate life cycle phase by writing in the number(s) next to the corresponding phase.

a. Development: ⎯⎯⎯⎯⎯⎯⎯⎯⎯⎯⎯

b. Investment: ⎯⎯⎯⎯⎯⎯⎯⎯⎯

c. Operations and support/ownership: ⎯⎯⎯⎯⎯⎯⎯⎯⎯⎯⎯⎯

d. Does not apply: ⎯⎯⎯⎯⎯⎯⎯⎯⎯⎯⎯

    1. Engineering design

    2. Production of all system elements

    3. Customer initial training and training equipment

    4. Sustaining maintenance

    5. Test and evaluation

    6. Replenishment spares

    7. Operator costs

    8. Demonstration of system operation concept

    9. Initial production facilitization and tooling

    10. Consumables (e.g., fuel)

    11. Maintenance management/data

    12. Initial spares

11

UNDERSTANDING AND
DEALING WITH
INFLATION AND ESCALATION

In proportion to the extent of the years, you shall increase its price and in proportion to the fewness of the years, you shall diminish its price.

Leviticus 25:16

An important question confronting the cost estimator is how to understand and deal with inflation and escalation. Although inflation and escalation have often been treated as one, they are distinctly different. Inflation is the time-oriented increase in costs brought about by rising prices and rising costs of materials, subcontracts, parts, supplies, goods, and services. It is caused principally by the injection of funds into the economy that unbalance the law of supply and demand for money. The distribution of more money than is collected in taxes and other income causes economic growth, but it also decreases the amount of work or goods that can be purchased with the dollar because the value of the dollar is thereby decreased.

Escalation, on the other hand, can be defined as the time-oriented increase in costs brought about by increases in labor-hours, wage rates, and nonproductive labor encountered in providing a given work output. Both escalation and inflation have been difficult to predict and control because very little has been known about their makeup and the factors that influence their magnitude. Let us explore inflation first and discuss some of its history, principal causes, and methods of dealing with it.

INFLATION: ITS HISTORY, CAUSES, AND EFFECTS

Figure 11.1 shows a history of the consumer price index, an indicator of inflation rate, since 1800. On this figure is plotted the consumer price index based on average prices in the years 1982 through 1984 at a baseline of 100. Notice that for a long period in our country's history, there was little or no inflation, but since the 1940s

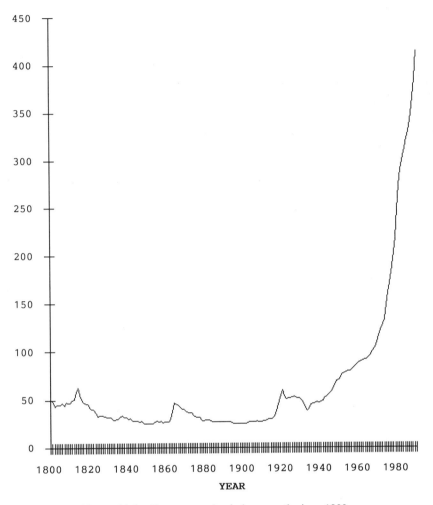

Figure 11.1 Consumer price index growth since 1800.

there has been an exponential rise in the inflation rate as indicated by the consumer price index. The government has had some success in recent years in stemming this rise, but there is little hope in reducing inflation further and even less hope in eliminating it altogether. Most economic forecasts show continued inflation well into the next century, for the following reasons:

1. Despite heroic attempts to quell inflation by legislation such as the Gramm-Rudman-Hollings Act and pressures for a constitutional amendment to balance the budget, lobbying and political pressure by special interest groups continues to put pressure on the Congress and the president to keep government spending above government income.

2. There are inflationary expectations imbedded in many of the financial forecasts, contracts, and loans already negotiated in both the public and private
   sectors. Examples are inflation provisions and clauses in union wage contracts, government budgeting and pricing rulings, adjustable loans, and government contracts. Other contract provisions that increase fringe benefits and
   permit less employee productivity tend to fuel inflation.

3. Periodic legislated or regulated increases in social security payments, minimum wages, and retirement benefits for military and government personnel
   are expected to continue.

4. Foreign divisions of U.S. companies and foreign competitors encounter inflationary influences throughout the world. Our inflation rate is influenced,
   therefore, by that of other countries.

Most projections show a leveling off or a slight decrease in the inflation rate, while
history shows a continued long-term trend upward. The twin problems of a high
inflation rate and a slower than desired rate of economic growth or development
give conflicting signals to economists and planners. Higher inflation augments
prices to offset rising production costs; however, slower growth means more competition for existing markets, which should result in lower prices. U.S. government
economic forecast data show that the expected average annual inflation rates for
various industries for the 1990–1995 period will be as low as 4 percent for some
products (electrical and electronics) and as high as 10.8 percent for others (copper
products).

Cost estimators must evaluate the effects of inflation on each specific work
element of a process, product, project, or service separately. The resource content
and inflation rate of each work element can vary within a work activity or work
output as well as between work outputs. The effects of uncontrolled fluctuation in
prices, such as in precious metals, the effect of consumer demand or production lead
times, and the dependence on foreign countries for rare minerals, all have a pro-
nounced effect on inflation in any specific business or industrial activity. In the
1970s, for example, when the price of gold and silver fluctuated widely, the defense
and aerospace industries encountered delivery problems with vendors holding firm
fixed-price orders for material with a high precious metal content. The orders did
not contain price adjustment clauses because most were placed before the price
surge of precious metals. Several vendors requested price increases, but there was
no legal basis for a price adjustment. Some refused to deliver without such an
adjustment, and the contractual differences were subject to resolution through the
disputes procedure or termination for default. Either of these avenues has the effect
of increasing the cost of the precious metal–containing item because a slip in
schedule usually means a loss of resources (labor-hours, equipment, facility usage)
and time. In this situation, inflation in the price of an item causes cost escalation in
other areas.

Among other factors that contribute to price inflation, delivery delays, and
resulting cost escalation is U.S. dependence on other countries for raw materials. In
addition to dependence on foreign oil, there are other rare raw materials needed by
emerging high-technology projects in the United States that are imported from

foreign countries. Two examples are cobalt and titanium. Cobalt is used in a particularly tough steel alloy called "maraging" steel. It contains 9 percent cobalt and is used widely in the defense and aerospace industries. Approximately 50 percent of the world's source of cobalt is from Zaire. Political disruption in Zaire and its neighbors severely reduces the production of maraging steel.

Titanium is another metal that has been in short supply because of historical dependence on the Soviet Union as a source. In the mid-1970s, the Soviet Union, which supplied over 50 percent of the West's supply of this metal, refused to enter into any new delivery agreements, partly because of the political environment and partly because its own demand sharply increased. This increased demand was primarily attributable to the Soviet submarine production program, which included titanium-hulled submarines requiring about 3 million pounds for each submarine. This situation may change if relations between the Soviet Union and the United States improve.

Supplies of materials and products from other countries have also affected the construction, electronics, steel, and automotive industries. Because of these influences of foreign business and foreign politics, the U.S. economy is enmeshed with the economies of other nations, primarily through the establishment and expansion of multinational corporations and increased dependence on other nations to supply essential materials and manufactured goods. Third World nations have begun to recognize the power at their disposal because of the industrialized nations' dependence on them for supplying raw materials. Some of these countries have established cartels and other confederations to control the supply and price of various items; the most prominent and powerful of these groups is the oil cartel.

The U.S. economy has felt the full effects of the reversal of a long history of price regulation of a wide variety of items and services. The practice of artificially supporting or restraining prices and/or wages was originally thought to be the solution to obtaining economic stability. However, it was found that this practice treated the symptoms rather than the basic problem, and there the trend toward decontrol of a wide variety of commodities, including gold, natural gas, and agricultural products, is continuing. Decontrol allows the free market law of supply and demand to work, but it can also have an inflationary effect. Decontrol of gold prices and allowing the price of gold and other precious metals to "float" on the world market, for example, resulted in tremendous price increases in these metals in the mid-1970s. Other related factors, such as the shifting of the balance of trade in such a way that the United States must import more of its goods and services, has decreased the value of the U.S. dollar, making the purchase of foreign products more costly. On the whole, however, the government's ability to control inflation has improved in recent years. Estimators must be alert to trends if they are to respond rapidly to any changes in the current environment.

ESCALATION: ITS CAUSES AND EFFECTS

Escalation, as defined for this discussion, includes mainly the continuing increase in the amount of resources, principally labor but including other cost elements, required to do a job. Two of the main culprits are "salary creep" and "grade creep" in an organization. In organizations with a relatively low turnover, salary and grade escalation is significant because employees must be upgraded, given an opportunity for career advancement, and provided periodic merit and cost-of-living salary or wage increases. Union agreements, fringe benefit increases, and legislatively imposed socioeconomic objectives also tend to foster continued cost escalation because these factors tend to reduce the number of productive labor-hours per worker per day or week. The combined effect of average wage increases and fewer productive hours per person continues to cause cost escalation. Escalation can also be caused by a continual modification, improvement, and upgrading of a work output beyond the actual output requirements.

Each year, the U.S. comptroller general publishes the estimated and actual costs of major federal acquisitions for both civil and military projects, and every year the actual costs have far exceeded the originally predicted costs even when the effects of erroneously predicted inflation rates are removed. This additional cost growth or cost increase above the inflation rate is the cost escalation encountered in major federal projects. The escalation numbers are improving somewhat (getting lower) but still represent a sizable percentage growth in a large number of projects. **Figure 11.2** shows a percentage breakout of escalation and inflation in defense industries.

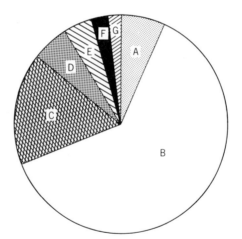

Cause of Cost Growth

A. Inflation	=	6.4%
B. Program Change Related Escalation	=	63.1%
C. Quantity	=	17.0%
D. Engineering	=	5.7%
E. Support	=	4.5%
F. Schedule	=	1.9%
G. Estimating and Other	=	1.4%
	Total =	**100.0%**

Figure 11.2 Mid-1980s analysis of program cost growth of the U.S. Defense Department by base year dollar changes.

Notice that 63.1 percent of the cost growth is caused by program changes. The Department of Defense has recently appealed to the Congress for increased program stability to help stem this trend.

THE IMPACT OF RISING ENERGY COSTS ON INFLATION

The impact of rising energy costs on inflation is treated separately because it is by far the most predominant potential factor in causing the rate of inflation to continue at a high or increasing level. The United States is vulnerable to unexpected energy cost increases more than any other country because it consumes 30 percent of the world's energy even though it contains only about 6 percent of the world's population. The United States uses more energy per dollar of gross national product (GNP) than any other nation. For example, its per capita energy consumption is twice that of West Germany, which enjoys about the same standard of living as the United States.

In the twentieth century we have evolved from an era when energy was thought of as in seemingly inexhaustible supply to one where we perceive energy as having a finite limit of supply. This is more of an attitude change than an energy supply change because the supply problem has always been there. We just did not realize it. It is human nature to be willing to pay more for things we perceive to be in short supply, and it is the right of profit-making corporations to charge more for products that are in high demand. The exact amount of energy that we have is not as important as what people perceive that amount to be. This is what establishes the price of energy. The United States has made two major energy transitions: from wood to coal and from coal to petroleum and natural gas.

Neither of these transitions was due to scarcity; the historical transitions were toward a more concentrated and convenient fuel. The next transition will most likely be to a combination of nuclear energy, nonrenewable energy sources, and renewable energy sources such as solar, wind, and ocean thermal energy and energy obtained from organic products. Coal consumption is expected to continue to rise slightly because coal represents 90 percent of the U.S. energy reserves but accounts for only 20 percent of consumption. The largest potential for expansion of coal usage is in the East and in the Midwest, where the coal supplies are most prevalent and where transportation costs from mine to user are lower. Although the cost of coal itself should not exceed the inflation rate significantly, pollution control devices required to use coal increase the cost of using coal considerably.

The supply of petroleum in the United States is slow in responding to price increases. Oil companies are spending more on exploration, and many domestic wells are being drilled at a higher frequency, but less oil is being found. As a result, U.S. petroleum reserves continue to decline, and a greater percentage of oil for the United States must be imported from foreign countries. About 55 percent of the petroleum used in the United States goes into fuels (45 percent for gasoline, 7 percent for jet fuel, and 5 percent for diesel fuel), and the remainder into home heating (17 percent), industrial fuel oil (12 percent), and asphalt, petrochemicals, and other uses (16 percent). Cost estimators must continue to use fuel inflation rates several percentage points above the general inflation rates because of potentially scarce supplies and because of the lack of commercially available alternate sources of energy.

Natural gas, sometimes called "the perfect fuel" because of its low cost and low environmental impact, rapidly decreased in supply because of the artificially low price set by federal regulation. Deregulation is causing it to increase in price. The overall historical trend for electricity rates since the 1940s has been downward, and the result has been widespread electrification of homes and businesses. A consumption growth rate of 6 to 7 percent annually has been supported by these decreasing prices. Annual growth rates of the use of electricity have decreased because of rising prices. All forms of energy could become more expensive at a rate that exceeds the rate of general inflation, a factor that must be accounted for and carefully analyzed in energy-intensive industries.

STRATEGIES TO DEAL WITH INFLATION

It is more in the purview of the cost estimator to recognize, predict, and account for inflation in cost estimates than to try to do something about it. Control of inflation is a multinational task entwined with political, geographical, and social policies and trends. Most economists agree that the inflation rate in the United States can be more successfully controlled by holding federal spending down to the level of federal income than by any other means.

In the meantime, the cost estimator must allow for inflation in cost estimates but cannot allow this practice to produce estimates that are not competitive. The cost estimator can approach this dilemma in two ways. The first is to study the economic price trends of the specific products and services needed to accomplish a specified work output. The sensitivity of each work and cost element to inflationary trends must be determined, and historical information and projection rationale must be developed for predicting the course of price changes for that element. In doing this, the cost estimator must realize that overall company production, purchasing, investment, and financing decisions can be made to gain strategic cost advantage over competitors. This method is the better one for dealing with inflation: know enough about the work output, its components, and the historical and forecasted economic influences on the resources required to provide the work output and its components.

Second, the cost estimator, in conjunction with company management and the contract negotiation function, can devise a contractual economic price adjustment clause for the contract. A contract cost adjustment can be tied to one of the several cost indexes formulated and periodically published by the government. Estimates prepared for government budgetary purposes are often made in constant dollars (say, 1995 dollars), and discrete escalation factors for each year are applied to determine real-year dollar forecasts. **Table 11.1** can be used to convert dollars from any year to any other year dollars by multiplying by the appropriate factor from the table. The type of contract used for procurement of a work output will depend to some extent on the ability to predict inflationary effects. Long-term fixed-price contracts must be avoided in an era of fluctuating inflation rates.

Other strategies designed to avoid the effects of inflationary prices are to purchase raw materials in quantity prior to bidding on a job, switch to in-house production to avoid purchasing items at a high cost, or negotiate contracts where the customer provides the materials and your company provides the labor, facilities, and equipment.

In contracting with the federal government, many fixed-price multiyear contracts contain an economic price adjustment (EPA) clause from the Federal Acquisition Regulations that allows for increases in price to occur because of unforeseen escalation amounts.

HOW TO DEAL WITH ESCALATION

To deal with escalation effectively, it is necessary to know the factors that cause and make up escalation and to deal with each separately. Escalation is usually attributed to one or more of the following factors—some of them easily controlled, some controlled only with difficulty, and some that cannot be controlled:

Accuracy of original cost estimate

Degree of completion of initial design work

Number of design changes

Increases in labor burden (fringe benefits)

Degree of customer involvement

Amount of government regulation and control

Adaptability and innovativeness of work force

Availability and hiring of new personnel

Accuracy of Original Cost Estimate

The question that always comes up in any discussion of escalation of a work activity is, "Was it an overrun or an underestimate?" Usually cost growth above the inflation rate is a combination of underestimating the amount of work that it would take to do the job and overrunning the amount of work that it should have taken to do the job. To account for potential cost escalation, many estimators add what is known as a contingency to their estimates. My opinion is that (1) the word "contingency" is incorrect for a cost amount added to an estimate to cover escalation and (2) the practice of adding this cost at the top level of an estimate is not a sound estimating practice. The reason "contingency" is an improper name is that it implies that cost growth may or may not occur. The contingency in every project I have known of has been consumed, which implies that it is a certainty rather than a contingency.

A better term for this added cost amount is "allowance for cost growth." The reason that addition of an allowance for cost growth at the top level of an estimate is not a sound estimating practice is that it becomes a self-fulfilling prophesy by virtue of its own existence. The provision of an allowance for cost growth in an estimate, contract, or budget provides an escape from close cost control until the allowance is

TABLE 11.1 U.S. Government Inflation Indexes of Conversion Factors

	To FY59	To FY60	To FY61	To FY62	To FY63	To FY64	To FY65	To FY66	To FY67	To FY68	To FY69	To FY70	To FY71
From FY59	1.0000	1.0430	1.0764	1.1194	1.1586	1.2107	1.2519	1.3270	1.3921	1.4672	1.5509	1.6579	1.7623
From FY60	0.9588	1.0000	1.0320	1.0733	1.1108	1.1608	1.2003	1.2723	1.3347	1.4067	1.4869	1.5895	1.6897
From FY61	0.9290	0.9690	1.0000	1.0400	1.0764	1.1248	1.1631	1.2329	1.2933	1.3631	1.4408	1.5402	1.6373
From FY62	0.8933	0.9317	0.9615	1.0000	1.0350	1.0816	1.1183	1.1854	1.2435	1.3107	1.3854	1.4810	1.5743
From FY63	0.8631	0.9002	0.9290	0.9662	1.0000	1.0450	1.0805	1.1454	1.2015	1.2664	1.3385	1.4309	1.5211
From FY64	0.8259	0.8615	0.8890	0.9246	0.9569	1.0000	1.0340	1.0960	1.1497	1.2118	1.2809	1.3693	1.4556
From FY65	0.7988	0.8331	0.8598	0.8942	0.9255	0.9671	1.0000	1.0600	1.1119	1.1720	1.2388	1.3243	1.4077
From FY66	0.7536	0.7860	0.8111	0.8436	0.8731	0.9124	0.9434	1.0000	1.0490	1.1056	1.1687	1.2493	1.3280
From FY67	0.7184	0.7493	0.7732	0.8042	0.8323	0.8698	0.8993	0.9533	1.0000	1.0540	1.1141	1.1909	1.2660
From FY68	0.6816	0.7109	0.7336	0.7630	0.7897	0.8252	0.8533	0.9044	0.9488	1.0000	1.0570	1.1299	1.2011
From FY69	0.6448	0.6725	0.6941	0.7218	0.7471	0.7807	0.8072	0.8557	0.8976	0.9461	1.0000	1.0690	1.1363
From FY70	0.6032	0.6291	0.6493	0.6752	0.6989	0.7303	0.7551	0.8004	0.8397	0.8850	0.9355	1.0000	1.0630
From FY71	0.5674	0.5918	0.6108	0.6352	0.6574	0.6870	0.7104	0.7530	0.7899	0.8326	0.8800	0.9407	1.0000
From FY72	0.5368	0.5599	0.5778	0.6010	0.6220	0.6500	0.6721	0.7124	0.7473	0.7877	0.8326	0.8900	0.9461
From FY73	0.5079	0.5297	0.5467	0.5685	0.5884	0.6149	0.6358	0.6740	0.7070	0.7452	0.7877	0.8420	0.8951
From FY74	0.4738	0.4941	0.5100	0.5304	0.5489	0.5736	0.5931	0.6287	0.6595	0.6951	0.7348	0.7855	0.8349
From FY75	0.4276	0.4460	0.4603	0.4787	0.4954	0.5177	0.5353	0.5674	0.5952	0.6274	0.6631	0.7089	0.7536
From FY76	0.3923	0.4092	0.4223	0.4391	0.4545	0.4750	0.4911	0.5206	0.5461	0.5756	0.6084	0.6504	0.6913

From FY77	0.3541	0.3693	0.3812	0.3964	0.4103	0.4288	0.4433	0.4699	0.4930	0.5196	0.5492	0.5871	0.6241
From FY78	0.3285	0.3426	0.3536	0.3677	0.3806	0.3977	0.4113	0.4359	0.4573	0.4820	0.5095	0.5446	0.5789
From FY79	0.3000	0.3129	0.3229	0.3358	0.3476	0.3632	0.3756	0.3981	0.4176	0.4402	0.4653	0.4974	0.5287
From FY80	0.2710	0.2827	0.2917	0.3034	0.3140	0.3281	0.3393	0.3596	0.3772	0.3976	0.4203	0.4493	0.4776
From FY81	0.2444	0.2549	0.2630	0.2735	0.2831	0.2959	0.3059	0.3243	0.3402	0.3585	0.3790	0.4051	0.4306
From FY82	0.2234	0.2330	0.2404	0.2500	0.2588	0.2704	0.2796	0.2964	0.3109	0.3277	0.3464	0.3703	0.3936
From FY83	0.2105	0.2196	0.2266	0.2357	0.2439	0.2549	0.2636	0.2794	0.2931	0.3089	0.3265	0.3490	0.3710
From FY84	0.1988	0.2073	0.2140	0.2225	0.2303	0.2407	0.2489	0.2638	0.2767	0.2917	0.3083	0.3296	0.3503
From FY85	0.1912	0.1994	0.2058	0.2140	0.2215	0.2314	0.2393	0.2537	0.2661	0.2805	0.2964	0.3169	0.3369
From FY86	0.1852	0.1932	0.1994	0.2073	0.2146	0.2243	0.2319	0.2458	0.2578	0.2718	0.2873	0.3071	0.3264
From FY87	0.1784	0.1861	0.1921	0.1998	0.2067	0.2160	0.2234	0.2368	0.2484	0.2618	0.2767	0.2958	0.3145
From FY88	0.1714	0.1788	0.1845	0.1919	0.1986	0.2075	0.2146	0.2275	0.2386	0.2515	0.2658	0.2842	0.3021
From FY89	0.1639	0.1709	0.1764	0.1834	0.1899	0.1984	0.2052	0.2175	0.2281	0.2404	0.2541	0.2717	0.2888
From FY90	0.1556	0.1623	0.1675	0.1742	0.1803	0.1884	0.1948	0.2065	0.2166	0.2283	0.2414	0.2580	0.2743
From FY91	0.1478	0.1542	0.1591	0.1654	0.1712	0.1789	0.1850	0.1961	0.2057	0.2168	0.2292	0.2450	0.2605
From FY92	0.1394	0.1454	0.1501	0.1561	0.1615	0.1688	0.1746	0.1850	0.1941	0.2046	0.2162	0.2312	0.2457
From FY93	0.1315	0.1372	0.1416	0.1472	0.1524	0.1593	0.1647	0.1746	0.1831	0.1930	0.2040	0.2181	0.2318
From FY94	0.1241	0.1294	0.1336	0.1389	0.1438	0.1502	0.1554	0.1647	0.1727	0.1821	0.1924	0.2057	0.2187
From FY95	0.1171	0.1221	0.1260	0.1310	0.1356	0.1417	0.1466	0.1554	0.1630	0.1718	0.1816	0.1941	0.2063
From FY96	0.1098	0.1145	0.1182	0.1229	0.1272	0.1330	0.1375	0.1457	0.1529	0.1611	0.1703	0.1821	0.1935
From FY97	0.1030	0.1075	0.1109	0.1153	0.1194	0.1247	0.1290	0.1367	0.1434	0.1512	0.1598	0.1708	0.1816

(continued)

TABLE 11.1 U.S. Government Inflation Indexes of Conversion Factors *(Continued)*

	To FY72	To FY73	To FY74	To FY75	To FY76	To FY77	To FY78	To FY79	To FY80	To FY81	To FY82	To FY83	To FY84
From FY59	1.8628	1.9689	2.1107	2.3387	2.5491	2.8239	3.0442	3.3334	3.6900	4.0922	4.4769	4.7500	5.0303
From FY60	1.7860	1.8878	2.0237	2.2422	2.4440	2.7075	2.9187	3.1959	3.5379	3.9235	4.2923	4.5542	4.8229
From FY61	1.7306	1.8292	1.9609	2.1727	2.3683	2.6235	2.8282	3.0968	3.4282	3.8019	4.1592	4.4130	4.6733
From FY62	1.6640	1.7589	1.8855	2.0891	2.2772	2.5226	2.7194	2.9777	3.2963	3.6556	3.9993	4.2432	4.4936
From FY63	1.6078	1.6994	1.8218	2.0185	2.2002	2.4373	2.6274	2.8770	3.1849	3.5320	3.8640	4.0997	4.3416
From FY64	1.5385	1.6262	1.7433	1.9316	2.1054	2.3324	2.5143	2.7531	3.0477	3.3799	3.6976	3.9232	4.1547
From FY65	1.4879	1.5727	1.6860	1.8681	2.0362	2.2557	2.4316	2.6626	2.9475	3.2688	3.5761	3.7942	4.0180
From FY66	1.4037	1.4837	1.5905	1.7623	1.9209	2.1280	2.2940	2.5119	2.7807	3.0838	3.3736	3.5794	3.7906
From FY67	1.3381	1.4144	1.5163	1.6800	1.8312	2.0286	2.1868	2.3946	2.6508	2.9397	3.2160	3.4122	3.6135
From FY68	1.2696	1.3419	1.4386	1.5939	1.7374	1.9247	2.0748	2.2719	2.5150	2.7891	3.0513	3.2374	3.4284
From FY69	1.2011	1.2696	1.3610	1.5080	1.6437	1.8209	1.9629	2.1494	2.3793	2.6387	2.8867	3.0628	3.2435
From FY70	1.1236	1.1876	1.2731	1.4106	1.5376	1.7033	1.8362	2.0106	2.2258	2.4684	2.7004	2.8651	3.0342
From FY71	1.0570	1.1172	1.1977	1.3270	1.4465	1.6024	1.7274	1.8915	2.0939	2.3221	2.5404	2.6953	2.8543
From FY72	1.0000	1.0570	1.1331	1.2555	1.3685	1.5160	1.6342	1.7895	1.9809	2.1969	2.4034	2.5500	2.7004
From FY73	0.9461	1.0000	1.0720	1.1878	1.2947	1.4342	1.5461	1.6930	1.8741	2.0784	2.2738	2.4125	2.5548
From FY74	0.8825	0.9328	1.0000	1.1080	1.2077	1.3379	1.4422	1.5793	1.7482	1.9388	2.1211	2.2504	2.3832
From FY75	0.7965	0.8419	0.9025	1.0000	1.0900	1.2075	1.3017	1.4253	1.5778	1.7498	1.9143	2.0311	2.1509
From FY76	0.7307	0.7724	0.8280	0.9174	1.0000	1.1078	1.1942	1.3076	1.4476	1.6053	1.7562	1.8634	1.9733
From FY77	0.6596	0.6972	0.7474	0.8282	0.9027	1.0000	1.0780	1.1804	1.3067	1.4491	1.5854	1.6821	1.7813

From												
From FY78	0.6119	0.6468	0.6934	0.7682	0.8374	0.9276	1.0000	1.0950	1.2122	1.3443	1.4707	1.5604	1.6524
From FY79	0.5588	0.5907	0.6332	0.7016	0.7647	0.8472	0.9132	1.0000	1.1070	1.2277	1.3431	1.4250	1.5091
From FY80	0.5048	0.5336	0.5720	0.6338	0.6908	0.7653	0.8250	0.9033	1.0000	1.1090	1.2132	1.2873	1.3632
From FY81	0.4552	0.4811	0.5158	0.5715	0.6229	0.6901	0.7439	0.8146	0.9017	1.0000	1.0940	1.1607	1.2292
From FY82	0.4161	0.4398	0.4715	0.5224	0.5694	0.6308	0.6800	0.7446	0.8242	0.9141	1.0000	1.0610	1.1236
From FY83	0.3922	0.4145	0.4444	0.4923	0.5367	0.5945	0.6409	0.7018	0.7768	0.8615	0.9425	1.0000	1.0590
From FY84	0.3703	0.3914	0.4196	0.4649	0.5068	0.5614	0.6052	0.6627	0.7336	0.8135	0.8900	0.9443	1.0000
From FY85	0.3561	0.3764	0.4035	0.4470	0.4873	0.5398	0.5819	0.6372	0.7054	0.7822	0.8558	0.9080	0.9615
From FY86	0.3450	0.3647	0.3910	0.4332	0.4722	0.5231	0.5639	0.6174	0.6835	0.7580	0.8292	0.8798	0.9317
From FY87	0.3324	0.3513	0.3766	0.4173	0.4549	0.5039	0.5432	0.5948	0.6585	0.7302	0.7989	0.8476	0.8976
From FY88	0.3193	0.3375	0.3618	0.4009	0.4370	0.4841	0.5218	0.5714	0.6325	0.7015	0.7674	0.8142	0.8623
From FY89	0.3053	0.3227	0.3459	0.3833	0.4177	0.4628	0.4989	0.5463	0.6047	0.6706	0.7337	0.7784	0.8243
From FY90	0.2899	0.3064	0.3285	0.3640	0.3967	0.4395	0.4738	0.5188	0.5743	0.6369	0.6967	0.7392	0.7829
From FY91	0.2753	0.2910	0.3120	0.3456	0.3768	0.4174	0.4499	0.4927	0.5145	0.6048	0.6617	0.6623	0.7434
From FY92	0.2597	0.2745	0.2943	0.3261	0.3554	0.3937	0.4244	0.4648	0.4854	0.5706	0.6242	0.6248	0.7014
From FY93	0.2450	0.2590	0.2776	0.3076	0.3353	0.3714	0.4004	0.4385	0.4579	0.5383	0.5889	0.5894	0.6617
From FY94	0.2312	0.2443	0.2619	0.2902	0.3163	0.3504	0.3778	0.4136	0.4320	0.5078	0.5555	0.5561	0.6242
From FY95	0.2181	0.2305	0.2471	0.2738	0.2984	0.3306	0.3564	0.3902	0.4052	0.4791	0.5241	0.5216	0.5889
From FY96	0.2046	0.2162	0.2318	0.2568	0.2799	0.3101	0.3343	0.3661	0.3801	0.4494	0.4917	0.4893	0.5524
From FY97	0.1919	0.2028	0.2174	0.2409	0.2626	0.2909	0.3136	0.3434	0.3801	0.4216	0.4612	0.4893	0.5182

(*continued*)

TABLE 11.1 U.S. Government Inflation Indexes of Conversion Factors (Continued)

	To FY85	To FY86	To FY87	To FY88	To FY89	To FY90	To FY91	To FY92	To FY93	To FY94	To FY95	To FY96	To FY97
From FY59	5.2315	5.3989	5.6040	5.8338	6.1021	6.4256	6.7661	7.1721	7.6024	8.0585	8.5421	9.1058	9.7068
From FY60	5.0158	5.1763	5.3730	5.5933	5.8506	6.1606	6.4872	6.8764	7.2890	7.7263	8.1899	8.7304	9.3066
From FY61	4.8603	5.0158	5.2064	5.4198	5.6692	5.9696	6.2860	6.6632	7.0630	7.4867	7.9359	8.4597	9.0181
From FY62	4.6733	4.8229	5.0061	5.2114	5.4511	5.7400	6.0442	6.4069	6.7913	7.1988	7.6307	8.1343	8.6712
From FY63	4.5153	4.6598	4.8368	5.0352	5.2668	5.5459	5.8398	6.1902	6.5617	6.9554	7.3727	7.8593	8.3780
From FY64	4.3208	4.4591	4.6286	4.8183	5.0400	5.3071	5.5884	5.9237	6.2791	6.6558	7.0552	7.5208	8.0172
From FY65	4.1788	4.3125	4.4764	4.6599	4.8743	5.1326	5.4046	5.7289	6.0726	6.4370	6.8232	7.2735	7.7536
From FY66	3.9422	4.0684	4.2230	4.3961	4.5984	4.8421	5.0987	5.4046	5.7289	6.0726	6.4370	6.8618	7.3147
From FY67	3.7581	3.8783	4.0257	4.1908	4.3836	4.6159	4.8605	5.1522	5.4613	5.7890	6.1363	6.5413	6.9730
From FY68	3.5655	3.6796	3.8195	3.9761	4.1590	4.3794	4.6115	4.8882	5.1815	5.4924	5.8219	6.2062	6.6158
From FY69	3.3733	3.4812	3.6135	3.7617	3.9347	4.1432	4.3628	4.6246	4.9021	5.1962	5.5080	5.8715	6.2590
From FY70	3.1555	3.2565	3.3803	3.5189	3.6807	3.8758	4.0812	4.3261	4.5857	4.8608	5.1524	5.4925	5.8550
From FY71	2.9685	3.0635	3.1799	3.3103	3.4626	3.6461	3.8393	4.0697	4.3139	4.5727	4.8471	5.1670	5.5080
From FY72	2.8084	2.8983	3.0084	3.1318	3.2759	3.4495	3.6323	3.8502	4.0813	4.3261	4.5857	4.8884	5.2110
From FY73	2.6570	2.7420	2.8462	2.9629	3.0992	3.2635	3.4364	3.6426	3.8612	4.0928	4.3384	4.6247	4.9300
From FY74	2.4785	2.5579	2.6551	2.7639	2.8910	3.0443	3.2056	3.3980	3.6018	3.8179	4.0470	4.3141	4.5989
From FY75	2.2369	2.3085	2.3963	2.4945	2.6092	2.7475	2.8932	3.0667	3.2508	3.4458	3.6525	3.8936	4.1506
From FY76	2.0522	2.1179	2.1984	2.2885	2.3938	2.5207	2.6543	2.8135	2.9823	3.1613	3.3510	3.5721	3.8079

From FY77	1.8526	1.9118	1.9845	2.0659	2.1609	2.2754	2.3960	2.5398	2.6922	2.8537	3.0249	3.2246	3.3274
From FY78	1.7185	1.7735	1.8409	1.9164	2.0045	2.1108	2.2227	2.3560	2.4974	2.6472	2.8060	2.9912	3.1887
From FY79	1.5694	1.6196	1.6812	1.7501	1.8306	1.9277	2.0298	2.1516	2.2807	2.4175	2.5626	2.7317	2.9120
From FY80	1.4177	1.4631	1.5187	1.5810	1.6537	1.7413	1.8336	1.9436	2.0603	2.1839	2.3149	2.4677	2.6306
From FY81	1.2784	1.3193	1.3694	1.4256	1.4912	1.5702	1.6534	1.7526	1.8578	1.9692	2.0874	2.2251	2.3720
From FY82	1.1685	1.2059	1.2518	1.3031	1.3630	1.4353	1.5113	1.6020	1.6981	1.8000	1.9080	2.0340	2.1682
From FY83	1.1014	1.1366	1.1798	1.2282	1.2847	1.3527	1.4244	1.5099	1.6005	1.6965	1.7983	1.9170	2.0435
From FY84	1.0400	1.0733	1.1141	1.1597	1.2131	1.2774	1.3351	1.4258	1.5113	1.6020	1.6981	1.8102	1.9297
From FY85	1.0000	1.0320	1.0712	1.1151	1.1664	1.2283	1.2934	1.3710	1.4532	1.5404	1.6328	1.7406	1.8555
From FY86	0.9690	1.0000	1.0380	1.0806	1.1303	1.1902	1.2532	1.3284	1.4081	1.4926	1.5822	1.6866	1.7979
From FY87	0.9335	0.9634	1.0000	1.0410	1.0889	1.1466	1.2074	1.2798	1.3566	1.4380	1.5243	1.6249	1.7321
From FY88	0.8968	0.9254	0.9606	1.0000	1.0460	1.1014	1.1598	1.2294	1.3032	1.3814	1.4642	1.5609	1.6639
From FY89	0.8573	0.8847	0.9184	0.9560	1.0000	1.0530	1.1088	1.1753	1.2459	1.3206	1.3998	1.4922	1.5907
From FY90	0.8142	0.8402	0.8721	0.9079	0.9497	1.0000	1.0530	1.1162	1.1832	1.2541	1.3294	1.4171	1.5107
From FY91	0.7732	0.7979	0.8282	0.8622	0.9019	0.9497	1.0000	1.0600	1.1236	1.1910	1.2625	1.3458	1.4346
From FY92	0.7294	0.7528	0.7814	0.8134	0.8508	0.8959	0.9434	1.0000	1.0600	1.1236	1.1910	1.2696	1.3534
From FY93	0.6881	0.7102	0.7371	0.7674	0.8027	0.8452	0.8900	0.9434	1.0000	1.0600	1.1236	1.1978	1.2768
From FY94	0.6492	0.6700	0.6954	0.7239	0.7572	0.7974	0.8396	0.8900	0.9434	1.0000	1.0600	1.1300	1.2045
From FY95	0.6124	0.6320	0.6561	0.6829	0.7144	0.7522	0.7921	0.8396	0.8900	0.9434	1.0000	1.0660	1.1364
From FY96	0.5745	0.5929	0.6154	0.6407	0.6701	0.7057	0.7431	0.7876	0.8349	0.8850	0.9381	1.0000	1.0660
From FY97	0.5389	0.5562	0.5773	0.6010	0.6286	0.6620	0.6970	0.7389	0.7832	0.8302	0.8800	0.9381	1.0000

Note: FY = fiscal year.

(continued)

gone. Unfortunately, this absence of cost control during the early part of the job creates an atmosphere of laxity that can continue long after the allowance is consumed, resulting in an overrun.

A much better way to provide a cost growth allowance is for each line supervisor to include an adequate amount of allowance within the estimate. Then the supervisor has to manage within his or her own budget because there is no fund from which additional resources can be drawn to do the job. This approach seems unrealistic to many managers and supervisors in American industry because they have lived with other methods for such a long time. The Japanese system, however, does not provide cost allowances at a high level in a project or organization, and the Japanese have one of the best records in the world for keeping their project costs within the allocated budget. Japanese projects are planned meticulously from the start. Knowledge that there is no more money to supplement ongoing work forces a rapid and timely retrenchment. Replanning, cost cutting, and disciplined management of the remaining resources are then possible. If a lower-level manager has to ask for additional funds, those funds must be taken from the budgets of other departments. Cost problems, then, work their way up through the organization, with each manager making difficult choices and decisions before going to the next higher level to request more money.

Another factor that enters into the accuracy of original cost estimates (particularly for multidisciplined, high-technology government contracts) is the prevalence of competitive optimism. The extent, causes, and suggested remedies for underestimates have been studied extensively by the U.S. government, industry, and educational institutions. The predominant recommendation from these studies is that the procuring government agency or company should have access to a level of competence sufficient for making sound, independent estimates and that these estimates should be used in evaluating bids to determine if any of the bids are overoptimistic and, if so, which ones. These bids would then be rejected or renegotiated to a point where both the buyer and the seller have confidence that the work specified can be accomplished within the allocated resources.

Degree of Completion of Initial Design Work

One cause of cost escalation is the absence of complete design documentation and planning prior to initiation of the work. There is no substitute for this planning, but many companies try to proceed into a project with plans only partially completed. When they do, they use rule-of-thumb estimating methods to forecast the costs. One predominant rule of thumb is to make a subjective judgment as to the degree of project definition that is in hand. If the degree of definition is assessed subjectively as 85 percent, the 85 percent is estimated and 15 percent is added as cost growth allowance. The 15 percent manifests itself as $15/85 = 17.6$ percent increase, and a 2.6 percent cost growth is already built in. This remaining work could be, and usually is, the portion of the work that has the highest cost content, causing an even higher overrun (or underestimate). The most acceptable and conservative method of avoiding this type of problem is to estimate accurately the cost of the initial design and planning effort and complete it before starting work on the project itself. This procedure is well established and usually carried out successfully by many architectural and engineering firms that design large construction projects.

Design Changes

Design configuration or work element specification changes usually fall into two categories: (1) those requested by the customer and (2) those made by the supplier as a result of unforeseen material substitutions, design inadequacies, or equipment adaptations. The first category is usually subject to advance payment or reimbursement by the customer. Since these changes are made at the customer's request, the supplier has a legal right to include all costs associated with that design change, including fee and profit. The cost of the second category of design change must be borne by the supplier if the supplier has agreed to deliver a certain product meeting certain specifications on an agreed-to time schedule. These changes can save money as well as require more money. A large number of costly changes can absorb profit in a short time, however. Adhering closely to the original specifications and schedule is a way to avoid a big driver of cost escalation.

Increases in Labor Burden

Increases in labor burden are brought about by increases in social security taxes, retirement benefits, paid holidays, sick leave, medical and dental insurance contributions by the company, and paid vacations. Increases in these employee benefits are caused by new legislation, renegotiation of union contracts, or changes in corporate employment policies to stay in competition for highly qualified personnel. These increases are also related to increases in overhead due to underutilized capacity. (See pp 134–138). Although these contributions to cost escalation fall into the category of "difficult to control," some positive steps can be taken to reduce them. For example, the hiring of younger personnel with less experience and the retirement of older employees may reduce the average paid vacation time, sick leave time, or other company-paid employee benefits. Estimators must keep abreast of changing company policies related to hiring, the latest statistics on turnover rates, and the most updated projections concerning projected company skill mix and skill levels to determine how increases in labor burden can be avoided.

Degree of Customer Involvement

The amount of customer involvement during the progress of any work activity can significantly affect costs. This effect can be either negative or positive, depending on the nature and personality of the customer and the content of the work. A customer who is flexible and understanding when it comes to approving minor changes in work content or schedule can go a long way toward helping hold costs in line. A customer whose reviews become increasingly frequent and demanding on the time of the work performer and whose questions and involvement cause the work activity to decelerate or temporarily stop while questions are being answered or while small changes are being made can cause a sizable cost escalation. In preparing a cost estimate, therefore, the estimator must be aware of the nature and content of the job and also of the personality and anticipated degree of involvement of the customer in the task or tasks being performed. The estimator must add time allowances in the labor estimates for customer contact, minor changes brought about by this customer contact, and feedback to the customer concerning progress.

A particularly important pitfall to avoid in a project of any kind is the involvement of a customer action as a "series function" in a work activity. If the customer must approve an intermediate milestone or scheduled action before subsequent actions can be accomplished, the work schedule has a built-in possibility of delay and resulting cost escalation. The best way to handle customer decisions, if they cannot be avoided altogether, is to limit severely the period in which the customer can make the decision, typically by notifying the customer that if a decision is not made by a certain time or date, work will proceed as scheduled.

One of the most unsatisfactory arrangements in this category of cost escalation causative actions occurs when the customer or an independent organization not under the control of the work performer must supply or make available a vital part, component, raw material, piece of equipment, or facility at a given point in the work activity schedule. Extensive schedule delays and resulting cost increases can result if the vital element is not supplied on time. To produce a realistic cost estimate, the cost estimator must carefully screen the work content to see if any such situation might exist and make allowances for the eventuality of cost escalation brought about by this type of customer or independent supplier action.

Amount of Government Regulation and Control

Because of the need for protecting the rights, privileges, freedom, and safety of citizens, innumerable laws, regulations, and directives are imposed on business and industry by federal, state, and local governments and government agencies. These laws, regulations, directives, and controls are sometimes called socioeconomic or geopolitical objectives. They cover a wide range of subjects and areas and have a significant effect on the cost of work activities and work outputs produced. Because these laws and directives are constantly changing and growing in number, they can have a widespread effect on cost escalation. Some of the areas where government laws, regulations, directives, and controls affect cost are as follows:

Affirmative action programs
Automotive safety
Buy American programs
Conflict of interest
Cost accounting standards
Fair employment practices
Freedom of Information Act

Industrial safety

Minimum wage (and other labor considerations)

Patents

Pollution control

Privacy Act

Reporting requirements

Small business utilization

Taxes

Laws, regulations, directives, and controls in these areas affect not only the activities of government contractors but also virtually every business, industry, or company in the United States. The cost estimator must be particularly sensitive to the impact of each of these areas on the cost of the work output or work activity being estimated. **Table 11.2** provides a listing of clauses from Federal Acquisition Regulations and Department of Defense Regulations that are included and/or referenced in a typical contract. Since all federal agencies use similar clauses that cover essentially the same subject matter, this list can be used as a checklist by the estimator of federal projects to determine if cost impact or assessment has been included for each area. Copies of the Federal Acquisition Regulations and the procurement regulations for each agency or service can be obtained from the Government Printing Office in Washington, D.C. A close understanding of these regulations is important for assessing socioeconomic and geopolitical cost impacts.

Adaptability and Innovativeness of the Work Force

A factor that affects an organization's ability to control or limit cost escalation is the adaptability and innovativeness of the organization's personnel. History has shown that improvements can always be made in the way that a job is done. Increased productivity and cost-effectiveness, the principal actions that combat cost escalation, are most prevalent in a work force that is adaptable, flexible, and innovative in its approach to the job. The timely application of new technologies, the use of labor-saving devices such as automation, computers, and computer graphics, and the freedom to innovate are important characteristics of any organization that wants to control costs. The capability to avoid cost growth in an organization is purely a subjective matter, but its existence and its degree must be considered and taken into account in the preparation of cost estimates for that organization. History is the best indicator of this characteristic unless significant organizational and/or personnel changes are anticipated. The availability and hiring and training of new personnel enters into the flexibility of the work force as a body, and every estimator should be aware of the organization's flexibility in this regard.

These factors individually and collectively affect cost escalation and cost control and can be assessed either individually or collectively. Most companies lump all allowances into just one or two adjustment factors that allow for cost growth. The most prevalent of these methods is the use of a "cost alignment ratio" or "cost

TABLE 11.2   Standard Procurement Clauses

Clause Title	Reference
Statutory compensation prohibitions and reporting requirements relating to certain former Department of Defense employees	252 203-7002
Required sources for miniature and instrument ball bearings	252 208-7000
Required sources for precision components and mechanical time devices	252 208-7001
Required sources for high-purity silicon	252 208-7002
Required sources for high carbon ferrochrome	252 208-7003
Required sources for forging and welded shipboard anchor chain items	252 208-7005
Acquisitions from defense contractors subject to on-site inspection under the Intermediate-Range Nuclear Forces (INF) Treaty	252 209-7001
IWIP productivity savings rewards	252 215-7001
Qualifying country sources as subcontractors	252 225-7002
Duty-free entry—qualifying country. End products and supplies	252 225-7008
Preference for domestic specialty metals (major programs)	252 225-7011
Duty-free entry—additional provisions	252 225-7014
Data requirements	252 227-7031
Supplemental cost principles	252 231-7000
Certification of requests for adjustment or relief exceeding $100,000	252 233-7000
Pricing of adjustments	252 243-7001
Transportation of supplies by sea	252 247-7203
Definitions	52 202-1
Officials not to benefit	52 203-1
Gratuities	52 203-3
Covenant against contingent fees.	52 203-5
Restrictions on subcontractor sales to the government	52 203-6
Antikickback procedures	52 203-7
Required sources for jewel bearings and related items	52 208-1
Protecting the government's interest when subcontracting with contractors debarred, suspended, or proposed for debarment	52 209-6
New material	52 210-5
Used or reconditioned material, residual inventory, and former government surplus property	52 210-7
Defense priority and allocation requirements	52 212-8
Examination of records by comptroller general	52 215-1
Audit-negotiation	52 215-26
Integrity of unit prices–(1987 Apr) alternate I	52 215-2b
Order of procedure	52 215-33
Notice of total small business set-aside	52 219-6
Utilization of small business concerns and small disadvantaged business concerns	52 219-8
Utilization of women-owned small business	52 219-13
Utilization of labor surplus area concerns	52 220-3
Labor surplus area subcontracting program	52 220-4
Walsh-Healey Public Contracts Act	52 222-20

(continued)

TABLE 11.2 (*Continued*)

Clause Title	Reference
Equal opportunity	52 222-26
Equal opportunity preaward clearance of subcontracts	52 222-28
Affirmative action for special disabled and Vietnam era veterans	52 222-35
Affirmative action for handicapped workers	52 222-36
Employment reports on special disabled veterans and veterans of the Vietnam era	52 222-37
Clean air and water	52 223-2
Drug free workplace	52 223-6
Duty-free entry	52 225-10
Authorization and consent	52 227-1
Notice and assistance regarding patent and copyright infringement	52 227-2
Federal, state, and local taxes	52 229-3
Taxes—Contracts performed in U.S. possessions or Puerto Rico	52 229-5
Payments	52 232-1
Extras	52 232-11
Interest	52 232-17
Prompt payment	52 232-25
Disputes	52 233-1
Protest after award	52 233-3
Changes—fixed-price	52 243-1
Notification of changes	52 243-7
Subcontracts (fixed-price contracts)	52 244-1
Limitation of liability	52 246-23
Termination for convenience of the government (fixed price)	52 249-2
Default (fixed-price supply and service)	52 249-8
Special prohibition on employment	252 203-7001
Overseas distribution of defense subcontracts	252 204-7005
Release of information to cooperative agreement holders	252 205-7000
Required sources for antifriction bearings	252 205-7006
Restrictions on federal public works projects	52 225-13
Discounts for prompt payment	52 232-8
Government property (fixed-price contracts)	52 245-2
Price reduction for defective cost or pricing data	52 215-22
Subcontractor cost or pricing data	52 215-24
Integrity of unit prices	52 215-26
Facilities capital cost of money	52 215-30
Waiver of facilities capital cost of money	52 215-31
Cost accounting standards	52 230-03
Administration of cost accounting standards	52 230-04
Disclosure and consistency of cost accounting practices	52 230-05
Aggregate pricing adjustment	252 215-7000

Note: 52, Federal Acquisition Regulations; 252, Defense Department Supplements to the Federal Acquisition Regulations.

adjustment ratio" to bring estimated labor-hours and other direct costs up from the "theoretically possible" values to the "actually achievable values". The ratio is developed by dividing actual hours spent doing a job by the hours predicted. Cost alignment ratios range from 1.0 to over 2.0, depending on the organization, its work output, and its history of efficiency or inefficiencies. Barring repeated unforeseen natural disasters, values of the cost alignment ratio close to 1.0 are possible.

The cost alignment ratio is actually an efficiency factor for the organization. It not only measures how well an organization performs but also how well the organization can predict its performance. Since there is a vagueness about where the dividing line between underestimates or underperformance lies, both are included in this one factor. The use of factors for estimating, in general, has been touched on only briefly in this book because a factor or multiplier of any type is used to bring estimated performance closer to actual expected performance.

A CHANGING ENVIRONMENT IN COST ESTIMATING

In the 1980s, many activities served to improve, expand, and increase the importance of cost estimates, cost estimators, and the cost estimating profession. Legislation introduced and enacted by Congress brought to the public attention the need for improved cost estimating in both the private and public sectors. Professional societies were formed and grew rapidly in membership, scope, and influence (among them are the Society of Cost Estimating and Analysis, the American Association of Cost Engineers, the American Society of Professional Estimators, and the International Society of Parametric Analysts). Colleges and universities are beginning to include more courses in economics, business, accounting, and management for technical as well as nontechnical degrees. More books and articles in technical, nontechnical, and media publications are including information on cost estimating, cost control, and cost management. Cost estimating is truly growing and expanding.

The disciplines, functions, and methodologies described in this book collectively make up this emerging field of cost estimating. Each aspect of cost estimating can and may very well grow into a profession of its own (parametric estimating, industrial engineering type estimating, etc.). Adherence to the belief that a good cost estimate is necessary to make informed management decisions will accelerate this growth, and further expansion of the estimating profession will result in cost estimates that can be relied on by managers in industry and government, and by the public, in accurately predicting and forecasting the resources required to produce work.

QUESTIONS

11.1. An inflation clause in a contract provides for an upward adjustment of the contract price.   T   F

11.2. Escalation is a forecasted increase in the amount of labor and materials required to accomplish a given job.   T   F

11.3. Inflation is a decrease in the general level of prices.   T   F

11.4. Assuming a mix of 40 percent labor and 60 percent material, inflate $1000 for three years at 5 percent labor inflation and 10% material inflation. The inflated value is closest to:

   a. $1080.

   b. $1167.

   c. $1227.

   d. $1262.

   e. None of the above

11.5. **a.** Inflate the rates in following table and display results to two decimal places.

Code	Base Rate	Annual % Escalation		
		1989	1990	1991
AA	$10.00	5.0	5.5	4.0
BB	$11.00	6.0	6.5	5.0
CC	$10.50	5.5	6.0	5.0
DD	$11.25	4.5	5.0	4.0

   b. If AA represents 20 percent of the effort, BB 30 percent, CC 40 percent, and DD 10 percent, what is the weighted percentage inflation in each year? (Show two decimal places.)

12

COMPUTER-AIDED COST ESTIMATING AND COST ANALYSIS

Who says, "Let Him make speed, let Him hasten His work, that we may see it?"

Isaiah 5:19

Speed and accuracy are of the essence in computing a cost estimate because the computation process occurs near the end of the cost estimating process when the proposal manager, the project manager, or the sales department are putting pressure on the estimating department for quick results. If the results are not acceptable to management, the estimating department may have to modify the estimate several times before approval. Because of the pressures for rapid results and because of the desirability of iteration of the cost estimate several, if not many, times during cost estimating preparation, the computer has become indispensable in cost estimating. The speed, accuracy, and increasingly large storehouse of software has made computerized estimating vital for businesses of all sizes.

This chapter (1) provides an overview of the types of computer and computer software tools available for computerized estimating and analysis, (2) describes typical software programs in each category, (3) summarizes desirable characteristics and what to look for in computer-aided and cost estimating and cost analysis systems, and (4) directs readers to sources of additional information on automated cost estimating and cost modeling systems.

Computer-aided cost estimating (CACE) and computer-aided cost analysis (CACA) include automated cost estimating systems, automated cost models, and computer tools that the cost estimator can use. **Figure 12.1** provides an overview of the spectrum of types and numbers of inputs required for a full range of computer-aided cost estimating and modeling tools starting with medium to low-fidelity or "low-granularity" modeling and analysis systems and proceeding to high-fidelity, high-granularity estimating and cost tracking systems. (The term "granularity" indicates the sizes of the elements being estimated. Elements of the top levels of the

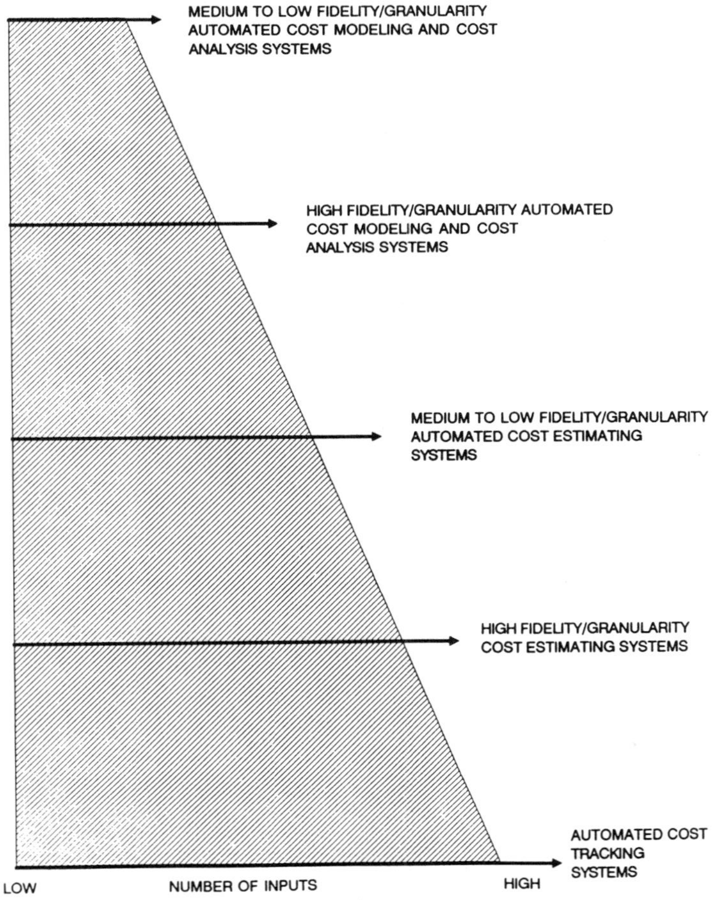

EXAMPLES OF TYPES OF INPUTS

HOME CONSTRUCTION	AEROSPACE	SOFTWARE
DOLLARS PER SQUARE FOOT FOR A GIVEN GEOGRAPHICAL AREA AND SQUARE FOOTAGE	COST PER POUND FOR A GIVEN VEHICLE TYPE AND WEIGHT IN POUNDS, AND QUANTITIES	DOLLARS OR HOURS PER LINES OF CODE, AND POSSIBLY, NUMBER AND TYPES OF FUNCTIONS PLUS OVERALL CASE PRODUCTIVITY
DOLLARS PER SQUARE FOOT FOR EACH TYPE OF ROOM, QUALITY FACTORS, TYPE CONSTRUCTION OR COMBINATIONS THEREOF; AND SQUARE FOOTAGE OF EACH	PERFORMANCE, THRUST, SPEED, RPM, HORSE-POWER, NO. OF FUNCTIONS, PAYLOAD, KW, CAPACITY, VOLUME, OR COMBINATIONS THEREOF; PLUS QUANTITIES AND LEARNING CURVE	DOLLARS OR HOURS PER LINES OF CODE, NUMBER OF FUNCTIONS, COMPLEXITY OF JOB, SKILL LEVELS OF ANALYSTS, TYPE OF LANGUAGE, APPLICATION(COCOMO) PLUS DETAILED CASE FACTORS
COMBINED LABOR AND MATERIAL DOLLAR PER BOARD-FT, YARD OF CONCRETE, SQUARE OF ROOFING, ELECTRICAL FIXTURE, CU YARD OF EXCAVATION, ETC.	STAFFING OF ENGINEERING BY FUNCTION, MANUFACTURING BY SHOP LOADING, TESTING, BY TEST CREW UTILIZATION; AND FACTORED MATERIAL COSTS AND OTHER DIRECT COSTS	STAFFING OF SYSTEM ANALYSTS, PROGRAMMERS, TECHNICAL WRITERS, AND MANAGERS BY LEVEL 2 OR 3 IN THE WORK BREAKDOWN STRUCTURE PLUS COMPUTER TIME AND OTHER DIRECT COSTS
DETAILED DRAWING QUANTITY TAKE-OFF TO ESTIMATE MATERIALS, LABOR, EQUIPMENT FOR EACH OPERATIONAL TASK BASED ON HANDBOOK VALUES	DETAILED TASK-BY-TASK ANALYSIS; DEVELOPMENT OF LABOR HOURS AND MATERIALS USING THE "PROCESS-PLAN" APPROACH	DETAILED TASK-BY-TASK ANALYSIS AND APPLICATION OF APPROPRIATE SKILLS TO EACH TASK: PLANNING, ANALYSIS, DESIGN, CODING, TESTING, DE-BUGGING, AND DOCUMENTATION
JOB-COST ACCOUNTING SYSTEM IN WHICH ALL LABOR SKILL CATEGORIES AND SKILL LEVELS ARE TRACKED BY HOURS AND MATERIALS DOLLARS	SCHEDULE OR NETWORK-BASED TRACKING OF EACH TASK IN THE WORK BREAKDOWN STRUCTURE, COMPARING ACTUALS WITH ESTIMATES	SCHEDULE OR NETWORK-BASED TRACKING OF EACH TASK IN THE WORK BREAKDOWN STRUCTURE, COMPARING ACTUALS WITH ESTIMATES, CACE TOOLS USED FOR TRACKING PRODUCTIVITY

MEDIUM TO LOW FIDELITY/GRANULARITY AUTOMATED COST MODELING AND COST ANALYSIS SYSTEMS

HIGH FIDELITY/GRANULARITY AUTOMATED COST MODELING AND COST ANALYSIS SYSTEMS

MEDIUM TO LOW FIDELITY/GRANULARITY AUTOMATED COST ESTIMATING SYSTEMS

HIGH FIDELITY/GRANULARITY COST ESTIMATING SYSTEMS

AUTOMATED COST TRACKING SYSTEMS

NUMBER OF INPUTS

LOW — HIGH

Figure 12.1 The cost modeling/cost estimating spectrum.

work breakdown structure are of low granularity, and elements of the lowest levels of the work breakdown structure are of high granularity. High fidelity means high responsiveness to minor variations in the smaller, lower level work elements.)

Since CACA tools normally estimate and analyze costs at the top end of the spectrum, they require fewer inputs than detailed estimates. Cost models, a subset of CACA, use cost estimating relationships (CERs) that are based on one or more performance or programmatic inputs. Medium- to low-fidelity cost models and analysis tools require only a few inputs, are quick and easy to operate, and produce rapid results for initial budgeting and estimating when a detailed design of the project, product, or service is not available. These top-level CACA tools usually are of low granularity with one exception: when higher-level derived costs are "allocated" or spread among lower work elements based on an apportioned percentage derived from historical data. High-fidelity, high-granularity CACA tools usually require an expanded list of both performance and programmatic inputs but require more knowledge about the project or system, as shown in the example boxes for home construction, aerospace projects, and computer software adjacent to the "High Fidelity/Granularity Automated Cost Modeling and Analysis Systems" arrow in Figure 12.1. In the mid-range of number of required inputs, the definition of automated systems changes from cost analysis systems to cost estimating systems. Automated cost modeling and analysis techniques use larger numbers of CERs and resource algorithms, and detailed automated cost estimates tend to require a number of different techniques, including automated quantity takeoffs from computer-aided design (CAD) systems, automated bill-of-materials generation, and estimator interjection of staffing or shop-loading estimates, firm bids, and catalog prices.

At the lowest level of the diagram in Figure 12.1, automated cost tracking systems require the largest number of inputs. If the diagram were extended downward even further, the number of inputs would reach the maximum at the cost accounting system level. Some organizations have been able to tie their cost accounting systems to their cost tracking and cost estimating systems, but generally only summary cost accounting data are used in cost tracking systems.

There are literally hundreds of software programs that perform the full spectrum of cost functions represented in Figure 12.1. These software programs fall into the following general categories:

Generic computer tools
Preprogrammed estimating templates for generic computer tools
Cost models
Schedule-based estimating tools
Vertical market estimating software
CAD–based estimating systems
Artificial intelligence and expert systems for estimating
Statistics software

(Unless otherwise stated, the CACE and CACA tools run on IBM-compatible personal computers.)

COMPUTER-AIDED COST ESTIMATING

The most valuable automated estimating tools available to the average cost estimator are the generic computer tools that can be used for any application but are put to use constantly in the field of cost estimating. These generic tools include electronic spreadsheets, database programs, integrated software packages, and special multidimensional spreadsheets and multidimensional database programs.

For simple cost estimates consisting of only a few elements, the spreadsheet program is usually the quickest and easiest to use. With skilled programming, however, spreadsheet programs can be used to develop large cost modeling programs, specialized cost estimating systems, and even schedule and cost tracking systems. Some commonly used spreadsheet programs are Lotus 1–2–3, EXCEL, 20/20, Ability Plus, Javelin Plus, Lucid 3-D, PFS: Professional Plan, PlanPerfect, Quattro, Silk, Smart Spreadsheet, Supercalc 5, Trapeze, and WingZ. For those who are not skilled in programming spreadsheets, there are spreadsheet add-ins and templates that turn the spreadsheet programs into customized estimating systems. Micro-Pricing Systems, Inc. of White House, Ohio, for example, markets templates called Curvefit, WBS/Tree, Cost of Money Factors, and several spreadsheet templates that automatically fill out government pricing and proposal estimating forms.

For high-fidelity, high-granularity cost estimating systems that require many inputs as well as many outputs, an automated database management system, with skillful programming, can be used to develop a sophisticated cost estimating system. Some of these programs are dBASE IIIplus and dBASE IV; RBASE; Clipper; dBASE MAC; dbXL; foxBASE+; McMax; Paradox 3.0; PC/Focus; PFS: Professional File; Quicksilver; Q&A; R&R; DataPerfect; Clarion Professional; Ask Sam; Dataease 4.0; Dataease Developer; Formula IV; and Advanced Revelation 2.0. For combined spreadsheet, database, graphics, and word processing capabilities, there are integrated software packages such as Symphony 3.0, PFS First Choice, Microsoft Works, Framework III, and Smart System. Mainstay, which will be covered later, is a multidimensional database that deserves special attention. Large model frameworks that accommodate flexible cost modeling such as PICES (Programmed Interactive Cost Estimating System) developed by the U.S. Army Missile Command and FAST (Freiman Analysis of Systems Technique), developed by Freiman Parametric Systems, Inc., have been developed and are used for estimating high-technology weapons systems and space projects.

The U.S. Army Corps of Engineers has developed an on-line estimating system and accompanying database for construction estimating called CACES (Computer-Aided Cost Estimating System), available for use by organizations providing construction estimates to the Corps of Engineers and other government organizations.[1]

COMPUTER-AIDED COST ANALYSIS

Computer-aided cost analysis is made possible by the use of cost models, model computer shells or frameworks, schedule models, and databases. In CACA, automated computer programs are used to depict various relationships between performance and cost for a wide variety of products, processes, projects, and services. Some cost models solve simple relationships, such as learning curves and linear regression problems, while others estimate program costs for complex jobs based on a number of performance and programmatic inputs. Cost models are commonly used for determining hardware and software costs for high-technology, multi-disciplinary projects for space, military, electronics, and information systems where detailed design has not been completed but certain performance and programmatic factors are known and can be correlated with historical data and/or emerging technology. Some cost models take into account program durations and funding profiles, while others develop "point" estimates (total costs in a given year dollars irrespective of timing) of total program costs. Cost models are also used to segregate and distribute costs into program phases, work elements in a work breakdown structure, and cost elements (labor, materials, travel, and other direct costs). Some cost models provide ranges of outputs based on built-in cost, schedule, and/or performance-risk analysis techniques.

Table 12.1 contains a listing of typical cost models from a few key companies that develop these models, apply them to specific cost estimating problems, and fit cost models to specific customer needs. These cost models are not usually sold for a given market price, as are commercially available computer software applications packages, but are used for fulfillment of specific consulting and contract customer needs as part of overall ongoing client services.

Applied Research, Inc., of Huntsville, Alabama, has developed the following models:

Engine Cost Model (ECM). With relatively few inputs, this model will produce detailed estimates of the development and production costs of future liquid propellant rocket engines based on historical costs of past liquid engines. Output data are available in work breakdown structure (WBS) format, by government fiscal year in constant-year dollars, and in various graphical formats.

Spacecraft Cost Model (SCM). This model is used to estimate the development and production costs of unmanned space hardware (satellites, instruments, platforms, etc.) at the subsystem level. The model provides time-phased outputs, graphics capabilities, and other state-of-the-art features.

TEAM Model. TEAM (Top-level Evaluation and Analysis Model) is a high-level model designed to construct and explore quickly and easily the costs of new strategic defense systems architectures, or other advanced systems, by selecting system types and quantities, entering critical design and performance factors, and selecting and displaying meaningful output reports and graphics

TABLE 12.1   General Areas of Cost Models

Acquisition cost models for infrared sensors	Nichols Research, Inc. Huntsville, AL
	Aerospace Corporation Los Angeles, CA
	MCR, Inc. Falls Church, VA
Life cycle cost models for ground- and space-based radars	Nichols Research, Inc. Huntsville, AL
	Applied Research, Inc. Huntsville, AL
	MCR, Inc. Falls Church, VA
Cost models for battle management and communications, command, and control systems	Applied Research, Inc. Huntsville, AL
	TITAN SYSTEMS, Inc. Arlington, VA
Cost models for large liquid rocket engines	Rocketdyne Canoga Park, CA
	Applied Research, Inc. Huntsville, AL
	Aerojet TechSystems Company Sacramento, CA
	Pratt & Whitney Aircraft West Palm Beach, FL
Electroptical laser production cost models	MCR, Inc. Falls Church, VA
	Applied Research, Inc. Huntsville, AL
Advanced composite airframe cost model	MCR, Inc. Falls Church, VA

(*continued*)

TABLE 12.1 (*Continued*)

Avionics and installation cost model	MCR, Inc. Falls Church, VA
Remotely piloted vehicle cost model	Applied Research, Inc. Huntsville, AL
Navy missile cost model	Naval Weapons Center Dahlgren, VA
Unmanned spacecraft cost model	AF Space Systems Div. Los Angeles, CA
Electronic black box estimating models	Tecolote Research Santa Barbara, CA

on-screen as well as in hard-copy format. This model (1) produces a most-likely-cost point estimate, (2) permits the user to select a fiscal base year dependent on an internally provided inflation-escalation table, (3) contains default types and numbers of subsystems in each of 19 systems or elements to permit faster architecture construction, (4) contains scaled (rather than linear) program-related costs for greater realism, and (5) provides documentation, including a tutorial, for novice or infrequent model users.

Brilliant Pebbles Model (BPM). Brilliant Pebbles is a computerized grass roots estimating tool that develops total life cycle costs, including R&D, production, military construction, and operations and support costs. The R&D phase is split into technology/concept development phase, demonstration and validation phase, and full-scale development phase. The estimates are time phased in constant and then-year dollars. The estimate is structured along functional lines with both contractor and government costs provided. The estimate uses the Programmed Interactive Cost Estimating System (PICES) as the model framework and is classified.

RAMLOG Model. RAMLOG combines the capabilities of the U.S. Army's LOGAM model with the U.S. Navy's TIGER reliability computer program to provide a capability to evaluate logistics support alternatives for any system. The model assists in the assessment of spares requirements, transportation requirements, repair levels, and maintenance concepts. This model runs on the VAX computer.

Cost Analysis Regression Program (CARP). This program produces best-fit logarithmic, linear, and exponential curves through sets of data points; produces a statistical analysis for each curve, including correlation coefficient, coefficient of determination, standard error adjusted, standard deviation, F value, T value, and others; and is capable of multiple regression to generate equations with up to four independent variables. It provides on-screen viewing of graphics.

COLOG Model. COLOG reads outputs from LOGAM and PICES, combines these outputs, and prepares a summary of the costs in several summary cost formats. This model runs on the VAX computer.

*Strategic Defense Initiatives Organization Life Cycle Cost Models (SDIOLCCM).** Life cycle cost models have been developed for eight elements of the Strategic Defense Initiative (SDI) program:

BSTS (Boost-Phase Surveillance and Tracking System Model)

SSTS (Space Surveillance and Tracking System Model)

SBI (Space-Based Interceptor Model)

GSTS (Ground-Launched Surveillance and Tracking System Model)

CC/SOIF (Command Control and Space Operations Information Facility Model)

SE&I (Systems Engineering and Integration Model)

GBR (Ground-Based Radar Model)

GBI (Ground-Based Interceptor Model)

LASER. LASER is a framework for building a work breakdown structure linked to a network diagram, which can be loaded with resources to produce a time-based cost estimate. The model uses ARTEMIS as a base software platform and runs on the HP–1000 computer.

*Strategic Defense Systems Life Cycle Cost Models (SDSLCCM).** Several life cycle cost models were developed for the U.S. Army's Strategic Defense Command:

ASAT (Antisatellite Cost Model)

AOA (Airborne Optical Adjunct Model)

GBL (Ground-Based Lasers Model)

ERIS (Exoatmospheric Reentry Interceptor System Mode)l

HEAC (High Endoatmospheric Interceptor Model)

NPB (Neutral Particle Beam Model)

HOE (Homing Overlay Experiment Model)

FEL (Free Electron Lasers Model)

HPV (Hypervelocity Gun Model)

SHAZAM: SDIO High-Level Affordability for Zero-Based Architecture Model. This model is a top-level cost algorithm that solves a broad variety of SDIO architectural scenarios.

[*Each of these models is capable of providing detailed, program-phased, time-phased parametric cost estimates. The models utilize the PICES framework and provide self-documenting backup as part of the computer output. The models are readily adaptable to program-unique requirements, including hardware learning, acquisition strategies, cost reduction innovations, technology advancement adjustments, and constant or then-year dollars. The models run on both the VAX minicomputer and IBM-compatible personal computers (PCs).]

Tecolote Research, Inc., of Santa Barbara, California, has developed several specific cost models:

LCURVE. LCURVE is an IBM-compatible PC software package that performs learning curve least-squares fits to data and estimates cost with either the results of the curve fit or with parameters input from the keyboard. It combines unit theory, cumulative average theory, unweighted/weighted regression options, curve fitting, and estimating in one package. In addition, LCURVE contains a brief tutorial, context-sensitive help windows, flexible inputs (lot total costs or lot average costs, log quantity or cumulative quantity), built-in inflation capabilities (input in constant-year [CY] or then-year [TY] dollars with conversion to user-desired CY, output in CY or TY dollars with weighted inflation indexes applied), graphics display of the data and curve fit with optional display of confidence intervals, data editing for "what-if" exercises, selective data point exclusion without reentering the data, extended statistical analysis tables including analysis of variance and confidence intervals, and storage, update, and retrieval of data files, output files (curve fit and estimates), and graphics files. The model was prepared for the Air Force Cost Center (AFCSTC/AD) in Washington, D.C.

Quick Reaction Cost Model (QRCM). QRCM is a PC-based, system-level cost model capable of rapidly reestimating program costs in response to changes in funding or procurement schedules. With built-in databases, cost drivers, and cost estimating routines, its main application is for quickly estimating the impact of funding changes in the Five-Year Defense Plan framework. QRCM provides for input and editing of system cost data in approved government format, calibrations of CERs, and file security for basic cost and CER data. Data and CERs for 11 aircraft programs are included. The model was prepared for the program Integration Division, Directorate of Planning and Integration, Washington, D.C.

Avionics Reliability-Cost Trade-Off Model (ARC). The ARC program is configured as a design aid for advanced technology avionics. It is intended to be used early in the design process to aid the designer in searching for cost-effective avionics implementations. The focus of the model is on technology advances promised by the next generation of integrated circuits typified by phase 1, and, ultimately, phase 2 VHSIC (very high speed integrated circuits). The model is designed to allow the study of trade-offs involving all phases of life cycle cost, but it is expected that the impact of VHSIC technology on operations and support costs, in particular, will lead to significantly different design parameters for circuit boards if costs are minimized. The model was prepared for the Aeronautical Systems Division, AFSC/AX, Wright-Patterson Air Force Base, Ohio.

The Black Box Estimators (BBEST) Electronics Cost Models. The Black Box Estimators (BBEST) are a family of 13 automated models estimating the costs of various black box electronics and electronics systems. Two of the models estimate prime mission equipment development cost of electronics—one at the total system or large subsystem level—and the other at the box level. Ten models estimate unit 100 production cost of specific types of military electronics items. These models estimate the costs of digital processors (computers, controllers, etc.), digital interface devices (modems, multiplexers, etc.), analog devices (servo controls, accelerometers, etc.), displays and controls, power supplies, low-power radio frequency devices (receivers, exciters, etc.), tube-type high-power radio frequency devices (transmitters and amplifiers), phased array antennas, and other antennas. The last BBEST model estimates the cost to integrate individual black boxes together into a system or large subsystem. The model was prepared for the Electronic Systems Division (ESD/ACC), Hanscom Air Force Base, Massachusetts.

Schedule Cost and Network System (SCANS). The SCANS model is a tool for structuring and evaluating critical path networks for both time and cost. The model operates in both a deterministic (critical path method) mode and a stochastic (risk) mode. In the deterministic mode, PC-SCANS presents expected time and cost estimates necessary to complete the network. As a stochastic network model, it evaluates the planned schedule for consistency, develops a full network representation, simulates the network using Monte Carlo techniques, and presents the results in terms of a cost distribution of the minimum, expected, and maximum cost values. SCANS features include user-defined cost and schedule risk distributions, activity simultaneity and lagging, time-cost correlation within an activity and time-cost correlation between activities, network and Gantt chart graphic output, flexible start/finish rules, and key milestone analysis.

Automated Cost Estimating Integrated Tools (ACEIT). The ACEIT system provides a standard user-friendly interface to an integrated set of automated tools. ACEIT provides the capability to define the program to be estimated and to build and document the cost estimate. ACEIT architecture consists of an automated estimating system integrated with a methodology library, databases, and a cost analysis statistics package. It includes built-in editors to enable cost organizations to tailor ACEIT to their needs. ACEIT has been installed at major air force centers and is being installed at the SDI National Test Bed, where it will be used as the centralized architecture and framework for SDI cost estimating. It provides factors, CERs, and cost models; document, source, and CER libraries; and databases of cost, schedule, technical, and programmatic information. It gives estimators the capability to search for and extract data from databases and to develop analogies and CERs from the data. ACEIT consists of eight modules or tools: (1) Automated Cost Estimator

(ACE), (2) Automated Cost Data Base (ACDB), (3) Automated Cost Document Library (ACDL), (4) MIDAS CER Relationship Library (MCRL), (5) Cost Estimating Models (CEM), (6) Software Cost Data Base (SCDB), (7) Software Site Data Base (SSDB), and (8) Statistics Package (STATPAK). The model was prepared for the Air Force's Electronic Systems Division at Hanscom Air Force Base and runs on both the VAX minicomputer and IBM-compatible PCs.

Fixed and Transportable Earth Station (FATES) Model Builder. FATES estimates the cost of fixed and transportable satellite ground stations performing either satellite control or communications functions. The greatest degree of detail is provided for individual hardware subsystems as defined by a generic hardware baseline. Development and support costs are scaled from these hardware costs. Model sensitivity to system parameters and mission requirements is provided.

FATES allows the user to custom tailor a model to specific needs by accessing a set of cost data libraries. Libraries are provided for equipment systems and subsystems as defined by a standard hardware cost breakdown structure (CBS). Libraries for support and design costs are also provided. The libraries provide the user with CERs and cost analogs, which can be "carried" back to the user's CBS automatically.

A series of cost equations is compiled by accessing libraries for the various line items of the CBS. By providing the quantities and parameters required to drive these equations, the final model is obtained. Once defined, this model can be easily modified to fit program requirements more accurately or to perform cost trade-off design to cost calculations. The model was prepared for the Air Force Space Systems Division.

Software Program Acquisition Network Simulation (SPANS) and Software Network and Parametric Analogy Database (SNAP). The SPANs model is a PC-based model for estimating the effort and schedule for a software development project. It can also be used for project management purposes such as tracking progress and status reporting, estimating the impact of changes, and achieving project history. The SNAP database was simultaneously developed in support of SPANs. It is populated with parametric software models as well as project schedule and cost data.

John M. Cockerham and Associates (JMCA) of Huntsville, Alabama, has developed the following models:

RISNET. Risk Information System and Network Evaluation Technique (RISNET), developed in the early 1970s, can generate baseline budget estimates; perform what-if exercises, sensitivity studies, and total risk assessing cost estimates; and conduct cost, schedule, and technical risk assessments.

Cost, schedule, and logic data input into RISNET define the interrelationships of the logic network. The network data are simulated deterministically and/or probabilistically to generate a variety of reports and graphs for display on a terminal or output on a printer or graphics plotter. RISNET also generates output files that interface with RISBAR, a GANTT-chart-plotting program, and RISPLOT, a time-phased network plotting program.

RISNET/A. RISNET/A is a menu-driven application that interfaces the RISNET software program with Metier's ARTEMIS program. RISNET/A extends the risk analysis capabilities of RISNET to ARTEMIS while providing RISNET the enhanced database management, statusing, and report capabilities available within ARTEMIS. The RISNET/A interface file is created within RISNET and loaded into the RISNET/A application. It analyzes the input data and generates output in the form of tabular reports, cumulative schedule and cost curves, bar charts, and arrow and precedence network diagrams.

MICRO Cost Model. The MICRO Cost Model is an analytical tool that combines modeling flexibility with quick turnaround. It was designed for use by project offices, command staff offices, and support contractors to perform budget analyses, baseline cost estimates, life cycle cost analyses, what-if exercises, cost reporting, and design to unit production cost analyses. Input can be parametric, throughput, or by CERs, with the output defined by the user. The model allows the user to "build" specialized reports or to output standard government-formatted reports. Costs can be output for time periods, functional categories, hardware categories, or other combinations. The model computes, spreads, and rolls up costs for desired elements.

CAAMS. CAAMS, a PC-based cost and schedule modeling system, was designed to be adaptable to various organizational data needs. It is composed of several software modules designed to work together or on a stand-alone basis. All modules feature graphics and tabular output for ease of understanding.

CAAMS-H (Hardware). This model develops cost and schedule estimates for engineering and manufacturing costs that include electronic and structural hardware. The user describes the hardware through a series of input screens. Multiple-level hardware runs are permitted at the same time.

CAAMS-WBS TREE. This estimating tool prepares system costs by a user-defined WBS structure, detailing labor, material, and associated costs by time period. It provides four-level WBS pricing. WBSTREE is used in pricing applications and evaluations and as a budgeting tool.

CAAMS-L (Life Cycle). CAAMS-L is a parametric cost model for developing the operating and maintenance cost for a hardware system over the lifetime of the system. It can be used to conduct sensitivity analyses of reliability factors, use rates, or maintenance and support concepts.

Management Consulting Research of Falls Church, Virginia, provides the following cost models:

Prototype-to-Production Step-Down Model (Airframes, Engines, and Avionics)
Space Based Radar Model (Recurring and Nonrecurring Costs)

Avionics and Missile Systems Installation Cost Model (Recurring, Nonrecurring, and Installation) for airframes and avionics

Ship Electronics Procurement Cost Model

Electro-Optical Cost Model

Radar Production Cost Model

RDT&E Cost Model

Tactical Missile Systems Cost Model

Space Defense Cost Model

In addition, there are cost models for aircraft, aircraft propulsion, airframes, avionics test equipment, software, tactical surveillance and fire control radars, intercontinental ballistic missiles, focal plane arrays, solid propellant rocket motors, airborne electronics, ground control facilities, and many others.

PRICE Systems, a division of General Electric, develops and supports on-line parametric cost estimating models that are broadly applicable to high-technology products and projects in specific areas. The PRICE-H model is used to estimate the cost of developing and producing electronic, electromechanical, and mechanical assemblies and systems hardware. The PRICE-HL model predicts the life cycle cost of the hardware. The PRICE-M model is used to estimate the development and production of custom microcircuit chips and printed circuit boards. The model can be used in conjunction with the PRICE-H model to estimate the cost of integrated circuitry at the finished product level. The PRICE-S model is used to estimate the cost of developing and implementing computer software. Modules of PRICE-S estimate the size of software to be developed and the cost of maintaining operational software.

Many more models are available, and even more are being developed each year. Among the organizations that have developed and are using cost models for high-technology projects are the National Aeronautics and Space Administration; the Air Force Space Systems Division in Los Angeles, California; Wright-Patterson Air Force Base in Dayton, Ohio; the Jet Propulsion Laboratory in Pasadena, California; and the Center for Naval Analysis, Army Cost Analysis Center, and Air Force Cost Analysis Centers in Arlington, Virginia. These public sector organizations are often willing to share their cost models with private sector firms and contractors that have a need for specialized computer-aided cost analysis tools.

SCHEDULE-BASED ESTIMATING TOOLS

Generic computer tools and cost models, unless specially constructed to spread costs over a time period that is dependent on the timing of milestones and the durations of tasks, usually do not yield calendar-based cost outputs that can be rapidly re-computed when the schedule changes. Since the *timing* of costs is vital in budgeting for new projects or updating the costs of current ones and because changes in schedule are not uncommon in projects of all sizes, schedule-based estimating systems are becoming essential for many projects. A good schedule-based estimating system should be able to transfer a WBS electronically from a "point-estimate" (nonschedule-based) system and to permit the work elements to be scheduled based on key milestone dates, element (activity) durations, and precedence of elements (activities).

To perform the estimate, the schedule-based estimating system should permit the "loading" or application of labor-hours, materials, and resources such as travel, computer time, and other direct costs to each work element. The system should then roll up the costs into the correct calendar units to produce a total cost estimate. Many schedule-based estimating systems also permit the collection, computation, and comparison of actual costs with estimated costs at all levels. At this point, the schedule-based estimating system becomes an automated cost tracking system. This type of cost estimating system is near the bottom of the chart of Figure 12.1 because a larger number of inputs are required, resulting in a high-granularity estimate. Systems that perform these functions are also called project management systems.

One of the most flexible project management systems is ARTEMIS, a critical path network–based system that runs on mainframe computers, minicomputers, and microcomputers. ARTEMIS is produced by Metier Management Systems, Incorporated, of Houston, Texas, and is available in the following versions:

ARTEMIS 2000, for IBM PCs.

ARTEMIS 6000, for Metier turnkey HP 1000 computers.

ARTEMIS 7000, for DEC VAX computers.

ARTEMIS 7000U, for the army standard UNISYS 5000-80 computers.

ARTEMIS 9000, for IBM mainframe computers.

A similar mainframe-minicomputer project system named PROJECT/2 is marketed by Project Software and Development, Inc. of Cambridge, Massachusetts. Other project management systems are the Primavera Project Planner, Vision, Prestige-PC, Harvard Project Manager, MacProject II, Micro-Planner, Microsoft Project, Project Scheduler 4, Project Workbench 3.0, SuperProject Plus, Time Line 3.0, Quiknet Professional, Plantrac, ViewPoint, Promis, and Pro-Path Plus.

Listings of project management software packages are available from the Project Management Institute (PMI), from *Constructor* magazine, and from P.M. Software Solutions.

VERTICAL MARKET COST ESTIMATING SYSTEMS

"Vertical market" cost estimating systems are designed for specific industries such as construction, chemical processing, manufacturing, or electronics. Even *within* each of the major industries, there are special vertical market packages for specific subdisciplines. For example, within the construction discipline, there are estimating systems for electrical systems, ductwork, and heating, ventilation, and air-conditioning systems. There are manufacturing estimating systems for turning small parts, estimating systems tied to numerical control machine program development, and many others. Professional and trade societies have lists of software that will help in estimating the costs of a specific product, project, process, or service.

COMPUTER-AIDED DESIGN-BASED ESTIMATING SYSTEMS

Digitized drawings in the correct electronic format can interface directly with bill of material estimating systems and automatic material quantity takeoff systems to eliminate the laborious steps of measuring and computing dimensions, areas, and volumes and the time-consuming process of counting identical parts, fixtures, appliances, doors, windows, bolts, rivets, or other subsystems. Most CAD systems permit the storage of the number of times an "entity" (part, fixture, appliance, or subsystem) appears on a given drawing. In many CAD programs, this information can be combined with "attributes" of each entity (cost, labor-hours, weight, or other features of the entity) to produce a priced estimate of the bill of materials of the object or system appearing in the drawing. This feature, coupled with automated area, volume, and distance takeoffs priced with prestored unit costs, permits virtual automated estimating of certain forms of CAD drawings. One CAD drawing system's brochure lists the following features:

- Automatically transfers dimensional takeoffs from CAD drawing to bid.
- Automatically converts dimensional takeoff units to order units.
- Generates 20 different reports, including bill of materials and cost lists.
- Recalculates any portions of the estimate affected by changes, allowing quick preparation of several estimates for one job.
- Prepares a checklist for taking off items to help protect against errors and omissions.
- Extends quantities and costs, eliminating the need to double-check calculations.
- Adjusts bid at the last minute for taxes, bonds, overhead, and profit.
- Estimates up to 16,000 different items.
- Takes off dimensions from CAD drawings and transfers them to the bid in the form of order units and costs.

Thus, in a CAD system, you are actually building the cost estimate as you build the drawing. As size is increased or entities (parts) are added to the drawing, you can check the takeoff summary to see the cost increase at any step in the design process. This feature goes a long way toward the objectives of design to cost, since you are able to observe the cost impact as you add to (or subtract from) the design of the item.

ARTIFICIAL INTELLIGENCE AND EXPERT SYSTEMS FOR COST ESTIMATING

Artificial intelligence (the ability of a computer software program to simulate "learning" during operation and interaction with an operator) and expert systems (systems that capture the intuitive and subjective knowledge of experts in a given field) made some inroads into the process of cost estimating during the 1980s, and I predict their greatly expanded usage for cost estimating in the 1990s and beyond. Two examples of systems incorporating characteristics of expert systems are the Teolote Expert Selection System for selecting a database of analogous systems for use in cost estimating and Cost Drivers expert system for sensors developed by Applied Research, Incorporated. Many other expert systems and artificial intelligence-based systems are emerging into the marketplace.[2]

STATISTICS SOFTWARE

Statistics software is useful to the cost estimator who wants to develop cost estimating relationships quickly for cost models. In these programs, the user enters historical cost and performance parameters into a table, and they are automatically plotted on a graph on the computer's display screen. Then the user chooses a linear, polynomial (first, second, third, or fourth order), exponential, or logarithmic curve fit. The computer automatically plots the chosen curve so it will best fit the plotted points, displays the mathematical equation for the curve, and provides a correlation coefficient that indicates the goodness of fit. Cricket Graphics on the Macintosh Personal Computer will perform the operation well. More sophisticated computer graphics and statistics programs are available on the Macintosh, IBM-compatible PCs, minicomputers, and mainframe computers. Some statistics programs for microcomputers are CSS, GAUSS Mathematics and Statistical System, G.B. Stat, MicrostatII, NWA StatPak, SPSS/PCplus, StatGraphics, StatPac Gold, and SYSTAT.

A MULTIDIMENSIONAL ANALYTICAL DATABASE FOR ESTIMATING AND FINANCIAL CONTROL

One type of software package that deserves considerable attention from the cost estimator or cost analyst who wants to make maximum use of the computer is the multidimensional analytical database, which represents a distinct and flexible methodology for rapid data collection, manipulation, and analysis. (Such a database is marketed by Mainstay Software Corporation of Denver, Colorado.) Specifically for the high-technology, multidisciplinary project, product, or service, the multidimensional analytical database addresses the need for looking at resource data from many different directions. Some of the directions or "dimensions" an estimator or analyst needs to observe are:

Work elements (work breakdown structure)

Cost elements (cost element structure)

Calendar spread of costs (schedule elements)

Multiple projects

Organizational costs (organizational elements)

Funding by sources

Tasks or work order (task elements)

Geographical locations

Program phases

Deliveries or quantities

In a simple spreadsheet, the analyst has two dimensions to work with: rows and columns. In a two-dimensional spreadsheet, only two dimensions can be observed at one time. Three-dimensional electronic spreadsheets permit ease of transfer of axes so the analyst can observe or plot values across several spreadsheets, but there are very few analytical tools available that will permit rapid interchange of axes, observation, and analysis of up to 10 dimensions. The multidimensional analytical database is designed to perform this function.

Cost estimators and analysts need to see work elements by calendar time, cost elements by calendar time, cost elements for each work element, cost elements by program phase, work elements by program phase, and many other views of the cost or resource data. In other words, they would like to have every item they need to see available for every view. They not only want to see cost, weight, quantity, for every box in every project for every time phase but also like to manipulate, calculate, and aggregate these data any way they want without any foreknowledge of this need. Within this framework, they would like to assess and define CERs, graph the scatter of points in the relationship and the curve of best fit, and then use this information to develop cost models that enable relevant forecasts of costs of future projects.

The first problem in responding to this need for an open-ended analytical process is that conventional microcomputer tools for performing data analysis are distinct from those for performing data manipulation. Spreadsheet products provide a two- to three-dimensional view of the data. For example, the ability to look at items of information as rows on a spreadsheet, with columns containing the data by time phase, and stacking a number of spreadsheets, one for each subdivision of work, can be done. Unfortunately, this provides only a partial and very limited view of the data. Only one project can be examined for one budget type, and any manipulation of data within the spreadsheets already established is difficult. What is required is the ability to select the views desired and have them available instantaneously without having to prepare another spreadsheet.

Among other deficiencies in the use of spreadsheets for complex projects is the lack of a database. Many cost estimators therefore interface a database system with a spreadsheet system to respond to this need. Although this appears to be the solution, it is not; the process of information analysis occurs when an individual can ask the computer a series of questions, each one based on information derived from one or more previous questions to which he or she has received answers. The process of analysis should be fluid and open-ended. The strength of this conversational process stems from the analyst's free flow of association.

Most software is not designed to provide the freedom to flow through an analysis and receive ready answers to any type of analytical question that occurs to the analyst. Spreadsheets were designed for relatively modest analytical analyses. Database systems were designed for processing repetitive transactions and have been extended to perform analyses; their underlying structure must be pre-programmed for specific views, and open-ended analysis is just not that effective. The multidimensional analytical database is designed to accommodate this analytic process. Its value evolves out of its original design focus: to create a tool for information analysis that contains the capabilities required to support comprehensive and sophisticated analytic processes.

Information analysis combines capabilities of database and analytics within one environment designed from the start to provide for rapid creation of an open-ended data manipulation environment expressly focused on the process of interactive data analysis. Given this focus, then, a cost analyst using a multidimensional database could as easily see data one way as another through the use of only one or two commands. A cost analyst can far better understand the cost environment by being able to determine and display data selectively in user-selected formats.

A multidimensional database provides complete flexibility. With no predetermined report format, the analyst can select any data stored, aggregate them any way desired, order the columns, rows, and page breaks, and present the data. Multidimensionality enables the creation of relational, hierarchical, network, and multidimensional relationships in a given application. Therefore, users and developers can create the precise environment the data imply. This is a far better and more natural approach than forcing naturally hierarchical data, for example, to fit the relational structure demanded by a particular software program.

Unlike other database systems, the multidimensional database does not have records and fields. Information is categorized as "variables" and "dimensions." Variables contain the information the user may need to see. Dimensions describe the way he or she wants to see the data. Thus, variables for the cost estimator would include cost, weight, quantity, labor-hours, and labor rate. Dimensions would include work elements, project, budget type, time phase, and cost element.

A multidimensional database could be the answer to rapid data analysis and cost estimating by the computer user who does not want to work in a customized environment imposed by prestructured models or estimating systems.

COMPUTERIZED CONSTRUCTION ESTIMATING SYSTEMS

Perhaps the most sophisticated and integrated computer estimating systems are those designed for estimating the costs of large construction projects. These systems not only perform the cost estimating function but accomplish most of the other tasks associated with running a large construction company, such as payroll, item billing,

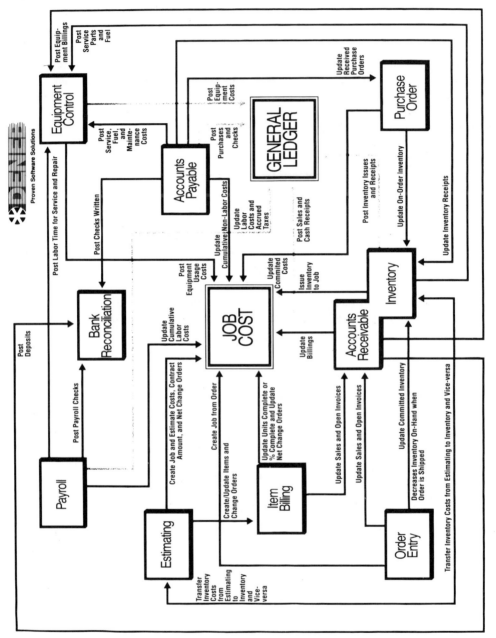

Figure 12.2 Construction estimating system capabilities (courtesy of DENEB Systems).

ESTIMATING

- Capability for multiple estimators and multiple companies
- Input and update line items for material, labor, sub-contractor, etc.
- Assembly mode or manual take-off
- Interface capabilities to materials pricing service and DENEB Inventory
- Can copy previous estimates or assemblies
- Standard phase descriptions
- On-screen calculator during input
- Allows transfer of the estimate into DENEB Job Cost and Item Billing

GENERAL LEDGER

- Supports multiple departments
- Allows current journal transaction entry, with edit list and journal
- Allows transaction entry for recurring journal entries
- Prints the general ledger worksheet and trial balance reports
- Allows on-line account inquiry in detail within specified date range
- User defined financial statements
- Maintains transaction detail for the year
- Prints budget or comparative statements with variances or ratio
- Interfaces Payroll, Accounts Payable, Accounts Receivable/Inventory, and Equipment Control
- Allows processing for multiple years

EQUIPMENT CONTROL

- Shows equipment profitability
- Maintains year-to-date costs and billings of equipment
- Posts equipment depreciation costs to General Ledger
- Allows equipment costs to be charged to a job in the DENEB Job Cost
- Provides fleet operations, equipment location and preventive maintenance reports

PAYROLL

- On-line timecard input by job, employee, or salaried employees
- Multiple city and state tax capacity
- Handles various pay frequencies
- User definable standard deductions
- User maintainable tax tables
- Prints payroll checks, check register, and deduction reports
- Prints certified payroll report (WH347)
- Labor distribution reports
- Detailed history and check register
- Monthly user defined union reports
- Monthly manpower utilization report
- Quarterly 941A and unemployment reports
- Quarterly and annual local tax reports
- Prints W-2 forms at year end
- Magnetic media W-2 reporting capability

ACCOUNTS PAYABLE

- Provides on-line inquiry and validation of input with distribution of input by Job, General Ledger Account, Inventory Item, Purchase Order
- Payments by invoice, job, or paydate
- Prints checks and register
- Handles retainers
- Monthly distribution reports of checks
- Monthly distribution of entries
- Prints waiver of liens
- Direct pay sales tax report
- Prints 1099 forms

PURCHASE ORDER

- Provides overall control of purchase orders
- Reports and inquiry by job or purchase order
- Purchase orders status reports
- Sub-contract report by sub-contractor or job

BANK RECONCILIATION

- Monitor up to fifteen bank accounts
- On-screen inquiry of current balances
- On-screen input for checks written, deposits, and miscellaneous entries
- Reports by bank account, time frame, cleared or uncleared transactions

JOB COST

- Consolidates expenses and billings from all aspects of a job
- Provides for labor analysis and job cost analysis of any or all jobs
- Inquiry and reports track information by job, phase, cost category, cost code, detail item
- Overhead Burden may be defined as a percentage factor at the company, job and phase levels
- Tracks current, month-to-date, and cumulative billings
- Reflects estimated, committed, projected and actual expenses
- Percentage of completion and unit of measure may be defined at the phase (sub-job) level
- Detail or summary reports on active or closed jobs are available by job, project manager, location, customer, or other user defined sort fields
- Handles labor costs plus five user defined cost types

ACCOUNTS RECEIVABLE WITH INVENTORY

- Provides invoices, statements, aging and detailed sales history
- On-line inquiry and updating of customer files
- Provides control over retainers
- Interactive invoice entry and printing of after the fact transaction entry with daily/period journals and totals
- Produces monthly analysis reports
- Inventory costing on LIFO, FIFO, Last Cost, or Average Cost

ITEM BILLING

- Generates progress billings or AIA type billings
- Maintains status of change orders
- Work performed and current stored materials worksheet
- Prints application for payment forms
- Control by unit or percent complete

ORDER ENTRY

- Open order, backorder control and reports
- Inquiry by order, customer, salesperson, job, purchase order number, inventory item
- Special pricing programs for recurring orders, promotional discounts, contracts
- Integration with Accounts Receivable/Inventory

Figure 12.3 Construction estimating system capabilities.

TABLE 12.2   Cost Estimating Software

MULTI/CAM:
AGS Management, Inc.
King of Prussia, PA

Advanced Project Workbench:
Applied Business Technology Corp.
New York, NY

Numerous cost estimating and cost analysis models:
Applied Research, Inc.
Huntsville, AL

Proposal pricing systems and government accounting systems:
Boeing Computer Services
Seattle, WA
Time Line, O&A, and ThinkTank:
Breakthrough Software
Novato, CA

Viewpoint:
Computer Aided Management
San Rafael, CA

SuperProject Expert:
Computer Associates
San Jose, CA

Plantrac:
Computerline Inc.
Pembroke, MA

CAAMS, RISNET, and other models (see text):
John M. Cockerham Associates, Inc.
Huntsville, AL

EASYTRAK, EASYBASE, Performance, Measurement Module (SCSC), ET/CETERA,
ET/GATEWAY:
Cullinet Software
Newport Beach, CA

Milestone:
Digital Marketing Corp.
Walnut Creek, CA

Advanced Mission Cost Model, SPACETRAN:
ECON, Inc.
McLean, VA

(*continued*)

Table 12.2 (*Continued*)

PRICE-H, PRICE-S, PRICE-HL, PRICE-M, and PRICECOM:
GE PRICE Systems
Moorestown, NJ

CP³ (Pricing System):
GovCon Systems, Inc.
Sunnyvale, CA

Project: Vision:
Inmax International Publishing Ltd.
Seattle, WA

Mainstay Multidimensional Database:
Mainstay Software Corp.
Denver, CO

Numerous cost estimating and cost analysis models (see text):
Management Consulting & Research, Inc.
Falls Church, VA

COSTIMATOR:
Manufacturers Technology
West Springfield, MA

ARTEMIS:
Metier Management Systems, Inc.
Houston, TX

Microsoft Project:
Microsoft Corp.
Redmond, WA

Primavera Project Planner:
Primavera Systems, Inc.
Bala Cynwyd, PA

Quiknet Professional:
Project Software and Development Inc.
Cambridge, MA

Project Scheduler 4:
Scitor Corp.
Foster City, CA

Pro-Path Plus:
SoftCorp
Clearwater, FL

(*continued*)

Table 12.2 (*Continued*)

Harvard Project Manager:
Software Publishing Corp.
Mountain View, CA

Vision, VES:
Systonetics
Vienna, VA

SSP's Promis:
Strategic Software Corp.
Cambridge, MA

ACEIT, ADAM, MICAS, NICE, PSM, SCATS, and other models (see text):
Tecolote Research, Inc.
Huntsville, AL

Cobra:
Welcom Software Technology
Houston, TX

---

order entry, accounts receivable, general ledger, accounts payable, equipment control, purchase orders, and bank reconciliation. There are many excellent systems of this type on the market, and others appear regularly.

Construction accounting and estimating were never easy. It took unending hours and a quick thinker to keep track of it all. Today it is even more confusing: a multitude of pay scales, work locations, deductions, taxes, government documentation, unions, and on and on. In this environment, it is important to have a system designed specifically for the construction industry that speaks the language. A general system that was adapted only to the business never seems quite adequate.

A typical construction estimating computer system for the 1990s is the DENEB estimating system marketed by DENEB Systems, Incorporated, of Dayton, Ohio. **Figure 12.2**, reproduced with the permission of DENEB systems, show the modules of the system and their interaction. **Figure 12.3** shows the capabilities of a fully integrated computerized construction cost estimating system. Another recommended construction estimating package is Estiplan produced by AGS Management Systems of King of Prussia, Pennsylvania.

Of the literally hundreds of construction computer-driven estimating systems, names that stand out are R. S. Means of Duxbury, Massachusetts; Contractor Management Systems of Reston, Virginia; Timberline of Seattle, Washington; G–2 Estimating of Boise, Idaho; and Primavera Systems of Bala Cynwyd, Pennsylvania. Each December *Constructor* magazine publishes a listing of dozens of automated construction estimating, management, and scheduling programs. An updated listing such as that shown in *Constructor* and software reviews provide information to help you identify the best system for your application.

This brief overview of the world of estimating with computers must be supplemented by your own investigations of computer magazines, professional magazines, computer software catalogs, and personal contacts with computer vendors. Estimating software is continually being upgraded. To make the job of keeping track of estimating software development easier, **Table 12.2** lists companies that specialize in cost modeling, cost estimating systems, cost estimating templates, and cost analysis tools and services.

NOTES

1. CACES is described in detail in Rodney L. Stewart and Ann L. Stewart, *Microestimating for Civil Engineers* (New York: McGraw-Hill, 1986).
2. James D. Johannes, *Cost Estimator's Reference Manual* (New York: Wiley, 1987).

QUESTIONS

12.1. What is the purpose of CACA tools?

12.2. Name three types of generic computer applications software suitable for cost estimating.

12.3. What is the most common use of a cost model?

12.4. Dollars per square foot or cost per pound are examples of inputs used in high-granularity cost estimating systems.   T   F

12.5. The process plan is used where a detailed cost estimate is required.   T   F

12.6. In what way can CAD systems be used for cost estimating?

12.7. Name some desirable features of a schedule-based computer-aided cost estimating system.

13
SOFTWARE COST ESTIMATING AND CASE

Present your case . . . set forth your arguments.

Isaiah 41:21

In the previous chapter, we discussed various forms of cost estimating software—automated programs that help the cost estimator do the jobs of cost modeling, scheduling, and computation of costs. But what about the task of estimating the cost of software itself? As early as 1973, Barry Boehm, author of the classic *Software Engineering Economics* and originator of COCOMO (COnstructive COst Model), predicted that software costs would reach or exceed 90 percent of the total costs of data processing (combined computer hardware and computer software costs) in the 1980s.[1] High-technology products, projects, processes, and services are requiring increasingly large proportions of software. Software costs have been the fastest growing and most elusive cost element to estimate. In the 1970s and 1980s it became common practice to estimate the cost of computer software based on the number of lines of code to be generated. In the 1990s and beyond this practice will need to be supplemented by productivity adjustments for two reasons. First, the lines of code to be generated depends to a large degree on the machine, high order or applications language to be used, and the approach taken by the system's analyst in interpreting user requirements. Second, a whole new set of productivity tools has emerged since the publication of the first edition of this book in 1982. These tools are generally categorized under the acronym CASE (computer-aided software engineering), a subset of computer-aided systems engineering (a related discipline with the same acronym) that promises to increase lines-of-code productivity by orders of magnitude.

THE CASE FOR CASE

Computer-aided software engineering (CASE) tools dramatically improve the productivity of computer software. They use the abilities of the computer itself to help

256

create software, a natural and logical but late-blooming development in the information age. The amount of software coding that can be produced in a given time period using CASE tools is phenomenal, and experts in software engineering predict huge reductions in cost not only in the programming of lines of code but in the front-end processes of software analysis and design. Software development tools are invading every stage of the software production and maintenance process, as well as every hardware and software environment, from microcomputers to mainframes and from spreadsheets to assembly languages.

The software estimator needs to be aware that CASE tools speed up virtually every step of the software process. Using CASE tools (themselves software programs), an information repository, and a development workstation, the software developer can accomplish many jobs in a hurry that used to take meticulous, line-by-line coding. Here are some examples:

Structured diagramming. CASE tools permit the rapid graphic layout of computer program flow diagrams using many structured diagramming approaches. CASE diagramming tools are available that support DeMarco, Gane-Sarson, Warnier-Orr, Yourdon, Immon, Jackson, Hatley-Pirbhai, Ward-Mellor, Constantine, Chenn, Codd, Merise, Harel-Statechart, Martin, Inforem, Wasserman, LBMS, DSDD, LSDM, and other structured computer software program diagramming methods. More than merely graphics tools, these structured diagramming methods store the relationships developed for use in subsequent steps of the software development process. This front-end set of CASE tools assists immeasurably in communication between the user and the software developer during the initial planning, analysis, and design stages of the software. Structured diagramming using the computer assists in visualizing and documenting the effects of the many changes and iterations that take place early in the software development cycle.

Screen, report, and menu generation. No more are programmers required to place each character or line on a computer screen, printed report, or menu with a location statement identifying its x and y coordinates. Screen generation utilities are available that automatically generate the program code for text and graphics displays on the video screen and on printed documents. These CASE tools are user friendly and easy to operate. Text inputs can be easily entered and located as in a word processor or imported from other programs. Graphic programming tools and subroutines are already available for a wide variety of outputs. Menu hierarchies can be easily generated, and "macros" that record the programmer's key strokes can be used to program repetitive functions. Screen forms for the input of data can be easily generated with all of the accompanying coding needed to permit user entry of data in appropriate fields. Prompts and error messages can be easily added without detailed line-by-line coding.

Command structures, subroutines, and data dictionaries. CASE development tools provide easy input and programming of command structures and even help in writing programs. The software developer can easily enter and rapidly retrieve the names, definitions, and characteristics of data tables, arrays, and fields. Libraries of subroutines are available with preprogrammed coding of many software functions, and the system developer can create custom subroutines that can be stored and used over and over. Twenty-five to 50 percent of the code is in reusable modules for many CASE programming environments, reducing the need to regenerate code for functions that have already been developed. Data dictionaries can be rapidly accessed, modified, deleted, or updated.

Program coding. The largest productivity gains from CASE result from automated code generation, eliminating the need for line-by-line coding. CASE tools develop new code as well as combine existing code in keeping with developed flow diagrams.

Transfer, interpretation, and bridging of coding. CASE tools have been developed that can interpret and modify existing coding, transfer coding into other hardware and software environments, and access information from data repositories.

Documentation generation. CASE tools are available that assist in the detailed documentation of software products. Documentation tools assist in the understanding of coding by other programmers and in the upgrading and maintenance of computer software. Computer generation of documentation assists in what has been one of the most time-consuming aspects of computer software development.

Testing, error checking, consistency, and completeness analysis. CASE tools provide many self-checking features that eliminate common errors that occur early in software development cycles. The visibility, speed, and user friendliness of these tools result not only in faster development but in improved, bug-free software.

Program management of software development. CASE tools help the software developer manage the development of the software. Automated software development monitoring techniques are being developed and perfected that will keep track of software development activities on the CASE system. By using date and time stamping of each operation, records of software development progress and productivity can be automatically recorded, computed, and reported by the CASE system itself. Schedules can be compared with actual progress to indicate progress, and software development costs can be estimated, tracked, and recorded by CASE tools.

Software cost estimating using CASE tools. As CASE tools become more fully developed, integrated, and widely used, they will become the tools for software cost estimating. With the capability for rapid prototyping of software, early estimates of the time and resources required to develop the software will be feasible, and as software development proceeds, updates and refinements of these software cost estimates will be feasible.

Software maintenance. One vital job for the emerging CASE tools is to assist in the maintenance and upgrading of the several hundred billion lines of code that have already been written. CASE developers have been able to develop tools that have the ability to interpret previously written code to determine the basic program structure. This "reverse-engineering" capability is essential for the reuse, refinement, upgrading, and modification of the thousands of existing programs that must be improved to meet constantly changing software requirements. The use of CASE tools for reengineered software maintenance has been accomplished for less than 10 percent of a complete program rewrite. In the mid-1980s, the F–16 jet fighter had an $85 million budget for software development. The software maintenance budget was $250 million— almost three times the software development cost. If CASE tools could be effectively applied for software maintenance for this type of project, hundreds of millions could be saved in this project alone. The cost of a CASE system (about $1 million at present but rapidly decreasing) is almost insignificant in comparison to the potential savings.

Computer-aided software engineering is revolutionizing the computer software industry because of its potential for dramatically improving the ease and speed of creating software. It has already gone through a first-generation and a second-generation phase in the few years it has been available (since 1984) and will be moving into third- and fourth-generation phases by the time this book is widely used by estimators. The productivity improvements that can be expected through the use of CASE can be predicted by projecting past improvements into future years. In terms of investments in CASE products, CASE usage is on an exponential curve that indicates a doubling of usage every four years. If this trend continues, virtually every software developer will have advanced CASE tools and methods in place in the first decade of the twenty-first century.

BASIC SOFTWARE TASKS

Software engineering can be subdivided into several overlapping steps or phases: (1) planning, (2) analysis, (3) specifications, (4) design, (5) implementation (coding and testing), (6) documentation, and (7) maintenance. These steps can be estimated by the two procedures: (1) by analyzing the work required to accomplish each step for a given software product, by applying the skills and hours required for each task, and by applying the appropriate labor rates, overhead, general and administrative expense, and fee values, and (2) by using one of a number of parametric software cost estimating models designed to approximate the costs of software development and maintenance. Chapter 12 of the *Cost Estimator's Reference Manual* lists and describes several computer software cost estimating models: (1) COCOMO by Barry Boehm, (2) Price S (produced by GE-Price Systems of Cherry Hill, New Jersey), (3) SLIM (Software Lifecycle Integration Model) (marketed by Quantitative Software Management, Inc., of McLean, Virginia), (4) the JPL Software Simulation Model (Jet Propulsion Laboratory, Pasadena, California), and (5) the ESD Parametric Software Cost Estimating Model originated by the U.S. Air Force

Electronics Systems Division at Bedford, Massachusetts).[2] (There are also other software cost models available in the software marketplace such as Softcost-R, REVIC, NASA/SEL, Tecolote #2, Jensen, Doty, Farr, Wolverton, Kustanowitz, Ruby, GRC, Schneider, Nelson, Boeing, Aaron, and Aerospace.) These software cost models, which require inputs of a number of parameters (one of them the expected number of lines of code), can be used to estimate labor-hours and costs for generation of software in the conventional manner by programmers who are not using computer-aided diagramming, specification development, coding, documentation, upgrading, and reverse engineering provided by CASE tools. To convert the output of these programs to the resources needed for software development and maintenance assisted by CASE tools requires the application of productivity factors such as those shown in **Figure 13.1**.

CASE AND ITS IMPACT ON SOFTWARE ESTIMATING

The increasing availability and emergence of sophisticated CASE tools is bringing about a transition in the software discipline that will affect the way software will be developed and maintained in the future. Just as PC spreadsheet and database applications programs have enabled PC users to develop sophisticated applications with-

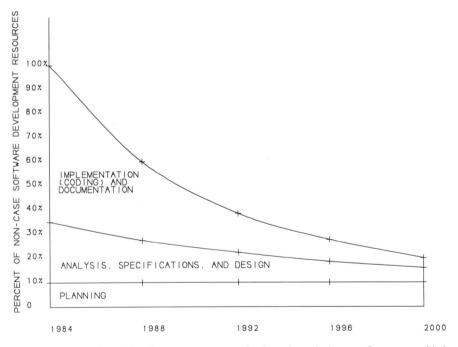

Figure 13.1 Projected development resource reductions through the use of computer-aided software engineering.

out producing computer code, so CASE tools are beginning to provide minicomputer and mainframe computer software developers with means of software development from analyst-generated flow diagrams and specifications. In developing a spreadsheet, the PC user becomes the end user, the analyst, the designer, and the programmer. Increasing use of CASE tools will gradually eliminate the boundaries between analysts, designers, and coders. Fewer skill categories for software development and maintenance will emerge. Today's systems professional will be called a developer or development engineer and will perform a job encompassing the functions of analysis, design, and coding. The job of maintenance programmer used to entail the review of documentation and the reanalysis of systems to understand the impact of the required changes and coding. In the evolving CASE environment, this person becomes more of an analyst and designer who uses the tool to determine where changes have to be made and then modifies the design to regenerate the program code automatically. The user also becomes a more active participant in the software development process. The role and skills of new computer professionals will be different from those of past software development technicians. The new skills, labor-hours required, and hourly rates will have to be considered in developing detailed labor-hour and material cost estimates of software creation using CASE tools.

THE ADA PROGRAMMING LANGUAGE

Ada is becoming the standard programming language for high-technology systems and aerospace projects. In 1973 the Department of Defense High Order Language Working Group began work to replace the several hundred languages and language versions then in use in order to provide a single, common programming language designed to serve the needs of the military services for mission-critical software. Use of that common language, Ada, has reduced software production and maintenance costs throughout the life cycle of deployed systems, reduced training costs, made programmers assignable across systems and agencies, and made software more portable from one system or installation to another.

In 1984 and 1985, all three Department of Defense services adopted Ada as their standard software language, and in 1985, Ada became the federal information processing standard. By 1987, Ada was at work in over 30 National Aeronautics and Space Administration projects totaling more than 740,000 lines of code in the major space centers. In 1988, there were approximately 200 validated Ada compilers reported by the Ada Information Clearinghouse. Technology-driven industrial history suggests that two to five firms will dominate the Ada industry in the 1990s. Increasing adoption of Ada by universities in the early 1990s will provide larger pools of Ada-fluent programmers to both government and commercial organizations.

CASE tools for Ada are rapidly becoming available for a variety of hardware platforms, supporting the entire software development and maintenance life cycle. For example, RATIONAL, of Mountain View, California, markets a seamless inte-

grated environment for the design, implementation, documentation, and maintenance of large software systems written in Ada. This CASE tool provides Ada-
compatible program design language, automatic generation of design documentation, interactive semantic analysis and design rule checking, incremental compilation, configuration management and version control, and source language debugging. Optimizing code generators and cross-debuggers provide support for several
application architectures. About 10 companies now provide CASE tools for Ada
system developers and maintainers. Productivity figures and costs for Ada CASE
tools can be supplied by the following companies:

Advanced Technology International, Inc., (212) 354–8280.

Cadre Technologies, Inc., (401) 351-CASE.

Concurrent Computer Corp., (201) 758–7569.

Digital Equipment Corp., (603) 881–2384.

Interactive Development Environments, Inc., (415) 543–0900.

Promd, Inc., (714) 855–3046.

RATIONAL, (415) 555–1212.

Ready Systems, (408) 736–2600.

Visible Systems, Inc., (617) 890–2273.

Yourdan, Inc., (212) 391–2828.

PROCEDURES FOR SOFTWARE COST ESTIMATING

The principal factors affecting the costs of computer software programs are the
computer equipment configuration and performance, the characteristics of the software product, and the extent of utilization of CASE tools in software development
and maintenance. For detailed cost estimates of computer software to be accurate,
these factors must be known or assumed prior to beginning the detailed cost estimating process. The following checklist will assist estimators in ensuring that vital
technical data about the hardware, the program's requirements, and the utilization
of CASE tools are known before the cost estimating process begins.

    A. Computer hardware configuration and performance
        1. Computer and peripheral designations (brand names and model num-
           bers).
        2. Numbers of each computer and peripheral units required.
        3. Computer speed (memory cycle time and add time).
        4. Memory type and capacity.
        5. Storage type and capacity.
        6. Bits per memory word.
        7. Input devices and channels, type, and transfer rate.

8. Output devices and channels, type, and transfer rate.

9. Time-sharing capability (multiuser).

10. Multiprocessing capability (multitasking).

11. Compiler requirements.

12. Communications transfer rates.

13. Number of separate operational sites.

14. Number and type of interfacing information processing hardware systems.

B. Computer software

1. Number of decision-making functions.

2. Number of computation functions.

3. Number of information and retrieval functions.

4. Number of subprograms.

5. Interrelation of subprograms.

6. Severity of storage and/or timing problems.

7. Degree of need for a common database.

8. Number of interfaces with other programs.

9. Number of fields in the database (if applicable).

10. Number of characters per field.

11. Number of input messages or variables.

12. Number of output messages or variables.

13. Degree of documentation required: User's manual, programmer's manual, written tutorial, programmed tutorial.

14. Testing requirements: Number of sites, number of users per site, duration of testing program.

15. User support requirements: Customization, on-site support, telephone support

16. Training.

C. Extent of utilization of CASE tools in software development and maintenance

1. Structured diagramming support.

2. Menu hierarchy generation and menu generation.

3. Report format and content generation.

4. Command structure generation.

5. Graphics generation.

6. Screen design and input format generation.

7. Utilization of presupplied subroutines.

8. Reuse of designer-generated subroutines.

9. Structuring and storage of CASE data dictionaries.

10. Database field specification generation.
11. Automated program coding and structuring.
12. Transfer, interpretation, and bridging of coding.
13. Automated documentation generation.
14. Testing, error checking, constancy, and completeness analysis.
15. Program management of software development.
16. Software maintenance, reengineering, and updating.

Lists A and B represent the requirements of the computer system. List C provides a structure or checklist that the software cost estimator can use to indicate the degree of utilization of CASE tools (hence, the productivity of the personnel developing or maintaining the software) for each function that CASE tools provide. Until CASE tools become fully used by organizations developing software and until they evolve to a point where they incorporate software development and maintenance resource estimating, the recommended estimating procedure is to use one of the two methods (detailed or parametric) to estimate software costs based on the use of manual or conventional planning, analysis, design, coding, testing, and documentation methods, and then to apply productivity factors resulting from the use of CASE tools in each area in list B. The two methods of estimating manual or conventional software development resources are: (1) detailed (labor-hour and material-based) software cost estimating and (2) parametric (conventional software estimating model-based) software cost estimating.

DETAILED SOFTWARE COST ESTIMATING

It is axiomatic that the degree of skill, competence, and experience of the software development personnel will have a large effect on the outcome of the detailed labor-hour resource estimates, as well as the final software cost estimate. Skill categories need to be carefully established, and there must be an appropriate mix of skill levels within these categories to accomplish the job in an efficient and effective manner. **Table 13.1** lists typical skill categories and skill levels for a software development project. These personnel will have capabilities and experience in management, analysis, engineering, computer science, programming, statistics, mathematics, technical writing, and publishing. Selection of quality personnel to fill all positions is of vital importance to completion of the software development project on time and within the allocated resources. The use of CASE tools will concentrate these skills into fewer skill categories and levels, principally in the systems analyst category.

Labor rates that are commensurate with experience, productivity, and skill levels should be established that will attract the high-quality individuals needed, and allowance should be made for merit increases during the project. Higher labor rates with higher corresponding productivities usually result in lower overall costs than lower labor rates with correspondingly lower productivities because productive personnel can be rapidly moved into new projects. When the work element struc-

TABLE 13.1   Typical Skill Categories and Skill Levels Used in Software Development

Skill Categories	Skill Levels
Program Management	Program manager
	Project manager
	Project engineer
	Cost estimator
Systems Analysts	Senior systems analyst
	Systems analyst
	Systems data analyst
Programmers	Senior programmer
	Programmer
	Coding specialist
Data entry personnel	Senior technician
	Technician
	Junior technician
	Clerical
Documentation specialists	Documentation manager
	Editor
	Senior technical writer
	Technical writer
	Proofreader

Source: Cost Estimator's Reference Manual Rodney D. Stewart and Richard M. Wyskida, eds., (New York: Wiley, 1987).

ture, schedule, skill categories, and levels, and labor rates are established, the estimation of labor-hours, computer time, and materials can begin.

Once the preliminary steps of the estimating process have been completed, the key remaining job is to forecast the labor-hours, computer time, travel, and materials required to accomplish the software development job. The remaining steps are routine in nature (but important) and will flow smoothly if the proper groundwork has been laid.

In the detailed estimating process of computer software, I recommend the expert opinion approach using experienced software development professionals. Often the people who are going to be doing the work, provided they are experienced, know better than anyone else how long it is going to take to accomplish the detailed tasks involved in software development. If the work has been broken down sufficiently and if the hardware and the product have been adequately defined, the one who is going to do the work, or his or her immediate supervisor, should make the resource estimates. These estimates will be reviewed and compared with parametrically developed estimates prior to final budget establishment as a check and balance, but the performer or supervisor must have an input in the early stages of the estimating process.

The iterative nature of software itself must be considered in estimating labor-hours for software development. Ample time must be allocated for checking, debugging, rerunning, editing, and limits testing of each submodule, module, and program. Care must be taken to ensure that labor skills are time-phased and that the skill mix is adjusted as the development schedule progresses to allow for the application of higher skill levels during the more difficult parts of the development process (startup and reevaluation after testing) and lower skill levels to accomplish routine data entry, error checking, proofreading, and maintenance functions. Mainframe and microcomputer programs are available to assist in the computerized pricing of software cost estimates. Many of these are the same programs that will perform the pricing functions of hardware projects or services. Computerized pricing includes the application of inflation and escalation factors, the addition of overhead, administrative costs, and fee or profit, and the adjustment of estimates if required to meet design-to-cost or budgetary criteria.

Once costs are developed for the lower levels of the work breakdown structure, the CASE applicability and utilization checklist can be used to determine the impact of CASE tools on reductions (or increases) in cost elements. Labor costs can be expected to decrease. Specifically, programming labor can be expected to decrease dramatically, as can testing, debugging, and documentation labor. Materials costs will increase by the cost of the CASE systems and tools themselves, and some front-end labor may need to be added for analysts and training personnel to train the software development and maintenance work force in the application of CASE tools. Unfortunately, specific productivity factors for the various aspects of CASE usage are not available. I recommend that the estimator obtain from CASE tool developers and suppliers productivity figures on specific CASE products and methods. Over 80 such products, along with the names, addresses, and telephone numbers of about 50 CASE tool developers appeared in the June 1989 *Systems Engineering* magazine. I presume that subsequent issues of the same magazine and similar publications will be available in the coming years to provide software cost estimators with up-to-date sources of information on CASE development tool productivity and CASE tool sources.

PARAMETRIC SOFTWARE COST ESTIMATING

There are over 20 parametric cost models available for estimating the cost of software development. These models do not take into account the potential effects of adopting CASE tools on increased productivity and potentially lower labor time or costs per line of code. But to form a base for subsequent application of CASE productivities, these tools can be used to develop baseline estimates. (You can expect to see CASE-based software cost estimating models emerge from the cost analysis profession in the near future.) The most well-known and widely followed parametric cost model for conventional manual programming methods is the COCOMO model.

Barry Boehm's COCOMO model is an essential reference for anyone who is planning, scheduling, estimating, or carrying out a software project. It contains detailed descriptions of the methodology for the cost estimating of software, as well as hard and factual numerical, quantitative data drawn from actual software projects. The in-depth discussions of all aspects of software engineering and its cost and resource requirements reflect the author's keen insight into the underlying problems in estimating the cost of computer software projects. His knowledge of the pitfalls, remedies, and the systematic procedures needed to gain some semblance of credibility in estimating the cost of software projects and products are clearly indicated. Because the book was written in 1981, well before CASE tools and related productivity enhancements in software development and maintenance were available, the methodology does not include consideration of CASE productivity improvements, but it provides an excellent, reasonable base of manual and conventional software cost estimating.

Two of the most important parts of the book are the definitions of "verification" and "validation":

1. *Verification:* Answers the question, "Are we building the product right?" (addresses the efficiency of the software)
2. *Validation:* Answers the question, "Are we building the right product?" (addresses the satisfaction of the user)

Since verification of software usually precedes validation, one can see that an iterative process must be used in software development (since we cannot usually tell if we have exactly the right product until it is already built).

The author provides an excellent "goal structure" and a detailed work or task element breakdown structure for a typical software project. The goal structure precisely defines specific goals under each of three general goal categories:

1. Human relations (includes user friendliness)
2. Resource engineering (cost of the software)
3. Program engineering (technical requirements)

Twenty-eight goals listed for successful software engineering must be fully defined before software design and subsequent estimating can begin. Boehm subdivides these software goals into product goals (to achieve a successful software development product), process goals (to carry out a successful software development process), and quantitative and qualitative descriptions of these goals.

Having developed a goal structure, the software cost estimator or cost analyst must then develop a work breakdown structure activity hierarchy against which resources can be estimated and allocated. Boehm advocates the following major subdivisions in this work breakdown structure:

Software management
Software systems engineering

Software programming

Software test and evaluation (verification and validation)

Software data (documentation)

Software implementation (field support)

Software maintenance (updates, corrections)

These major work elements are subdivided into a total of 61 subelements.

The procedures Boehm recommends are applicable to a wide variety of types and sizes of software projects, and the procedures are written in a generic manner. For example, the database on which resource algorithms are based covers projects requiring from 7 to 7000 labor-months to complete, and the database of 63 projects contains 7 business systems or applications, 10 control systems or applications, 13 human/machine interface applications, 17 scientific applications, 8 support applications, and 8 systems applications. The user can select the part of the database that is most applicable.

The cost model is presented in three levels for top-level, intermediate, and lower-level parametric estimating. The level of estimating depends on the degree of definition of the project.

The book also contains other useful features and information:

1. Typical project phases, activities, and milestones ("waterfall" scheduling model) are listed.

2. The author's seven basic steps in software cost estimation are discussed: (a) establish objectives, (b) plan for required data and resources, (c) pin down software requirements, (d) work out as much detail as possible, (e) use several independent techniques and sources, (f) compare and iterate estimates, and (g) follow up.

3. Levels of software complexity are defined.

4. A list of factors not included in the parametric software resource database is given.

5. Answers to the following questions are provided:

   a. Why does software development cost as much as it does?

   b. What factors make the cost of software go up or down, and how do they interact?

   c. What activities consume most of the cost?

   d. How can new software techniques reduce software cost?

6. A distinction between material economics and human economics in software development is provided.

7. A discussion of "advancemanship," which is the *premium value of early definition* of requirements, design specifications, and validation, even for small projects, is furnished.

8. A listing, along with detailed equations, charts, and text descriptions of the

estimating and use of 15 software, computer, project, and personnel attributes is furnished.

9. A detailed discussion of software project planning and control is provided.

10. Forms, checklists, and an extensive bibliography of software reference books are included.

The most astute conclusion in the book regards software estimating databases: *The only really reliable database for software cost estimating is that which has been developed by the organization that is going to do the work.* The software cost estimator must take this fact into account no matter what cost estimating method is used because productivities, even with CASE tools, vary from organization to organization.

Whether COCOMO or another software cost estimating tool is used, the impact of CASE tool usage must be considered in the final software estimates. For parametric model-based estimates, improvements such as that shown in **Figure 13.1** could be considered. Although these are only estimates, which will have to be updated frequently to hold any real credibility over a long period of time, it can be seen that dramatic improvements in lines of code per resource spent can be expected by the end of the century. The eventual result of CASE tool application will be that the average applications software developer and maintainer, as well as those involved in processing, monitoring, and control software, will be involved more in systems planning and analysis and less in program coding, testing, and documentation. In the coming century, CASE tools will take the tiresome work out of software development and maintenance and will eventually help the estimator predict the costs of the software itself.

NOTES

1. Barry Boehm, *Software Engineering Economics* (Englewood Cliffs, N.J.: Prentice-Hall, 1973).

2. Rodney D. Stewart and Richard M. Wyskida, eds., *Cost Estimator's Reference Manual* (New York: Wiley, 1987).

QUESTIONS

13.1. List five examples of areas where the use of CASE tools improves productivity of computer software.

13.2. List six basic steps of software engineering. Tell how these steps can be estimated.

13.3. What are the principal factors affecting the life cycle costs of computer software programs?

13.4. List three cost drivers in software development that affect the number of labor-hours.

13.5. What is the most common method of estimating the cost of software?

13.6. What major subdivisions of the work breakdown structure are advocated by the COCOMO model?

13.7. Cite two reasons why the use of the number of lines of code to develop a software cost estimate may produce erroneous results.

APPENDIX I

MANUFACTURING STANDARDS AND ESTIMATING FACTORS*

SHEET METAL OPERATIONS

Sheet metal (aluminum, steel, copper, brass, or magnesium) is often the least costly material from which to form industrial and commercial products because it usually results in less waste or scrap than machining and results in high-strength, lightweight brackets, enclosures, ducts, housings, and containers.

Steel is the least expensive kind of material for use in making sheet metal parts because it requires less cleaning and finishing than either aluminum or magnesium; however, the lighter weight of the latter two makes them desirable for use in some applications. Magnesium requires the heating of parts and dies in shaping and forming, adding time to the fabrication of parts and causing a fire hazard. The standards that follow are in three representative sizes, and it is expected that intermediate sizes or special configurations will require an intelligent deviation from the values shown. Small is 3 × 3 inches; medium is 18 × 18 inches; and large is 30 × 30 inches.

Handling time for parts is included in operation time unless it is shown separately.

In general, the sequence in which the various operations are given is the shop operating sequence of events.

SHEET METAL BLANK CUT STANDARDS:

Equipment: Power gate shear
  Setup time:
    Set stops (front or rear)
    for gauging test cut and check
    measurements and periodically check
    holddowns

*Note: For manual operations only: Adjustments must be made for specific automation techniques.

	0.2 hr Minutes per Operation		
	Small	Medium	Large
Run time:			
Average time per cut	0.10	0.20	0.40

The maximum cuts for a rectangular blank would be four; however, in actual practice, one cut is all that is required because each cut along one side of a blank is also the side of another. Also, on initial cuts, one cut actually cuts several blank sides.

SHEET METAL NOTCHING STANDARDS

Equipment: Power notcher
  Setup time:
    Set stops; trail cut; check
    measurements

	0.1 hr Minutes per Operation		
	Small	Medium	Large
Run time:			
Pick up part and position, depress foot pedal, and lay aside or position for next cut	0.10	0.20	0.40

MAKING HOLES IN SHEET METAL

Various methods may be used in making holes in sheet metal. There are punchers, drills, fly cutters, circle sheers, hole saws, profilers, routers, and milling machines. The standards shown here are for a turret punch: Weideman RA41P with pantograph, styles, template, and work holder.

	Hours
Setup time:	
To tool crib for template, locate template and secure.	0.1
Line up and adjust holding device.	0.1
Total	0.2
Add for each change of punch size.	0.05

	Minutes per Operation		
	Small	Medium	Large
Run time:			
Pick up blank, match tooling holes to locator pins, clamp, rotate turret to right punch size, and unclamp piece after piercing and remove.	0.20	0.40	0.80
Punch holes, move stylus to template, and remove stylus and transfer to next position.	0.05	0.05	0.05

METAL DRILLING

Drilling $1/16$ to 1 inch in diameter requires a fairly constant run time. For holes less than $1/16$ inch, feed time must be carefully regulated to avoid breaking the drill. One- and two-inch holes can be drilled in approximately the same time since drill bits are stout, heavy-duty presses are used, and high feed rates can be accommodated. It takes more time to drill without a template since the operator must sight the exact point of drilling.

The following table is an example of standards for hole-drilling times in minutes for aluminum.

Hole Size (Diameter)	Number of $1/16$ in. Sheets in Stack	Move Time (Hole to Hole)	Machine Time	Total	Time per Sheet
$1/16$ in. to 1 in.	1 (No template)	0.075	0.024	0.099	0.099
	1 (Template)	0.047	0.024	0.071	0.071
	2 (Template)	0.047	0.037	0.084	0.042
	3 (Template)	0.047	0.049	0.096	0.032
	4 (Template)	0.047	0.064	0.111	0.028
2 in. to 4 in.	1 (No template)	0.075	0.400	0.475	0.475

SHEET METAL BLANKING AND PIERCING OPERATIONS (20- to 75-Ton Press)

For sheet metal blanking and piercing operations, transporting parts to the die on an individual basis is the most time-consuming operation. When raw material can be fed from strip or coil, the output is a function of the steady run rate. Generally, press cycles are in the range of 10 to 200 cycles per minute, which means that theoretically with continuous stock feed one could expect 10 to 200 pieces per minute. The full theoretical output, however, can never be reached because of the necessity to set up new stock, remove scrap, and other maintenance.

Setup time:
The punch and die elements are mounted in a common die shoe-guide post-punch holder, the punch and die elements are permanently aligned in the die set, a trip to tool crib is included, die shoe is fastened to press bed, and height of press bed is adjusted to achieve desired depth.

4 hr

	Minutes per Operation		
	Small	Medium	Large

Run time:
Pick up blank, place on die, activate, remove piece to tray, and clear scrap.

	Small	Medium	Large
	0.20	0.30	0.50

Sheet metal dimple and joggle operations are done on the same kind of machine as blank and pierce operations, the difference being that dimple and joggle use a form die. Dimples are formed around lightening hole to give added stiffening to a flat surface. Joggles are used to make lap joints so that the surface at the lap is more or less flush. Setup and run times are the same as for blank and pierce operations.

BRAKE-FORMING OF SHEET METAL

Equipment: Power brake
Setup time:
Adjust position stops, adjust ram blade for proper thickness, and change dies.

0.6 hr

	Minutes per Operation		
	Small	Medium	Large

Run time:
(Same as blank and pierce.)

	Small	Medium	Large
	0.20	0.30	0.50

ROLL-FORMING OF SHEET METAL

Equipment: Three-roll power mangle
   Setup time:
      Adjust front rolls to metal thickness,
      adjust rear roll to desired radius.

	0.2 hr Minutes per Operation		
	Small	Medium	Large
Run time: Activate rolls, and feed blank into mangle	0.20	0.90	1.50

Run times are for one pass through the rolls. Usually after the first few pieces are run, the mangle will be adjusted so that the desired radius can be formed in one pass (including a complete cylinder). If more than one radius is involved, standard values should be multiplied by the number of radii.

DEEP DRAWING OF METAL

Deep drawing is done with relatively expensive dies, the cost of which will not be warranted unless significant quantities are involved. Three controlling factors are important in drawing: height to diameter ratio, ductility of metal to be formed, and the corner radius. Where more than one draw is necessary to completely form the part, the metal may have to be annealed between each draw. If a new design is being estimated, the following can be used as a guide:

   One draw: if depth is one-third of the punch diameter

   Two draws: if depth is one-half of the punch diameter

   Three draws: if depth is three-quarters of the punch diameter

   Four draws: if depth is equal to the punch diameter

Equipment: 70-Ton hydraulic press, male and female dies
   Setup time:
      Install dies on platform and ram.

	0.5 Minutes per Operation		
	Small	Medium	Large
Run time: Place part on conveyor rack, close door, and remove.	0.10	0.20	0.40

HYDRO-FORMING OF SHEET METAL

The chief advantage of this kind of forming is the lower cost of tooling involved. Only the male portion of the die is required. A caged rubber mat forces the blank to take the form of the male die as pressure is applied.

Equipment: 70-Ton press, male die
  Setup time:

	0.3 hr		
Install male die on lower press platen, and install caged rubber mat on upper platen.	Minutes per Operation		
	Small	Medium	Large
Run time:			
Pick up and position blank, actuate, remove part to pallet, and blow die clear.	1.40	1.70	2.40

DE-BURRING SHEET METAL

Equipment: Belt sander or portable power vibrator
  Setup time:

	0.1 hr		
Trip to tool crib.	Minutes per Operation		
	Small	Medium	Large
Handling time:			
Pick up and position and place in tray.	0.10	0.20	0.40
De-burr edge: aluminum, epoxy laminate, belt sander, file, and emery cloth. Machine time per inch.	0.02	0.02	0.02
De-burr flat surface: portable sander. Machine time per square foot.	0.20	0.30	0.50
Deburr hole: hand scraper or end file, per hole. Time per hole.	0.03	0.03	0.03

WELDING SHEET METAL

Equipment: Oxyacetylene welding equipment
  Setup time:
    Obtain degreaser, and position
    exhaust duct.

	0.3 hr		
	Minutes per Operation		
	Small	Medium	Large
Cleaning:			
Clean faying or butt surfaces.	0.25	0.70	1.80
Handling:			
Place part on fixture and remove.	0.10	0.20	0.40
		Hours	

Run time:
  Weld with 0.062-in. rod.   0.25 min/in.
  Weld with 0.125-in. rod.   0.40 min/in.
  Weld with 0.250-in. rod.   0.75 min/in.

STRESS-RELIEVING AFTER WELDING

Equipment: Controlled heat furnace
  Setup time:
    Adjust furnace temperature.

	0.1 hr		
	Minutes per Operation		
	Small	Medium	Large
Run time:			
Put parts in furnace and remove.	0.10	0.20	0.40

GRIND FITLET WELD

Equipment: Floor grinder or portable sander
  Setup time:
    Clamp part to bench

	0.1 hr		
	Minutes per Operation		
	Small	Medium	Large
Run time:			
Handle parts. Machine time.	0.10	0.20	0.40
	(103 min/in.)		

SPOT-WELDING OF SHEET METAL

Equipment: Single head spot welder, 10 A
   Setup time:
      Install and adjust contact points,
      current timing, and holding fixture

	0.4 hr		
	Minutes per Operation		
	Small	Medium	Large
Run time:			
Handling: convey parts to welder, and remove and place in tray	0.10	0.20	0.40
Welding: move from spot to spot, press foot pedal, and machine cycle	0.05	0.05	0.05

If more than one size is being joined, the proper handling values should be used (*example:* If three small parts are being welded to one medium part, the handling time would be 0.50 minute).

RIVETING SHEET METAL

Equipment: Hammer, rivet set, anvil
   Setup time:
      Obtain hammer, rivet set, and anvil

	0.4 hr		
	Minutes per Operation		
	Small	Medium	Large
Run time:			
Handle parts	0.10	0.20	0.40
Pickup and insert rivet	0.05	0.05	0.05
Upset and tighten rivet	0.05	0.05	0.05

If more than one size is being joined, the proper handling value should be used (*example:* If three small parts are being riveted to one medium part, the handling time would be 0.50 minute).

ELECTROPLATING AND METAL TREATING

There are standards for the electroplating and/or heat treating of various metals. The purpose of the treatments, the applicable military or other specifications, and two standard time values are presented in tabular form in the following sections. The soak time value in the first column is the time each batch should remain in the bath or in treatment. The handling value in the second column is the time required (labor-minutes) to handle the batch in the given operation.

The time values listed are based on manually dipping the parts, and these values are based on averages. They consider average amounts of corrosion on parts to be cleaned, average plating thickness, and average time per bath. While individual cases may vary from the given values over a period of time, the actual values will generally coincide with those provided.

Aluminum Anodizing

Baths	Minutes/Batch	
	Soak	Handle
Alkaline cleanse	4.0	2.5
Rinse	0.5	0.5
Deoxidize	7.0	2.5
Rinse	0.5	0.5
Anodize	30.0	2.5
Rinse	0.5	0.5
Seal	15.0	2.5
Rinse	0.5	0.5
Total	58.0	12.0

Note: Purpose: paint base and corrosion resistance
Specification: MIL-A-8625, anodic coating for aluminum, Type II.
Thickness: 600 mg/ft^2.
Time: based on tank size: 36 in. $\times$ 30 in. $\times$ 36 in.; 15 ft^2 of parts plated (10 A/ft^2 at 150 A).

Aluminum: Chemical Film (Iridite)

Baths	Minutes/Batch	
	Soak	Handle
Alkaline clean	4.0	2.5
Rinse	0.5	0.5
Dioxidize	7.0	2.5
Rinse	0.5	0.5
Iridite	2.0	2.5
Rinse	0.5	0.5
Total	14.5	9.0

Note: Purpose: paint base and corrosion resistance (salt spray 168 hr).
Specification: MIL-C-5541, chemical films for aluminum and aluminum alloys.
Thickness: not specified.

Aluminum: Gold Plate

	Minutes/Batch	
Baths	Soak	Handle
Alkaline cleaner	4.0	2.5
Rinse	0.5	2.5
Dioxidize	7.0	2.5
Rinse	0.5	0.5
Acid dip	0.5	1.0
Rinse	0.5	0.5
Zinc immersion	1.5	2.0
Rinse	0.5	0.5
Copper strike	0.5	1.0
Rinse	0.5	0.5
Silver strike	0.5	1.0
Rinse	0.5	0.5
Gold plate	10.0	2.5
Rinse	0.5	0.5
Rinse	0.5	0.5
Total	28.0	18.5

Note: Purpose: conductivity, solderability, and corrosion resistance.
Specification: none.
Thickness: 50 to 100 millionths of an inch.
Time: based on tank size, 18 in. $\times$ 12 in. $\times$ 18 in.

Aluminum: Silver Plate

	Minutes/Batch	
Baths	Soak	Handle
Alkaline cleaner	4.0	2.5
Rinse	0.5	0.5
Dioxidize	7.0	2.5
Rinse	0.5	0.5
Acid dip	0.5	1.0
Rinse	0.5	0.5
Zinc immersion	1.5	2.0
Rinse	0.5	0.5
Copper strike	0.5	1.0
Rinse	0.5	0.5
Silver strike	0.5	1.0
Rinse	0.5	0.5
Silver plate	20.0	2.5
Rinse	0.5	0.5
Total	37.5	16.0

Note: Purpose: conductivity, corrosion resistance, and solderability.
Specification: QQ-S-365, Type III (bright).
Thickness: 0.0005 to 0.0010 in.
Time: based on tank size, 18 in. × 12 in. × 18 in.

Aluminum: Tin Plate (Hot Oil Fuse)

Baths	Minutes/Batch	
	Soak	Handle
Alkaline cleaner	4.0	2.5
Rinse	0.5	0.5
Deoxidize	7.0	2.5
Rinse	0.5	0.5
Acid dip	0.5	1.0
Rinse	0.5	0.5
Zinc immersion	1.5	2.0
Rinse	0.5	0.5
Copper strike	0.5	1.0
Rinse	0.5	0.5
Tin plate	40.0	2.5
Rinse	0.5	0.5
Hot oil fuse	2.0	2.5
Vapor degrease	1.5	2.0
Total	60.0	19.0

Note: Purpose: solderability.
Specification: MIL-T-10727, Type I.
Thickness: 0.005 to 0.0010 in.
Time: based on tank size, 18 in. × 12 in. × 18 in.

Copper: Chromium Plate

Baths	Minutes/Batch	
	Soak	Handle
Electroclean	3.0	2.5
Rinse	0.5	0.5
Acid dip	0.5	1.0
Rinse	0.5	0.5
Chrome plate	180.0	2.5
Rinse	0.5	0.5
Total	185.0	7.5

Note: Purpose: decorative, creates wear resistance.
Specification: QQ-C-320, C1. I, bright and stain.
Thickness: 0.001 to 0.010 in.
Time: based on tank size, 18 in. $\times$ 12 in. $\times$ 18 in.,
or 50 in.^{2} area of parts (1 A/in.^{2} at 50 A).

Copper: Gold Plate

	Minutes/Batch	
Baths	Soak	Handle
Electrocleaner	3.0	2.5
Rinse	0.5	0.5
Cyanide dip	0.5	1.0
Rinse	0.5	0.5
Silver strike	1.0	1.5
Rinse	0.5	0.5
Gold plate	10.0	2.5
Rinse	0.5	0.5
Rinse	0.5	0.5
Total	17.0	10.0

Note: Purpose: conductivity, solderability, and corrosion
resistance.
Specifications: none
Thickness: 59 to 110 millionths of an inch.
Time: based on tank size, 18 in. $\times$ 12 in. $\times$ 18 in.

Copper: Nickle and Rhodium Plate

	Minutes/Batch	
Baths	Soak	Handle
Electrocleaner	3.0	2.5
Rinse	0.5	0.5
Acid dip	0.5	1.0
Rinse	0.5	0.5
Nickel plate	10.0	2.5
Rinse	0.5	0.5
Rhodium plate	15.0	2.5
Rinse	0.5	0.5
Rinse	0.5	0.5
Total	31.0	11.0

Note: Purpose: corrosion and wear resistance.
Specifiction: none.
Thickness: nickel base 0.0004 in.
Rhodium base: 0 to 20 millionths of an inch.
Time: based on tank size, 18 in. × 12 in. × 18 in.

Copper: Silver Plate

| | Minutes/Batch | |
Baths	Soak	Handle
Electrocleaner	3.0	2.5
Rinse	0.5	0.5
Cyanide	0.5	1.0
Rinse	0.5	0.5
Silver strike	0.5	1.0
Silver plate	20.0	2.5
Rinse	0.5	0.5
Rinse	0.5	0.5
Total	26.0	9.0

Note: Purpose: conductivity, corrosion resistance, and solderability.
Specification: QQ-S-365, Type III (bright).
Thickness: 0.0005 to 0.0010 in.
Time: based on tank size, 18 in. × 12 in. × 18 in.

Copper: Tin Plate

| | Minutes/Batch | |
Baths	Soak	Handle
Electrocleaner	3.0	2.5
Rinse	0.5	0.5
Acid dip	0.5	1.0
Rinse	0.5	0.5
Tin plate	40.0	2.5
Rinse	0.5	0.5
Total	45.0	7.5

Note: Purpose: solderability.
Specification: MIL-T-10727, Type I.
Thickness: 0.0005 to 0.0010 in.
Time: based on tank size, 18 in. × 12 in. × 18 in.

Steel and Iron: Black Oxide Coating

	Minutes/Batch	
Baths	Soak	Handle
Alkaline clean	4.0	2.5
Rinse	0.5	0.5
Acid pickle	15.0	2.5
Rinse	0.5	0.5
Rinse	0.5	0.5
Black oxide	4.0	2.5
Rinse	0.5	0.5
Wax coat	2.5	2.5
Total	27.5	12.0

Note: Purpose: decorative black oxide coating for ferrous metals.
Specification: MIL-C-13924, black oxide coating for ferrous metals, Class I.
Thickness: not specified.
Time: based on tank size: 30 in. $\times$ 18 in. $\times$ 36 in.

Steel: Cadmium Plating

	Minutes/Batch	
Baths	Soak	Handle
Electroclean	3.0	2.0
Rinse	0.5	0.5
Acid dip	0.5	1.0
Rinse	0.5	0.5
Cad plate	15.0	2.5
Rinse	0.5	0.5
Post treat	0.5	1.0
Rinse	0.5	0.5
Total	21.0	8.5

Note: Purpose: corrosion resistance (salt spray 192 hr).
Specification: QQP-416, Type I, without supplemental phosphate treatment.
Thickness: 0.0003 to 0.0010 in.
Time: based on tank size: 36 in. $\times$ 30 in. $\times$ 36 in.

Steel: Chromium Plate

| | Minutes/Batch | |
Baths	Soak	Handle
Electrocleaner	3.0	2.5
Rinse	0.5	0.5
Acid dip	0.5	1.0
Rinse	0.5	0.5
Chrome reverse etch	1.0	1.5
Chrome plate	180.0	2.5
Rinse	0.5	0.5
Total	186.0	9.0

Note: Purpose: decorative, creates wear resistance.
Specification: QQC-370, CI. I, bright and stain.
Thickness: 0.001 to 0.010 in.
Time: based on tank size, 18 in. $\times$ 12 in. $\times$ 18 in., or
50 in.^{2} area of parts (1 A/in.^{2} at 50 A).

Stainless Steel: Passivate

| | Minutes/Batch | |
Baths	Soak	Handle
Vapor degrease	1.5	2.0
Passivate	60.0	2.5
Rinse	0.5	0.5
Total	62.0	5.0

Note: Purpose: corrosion resistance.
Specification: MIL-S-5002, treatment for metal parts.
Thickness: not specified.
Time: based on tank size, 18 in. $\times$ 12 in. $\times$ 18 in.

Steel: Phosphate Treat

	Minutes/Batch	
Baths	Soak	Handle
Electrocleaner	4.0	2.5
Rinse	0.5	0.5
Oxalic acid	1.5	2.0
Rinse	0.5	0.5
Phosphate treat	4.0	2.5
Rinse	0.5	0.5
Phosphate seal	1.0	1.5
Total	12.0	10.0

Note: Purpose: corrosion resistance, paint adhesion, and
dry film lubricant adhesion.
Specification: MIL-C-490, Grade I.
Thickness: 300 mg/ft^2.
Time: based on tank size, 30 in. × 18 in. × 36 in.

PAINTING STANDARDS

Standards included in the following sections are primarily for typical operations required to paint metal chassis, panels, and cabinets. With judgment, larger surface areas could be estimated by using the data given. The time values are based on using an individual spray booth type of operation as opposed to a continuous conveyor method.

Primers require one pass. A high gloss finish coat will usually require two passes. The thinner the paint or primer, the more quickly a coat can be applied.

Time values are for a box-shaped item of the dimension given. If inside surfaces must be coated, the given values must be doubled. The values given include time for picking up parts, moving to and from the booth, and replacing on a pallet.

A listing follows of representative piece sizes and time values for cleaning by grit blasting or power wire brushing in preparation for painting.

Part Size	Minutes per Part
1½ in. × ½ in.	0.20
2 in. × 2 in.	0.40
4 in. × 4 in.	0.60
4 in. × 12 in.	0.90
4 in. × 18 in.	1.00
12 in. × 18 in.	1.5

	Minutes
Per square foot	1.00
Sand by hand per square foot	2.00
Surface wash with solvent per square foot	0.05
Surface spray paint (primer, one coat) per square foot	0.05
Surface spray paint (two coats gloss finish) per square foot	0.10
Compressed air blow down per square foot	0.05
Brush paint per coat per square inch	0.20

Mask and Unmask

	Minutes
Apply	
Pick up tape	0.015
Pick end loose	0.020
Pull off 10 in. tape	0.010
Position to part	0.015
Apply to 10 linear in.	0.050
Tear tape	0.010
Lay aside tape roll	0.010
Total apply	0.130
Remove	
Pick end loose	0.020
Grasp and pull off (avg. 1½ pulls)	0.045
Dispose of tape	0.030
Wipe surface with solvent rag	0.060
Total remove	0.155
Total apply and remove 10 in.	0.285
Per inch	0.03
Plugs, stencils, and shields for masking	
Install and remove average each 0.10 min	
Painting	
Equipment: Paint booth, turntable, spray gun	
Setup time	
Obtain paint	
Obtain liquid tank	
Thin paint as required	
Transfer to tank	
Obtain air and paint hoses	
Clear air hose and attach spray gun	
Attach nozzle	
Adjust and try out	
Upon job completion, clean paint apparatus with solvent	
Total setup hours	0.3

Application of Primer

Time value analysis	Minutes/Unit/Coat			
	3 in.	8 in.	20 in.	30 in.
To booth turntable				
Pick up and position on table	0.05	0.10	0.15	0.20
Pick up and put down spray gun	not reqd.	0.10	0.10	0.10
Lay aside part	0.05	0.10	0.15	0.20
Subtotal	0.10	0.30	0.40	0.50
To drying rack or oven				
Pick up and position part	0.05	0.10	0.15	0.20
Lay aside part	0.05	0.10	0.15	0.20
Subtotal	0.10	0.20	0.30	0.40
Total handling per part	0.20	0.50	0.70	0.90
Spray time				
Varies by paint type	0.10	to		1.25
Total wash primer	0.30	0.65	1.00	1.30
Total chromate (zinc)	0.60	1.10	1.70	2.15

Application of a Surfacer

A surfacer is used where a high gloss finish is wanted. It is a filler to fill in minor tooling and other marks on cabinets and face plates. It is applied by brush or spray. A very smooth base for the finish coat is obtained by hand rubbing or buffing.

Time value analysis	Minutes/Unit/Coat			
	3 in.	8 in.	20 in.	30 in.
Handle (as in primer)	0.20	0.50	0.70	0.90
Spray paint	0.60	0.90	1.00	1.25
Buff (power)	1.40	2.00	2.40	3.85
Total	2.20	3.40	4.10	6.00

Apply Lacquer or Enamel

Time value analysis	Minutes/Unit/Coat			
	3 in.	8 in.	20 in.	30 in.
Flat finish, handle (as in primer)	0.20	0.50	0.70	0.90
Spray time	0.40	0.60	1.00	1.25
Total	0.60	1.10	1.70	2.15
Gloss, handle (as in primer)	0.20	0.50	0.70	0.90
Spray time	0.70	1.20	1.80	2.30
Total	0.90	1.70	2.50	3.20

Apply Varnish

Time value analysis	Minutes/Unit/Coat			
	3 in.	8 in.	20 in.	30 in.
Clear, handle (as in primer)	0.20	0.50	0.70	0.90
Spray time	0.50	0.80	1.30	1.60
Total	0.70	1.30	2.00	2.50
Pigmented (16 oz paste/gal), handle (as in primer)	0.20	0.50	0.70	0.90
Spray time	0.70	1.20	1.85	2.30
Total	0.90	1.70	2.55	3.20

Apply Strippable Plastic Protective Film

Time value analysis	Minutes/Unit/Coat			
	3 in.	8 in.	20 in.	30 in.
Handling (as in primer)	0.20	0.50	0.70	0.90
Spray time	0.30	0.50	0.85	1.00
Total	0.50	1.00	1.55	1.90

Spray Application of Fungicide

Time value analysis	Minutes/Unit/Coat			
	3 in.	8 in.	20 in.	30 in.
Handling (as in primer)	0.20	0.50	0.70	0.90
Spray time	0.50	0.80	1.30	1.60
Total	0.70	1.30	2.00	2.50

APPENDIX II

MANUFACTURING OF ELECTRONICS AND ELECTRICAL COMPONENTS*

ETCHED ELECTRICAL/ELECTRONIC CIRCUIT AND TERMINAL BOARDS

Etched electrical and electronic circuit and terminal boards require the use of sheet metal, machine shop, and other process operations. The most common of these operations are combined into tables that can be used to estimate the time to produce various types of circuit boards. Etched circuit board standards are based on using epoxy laminate 0.062-inch thick, 2 ounce copper clad. Standards for terminal boards are based on using phenolic laminate sheet stock 0.125-inch thick.

Setup time shown in Table A.2.2, "Terminal Board Operations," includes silk screening, which includes making a negative, a positive, and a silk screen stencil, as well as setting up the screen jig for production.

Table A.2.1.   Circuit boards (composite jig handling and drilling time)

Number of $\frac{1}{16}$-in. Boards in Stack	Jig Handling Time	Proration at 100 Holes per Board	Move from Hole to Hole	Drill Time at 0.32 min/in.	Total per Board in Jig	Total per Hole per Board
1[a]	0	0	0.060	0.020	0.080	0.080
1	0.20	0.002	0.047	0.020	0.069	0.069
2	1.20	0.012	0.047	0.040	0.099	0.050
3	1.30	0.013	0.047	0.060	0.120	0.040
4	1.40	0.014	0.047	0.080	0.141	0.035
5	1.50	0.015	0.047	0.100	0.162	0.033

[a]No drill plate. Align and position drill per circuit pattern.

*Note: For manual operations only: Adjustments must be made for specific automation techniques.

290

Table A.2.2. Terminal board operations

Operation (4 in. × 4 in. board)	Setup (hr)	Run Time		
		Operation Time (min)	Number of Operations	Total (min)
Cut blank to size				
Handle board				
1 in. × 2 in.		0.03		
4 in. × 4 in.		0.04	1	0.04
4 in. × 12 in.		0.08		
Diamond saw, 2 sides (⅛ in.) per inch	0.1	0.02	8	0.16
Deburr 4 edges per inch		0.02	16	0.32
Drill terminal holes per drawing dimension	0.3	0.08		
Per drill jig				
1/ stack	0.3	0.07	1	0.07
2/ stack	0.3	0.05		
3/ stack	0.3	0.04		
Deburr holes with vibrator				
1 in. × 2 in. board	0.1	0.20		
4 in. × 4 in. board	0.1	0.40	1	0.40
Silk screen identification data to board				
1 in. × 2 in. board	1.3	0.25		
4 in. × 4 in. board	1.3	0.40	1	0.40
4 in. × 12 in. board	1.3	0.60		
Stake terminal, handle				
1 in. × 2 in. board		0.03		
4 in. × 4 in. board		0.04		
4 in. × 12 in. board		0.08		
Pick up and stake terminal	0.4	0.06	1	0.06
Epoxy coat after assembly, per side		0.35		
Total constant time/board	(2.2)			(1.32)
Total variable time/board/hole				0.13

Table A.2.3. Fabrication of one-sided etched circuit board

Operation [one side, (4 in. × 4 in.)]	Setup (hr)	Run Time Operation Time (min)	Run Time Number of Operations	Run Time Total (min)
Stamp blank with tool holes, punch press	0.4	0.20		
Shear blank	0.2	0.10	1	0.10
Drill 2 tooling holes	0.3	0.50	1	0.50
Drill circuit holes per circuit pattern	0.3	0.08		
Per drill jig				
1/ stack	0.3	0.07		
2/ stack	0.3	0.05		
3/ stack	0.3	0.04	1	0.04
4/ stack	0.3	0.035		
Deburr holes with vibrator, per board	0.1	0.50	1	0.50
Silk screen resist				
1 side	1.3	1.10	1	1.10
2 sides	2.5	3.30		
Add per hole for ± 0.005 tolerance		0.01		
Etch and deresist				
1 side	0.1	1.40	1	1.40
2 sides	0.1	2.85		
Add to deresist plate through holes		0.01		
Rout blank to size ($\frac{1}{16}$ in.) per inch	0.3	0.04	16	0.64
Deburr edges, per inch		0.02	16	0.32
Clean and plate				
Copper through holes (in.²)	0.6	0.07		
Nickel-rhodium tab (in.²)	0.4	0.10	16	1.60
Gold flash circuit (in.²)	0.4	0.09		
Connector tab and key slot				
Punch press both	0.4	0.20		
Shear tab	0.2	0.10	1	0.10
Saw and bevel slot	0.1	0.40	1	0.40
Connector tab, chamber 3-in. tab	0.1	0.20	1	0.20
Eyelet, handle board		0.10		
Install eyelet, automatic feed	0.4	0.04		
Solder both sides, handiron		0.10		
Epoxy coat after assembly, per side		0.35		
Total constant time/board	(3.4)			(6.86)
Total variable time/board/hole				(0.04)

Table A.2.4.   Values: Fabrication of two-sided etched circuit board

Operation [two side, (4 in. × 4 in.)]	Setup (hr)	Run Time Operation Time (min)	Run Time Number of Operations	Run Time Total (min)
Stamp blank with tool holes, punch press	0.4	0.20		
Shear blank	0.2	0.10	1	0.10
Drill 2 tooling holes	0.3	0.50	1	0.50
Drill circuit holes per circuit pattern	0.3	0.08		
Per drill jib				
1/ stack	0.3	0.07		
2/ stack	0.3	0.05		
3/ stack	0.3	0.04	1	0.04
4/ stack	0.3	0.035		
Deburr holes, per board	0.1	0.50	1	0.50
Silk screen resist				
1 side	1.3	1.10		
2 sides	2.5	3.30	1	3.30
Add to deresist plate through holes		0.01	1	0.01
Etch and deresist				
1 side	0.1	1.40		
2 sides	0.1	2.85	1	2.85
Rout blank to size ($1\frac{1}{16}$ in.) per inch	0.3	0.04	16	0.64
Clean and plate				
Copper through holes (in.^{2})	0.6	0.07	16	1.12
Nickel-rhodium tab (in.^{2})	0.4	0.10	16	1.60
Gold flash circuit (in.^{2})	0.4	0.09		
Connector tab and key slot				
Punch press both	0.4	0.20		
Shear tab	0.2	0.10	1	0.10
Saw and bevel slot	0.1	0.40	1	0.40
Connector tab, chamber 3-in. tab	0.1	0.20	1	0.20
Eyelet, handle board		0.10		
Install eyelet, automatic feed	0.4	0.04		
Solder both sides, handiron		0.10		
Epoxy coat after assembly, per side		0.35		
Deburr edges, per inch		0.02	16	0.32
Total constant tie/board	(5.2)			(11.28)

SILK-SCREENING PROCESSES FOR ELECTRONIC PRINTED CIRCUIT (PC) BOARDS

Photographic Operations

Equipment: Darkroom with developer, fix and rinse baths, industrial copy camera, contact printer enlarger, viewing table, and drying cabinet.

Note: For convenience, the following listing gives time values for preparation of negatives, positives, and halftone negatives.

Element	Machine Time	Labor Time (min) Line Negative	Positive from Negative	Halftone Negative
Expose film				
Assemble copy to camera		1.00		1.00
Turn light switch and adjust		0.30	0.30	0.30
Set lens opening		0.50		0.50
Set timer		0.30	0.30	0.30
Adjust lens board to center image		0.50		0.50
Cut film, position to vacuum holder		0.70	0.70	0.70
Position halftone contact screen over film				1.00
Position negative over film			0.50	
Position glass over negative	0.6 to 5.0	0.60	0.60	2.50
Disassemble film from camera		0.30	0.30	0.30
Subtotal	0.6 to 5.0	4.20	2.70	7.10
Develop film				
Place film in developer bath	2.5	2.50	2.50	2.50
Rinse	0.2	0.20	0.20	0.20
Place film in fix bath	3.0	3.00	3.00	3.00
Place film in wash bath	10.0	2.50	2.50	2.50
Dry in film dryer	25.0	0.50	0.50	0.50
Subtotal	40.7	8.70	8.70	8.70
Total expose and develop		12.90	11.40	15.80

Fabricate Silk Screen Stencil

Included are two methods. One is the PC board for presensitized screen process film and the other is letter artwork for unsensitized screen process film.

	Minutes/Job	
	PC Boards	Letter Artwork
Sensitize		
Cut film to size	1.00	1.00
Immerse in sensitizing solvent		
Rub surface		
Remove air bubbles		1.00
Transfer file to transparent vinyl support, emulsion		
side down		0.50
Squeegee excess sensitizer and air bubbles from film		0.50
Wipe dry		0.50
Expose		
Place vinyl support with film on emulsion side		
of positive	0.50	0.50
Place support and positive in vaccum frame	0.50	0.50
Cut to length and assemble opaque tape around border		
of positive	1.00	1.00
Expose film	3.00	5.00
Develop film in "A" and "B" developer solution	2.50	
Wash out		
Immerse film and support in 110°F water	0.50	0.50
Soak 0.5 min and peel backing	1.00	1.00
Agitate and dissolve unexposed gelatin	1:00	1.00
Attach developed film to screen		
Clean silk screen with cleaner or solvent and brush		
under running water	4.00	4.00
Place silk screen over film	0.50	0.50
Place paper towel over screen to absorb moisture		
Remove	1.00	1.00
Weigh frame down and allow to air dry	2.00	2.00
Peel vinyl support from screen stencil	2.00	2.00
Total	20.50	22.50
Multiplier	0.022	0.022
Setup and run hours	0.45	0.50

Note: Recall that the multiplier incorporates a factor for unproductive time as well as converting minutes to hours.

Set Up Silk Screen for Production

	Minutes/Job	
	Single-Side PC	Double-Side PC
Receive work order, drawings, blank boards	2.00	2.00
Set up to clean boards	1.00	1.00
Silk screen setup		
Draw screen from storage	0.30	0.30
Clamp to 2 bench hinges	1.00	1.00
Mark tool pin holes on ink board per PC board	0.30	0.30
Drill and pin ink board	2.00	2.00
Position PC board to 2 pins	0.10	0.10
Line up ink board to screen pattern	0.50	0.50
Staple base down	0.30	0.30
Screen first PC board		
Mix ink	1.00	1.00
Squeegee	1.00	1.00
Check registration	3.00	3.00
Put aside PC board for inspection	0.10	0.10
Add time values from "position board to 2 pins" down for double-sided board		6.00
Set up for touchup		
Resist ink, brush, neg., pos., or sample	2.00	2.00
Total	14.60	20.60
Multiplier	0.022	0.022
Setup hours/job	0.32	0.45

Silk-Screening Operations

Details follow of the setup for a single-sided PC board, a double-sided PC board, letter artwork per stencil, or single side of panel.

	Setup Hour/Job		
	Single-Side PC	Double-Side PC	Letter PC
Setup Analysis			
Fabricate negative and positive	0.5	1.0	0.5
Fabricate silk screen	0.5	1.0	0.5
Set up silk screen for production	0.3	0.5	0.3
Total	1.3	2.5	1.3
All per character to draw artwork (LeRoy or similar)			0.01

	Minutes/Unit		
Run time (avg. 6 in. × 6-in. board)			
Clean PC board with cleaner	0.30	0.40	
Silk screen resist board			
Fill plate through holes with resist			
Squeegee one side		0.40	
Squeegee second side		0.40	
Clean two sides with solvent		0.50	
Silk screen board			
Handle board to and from pins	0.20	0.40	
Squeegee ink through screen	0.40	0.80	0.40
Dry in oven (handling only)	0.20	0.40	0.20
Total	1.10	3.30	0.60

Decals (Made by Silk Screen)

	Hours/Job
Setup time	
Fabricate negative and positive (see previous description)	0.5
Fabricate silk screen	0.5
Set up silk screen for production	0.3
Total	1.3

	Minutes/Unit
Run time	
Average 3 in. × 3 in. decal	
Fabricate decal	
Clear screen (screen clear lacquer to base paper)	0.30
Stencilled screen (screen colored lacquer to base paper)	0.30
Clear screen (screen clear lacquer over color pattern)	0.30
Total	0.90
Assemble decal to part of chassis	
Place decal in water to loosen backing	0.05
Pick up and peel off backing	0.15
Position decal to part	0.10
Wipe smooth	0.20
Total	0.50

Etch Printed Circuit Boards

Equipment: Paddle agitation rack. Loaded etching machine (using ferric chloride as etching agent).

	Hours
Setup time: Keep etching solution at 105°F to 115°F; maintain ferric chloride and distilled water solution; provide lacquer thinner to deresist boards; setup hours/job.	0.1

	Minutes/Job	
	Single-Side PC	Double-Side PC
Run time		
Position board on rack	1.10	2.20
Position rack to etching machine	0.04	0.08
Turn on	0.01	0.02
Machine time	0.60	1.20
Remove rack	0.02	0.04
Rinse rack	0.10	0.20
Remove board from rack	0.05	0.10
Deresist board with thinner and brush	0.50	1.00
Total	2.42	4.84

Note: Add to deresist holes 0.01 min/hole.

Vacuum Encapsulating

Equipment: Vacuum impregnator oven, Split type mold.

	Minutes/Job
Setup times: trip to tool crib, set up oven, obtain accessories.	14.0
Portion out resin	2.5
Set up mold release	2.5
Prepare epoxy with catalyst (A and B)	5.0
Portion out amount of mixture required	1.0
Place in oven (heat time 30 min)	1.0
Place in encapsulator	2.0
Draw 28 in. vac (approximately 7 min)	
Hold for approximately 15 min	
Check while in process	2.0
Remove compound and heat in oven	2.0
Total	32.00

	Hours
Add for optional operations	
Shield with silver foil	
Set per job	
Total	0.1

	Minutes/Job
Run time	
Clean capsule with solvent	0.30
Brush cement on capsule	0.20
Bake 10 min (handle only)	0.20
Cut foil to length	0.20
Wrap capsule with foil	0.50
Seal corners with solder	0.40
Clean resin with solvent	0.30
Brush lacquer on capsule (dry 1 hr)	0.20
Bake in oven 1 hr	0.20
Total	2.50

Coil Winding

	Minutes/Job	
	Hand Wind	Machine Wind
Setup times:		
Trip to tool crib and supply room	5.00	5.00
Calculate proper gear ratio (turns/inch)	0	2.50
Calculate cam size (coil width)	0	2.50
Cam disassemble, reassemble	0	0.20
Nut disassemble, reassemble	0	0.30
Allen screw, unlock, relock	0	0.80
Readjust (at halfway point)	0	0.70
Gear disassemble, assemble	0	0.60
Allen screw disassemble, reassemble	0	0.90
Line up and adjust	0	1.00
Spindle assemble arbor base	0.30	0.30
Winding finger screw, unlock and relock	0	1.20
Fail stock nut, unlock and relock	0	0.30
Counter—adjust to stop	0.40	0.40
Division control adjust	0	0.20
Tension and spool holder	0	3.00
Total	5.70	19.90
Multiplier	0.022	0.022
Setup hours/job	0.13	0.44

	Minutes/Job
Add for each additional coil for multiple winding	
Adjust winding finger	1.20
Tension and spool holder	3.00
Minutes/job	4.20
Multiplier	0.022
Setup hours/each added coil	0.09

	Minutes/Job
Coil winding elements	
Advance arbor	0.005
Assemble tube or bobbin to arbor	
Random position	0.04
Chuck arbor	0.03
Assemble nut	0.05
Expansion arbor	0.04
Spring arbor	0.03
Align tube to specific lead position	
Chuck arbor	0.045
Wing nut arbor	0.04
Assembly nut	0.05
Expansion arbor	0.05
Spring arbor	0.04
Assemble spacer to arbor	0.02
Close tail stock	0.03
Press and secure leads of previous winding	
Unroll tape and position	0.04
Application per lead	0.01
Wrap lead to terminal	0.035
Anchor start lead to wind	
Thread to hole through coil form and dress coil on arbor	
18 to 22 gauge	0.13
24 to 36 gauge	0.11
38 to 40 gauge	0.12
Wrap to terminal	
18 to 22 gauge	0.07
24 to 28 gauge	0.05
30 to 40 gauge	0.03
Wrap to tube and tape (wrap lead two turns, unroll tape and apply)	0.08
Double back start lead to reinforce	0.035
Twist precut and stripped reinforcement lead to coil led	0.05
Index wire guide	0.015

	Minutes/Job
Position wire around guide buttons	0.03
Set counter	
Feeder root type, clear to zero	0.025
Self-braking type, set up to 99 turns	0.045
Per additional digit	0.015
Hand wind initial turns	
1 turn	0.044
2 turns	0.053
3 turns	0.062
4 turns	0.072
Cement start of winding	
Handle applicator	0.025
Apply cement per lead	0.015
Wind	
Machine wind using machine lead spacer	
Start, stop, and brake machine	0.045
Space wind	
14–16 gauge 300 rpm	0.003
18–20 gauge 500 rpm	0.002
22–24 gauge 1000 rpm	0.001
26–up gauge 1500 rpm	0.0007
Close or universal	
14–16 gauge 200 rpm	0.005
18–20 gauge 300 rpm	0.003
22–24 gauge 500 rpm	0.002
26–up gauge 1000 rpm	0.001
Groove wind on threaded core	
16–18 gauge 200 rpm	0.005
20–22 gauge 300 rpm	0.003
24–up gauge 500 rpm	0.002
Hand wind	
Hand feed wire to required turns per inch	
Start, stop, and brake machine	0.02
Close wind or groove wind	
14–16 gauge 60 rpm	0.017
18–20 gauge 80 rpm	0.013
22–up gauge 100 rpm	0.01
Taps and insulation strips	
Release brake, position arbor	0.025
Make tap	
Twist tape and knot	0.13
Twist tape and wrap one turn to terminal	0.15
Loop tap, anchored with tape	0.19
Anchored with tape and cement	0.21
Wrap to terminal	0.18

	Minutes/Job
Add for second tape around tap	0.07
Cambric type insulation strip	
Insert under lead	0.07
Spread and position preformed tap	0.11
Form and position flat tap	0.12
Hand wind one turn, dress cambric, and tap together	0.06
Kraft paper type insulation strip	
Position to coil	0.04
Brush with cement (per $\frac{1}{2}$ in.)	0.035
Handle brush	0.03
After wind	
Release brake, position arbor	0.025
Anchor finish lead to coil with tape, unroll tape, and apply	0.06
Push back guide	0.015
Cut leads	
Approximate length	0.005
Exact length	0.02
Handle scissors	0.03
Thread finish lead one hole through coil form and dress	
18–22 gauge	0.07
24–22 gauge	0.05
30–40 gauge	0.03
Trim leads wrapped to terminal	0.01
Handle cutters or tweezers	0.025
Unwrap start leads	
From arbor to tube	0.015
From terminal	0.03
Solder start, finish, or splice leads per joint	0.04
Handle iron (solder)	0.045
Disassembly lead of previous winding	
Taped to arbor	0.02
Taped to tube	0.03
Unwrap from terminal	0.03
Open fail stock	0.03
Disassemble arbor from chuck	0.04
Disassemble coil from arbor	
Chuck arbor	0.03
Wind nut arbor	0.02
Disassembly nut	0.04
Expansion arbor	0.035
Spring arbor	0.02
Disassemble lead from spacer slot	0.012

WIRE PREPARATION AND WIRING

This section contains information relative to preparation of wire for the application of various kinds or types of terminals. There is also information for layout and manufacture of wiring harnesses. Both machine wire preparation and hand preparation of wiring are addressed.

Table A.2.5. Machine preparation of wire[a]

Operation 14–22 Gauge	Number of Ends	Wire Length (in.)					
		2 to 3	3 to 15	15 to 20	20 to 30	30 to 45	45 to 60
Machine cut and strip	1	0.020	0.020	0.040	0.040	0.060	0.080
	2	0.020	0.020	0.040	0.040	0.060	0.080
Twist strands	1	0.035	0.025	0.032	0.032	0.032	0.037
	2	0.060	0.043	0.056	0.056	0.056	0.062
Tin strands	1	0.026	0.017	0.021	0.030	0.030	0.035
	2	0.038	0.024	0.030	0.056	0.056	0.061
Stamp wire—simultaneous with machine cut	1	00	00	00	00	00	00
	2						
Stamp wire—separate operation	1	0.090	0.130	0.160	0.190	0.230	0.270
	2	0.090	0.130	0.160	0.190	0.230	0.270
Total—cut and stamp simultaneously	1	0.081	0.062	0.093	0.102	0.122	0.152
	2	0.118	0.087	0.126	0.152	0.172	0.203
Total—stamp separate	1	0.171	0.192	0.253	0.292	0.352	0.422
	2	0.208	0.217	0.286	0.342	0.402	0.473
Operation 22–26 Gauge							
Machine cut and strip	1	0.020	0.020	0.040	0.040	0.060	0.080
	2	0.020	0.020	0.040	0.040	0.060	0.080
Twist strands	1	0.035	0.025	0.032	0.032	0.032	0.037
	2	0.060	0.043	0.056	0.062	0.062	0.068
Tin strands	1	0.030	0.017	0.028	0.030	0.030	0.035
	2	0.042	0.024	0.038	0.056	0.056	0.061
Stamp wire—simultaneous with cut	1	00	00	00	00	00	00
	2						
Stamp wire—separate	1	0.090	0.130	0.160	0.190	0.230	0.270
	2	0.090	0.130	0.160	0.190	0.230	0.270
Total—cut and stamp simultaneously	1	0.083	0.062	0.097	0.102	0.122	0.152
	2	0.122	0.087	0.134	0.158	0.178	0.209
Total—stamp separate	1	0.175	0.192	0.258	0.292	0.352	0.422
	2	0.212	0.217	0.294	0.348	0.408	0.479

[a]The Artos machine automatically unreels, cuts to length, and strips solid or stranded wire.

Hand Preparation of Insulated Wire

	Minutes (Any Length)	Minutes	
		15 in.	60 in.
Pull wire from reel			
Grasp wire end		0.031	0.031
Pull off of reel: 0.001/in.			
Measure			
Line up to marker		0.028	0.028
Cut with hand pliers			
Tool handling		0.003	0.003
Identify (temporary)			
Tear tape	0.030		
Apply to wire	0.050		
Check drawing for identification	0.050		
Write identification	0.050		
Remove after hookup	0.020		
Total	0.200		
Strip with hand pliers		N.R.[a]	0.200
Tool handling		0.110	0.110
Tin with solder iron		0.003	0.003
Tool handling		0.120	0.120
Pick up and bundle wires		0.004	0.004
Tool handling		0.020	0.080
Total		0.320	0.580

[a]Not required.

Stake Taper Pin to Wire

	Hours
Setup time	0.4

AMP type machine: Taper pins are supplied in a continuous chain on a reel. When one staking action is made, the machine automatically cuts the pin free from the chain, stakes it to the wire, and positions the next pin to anvil.

	Minutes/Unit
Run time—machine	
Separate wire from group	0.005
Grasp	0.002
Position to taper pin on anvil	0.022

(*continued*)

	Minutes/Job
Press foot pedal and machine cycle	0.010
Remove wire from anvil and aside	<u>0.005</u>
Total—one end	0.040
Add for second end	<u>0.040</u>
Total—two ends	0.080
Run time—hand	
Pick up, position pin to pliers	0.045
Pick up, position wire to pin	0.040
Squeeze	0.015
Release pliers, set aside wire	<u>0.010</u>
Total—one end	0.11
Add for second end	<u>0.11 </u>
Total—two ends	0.22
Add for tool handling (pliers)	<u>0.03 </u>
Total	0.25

Table A.2.6. Values: wiring

		Run Time Values (min)			
		Machine Preparation Length (in.)		Hand Preparation Length (in.)	
Wiring Operation	Setup (hr)	15	60	15	60
Insulated wire—prepare and install two ends					
Crimp and solder					
Point to point	0.10	0.65	1.00	0.95	1.15
Lay in U channel	0.10	0.70	1.15	1.00	1.35
Lace harness	0.10	0.95	1.60	1.25	1.80
Taper pin (solderless)					
Point to point	0.10	0.50	0.85	0.95	1.15
Lay in U channel	0.10	0.55	1.00	1.00	1.35
Lace harness	0.10	0.80	1.45	1.25	1.80
Pneumatic wrap (solderless)					
Point to point	0.10	0.30	0.60	0.55	0.75
Lay in U channel	0.10	0.35	0.75	0.60	0.95
Lace harness	0.10	0.60	1.20	0.85	1.40
Bus—wire—cut crimp solder two ends	[a]	0.40		0.45	
Resistor—two ends					
Crimp and solder to terminals	0.01	0.45		0.50	
Crimp to PC board and dip solder	0.01	0.30		0.35	
Transistor, 3 lead component					
Crimp and solder to terminals	0.01	0.65		0.70	
Crimp to PC board and dip solder	0.01	0.40	0.45		

Table A.2.6. (Continued)

		Run Time Values (min)			
		Machine Preparation Length (in.)		Hand Preparation Length (in.)	
Wiring Operation	Setup (hr)	15	60	15	60
Sleeving—cut to length—thread to lead	[a]	0.05		0.10	
Shielded cable—prepare and install two ends					
Single conductor				3.95	4.35
Double conductor				5.00	5.40
Coax cable—prepare and install two ends					
Ground lead termination	0.10			4.15	4.55
Connector termination	0.10	8.50		9.20	
Connect first end, ground lead second end	0.10			6.30	6.85
Connector-mechanical assembly to harness					
Small: 5 to 10 pin				2.70	
Medium: 10 to 25 pin				4.25	
Large: 25 to 40 pin				6.15	
Pull tubing over cable					
1 to 2 ft/ft				0.70	
3 to 5 ft/ft				0.80	
6 to 15 ft/ft				0.90	
Twist cable wire per foot				0.06	
Spot tie harness per foot				0.90	
Seam solder per inch				0.10	
Develop wire list from schematic per wire	0.10				
Fabricate harness nail board—basic	3.50				
Add for each wire	0.06				
Set up components at work station	0.02				
Buzz wire to identify				0.20	

[a] Negligible.

SOLDERING

Soldering covered here is concerned with soft solder, an alloy of 63 percent tin and 37 percent lead. Silver solder or brazing is not generally applicable to soldering electronic wiring connections.

Time values shown herein are based on the use of solder of 63 percent tin and 37 percent lead solder, 0.062-in. diameter with resin core.

Table A.2.7.   "Solder-wire-to-terminal" values

Wire Gauge	Number Wires on Terminal	Solid Terminal	Hole Terminal	Hollow Term		Solder to Chassis	
				Prefill	Heat and Insert Lead	Heat to Cool	Without Cooling Time
18 to 24	1	0.047	0.400	0.070	0.080	0.135	0.080
	2	0.057	0.045				
	3	0.061	0.005				
16	1	0.060	0.053	0.080	0.090	0.148	0.093
	2	0.071	0.059				
	3	0.077	0.071				
14	1	0.073	0.066	0.090	0.100	0.161	0.106
Spot Solder Braid	0						0.070
Pigtail	1					0.165	0.100

Dip Soldering of Etched Circuit Boards

Equipment: Semiautomatic machine
    Automatic machine lowers board into solder bath,
    removes, and positions for manual unloading. Pot
    size is approximately 16 in. × 16 in. by appropriate
    depth.
    Setup time: obtain solder stock, adjust dwell time of
    mechanism, turn on heat, and cut and dry out
    sample board.   0.4 hr

	Minutes		
	4 in. × 4 in.	4 in. × 6 in.	4 in. × 12 in.
Run time			
Mask board with tape	0.18	0.42	0.63
Brush flux on board	0.10	0.20	0.30
Assemble board on holding fixture	0.08	0.10	0.13
Actuate machine switch	0.02	0.02	0.02
Machine cycle	0.35	0.35	0.35
Remove board from fixture	0.05	0.07	0.10
Wash off flux residue	0.30	0.50	0.70
Blow dry	0.15	0.25	0.35
Subtotal	1.23	1.91	2.58
Touch up with handiron (avg.)	0.30	0.60	0.90
Total/board	1.53	2.51	3.48

Seam Solder

Equipment: 150 W electric solder iron

	Minutes
Run time	
Handiron—pick up and lay aside	0.045
First inch	0.120
Each additional inch	0.080

APPENDIX III
SAMPLE WORK BREAKDOWN STRUCTURE DICTIONARY

1.0 SPACE PROJECT

This overall category includes the total complex of labor, travel expenses, services, materials, tooling and equipment, facilities, prime contracting and subcontracting required for the concept selection, design, development, manufacture, assembly, test, modification, checkout, transportation, preparation to launch, launch, and flight operations. Subordinate element descriptions indicate specific inclusions and exclusions in this summary category.

1.1 PROJECT MANAGEMENT

Project management includes the overall administrative effort of planning, organizing, coordinating, directing, controlling, and approving the work activities required to accomplish the program objectives. The subelements of project management are defined below.

1.1.1 Cost Control Management

This refers to those activities that ensure the integrated planning, scheduling, budgeting, work authorization, and cost accumulation of all tasks performed during the project. It provides project performance planning, including preparation and maintenance of a project management plan, project schedules, resource status reports, and cost forecasting. Also included are the establishment of project performance criteria, the control of change parameters, and the analysis and summary of measured data. Continuous monitoring of all functional management disciplines is provided for central direction and control of the overall project, including timely resolution of problem areas to ensure that established schedules are met. Establishment, operation, and maintenance of a management information system is a portion of this element. Other task elements include interface with the customer, contract administration, and proposal administration.

Specific Inclusions

1. Updating of the work breakdown structure (WBS)/dictionary.
2. Preparation and maintenance of a cost distribution coding system.
3. Monitoring of all budget allocations.
4. Maintenance of surveillance of cost accounts in order to ensure reasonably accurate accrued charges.
5. Identification of technical performance measurement parameters and values, and technical achievement planning including preparation, submittal, and maintenance of a technical performance report.

1.1.2   Logistics Management

This element provides the effort to implement, operate, and maintain a logistics management activity for support of the project. Included in this element are the preparation and maintenance of the following documents:

1. Systems support and logistics plan.
2. Recommended spare parts list.
3. Maintenance analysis.
4. Analysis of support requirements.

Other examples of policy and procedures generated by this WBS element are:

Spares management.
Inventory management.
Repair and overhaul policy.
Propellants, gases, and fluids.
Forecasts and usage reports.
Warehousing and storage policy.
Transportation analysis and planning.

Specific Exclusions

The operating functions that implement policy, practices, and procedures set by logistics management are covered by WBS 1.4.5, Logistics Support.

1.1.3   Procurement Management

Management and technical control of interdivisional work, subcontractors, and vendors is provided by this element. Tasks included are providing contractual direction to other divisions within a company, subcontractors, and vendors; authorizing subcontractor tooling and equipment; analyzing subcontractor reports; conducting subcontractor and vendor reviews; and on-site coordination and evaluation of procurements. Also included are the maintenance of records and submittal of required reports relating to the geographic dispersion of minority and small business participation in procurements.

Specific Inclusion

1. Coordinate and review all vendor data.
2. Maintain vendor data specification.
3. Maintain vendor technical data file.

Specific Exclusions

1. Responses to vendor inquiries concerning changes to, deviation from, or interpretation of design or other requirements are included in the appropriate hardware or service element.
2. Establishment of supplier performance measurement criteria and survey of vendor facilities and procedures to determine adequacy are included under the management elements of cost control, quality and reliability assurance, and safety.

1.1.4 Configuration Management

This element provides a system for defining the hardware and software configurations at any time throughout the project life cycle. This system provides identification of configuration baselines and a progressive verification that the as-built configuration agrees with the current baseline or that differences are identified. Included in this element are the tasks associated with preparation, maintenance, and submittal of the following:

1. Configuration management plan.
2. Configuration status accounting report.
3. Configuration baseline document.
4. As-built configuration reports.
5. Engineering change proposals and requests.

Also included are establishment, implementation, and maintenance of specification formats; end-item selection criteria; and procedures for control and accounting of configuration changes. Provisions for design support; conducting design reviews, audits, and analyses; and change control are included in the element. Participation in configuration verification to support acceptance inspections are also covered.

1.1.5   Information Management

This element refers to the overall management process and activities required to ensure proper information control. Services are provided to identify, control, and monitor the preparation of and maintain status of the documentation for the project. Establishment, implementation, and maintenance of a data management plan and procedures are part of this element. Monitoring and preparation of data required by the appropriate engineering task order, agreement, or directive are included in this element along with submittal of the data as required. Acquisition of data from subcontractors and vendors is also included. Establishment, operation, and maintenance of a project-level information file are included. Efforts associated with data acquisition, reproduction, and dissemination required for proper management, control, and definition of the project are included in the appropriate hardware WBS elements. Any audiovisual and photography support and training presentations are also included under the appropriate hardware WBS elements.

1.1.6   Quality and Reliability Assurance Management

This element covers the effort associated with the establishment, implementation, and maintenance of a quality and reliability assurance activity in order to provide high-quality hardware through systemic procedures, training, analysis, review, and assessment. It includes development and implementation of plans, requirements, procedures, and controls; design participation; quality audits; identification and data retrieval; procurement-related quality control activities; nonconformance reporting and disposition; metrology; laboratory test support; packaging, handling, and storage-related activities; establishment and monitoring of a failure mode and effect analyses; statistical analysis; government property control; and flight test/ground operations–related activities. Work in this element includes the preparation, submittal, and maintenance of a reliability program plan and quality control plan. Training of quality assurance personnel is included under this category.

Specific Exclusions

1. Those engineering-oriented quality, reliability, and safety activities specifically included under 1.2.2, Internal Analysis and Integration.
2. Implementation of the plans prepared by this element are included under 1.2.2, Internal Analysis and Integration.
3. Quality control inspections are charged under the applicable hardware-oriented WBS elements.

1.1.7   Safety Management

This element covers items required in the definition, direction, and monitoring of a safety program that will ensure the development of a safe product, prevent accidents and incidents, and minimize hazards to personnel and property. Safety will be an integral part of design, development, manufacturing, testing, handling, storage, and operation. This will be accomplished through training, analysis, safety program assessments, and preparation of a project hazard summary; and development and implementation of procedures, controls, reviews, audits, safety analyses, safety design, and a safety plan that covers the safety program and its implementation.

Specific Inclusions

1. Safety training exercises.
2. Periodic reporting, auditing, certification, working group meetings, and accident investigations.
3. Review of all designs and procedures for compliance with established safety requirements.

Specific Exclusions

1. Labor and materials used in the making of signs or training aids are charged to the specific hardware WBS element.
2. Implementation of safety programs and practices that can be identified with specific hardware WBS items.

1.1.8 Project Direction

This function integrates the elements defined above while providing day-to-day management direction of the project. Specifically excluded are activities of higher management and staff. Management activities identifiable with single project management elements or specific hardware items are included in those items.

1.1.9 Checkout

Included are those quality and manufacturing operations required from the time of final assembly until the vehicle is shipped to the launch site.

Specific Inclusions

1. The final acceptance tests that confirm that all systems will perform in accordance with engineering documentation, that the system meets all design criteria, that all specified operating parameters are within tolerance, and that the system will interface physically and functionally with all flight and ground support equipment items as required.
2. Tool liaison and maintenance during checkout.
3. Final vehicle weighing, including preparation, maintenance, and submittal of a final vehicle weight report.
4. Data reduction and analysis.

5. Alignment.

6. Operations required to prepare the vehicle for shipment, includin .emoval of appropriate hardware, installation of protective equipment and covers, packing, and crating.

7. Storage of the vehicle between checkout and transportation to the launch site.

Specific Exclusions

1. Final assembly is included under integration, WBS 1.2.1.6, 1.3.2.5, 1.3.3.7, and 1.3.4.4.

2. Installation of pyrotechnic devices, if any, are covered under WBS 1.5.

3. Preparations for launching are covered under launch support.

4. Acceptance testing of hardware at levels 5 and below before final assembly is covered under the specific hardware element.

1.2   SYSTEMS ENGINEERING

This summary element deals with the application of scientific and engineering endeavors toward the planning and control of a totally integrated project. The work, involving more than one element, includes (1) transformation of an operational need to a description of performance parameters and a configuration through an iterative process of definition, synthesis, analysis, design, test, and evaluation; (2) integration of related technical parameters in order to ensure compatibility of all physical, functional, and program interfaces in a manner that optimizes the total project definition and design; and (3) integration of maintainability, producibility, and human factors into the total engineering effort.

Specific Inclusions

1. An especially important requirement of systems engineering is materials and processes investigations that span more than one hardware element. Facets of this area are metals, nonmetals, composite materials, manufacturing processes, and compatibility of materials.

2. Traceability of significant engineering decisions and the rationale upon which the decisions were based are included.

3. Assurance that engineering decisions on design alternatives consider a system/cost-effectiveness analysis based on merit, performance parameters, and available resources.

4. Mission concepts and analysis, including space vehicle interface trades, time lines, delta velocities, and payload placement accuracies.

5. Monitoring the conduct of the technical program.

6. A systems engineering management plan for satisfying the systems engineering objectives is included.

7. Preliminary design reviews, critical design reviews, flight readiness reviews, and production configuration audits that pertain to combinations of two or more subsystems (for instance, subsystem interface reviews) are included.
8. Technical risk assessment to identify potential major problems. Development and maintenance of hazard tracking and reporting systems.
9. Integration of test results and analyses into system design.
10. Review of specifications and procedures.

Specific Exclusions

1. Engineering efforts (for instance, test plans, specifications, and design reviews) directed toward specific WBS elements are charged to those elements.
2. Hardware item redesign required because of problems identified during design reviews is included under the specific WBS element.
3. Materials and processes investigations relating to one hardware item are included in that particular element.

1.2.1 External Integration

This element represents that portion of systems engineering that pertains specifically to the space project's interface with its launch vehicle.

Specific Inclusions

1. Participation in system analysis, design, and test and evaluation to ensure the efficient integration into the launch vehicle.
2. Preparation, submittal, and maintenance of interface control documents.
3. Test integration and preparation, submittal, and maintenance of the test plan and instrumentation and measurement lists.

1.2.2 Internal Analysis and Integration

This element covers the analysis and integration portion of systems engineering. The subelements are (1) mission operations requirements analysis, (2) systems requirements analysis, (3) system verification, (4) systems requirements control, and (5) vehicle integration. Details of these are:

1. Mission/Operation Requirements Analysis

   A. System Mission/Operations Analysis defines the operational requirements of the space system.
   B. Ground Operations Timelines are prepared to define the sequence and duration of the preflight phase events until launch. The phases covered are prelaunch, launch, and postlaunch. These timelines provide data for support systems design and for reliability analysis.

C. Flight Operations Timelines define the sequence and duration of the flight phase events. These lead to the definition of flight sequence requirements and are utilized for reliability and failure effects analysis.

D. Contingency Analysis is performed to define the parameters to be utilized as cues for off-nominal operations and to define the actions to be taken in case of abnormalities during prelaunch and flight phases.

E. Prelaunch Systems Integrity Verification Analysis is conducted to define the parameters and the limits of these parameters to ensure systems integrity prior to launch. The task also defines whether the parameters are automatically verified or verified by an observer.

F. Fleet Size Analysis. The mission model, on-orbit stay time, and ground turnaround times are modeled to define the fleet size required during the operational phase.

G. Other analyses that are included are consumables analysis, power profiles, payload deployment event timelines, capture analysis, launch rates, reference mission profiles, trajectory analysis, minimum duration deployment analysis, analysis of servicing satellites on orbit, retrieval capability analysis, design reference trajectory analysis, functional flow diagrams, and abort capability analysis.

2. Systems Requirements Analysis involves the following analyses and functions:

A. Vehicle sizing analysis, which is utilized in determining optimum performance.

B. Control, loads, and thermal analyses, which establish structure and subsystem requirements.

C. Identification of requirements for ground support operations, equipment, and facilities in support of the flight system.

D. Incorporation of safety, reliability, and quality requirements generated under WBS 1.1.6 and 1.1.7 into the system and end item specifications, interface control documents, and subsystem requirements handbooks, and the establishment of a requirements baseline based on these documents.

E. Consolidation of the subsystem requirements in the requirements handbooks for use by the designers and for ensuring compatibility of the subsystem interfaces.

F. Preparation of the technical portion of the procurement packages.

G. Preparation, submittal, and maintenance of an engineering program plan providing planning and control of all engineering and development tasks.

H. Configuration trade studies and design definitions.

I. Performance of mass properties analysis, induced environments analysis, and subsystem requirements analysis.

3. System Verification consists of the establishment of test requirements and

integration, definition of requirements for a certification program, and assessment of the design definition and test data to verify that the requirements have been met by the defined system. Analytical verification and certification status are also included.

4. Systems Requirements Control is composed of the following:
   A. Preparation and maintenance of a technical plan.
   B. Engineering change control.
   C. Support to cost control management.
   D. Technology utilization.
   E. Preparation and maintenance of specifications.
   F. Preparation, coordination, and support of interface control documents.
   G. Procurement specification formulation.

5. Vehicle Integration covers those efforts directed toward assembling the level 5 hardware systems into a vehicle or test article. Those overall integration endeavors outside the scope of the WBS elements 1.3.1.6, 1.3.2.5, 1.3.3.7, and 1.3.4.4 are included.

Specific Inclusions

1. Provision of engineering support to manufacturing during hardware build, including assistance in performance trades.

2. Preparation, submittal, and maintenance of a prelaunch-postlanding operations analysis document. It provides a logical functional flow of the activities from factory through prelaunch. The analysis includes event sheets that describe or summarize the individual events in the functional flow and identifies requirements for ground support equipment, handling hardware, and transportation equipment to support the activities of each event. The necessary documentation required to support each activity includes:
   A. Interface control documents.
   B. Test and checkout documents.
   C. Composite mechanical schematics.

3. Integration of failure mode and effect analyses on hardware and systems that affect the launch and mission, including preparation, maintenance, and submittal of data required.

4. Implementation of a safety program plan, a reliability program plan, and a quality control plan.

5. Review of all designs and procedures for compliance with human engineering requirements.

6. Developing and maintaining the necessary training requirements for engineering, fabrication, test, procurement, reliability and quality assurance, and other personnel who may have an effect on or are responsible for the determination of reliability or quality.

7. Activities to determine and control the weight of the subsystems and compo-

nents, including the preparation and submittal of required mass properties reports.

8. In-scope basic design maintenance for flight test hardware. Maintenance includes in-scope changes identified by factory liaison calls, field liaison calls, and engineering evaluation in the course of checkout, launch, and flight operations.

9. Establishment and control of an electromagnetic interference control plan.

10. Standards and calibration services.

Specific Exclusions

1. Parts selection and control of electronic, electrical, and mechanical parts, including preparation, maintenance, and submittal of data required.

2. Preparing, maintaining, and updating equipment logs for each subsystem and system as a means of documenting its history, including preparation and submittal of the data required.

1.2.3   Continuing Engineering

This subelement of systems engineering covers all sustaining engineering support of the project after the completed space vehicle has been assembled and checked out. Sustaining tooling engineering effort is included.

Specific Inclusions

1. Design, development, test, and analysis; tool design, fabrication, and maintenance; manufacturing of detail parts, components, assemblies, and subassemblies; support to reliability and safety; inspection; and the procurement activities to provide the lower-level elements for installation and integration into the space vehicle.

2. Test and support articles.

3. Design and fabrication of specified models relating to this system.

4. Fabrication of spare parts in support of the test units.

5. Tooling and fabrication efforts required to install wiring harnesses, conduits, plumbing assemblies, ducting, and attachment provisions.

6. Quality control and reliability inspection, including suppliers' source inspections.

7. Fabrication, repair, and overhaul of spare parts in support of operational flights.

8. Sustaining engineering that can be identified with a single WBS element.

Specific Exclusions

Checkout of the fully assembled vehicle is covered by 1.1.9.

1.3   SPACE VEHICLE

This summary element comprises the design, development, procurement, manufacturing, testing, quality control inspection, safety, tooling, checkout of space vehicle elements, and rework required in order to produce a complete space vehicle with its full complement of spares. Facilities are covered under WBS 1.4.2.

1.3.1   Structural System

This element refers to the assembled structural and aerodynamic components of the space vehicle, integration of the subelements, integration of structural system into the space vehicle, and support of major vehicle tests and launch support. Included is the effort required to monitor in-scope engineering design changes for producibility, to establish the incorporation points and prepare advanced planning instructions, process plans, log changes, tool orders, tool drawings for new or changed tools, and the liaison and tool fabrication effort. This also covers the preventive maintenance, calibration, improvement, and periodic inspection of tooling, tool control and storage, and the maintenance of tooling and planning files.

1.3.1.1   Propellant Tanks. This element covers the structural details and structural subassemblies of the propellant tanks. It encompasses subordinate features such as necessary frames and struts; multilayered insulation including purge bag, reflector, separator, face sheets, studs and fasteners, and baffles; level sensor support structures; basic tank shells; feedline support structures; manhole covers; access doors and lesser openings; attach mechanisms for wiring and other such provisions; and mounting devices for propellant lines and pumps.

Specific Inclusions

1. Detail design and analysis, including preparation, maintenance, and submittal of drawings and technical studies and analyses.
2. Tool engineering, tool manufacture, and associated manufacturing aids, including preparation and maintenance of tool and fixture drawings.
3. Detail manufacture and associated support activities, including quality control and the preparation and maintenance of manufacturing planning data, and manufacturing specifications and procedures.
4. Procurement of material and services, including supplier nonrecurring and recurring costs.
5. Joining of subordinate elements listed in the above definitions.
6. Details and subassemblies for development test, qualification test. and production.
7. Development and qualification test fixtures, tests, test rigs, test setups, and instrumentation in support of the test. Also includes the preparation, maintenance, and submittal of test procedures, test reports, and qualification status reports.

8. Tool liaison and tool maintenance during production and test.
9. Subsystem models.
10. Manufacture of spares and repair parts in support of production and test.
11. Materials research and analysis.
12. Design, fabrication, and test of spare parts in support of operational flights.

1.3.1.2   Thrust Structure. This element is composed of all structural members and subassemblies comprising the interface between the main shell and the engine. It includes fiberglass layups, thrust struts, engine mounting provisions, feedline supports, actuator attach points, and mounting supports for engine fluid and electrical interface lines, cables, and couplings.

For specific inclusions and specific exclusions, refer to 1.3.1.1.

1.3.1.3   Main Shell. This element is the principal structural entity on which the propellant tanks mount. It consists of the shell structure, manipulator attach points, and support bracketry for the feed system, vent system, pressurization system, electrical cabling and avionics components, access ports, and stage side umbilicals.

For specific inclusions and exclusions, refer to 1.3.1.1. Excluded are any materials bonded to the main shell for the purpose of dampening heat caused by impingement of effluent from the auxiliary power system.

1.3.1.4   Interface Structures. This element covers the structural portion of the forward support cradle and the aft adapter (support skirt) situated between the stage and the launch vehicle. Excluded are electrical, propulsion, and mechanical aspects, which are included under WBS elements 1.3.2, 1.3.3, and 1.3.4, respectively.

For specific inclusions and exclusions, refer to 1.3.1.1.

1.3.1.5   Micrometeoroid Protection. This item is comprised of special micrometeoroid protection that is necessary beyond that provided by the main shell and the multilayered insulation.

For specific inclusions and specific exclusions, refer to 1.3.1.1.

1.3.1.6   Integration. This element covers assembly of the structural system and its subelements into the space vehicle and testing the assembled system.

Specific Inclusions

1. Detail design and analysis, including preparation, maintenance, and submittal of installation and final assembly drawings and technical studies and analyses.
2. Tool engineering, tool manufacture and associated manufacturing aids required for installation, mating, and in-process checking.
3. Fabrication and installation of simulated parts, components, or assemblies

necessary for later installation or mating operations, including preparation and maintenance of manufacturing planning data, manufacturing specifications, and manufacturing procedures.

4. Interface alignment documentation.
5. Inboard profile drawings.
6. Quality assurance effort consists of performing inspection verification during installation and mating of structural assemblies, systems, and interfacing checks. Nondestructive evaluation inspection, verification of cleaning process controls, and component closeout are included.
7. Procurement of material and services, including supplier nonrecurring and recurring costs, required to support installation.
8. In-process verification test of subsystems during installation.
9. Tool liaison and tool maintenance during mating and final assembly.
10. Mating of structural system elements.
11. Data reduction and analysis.
12. Analysis of thermal control systems relating to the structural system.
13. Design and development of active thermal control systems, such as radiators, that pertain to the structural system.

1.3.2 Avionics System

This element refers to those electrical and electronic subsystems that provide electrical power, navigation, guidance and control, telecommunication instrumentation, data management, tracking and command, and systems integration functions. Any required thermal conditioning relating to an avionics element is included in that element. It includes the effort required to monitor the in-scope engineering design changes for producibility and to establish the incorporation points and prepare advanced planning instructions, process plans, log changes, tool orders, tool drawings for new or changed tools, and the liaison and tool fabrication effort. This also covers the preventive maintenance, calibration, improvement, and periodic inspection of tooling, tool control, and storage and the maintenance of tooling and planning files. Umbilical disconnects and actuators are covered under 1.3.4.1 and 1.3.4.3.

Specific Inclusions

1. Design, development, test, and analysis; tool design, fabrication, and maintenance; manufacturing of detail parts, components, assemblies, and subassemblies; support to reliability and safety; inspection; and the procurement activities to provide the lower-level elements for installation and integration.
2. Test and support articles.
3. Design and fabrication of specified models relating to this system.
4. Fabrication of spare parts in support of production and test.

5. Tooling and fabrication efforts required to install wiring harnesses, conduits, plumbing assemblies, and ducting attachment provisions.

6. Quality control and reliability inspection, including suppliers' source inspections.

7. Fabrication, repair, and overhaul of spare parts in support of operational flights.

Specific Exclusion

Checkout of the fully assembled spare vehicle is covered by 1.1.9.

1.3.2.1   Electrical Power.   This level 4 element refers to the equipment that generates, conditions, controls, and distributes electrical power throughout the space vehicle. It includes fuel cells, batteries, voltage sensors, connectors, static inverters, power amplifiers, power conditioners, distributors, switching elements, and wiring. Electrical power to the space vehicle is covered to the interfaces of the disconnects.

1.3.2.2   Navigation, Guidance, and Control.   This element includes a star tracker, horizon sensor, inertial measuring unit, platform, gyros, accelerometer, rate stabilization system, attitude control equipment, rendezvous and docking equipment, data acquisition teleoperation, as well as navigation, guidance and control analysis, and flight dynamics. Actuators are included under 1.3.4.3.

1.3.2.3   Data Management and Processing.   This element consists of a computer, data storage, data bus, data terminals, computer operations, data processing, and software.

1.3.2.4   Instrumentation and Communication.   This element covers the development and operational flight instrumentation and communication systems, including establishment of detailed requirements. It includes measuring equipment, signal conditioning equipment, instrumentation sensors, digital interface units, transmitters, transponders, antennas, multiplexers, camera lights, relay assemblies, malfunction detection packages, cable harnesses, rate pulse beacons, command control receivers, imaging devices, and transducers not readily identifiable with another avionics item.

1.3.2.5   Integration.   This covers all work relating to incorporating the avionics system hardware elements into the space vehicle and testing the system.

Specific Inclusions

1. Detail design and analysis, including preparation, maintenance, and submittal of installation and final assembly drawings and technical studies and analyses.

2. Tool engineering, tool manufacture, and associated manufacturing aids required for installation, mating, and in-process checking.
3. Fabrication and installation of simulated parts, components, or assemblies necessary to later installation or mating operations, including preparation and maintenance of manufacturing planning data, and manufacturing specifications and procedures.
4. Quality assurance effort consists of performing inspection verification during installation and mating of avionics system assemblies, electrical systems, and interfacing checks. Nondestructive evaluation inspection, verification of cleaning process controls, proof pressure and leak checks, component closeout, and continuity checks are included.
5. Procurement of material and services, including supplier nonrecurring and recurring costs, required to support the subsystem installation.
6. In-process verification test of subsystems during installation.
7. Tool liaison and tool maintenance during mating and final assembly.
8. Mating of all avionics system elements.

1.3.3 Propulsion System

This summary category work element is comprised of those elements that provide impulse for translation and attitude control. Also covered is thermal conditioning of propulsion elements. Actuators are covered under 1.3.4.3.

Specific Inclusions

1. Design, development, test, and analysis; tool design, fabrication, and maintenance; manufacturing of detail parts, components assemblies, and subassemblies; support to reliability and safety; inspection; and the procurement activities to provide the lower-level elements for installation and integration.
2. Test and support articles.
3. Design and fabrication of specified models relating to this system.
4. Fabrication of spare parts in support of production and test.
5. Tooling and fabrication efforts required to install wiring harnesses, conduits, plumbing assemblies, ducting, and attachment provisions.
6. Quality control and reliability inspection, including supplier source inspections.
7. Fabrication, repair, and overhaul of spare parts in support of operational flights.
8. Valve actuators.

Specific Exclusion

Checkout of the fully assembled space vehicle is covered by 1.1.9.

1.3.3.1 Main Engine. This item covers that device that imparts the basic thrust to the space vehicle. Gimbals and thermal control are included.

1.3.3.2 Propellant Feed. This element is comprised of all lines, valves, ducts, bellows, and other components that transfer the main engine oxidizer/fuel from the tanks to the main engine. Attendant thermal conditioning is covered by the thermal conditioning, WBS element 1.3.3.6.

1.3.3.3 Main Tank Pressurization and Vent. This element is composed of all lines, valves, ducts, bellows, and other components that take pressurization gases from the engine to the main fuel tank and the lines, valves, ducts, bellows, storage tank, and other components that provide pressurization gas to the fuel tanks. Also covered are those components that carry pressurization gas for dumping overboard.

1.3.3.4 Main Tank Fill and Drain. This element covers all lines, ducts, valves, and other components required to fill and drain the main propellant tanks. Propellant provisions are also covered.

1.3.3.5 Auxiliary Propulsion. This element in the propulsion system covers the thrusters, valves, lines, and storage tanks that provide impulse for small translation and attitude control maneuvers. Also covered are materials and equipment designed to control or dampen heat caused by impingement of effluent from the auxiliary power system.

1.3.3.6 Thermal Conditioning. This element includes all devices provided especially to control temperatures of hardware elements in the propulsion system. As an example, this covers the thermal control of the engine and propellant feed but not of the auxiliary power system.

1.3.3.7 Integration. This element covers all work required to incorporate the propulsion system into the space vehicle, and testing the system.

Specific Inclusions

1. Detail design and analysis, including preparation, maintenance, and submittal of installation and final assembly drawings and technical studies and analyses.
2. Tool engineering, tool manufacture, and associated manufacturing aids required for installation, mating, and in-process checking.
3. Fabrication and installation of simulated parts, components, or assemblies necessary for later installation or mating operations, including preparation and maintenance of manufacturing planning data, manufacturing specifications, and procedures.
4. Quality assurance effort consists of performing inspection verification dur-

ing installation and mating of fluid systems and interfacing checks. Non-destructive evaluation, inspection verification of cleaning process controls, proof pressure and leak checks, and component closeout are included.

5. Materials and services, including supplier nonrecurring and recurring costs, required to support installation.
6. In-process verification test of subsystems during installation.
7. Tool liaison and tool maintenance during mating and final assembly.
8. Mating of all propulsion system elements.
9. Tank cleaning.
10. Data reduction and analysis.

1.3.4 Mechanical System

This WBS element includes all machinery or mechanisms imparting some action to a subordinate structural member or members. Included is the effort required to monitor the in-scope engineering design changes for producibility; to establish the incorporation point and prepare advanced planning instructions, process plans, log changes, tool orders, and tool drawing for new or changed tools; and the liaison and tool fabrication effort. This element also covers the preventive maintenance, calibration, improvement and periodic inspection of tooling, tool control, and storage, and the maintenance of tooling and planning files. Individual components include latches, vent closing and opening devices, holding devices, actuators, and hinges.

Specific Inclusions

1. Design, development, test, and analysis; tool design, fabrication, and maintenance; manufacturing of detail parts, components, assemblies, and subassemblies; support to reliability and safety; inspection; and the procurement activities to provide the lower-level elements for installation and integration.
2. Test and support articles.
3. Design and fabrication of specified models relating to the mechanical system.
4. Fabrication of spare parts in support of production and test.
5. Tooling and fabrication efforts required to install wiring harnesses, conduits, plumbing assemblies, ducting, and attachment provisions.
6. Quality control and reliability inspection, including supplier source inspections.
7. Fabrication, repair, and overhaul of spare parts in support of operational flights.

Specific Exclusions

1. Checkout of the fully assembled space vehicle is covered by 1.1.9.
2. Valves are covered in the propulsion system.

1.3.4.1   Launch Vehicle Interface. This covers all the mechanical hardware enabling the space vehicle to link with the launch vehicle and to separate from it in
flight. Included is the alignment and energy absorption subsystem, the retrac-
tion/extension support subsystem, the reentry purge subsystem, and the umbilical
disconnects in the fluid/electrical interface. Tubing, fittings, hoses, cables, connectors, adapters, and interface supports are excluded and are covered under other
appropriate hardware WBS elements.

1.3.4.2   Payload Interface. This element is comprised of all mechanical devices
associated with attachment of the payload to the space vehicle. The structural
entities are covered under the appropriate structural system element.

1.3.4.3   Actuators and Other Mechanical Components. This element covers all
engine actuators and other mechanical components necessary to orient the thrust
vector control of the main engine and those actuators necessary to actuate all valves.
Related structural members are covered under 1.3.1. This element also includes all
mechanical devices associated with the space vehicle ground support equipment
interfacing with the launch facility.

1.3.4.4   Integration

1. Detail design and analysis, including preparation, maintenance, and submittal
   of installation and final assembly drawings and technical studies and analyses.
2. Tool engineering, tool manufacture, and associated manufacturing aids required for installation, mating, and in-process checking.
3. Fabrication and installation of simulated parts, components, or assemblies
   necessary for later installation or mating operations, including preparation
   and maintenance of manufacturing planning data, manufacturing specifications, and procedures.
4. Quality assurance effort consists of performing inspection verification during
   installation and mating of mechanical systems and interfacing checks. Nondestructive evaluation inspections, verification of cleaning process, controls,
   and component closeout are included.
5. Procurement of materials and services, including supplier nonrecurring and
   recurring costs required to support installation.
6. In-process verification test of subsystems during installation.
7. Tool liaison and tool maintenance during mating and final assembly.
8. Mating of all mechanical system elements.
9. Data reduction and analysis.

1.4   SYSTEM SUPPORT

This summary WBS element covers miscellaneous system support activities not
identifiable with any of the previously defined WBS elements. Specifically included

are design, development testing, qualification testing, tool design, tool manufacture, tool maintenance, test hardware, procurement, manufacturing, assembly, transportation, and installation of items defined below.

1.4.1 Support Equipment

This element covers ground support equipment, factory support equipment, special test equipment, software, and support equipment integration not relatable to a single space vehicle item.

1.4.1.1 Ground Support Equipment. The ground support equipment element is composed of deliverable equipment of those categories described in the following subelements:

1. Servicing equipment is that required to supply, distribute, and condition fluids or electrical power to the space vehicle.
2. Handling equipment is that required to support and handle the space vehicle, assemblies, and subassemblies.
3. Transportation equipment is that required to package and/or transport the space vehicle, assemblies, and subassemblies.
4. Checkout equipment is that required to verify flight systems and ground support equipment, provide controls and monitoring, and distribute electrical signals.
5. Auxiliary equipment includes access platforms and work stands.

1.4.1.2 Factory Support Equipment. The factory support equipment element covers the design and manufacture of those items of nondeliverable support equipment that satisfy unique space vehicle manufacturing, test, checkout, access, and handling requirements.

Specific Inclusions

1. Test and support articles
2. Propellant tank multilayered insulation purge equipment.
3. Spare parts for those support equipments listed above.
4. Vehicles, equipment, and tools used to fuel, service, transport and hoist, repair, overhaul, assemble, disassemble, test, inspect, or otherwise maintain the space vehicle and its ground support equipment.
5. Installation and activation of support equipment necessary to support the ground and flight tests.

Specific Exclusions

1. Spare parts provided for space vehicle hardware items.
2. Dimensional and fabrication tooling, materials handling equipment, facilities, or laboratory test fixtures.

3. System engineering integration activity, including reliability, maintainability, human engineering, and integration with the launch vehicle is included in the subelements of WBS element 1.2.
4. Standards and calibration services are included in element 1.2.2.
5. The purge bag integral to the multilayered insulation is included in 1.3.1.1.
6. Integration effort is included in WBS 1.2.
7. Development testing and quality testing are included in appropriate WBS hardware element.

1.4.2 Facilities

"Facilities" encompasses the activation, modification, construction, and maintenance of all buildings, furniture, roads, utilities, equipment foundations, rail appurtenances, drainage ways, test stands, block houses, cable passages, trailers, and docks required for the administration, engineering, manufacturing, checkout, test, and flight of the vehicle and its related support equipment. Installation of tooling and support equipment in the buildings or on the foundations is covered under WBS 1.3 and 1.4.1.

Specific Inclusions

1. Preproduction studies.
2. Formulation and maintenance of a facility plan, progress reports, and change control activities that relate to facilities.
3. Planning of use of facilities.
4. Capability surveys.
5. Drawings depicting installation of support equipment.
6. Implementation of safety and environmental obligations.
7. Inspection of new facilities or modifications.
8. Analyzing requirements against existing facilities and planning the utilization of all facilities and facility equipment required for design, development, production test, and checkout associated with the space vehicle, including preparation, maintenance, and submittal of the facilities plan.
9. Maintenance of real property records.
10. Coordination of facility planning and activation, including preparation, maintenance and submittal of the facility construction, activities, utilization, and maintenance reports.
11. Activation of administration, manufacturing, and flight test facilities, including site readiness reviews. Activation includes the installation of all equipment and verification of facility-equipment-hardware interfaces.
12. Supervision and accomplishment of facility design, modification, and new construction.

Specific Exclusion

Auxiliary equipment that facilitates fabrication.

1.4.3   Transportation

This element refers to the services required to transport the space vehicle, its subassemblies, and associated ground equipment from the point where it is finally assembled through the point of ultimate use.

Specific Inclusions

1. The effort required to provide monitoring while in transit to the launch site.
2. Preparation and maintenance of a transportation plan is included as part of a systems support and logistics plan.
3. The transporter crew and incidental materials and equipment for protection of the space vehicle during shipment.

Specific Exclusions

1. In-plant transportation required during manufacturing buildup, test, and checkout.
2. Protective covers, shipping containers, handling equipment, etc., are included under checkout, 1.1.9.
3. Shipment of manufactured parts and components from the manufacturing site to the final assembly site are included in the element under which the item was manufactured.

1.4.4   Training

This element refers to training services, devices, accessories, aids, equipment, and parts used to facilitate instruction through which personnel will acquire efficient concepts, skills, cost-consciousness, and attitudes to operate and maintain the space vehicle with maximum efficiency. This includes all endeavors associated with the design, development, and production of training equipment, as well as the conduct of training activities.

Specific Inclusions

1. Instructor and personnel training, including the preparation and maintenance of a training plan and a training manual, and the preparation, maintenance, and submittal of a training requirements analysis.
2. Detailed design and development of unique training equipment, including the preparation and maintenance of drawings.
3. Training aids.

4. Training in support of flight operations.
5. Travel allowances in connection with training exercises.
6. Maintenance and shop support of training equipment and maintenance of tooling in support of flight operations phase.

Specific Exclusions

1. Safety training is covered under 1.1.7.
2. Quality training is covered under 1.1.6.

1.4.5 Logistics Support

This element provides the effort to implement and operate a logistics activity for the space vehicle and its related ground equipment.

Specific Inclusions

1. Spares handling.
2. Fabrication, maintenance, repair, and testing of spares.
3. Warehousing of spares.
4. Inventory control.
5. Propellant and gases handling and control.
6. Shipping and receiving.
7. Receiving inspection.

Specific Exclusions

1. Planning and management functions are covered under 1.1.2, Logistics Management.
2. The spares themselves are covered under the specific hardware categories.

1.5 VEHICLE TESTS AND OPERATIONS

This summary element encompasses all labor, materials, and other expenses required to conduct all major tests and mission operations.

Specific Inclusions

1. Provision of engineering/technical effort required for the formulation of procedures, plans, checklists, and test reports.
2. Liaison engineering for the support of planning for system support activities.
3. Removal of protective covers installed during transportation.

4. Reassembly of elements that were removed from the vehicle in preparation for transportation.

5. Tool engineering, tool manufacture, and associated manufacturing aids required for reassembly and checkout after arrival at the test or launch site.

6. Manufacturing planning data, specifications, and procedures specifying removal of equipment, reassembly, and site installation tasks.

7. Quality inspection during assembly and installation, final vehicle inspection, and inspection support to tooling fabrication and tool maintenance.

8. Materials and services required during reassembly and installation.

9. Tool liaison and maintenance.

10. Data reduction and analysis.

11. Installation of pyrotechnic devices, if any.

12. Test and operations planning and control.

Specific Exclusions

1. Final assembly drawing, which is covered by 1.2.2.

2. Manufacturing aids, which are used in integration elements, are included under 1.3.1.6, 1.3.2.5, 1.3.3.7, and 1.3.4.4.

3. Identification and activation of all facilities and support equipment required at the site is included in the appropriate subelements of WBS element 1.4, System Support.

1.5.1   Structural Test Support

This element covers all work required to prepare the structural test article for test, conduct the test, acquire and analyze data, and refurbish the hardware in preparation for follow-on tests.

Specific Inclusions

1. Transportation of the test article to the test site.

2. Installation of test article in structural test stand.

3. Installation of strain gauges.

4. Checkout and quality inspection during test.

5. Reports preparation.

Specific Exclusions

1. Costs of manufacturing test hardware are included under 1.3 and 1.4.1.

2. Facilities expenses are included under 1.4.2.

3. Logistics support costs are covered under 1.4.5.

1.5.2   Dynamics Test Support

This element includes all work required to prepare the structural test article for dynamics test, conduct the test, acquire and analyze data, and refurbish in preparation for further tests.

Specific Inclusions

1. Transportation of the test article to the test site.
2. Installation of the test article in the test stand.
3. Installation of any special measuring devices, such as strain gauges.
4. Quality inspection during test.
5. Reports preparation.

Specific Exclusions

1. Test hardware and ground support equipment are included under 1.3 and 1.4.1.
2. Facilities are included under 1.4.2.
3. Logistics support is included under 1.4.5.

1.5.3   Propulsion Test Support

Covered are all resources required to prepare the propulsion test article for test, install the engine, load the propellants, conduct the test, gather and analyze the data, and refurbish the vehicle in preparation for flight.

Specific Inclusions

1. Transportation of the assembled space vehicle from the point of manufacture to the test site.
2. Installation of the test vehicle into the test stand.
3. Quality inspection.
4. Reports preparation.

Specific Exclusions

1. Hardware and ground support equipment costs are included in 1.3 and 1.4.1.
2. Facilities are covered under 1.4.2.
3. Logistics support costs are covered under 1.4.5.
4. Integration of avionics components into the propulsion test vehicle after the test is included under 1.3.2.5.

1.5.4   Launch Operations

This element covers all the work required to receive, assemble, install in the launch vehicle, service and prepare, check out and perform countdown for launch, and command during launch operations. The work applies to flight tests and mission operations.

Specific Inclusions

1. Management of launch operations activities.
2. Data acquisition and analyses.
3. Tracking.
4. Report preparation.

1.5.5   Flight Operations

This element covers all the work required to control the mission operations from the end of launch operations through reentry and landing. The work applies to flight tests and mission operations. The following tasks are included:

1. Management of flight operations activities.
2. Flight control.
3. Mission planning.
4. Data acquisition and analyses.
5. Tracking (from launch operations handover).
6. Flight operations procedures preparation.
7. Mission evaluation.
8. Flight software.

ANSWERS

CHAPTER 1

1.1. Three reasons for good cost estimating are (any three of the following are acceptable answers):
- **a.** To provide greater assurance that a profit can be achieved.
- **b.** To enhance the efficient allocation of resources.
- **c.** To account for inflationary influences.
- **d.** To pinpoint areas for needed productivity improvements.
- **e.** To protect the organization's reputation for estimate accuracy.
- **f.** To ensure a continuously competitive skill mix.
- **g.** To quantify the effects of planning and scheduling.
- **h.** To keep the price of a work output or work activity compatible with changing market conditions.

1.2. Any two of the following are acceptable answers:
- **a.** Depletion of natural resources.
- **b.** Changes in demand for natural, labor, or capital resources.
- **c.** Changes in technology causing changes in resource usage.
- **d.** Changes in the national money supply.
- **e.** Changes in interest rates: the cost of "using" financial resources.

1.3. Any three of the following are acceptable answers:
- **a.** Changes in employee fringe benefits.
- **b.** Changes in the consumer price index.
- **c.** Changes in wages based on merit, contract negotiation, productivity, or the minimum wage.
- **d.** Material price changes.
- **e.** Utility price changes (electricity, gas, water, waste disposal).
- **f.** Changes in the cost of taxes, insurance, depreciation, or compliance to government regulations.

g. Changes in the company's productivity level.

h. Changes in required combinations of resources (natural, labor, or capital).

1.4. A credible, supportable, and accurate detailed cost estimate can be completed by using the following approaches: (Any three of the following are acceptable answers.)

    a. Prepare a complete list of all materials (drawings, documents, publications, materials, and equipment) required to perform the job.

    b. Prepare a manufacturing analysis showing detailed procedures and tooling and special equipment required.

    c. Apply labor work standards and variances to them to determine the labor time necessary to perform the manufacturing work.

    d. Define and identify labor required to perform administrative, engineering, and other nonmanufacturing tasks.

    e. Determine costs for material from inventory, catalogs, vendor quotes, or other means.

    f. Determine predicted costs for travel, computer usage, consultants, or other direct charges not otherwise allocated.

    g. Apply labor rates by category of labor, overhead and general and administrative costs, material handling fees, allowance for profit, and any allowance for inflation.

1.5. False

CHAPTER 2

2.1. The four kinds of work output are processes, products, projects, and services.

2.2. Cost estimating is "the art of approximating the probable worth or cost of an activity based on information available at the time."

2.3. Cost is the total amount of all the resources required to perform the activity, normally measured in dollars. Price is the total amount paid for that activity, normally measured in dollars, that accommodates the effects of such forces as supply and demand, competition, and negotiation. Price is established by the marketplace, and should equal the cost plus the desired profit. Price = Cost + Profit.

2.4. The basic ingredients of an estimate are labor-hours, materials and subcontracts, travel costs, other direct costs, labor rates, indirect costs, administrative costs, and fee or profit.

2.5. The five basic tools of the estimating process are:

    a. The estimators who prepare the estimate.

    b. The methodological approach to be used to prepare the estimate.

    c. Knowledge or data concerning the project, process, product, or service being estimated.

    d. Capability to compute the estimate.

    e. Capability to publish and distribute the estimate.

2.6. True.

2.7. The typical cost estimating exercise follows this sequence:

    h

    a

    d

    b

    g

    c

    f

    e

CHAPTER 3

3.1. c.

3.2. Parameters defining hardware in a technical specification may include: (five of the following typical answers are acceptable)

Accuracy	Resistance to environ-
Capacity	mental conditions
Color and markings	Security and protection
Life expectancy	requirements
Material type	Shape
Power	Size
Quality	Speed
	Weight

3.3. The items, listed from most important to least important, are **(a)** Statement of Work, **(b)** technical specifications, **(d)** delivery schedule, **(c)** contract work breakdown structure.

3.4. a.

3.5. b.

CHAPTER 4

4.1. The curves intersect at 32.68 units where the cost is 441.44.

Two solutions are provided for this question. Refer to a college algebra textbook for further explanation on setting up these types of problems for solution.

First Solution:

Solve by using exponents. This is a problem of simultaneous equations, solving for x. By definition y must be equal in both equations.

Given: $y = 1000x^{-0.2345}$.

$y = 750x^{-0.1520}$.

Solution: $1000x^{-0.2345} = 750x^{-0.1520}$

$$\frac{1000x^{-0.2345}}{750x^{-0.1520}} = 1$$

$$x^{-.2345 \,+\, .1520} + \frac{750}{1000}$$

$$x^{-.0825} = .75$$
$$x = .75^{-1/.0825}$$
$$x = 32.68954$$

Substituting x, solve for y in the original equations

$$y = 1000(32.68954)^{-0.2345}$$
$$y = \underline{441.44}$$

Check: $y = 750(32.68954)^{-0.1520}$
$y = \underline{441.44}$

Second Solution: Solve by using logarithms and using simultaneous equations, solving for x and finding y in substitution.

Given: $y = 1000x^{-(0.2345)}$
$y = 750x^{-(0.1520)}$

Solution: $\dfrac{y}{1000} = x^{-(0.2345)}$

$$\frac{y}{750} = x^{-(0.1520)}$$

$$-0.1520 \times \frac{\text{Log } y}{\text{Log } 1000} = (-0.152) \times (-0.2345) \times \text{Log } x$$

$$-0.2345 \times \frac{\text{Log } y}{\text{Log } 750} = (0.1520) \times (-0.2345) \times \text{Log } x$$

.2345 Log y/750 −0.152 Log (y/1000) = 0
0.2345 (Log y − Log 750) − 0.152 (Log y − Log 1000) = 0
0.2345 Log y − 0.2345 × (2.875) −0.152 Log y + .152(3) = 0
0.2345 Log y − 0.6742 −0.152 Log y + 0.456 = 0
0.2345 Log y − 0.152 Log y −0.2182 = 0
(Log y) (.0825) = 0.2182
Log y = 2.645 y = 441.44

Check: $y = 1000x^{-0.2345}$

$$\frac{441.44}{1000} = x^{-0.2345}$$

Log .4414 = −0.2345 Log x
−0.3552 = −0.2345 Log x
Log x = 1.515
x = 32.7

4.2. a. $y = Ax^b$
$y = 2000(1024)^{-0.1520}$
$y = 2000(0.3487)$
$y = 697.37$

b. $\dfrac{\text{Unit cost at } 1024}{\text{Unit cost at } \#1} = \dfrac{697.37}{2000.00} = 0.3487$, or 34.87%

c.   This is a two-part answer. First compute the unit cost of unit number 8:
$y = Ax^b$
$\quad = 2000(8)^{-0.1520}$
$\quad = 2000 \times 0.7290$
$\quad = 1458.01.$
Then compute the efficiency factor:

$$\frac{\text{Unit cost at } 1024}{\text{Unit cost at } 8} = \frac{697.36}{1458.01} = 0.4783, \text{ or } 47.83\%$$

4.3. Given:

Lot	Units	Cost
1	400	$ 900
2	350	750
3	600	1400
4	650	1350

Solution by using the method of least squares. (You may have some interpolation of answers depending on your calculator.)

Column 1	Column 2	Column 3 y Lot	Column 4	Column 5	Column 6 Avg Cost
Lot	x Units	Cost	x^2	xy	(y)
1	400	900	160,000	360,000	2.25
2	350	750	122,500	262,500	2.14
3	600	1,400	360,000	840,000	2.33
4	650	1,350	422,500	877,500	2.08
Σ	2,000	4,400	1,065,000	2,340,000	8.80

$\bar{x} = 2000/4 = 500$

$\bar{y} = 4400/4 = 1100$

$b = \dfrac{\Sigma(xy) - \bar{x}(\Sigma(y))}{\Sigma(x^2) - \bar{x}(\Sigma(x))}$

$b = \dfrac{2,340,000 - (500)(4400)}{1,065,000 - (500)(2000)} = \dfrac{2,340,000 - 2,300,000}{1,065,000 - 1,000,000} = \dfrac{140,000}{65,000} = 2.15$

$a = \bar{y} - b\bar{x} = 1100 - (2.15)(500) = 1100 - 1075 = 25.$

Check:

$$y = a + bx = 25 + 2.15(500) = 25 + 1075 = 1100$$

For 460 units:

$$y = a + bx = 25 + 2.15(460) = 25 + 989 = 1014$$

b. Average cost of each lot: column 6 above.

c. Average cost of all lots: $8.80/4 = 2.20$

d. Weighted average cost: $4400/2000 = 2.20$ (by coincidence this is the same as the average cost)

e. $460 \times 2.20 = 1012.$

4.4. b

4.5. e
4.6. b

4.7. a

4.8. True

4.9. False

CHAPTER 5

5.1. True.

5.2. c

5.3. Identify skill categories.
Identity skill levels.
Time-phase skill levels.
Adjust skill levels to available personnel.

5.4. Any 10 of the following answers, or their general intent, are acceptable.
- Competitive or single-source RFP.
- Type of contract.
- Phases of the program involved: Research, design, prototype development, production.
- Composition of the team to prepare the proposal.
- Period of performance of the proposed contract.
- Place(s) of performance for the proposed contract.
- Types and quantities of deliverable items (hardware, data, software).
- Schedule of delivery.
- Type and location of customer inspection and acceptance.
- Test requirements.
- Shipping requirements.
- Types of facilities required.
- Areas of potential risk.
- Data rights (retention by the company or passed on to the customer).
- Warranty requirements.
- Statement of Work requirements (their availability, clarity, and completeness).
- Proposal submission date.
- Contract award date.
- Proposal delivery requirements.
- Type of funding (incremental, one lump sum, progress payments, full or partial).
- Types of clauses in the proposed contract.
- Legal issues.
- Patents and royalties.
- Proposal evaluation factors (technical, schedule, price).

5.5. True.

5.6. d.

5.7. True.

5.8. False.

CHAPTER 6

6.1. $660,000

6.2. e.

6.3. A process plan contains a listing of all operations that must be performed, including labor-hours required to perform the tasks. From this plan and the estimated labor-hours, the labor portion of the cost estimate is made.

6.4. a.

Manufacturing,	10,000	labor-hours
Quality assurance,	1,500	(manufacturing labor times 15 percent)
Tooling	2,500	
Manufacturing Eng	750	(Quality assurance labor $\times$ 50%)
Total labor-hours	14,750	Hours

b.

$$\frac{\text{Quality assurance labor hours}}{\text{Total labor-hours}} = \frac{1,500 \text{ hours}}{14,750} = 10.17 \text{ percent}$$

6.5. True

6.6. d.

CHAPTER 7

7.1. a. Administrative costs are those costs that have to do with phases of operations not directly identifiable with the production, sale, or financing of operations. They are costs incurred in connection with policy formation and the overall direction of a business. Salaries of major executives and general services such as accounting, contracting, and industrial relations are included in this category.

b. Material overhead is the overhead cost that is attributable to purchasing, receiving, storing, warehousing, delivering, or expediting materials. It is also termed "material burden" and "material procurement (indirect) costs."

7.2. True.

7.3. Indirect costs may fall into five general categories, depending on the structure of the company and its products or services offered. These typical categories include engineering overhead, manufacturing overhead, material overhead, general and administrative expenses, and internal research and development and bid and proposal expenses. These indirect costs are normally calculated and used as a percentage of various cost bases. Typically the engineering overhead rate is based on total direct engineering labor, manufacturing overhead on direct manufacturing labor; and material overhead on all material and subcontracts. General and administrative expenses are based on the sum of direct labor, materials, and subcontracts, their respective overhead amounts, and other direct costs such as travel and consultants. Internal research and development and bid and proposal expenses are based on all previous costs, including general and administrative expenses and any interdivisional transfers.

Indirect costs are normally forecast on an annual basis. These forecast rates can be used by the estimator in accordance with company policy and customer requirements. Firms doing business with the U.S. government need to refer to the Federal Cost Accounting Standards, which are issued by the Cost Accounting Standards Board and are included in the Federal Acquisition Regulations.

7.4., 7.5., 7.6. Questions 4, 5, and 6. Computation of in-house make cost for make-or-buy decision.

Lot of 50 computation. Assume both lots have equal costs.

Direct Costs:

Labor: Shear operation

Time:	Setup: 0.3 hours × 2 operators =	0.6 hours
	Run time: 25 units/hour × 50 units × 2 operators =	4.0 hours
	Total:	4.6 hours
Cost:	4.6 hours × $12.50 per hour =	$57.50
	Machining operation	
Time:	Setup: 2.0 hours × 1 operator =	2.0 hours
	Run time: 0.20 hours each unit × 50 units =	10.0 hours
	Total:	12.0 hours
Cost:	12.0 hours × $14.30 per hour =	$171.60
	Total direct labor cost =	$229.10
	Materials	
	Raw materials	
	$19.68 per unit × 50 units = $984.00	
	Total direct materials =	$984.00

Indirect Costs: (for make-or-buy comparison)

Labor: Direct labor cost × labor overhead rate

$229.10 × 170% = $389.47

Materials: Materials cost × materials overhead rate

$984.00 × 4% = $39.36

Total direct and indirect cost (for evaluation purposes) = $1641.93
In-house unit cost (for evaluation purposes) =   32.84

No G&A should be applied when evaluating for make or buy.

7.4. Buy outside. The vendor quote is $32.51 versus the comparable in-house cost of $32.84, a savings of $.33 per unit.

7.5. If the company plans to buy the weldment outside, it should include the vendor quote.

7.6. If the vendor quote were $33.00, use the in-house estimate of $32.84 and plan on making the weldment in-house.

7.7. *Materials*

1000 brackets, purchased at $6.25 each	$ 6,250.00
1000 canisters castings at $80.00 each	80,000.00
2000 covers material at $0.50 each	1,000.00
Direct material subtotal	$87,250.00
Material overhead (3% of direct material)	2,617.50
Subtotal material	$89,867.50

Labor
1000 canisters
Run time:

2 hours each × 1000 units × $14.00/hr =	28,000
Setup: 12 hours × 2 lots × 14.00 =	1,008

2000 covers
Run time:

0.2 hours each × 2,000 units × $14.00/hr =	5,600.00
4.0 hours × 5 lots × $14.00	280.00
Direct labor subtotal	34,888.00
Labor overhead (175% of direct labor)	61,054
Subtotal labor	$95,942.00
Labor and material subtotal	185,809.50
General and administrative expenses (10% of labor and materials)	18,580.95
Total cost with G&A	$204,390.45

Unit cost = $204.39

CHAPTER 8

8.1. b.

Solution: Total price is $20,000. Price equals total cost plus profit.

$P = TC + X$, where X is profit and TC is total cost.
$X = TC \times$ profit margin.

Substituting known values, we have:

$P = TC + X$
$\$20,000 = TC + (TC \times 0.2)$
$\$20,000 = 1.2 \times TC$
$\$20,000/1.2 = TC$
$\$16,667 = TC$

Placing this value of TC in the original equation, we solve for X:

$\$20,000 = \$16,667 + X$
$\$20,000 - 16,667 = X$
$X = \$3,333$

8.2. d. Financial analysis is a key tool in business decision making. Without understanding the potential financial implications of any decision, business management would not be looking after the fiscal health of the firm. Using financial analysis will enable the management to determine the course of action that best accomplishes the firm's objectives.

8.3. b.

8.4. c. Normally funds flows are negative at the first unit because the break-even point is normally greater than the first unit.

8.5. c. Refer to the discussion in question 8.1 for more details on setting up this problem.

$P = TC + X$
$\$10,000 = TC + X$
$\$10,000 = TC + (TC \times 0.16)$
$\$10,000 = 1.16 \times TC$
$\$10,000/1.16 = TC$
$\$8,620 = TC$
$\$10,000 - \$8,620 = X$
$X = \$1,380$

8.6. $552

Screen print	$40	
setup 4 hours × $10/hour =		
run time 0.05 hour × $10/hour × 100 pcs. =	$50	
Subtotal screen print labor		$90
Punch press		
setup 2 hours × $10/hour × 2 setups	$40	
run time 0.01 hour × $10/hour × 100 pcs. =	$10	
Subtotal punch press labor		$50

Materials cost $0.50 per piece × 100 pcs =		$50
Total labor =	$140	
Labor overhead at 150% =	$210	
Subtotal		$350
Materials cost =		$ 50
Subtotal labor, overhead & materials		$400
General & administrative expense (20%)		$ 80
Subtotal through G&A		$480
Profit at 15%		$ 72
Total Price		$552

8.7. c.

CHAPTER 9

9.1. Any five of the following answers are acceptable:
  a. To verify estimate accuracy.
  b. To verify estimate completeness.
  c. To confirm estimate credibility.
  d. To identify inconsistencies.
  e. To identify overlaps.
  f. To identify duplications.
  g. To identify omissions.

9.2. Any two of the following answers are acceptable:
  a. Incompatibility of the total estimated cost with the price derived from a market analysis.
  b. Incompatibility of the total estimated costs with a management target.
  c. Inappropriate time-phasing of estimated funding requirements.

9.3. c.

9.4. Any two of the following answers are acceptable:
  a. Combining work elements.
  b. Relocating work areas.
  c. Effective utilization of skills.
  d. General productivity improvement.

9.5. Any five of the following answers are acceptable:
  a. Environmental factors.
  b. Motivational factors.
  c. Effectiveness of machine maintenance.
  d. Effectiveness of tooling support.
  e. Efficiency of shop workload planning.

  f. Adaptability of product design to machine capabilities.

  g. Human engineering of product design.

9.6. Any six of the following answers are acceptable:

  a. Labor hours required for each task.

  b. A description of the work.

  c. A delivery or time schedule.

  d. A list of ground rules or assumptions used in preparing the estimate.

  e. Name(s) of the person(s) who prepared the estimate.

  f. Supporting rationale for each of the estimate inputs.

  g. Total estimated cost.

  h. Cost for each fiscal period.

  i. Cost for each work element.

  j. Rates and factors.

  k. Detailed cost breakouts.

CHAPTER 10

10.1. a. *Constant dollars* are dollars calculated at a fixed level of inflation.

  b. *Current dollars* are amounts that occurred historically or are projected using inflation rates for each year.

  c. *Discounted dollars* express the future value of money based on an earlier year as a base.

10.2. True. Acquisition and operating costs account for the majority of the program life cycle cost.

10.3. True.

10.4. a.

10.5. a. 1, 5, 8.

  b. 2, 3, 9, 12.

  c. 4, 6, 7, 10, 11.

  d. none

CHAPTER 11

11.1. True.

11.2. True.

11.3. False.

11.4. $1000 Total

  40% labor, 60% material of total amount

  5% labor escalation, 10% material escalation

Labor: $100 × 40% = $400
            5% labor escalation per year

Year 1	Year 2	Year 3
400 × 1.05 = $420	$420 × 1.05 = $441	$441 × 1.05 = $463

Materials:

$1000 × 60 % = $600
10% material escalation per year

Year 1	Year 2	Year 3
600 × 1.10 = $660	$660 × 1.10 = $726	$726 × 1.1 = $799

Total:

Year 1	Year 2	Year 3
420	441	463
660	726	799
1080	1167	1262

For labor:

$F = P(1 + i)^n$ (from Chapter 10)
$i = 5\%$, $n = 3$ years, $P = \$400$
$F = 463$

For materials:

$F = P(1 + i)^n$ (from Chapter 10)
$i = 10\%$, $n = 3$ years, $P = 600$
$F = 799$

Total:

F (for labor)   =   463
F (for materials) =   799
    Sum   = 1262 (expressed to the nearest whole dollar)

11.5. a.

	1989	1990	1991
AA	$10.50	$11.08	$11.52
BB	$11.66	$12.42	$13.04
CC	$11.08	$11.74	$12.33
DD	$11.76	$12.34	$12.84
b.	5.45%	5.95%	4.70%

CHAPTER 12

12.1. To estimate and analyze costs at the top end of the cost modeling/cost estimating spectrum.

12.2. Any three from the list below are acceptable answers:
Spreadsheets.
Databases.
Integrated software packages.
Multidimensional spreadsheets.
Multidimensional databases.
Schedule-based software packages that permit loading of resources.

12.3. To determine hardware and software costs where detailed design has not been completed.

12.4. False.

12.5. True.

12.6. By automated takeoff of lengths, areas, volumes, and quantities.

12.7. Provides for lead and lag times between activities; displays resource histograms; permits variable resource loading of activities; summarizes costs by work breakdown structure; displays Gantt charts, displays network charts, permits easy updates.

CHAPTER 13

13.1. Any five from the following list:
a. Structured diagramming.
b. Screen, report, and menu generation.
c. Command structures, subroutines, and data dictionaries.
d. Program coding.
e. Transfer, interpretation, and bridging of coding.
f. Documentation generation.
g. Testing, error checking, consistency, and completeness analysis.

h. Program management of software development.

i. Software cost estimating using CASE tools.

j. Software maintenance.

13.2. a. Planning, analysis, specifications, design, implementation and coding, documentation.

b. (1) By analyzing the work required to accomplish each step for a given software product; by applying the skills and hours required for each task; by applying the appropriate labor rates, overhead, G&A, and fee values, and (2) by using a parametric software cost estimating model designed to approximate the costs of software development and maintenance.

13.3. Computer equipment configuration and performance; characteristics of software product; and extent of utilization of CASE tools in software development and software maintenance.

13.4. List any three from the following list:

a. Testing.

b. Debugging.

c. Rerunning.

d. Editing.

e. Limits testing.

13.5. By basing costs on the number of lines of code to be generated.

13.6. a. Software management.

b. Software systems engineering.

c. Software programming.

d. Software test and evaluation (verification and validation).

e. Software data (documentation).

f. Software implementation (field support).

g. Software maintenance (updates, corrections).

13.7. a. The fact that the number of lines of code itself, is often difficult to estimate.

b. Resources per lines of code often do not take into account the use of advanced productivity tools like CASE.

BIBLIOGRAPHY

Boehm, Barry W. *Software Engineering Economics*. Englewood Cliffs, N.J.: Prentice-Hall, 1981.

Burt, David N. *Proactive Procurement*. Englewood Cliffs, N.J.: Prentice-Hall, 1984.

Clark, Forrest D. and A. B. Lovenzoni. *Applied Cost Engineering*. New York: Dekker, 1985.

Couper, James R., and William H. Rader. *Applied Finance and Economic Analysis for Scientists and Engineers*. New York: Van Nostrand Reinhold, 1986.

Del Mar, Donald. *Operations and Industrial Management*. New York: McGraw-Hill, 1985.

Draper, N. R., and N. Smith. *Applied Regression Analysis*. 2d ed. New York: Wiley, 1981.

Earles, Mary Eddins. *Factors, Formulas, and Structures for Life Cycle Costing*. 2d ed. Concord, Mass.: Eddins-Earles Publishing, 1981.

Fisher, Gene H. *Cost Considerations in Systems Analysis*. New York: American Elsevier, 1971.

Goldman, Thomas A. *Cost Effectiveness Analysis*. New York: Praeger, 1971.

Grant, Eugene L., et al. *Principles of Engineering Economy*. New York: Wiley, 1982.

Hillier, Frederick S. and Gerald J. Lieberman. *Introduction to Operations Research*, 4th ed. San Francisco: Holden-Day, 1986.

Jelen, Frederic C., and James H. Black. *Cost and Optimization Engineering*. 2d ed. New York: McGraw-Hill, 1983.

Jordan, Raymond B. *How to Use the Learning Curve*. Boston: Cahner Books, 1972.

Kaplan, Marshall H. *Acquiring Major Systems Contracts*. New York: Wiley, 1988.

Kaplan, Seymour. *Energy Economics*. New York: McGraw-Hill, 1983.

McNichols, Gerald R., ed. *Cost Analysis*. Arlington, Va.: Operations Research Society of America, 1984.

Michaels, Jack V., and William P. Wood. *Design to Cost*. Wiley Series in New Dimensions in Engineering. New York: Wiley, 1989.

Miller, Irwin, and John E. Freund. *Probability and Statistics for Engineers*. 3d ed. Englewood Cliffs, N.J.: Prentice-Hall, 1985.

Moder, Joseph J. et al. *Project Management with CPM, PERT, and Precedence Diagramming*. 3d ed. New York: Van Nostrand Reinhold, 1983.

Newnan, Donald G. *Engineering Economic Analysis*. 2d ed. San Jose, Calif.: Engineering Press, 1983.

Ostwald, Phillip F. *Cost Estimating*. 2d ed. Englewood Cliffs, N.J.: Prentice-Hall, 1984.

Park, William R., and Dale E. Jackson. *Cost Engineering Analysis*. 2d ed. New York: Wiley, 1984.

Riggs, James L. *Production Systems: Planning, Analysis and Control*. 3d ed. New York: Wiley, 1981.

Salvendy, Gavriel. *Handbook of Industrial Engineering*. New York: Wiley, 1982.

Seldon, M. Robert. *Life Cycle Costing: A Better Method of Government Procurement*. Boulder, Colo.: Westview Press, 1979.

Shannon, Robert E. *Systems Simulation, The Art and Science*. Englewood Cliffs, N.J.: Prentice-Hall, 1975.

Shelly, Gary B., and Thomas J. Cashman. *Complete Fundamentals for an Information Age*. Brea, Calif.: Anahiem Publishing, 1984.

Stewart, Rodney D., and Ann L. Stewart. *Managing Millions*. New York: Wiley, 1988.

Stewart, Rodney D., and Ann L. Stewart. *Microestimating for Civil Engineers, Microestimating for Mechanical Engineers*. New York: McGraw-Hill, 1986/1987.

Stewart, Rodney D., and Ann L. Stewart. *Proposal Preparation*. New York: Wiley, 1984.

Stewart, Rodney D., and Richard M. Wyskida, eds. *Cost Estimator's Reference Manual*. New York: Wiley, 1987.

Wilson, Frank C. *Industrial Cost Controls*. Englewood Cliffs, N.J.: Prentice-Hall, 1971.

PITFALLS AND COMMON ERRORS TO AVOID IN COST ESTIMATING

The following list gives pitfalls and common errors encountered in the practice of cost estimating. They are extracted from the text of this book for ease of visibility and for use as a readily available checklist:

1. Failure to define fully the work activity or work output being estimated.
2. Failure to eliminate duplications, overlaps, and omissions.
3. Lack of a well thought out time schedule for conducting the work.
4. Application of improper skill levels and skill categories to the job.
5. Incomplete analysis of indirect, general, and administrative costs.
6. Failure to include adequate allowances for the "*certainty*" of cost growth.
7. Failure to understand and to deal successfully with cost escalation and inflation.
8. Failure to account for productivity improvements made possible by high technology advances (ie: Computer-Aided-Design Systems, Computer-Aided Software Engineering, Automation and Robotics).

INDEX

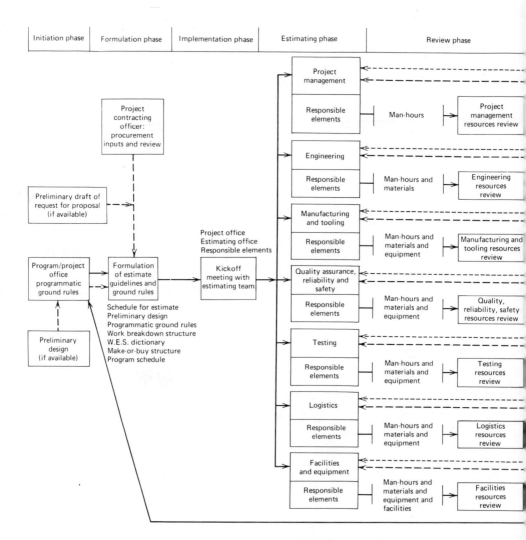

Figure 9.1 Flow diagram of the cost estimating process. See page 177.